Brabham: The Grand Prix Cars

Brabham: The Grand Prix Cars

Alan Henry

Hazleton Publishing, Richmond, Surrey

This first edition published in 1985 by Hazleton Publishing,
3 Richmond Hill, Richmond, Surrey TW10 6RE.

ISBN 0 905138 36 8

Printed in Holland by Drukkerij Veenman b.v., Wageningen.
Typesetting by C. Leggett & Son Ltd., Mitcham, Surrey, England.

Cover photographs by LAT Photographic and Phipps Photographic.

Colour Photography by:

Diana Burnett
Geoffrey Goddard
LAT Photographic
Phipps Photographic
Nigel Snowdon

Black & White Photography by:

BMW Motorsport
Bernard Ecclestone
Andrew Frankl
Geoffrey Goddard
Alan Henry
Jeff Hutchinson
LAT Photographic
Gordon Murray
Phipps Photographic
Repco Ltd
Nigel Snowdon
Keith Sutton
Ron Tauranac
John Townsend
Leslie Wright

***(frontispiece)* Beaming with relaxed pleasure. Jack Brabham celebrates his fourth Repco-powered victory of the 1966 season on the winner's rostrum at Nürburgring. His German Grand Prix triumph over John Surtees's Cooper-Maserati on a streaming wet circuit was one of the most satisfying of his career.**

DISTRIBUTORS

USA
Motorbooks International,
PO Box 2, 729 Prospect Av.,
Osceola, Wisconsin 54020

Australia
Technical Book & Magazine Co.,
289-299 Swanston Street,
Melbourne, Victoria 3000

New Zealand
David Bateman Ltd.,
PO Box 65062,
Mairangi Bay,
Auckland 10

UK and Other Markets
Osprey Publishing Ltd.
12-14 Long Acre
London WC2E 9LP

Contents

Foreword by John Watson 11

Introduction and Acknowledgements 12

Section 1: Jack's Brabham years, 1962-70

Chapter 1 A fortuitous partnership 17

Chapter 2 Champion on his own terms: the Brabham-Repcos, 1966-68 53

Chapter 3 First time round for the Cosworth DFV 79

Section 2: The Ecclestone era

Chapter 1 The Brabham team in transition 119

Chapter 2 The first Gordon Murray cars 133

Chapter 3 The Brabham-Alfas, 1976-79 159

Chapter 4 A return to the Cosworth route 215

Chapter 5 The Brabham-BMW turbos 239

Appendix 276

Race results

Foreword:

John Watson

Long before I ever drove in Formula 1, Brabham cars played a very significant part in the development of my professional racing career, so it is not surprising that I have always felt a strong affinity for the marque. Some of my first single seater experience was gained in Irish formule libre events with a hybrid BT14 which had started out life as a works F2 car fitted with a Honda engine, and I later enjoyed two seasons contesting the European F2 Championship with my own BT30, a delighfully progressive and responsive car to handle.

In fact, a consistent Brabham theme continued throughout much of my career. I made my Grand Prix debut at Silverstone in 1973 with a Ralph Bellamy designed BT37 and campaigned my first full World Championship season the following year with a BT42 and a BT44, Gordon Murray's two earliest creations. Eventually my good fortunes led me back to the Brabham works team for 1977 and 78 at a time when they were using Alfa Romeo's powerful, yet often unreliable engines. I particularly enjoyed my 1978 season partnering Niki Lauda: it was a difficult year from the point of view of results, but we struck up a first class working relationship which we were later to continue at Marlboro McLaren.

It is a source of regret to me that I never managed to win a Grand Prix in a Brabham, for they always seemed to have a good feeling about them. Like the old Formula 2 BT30, the F1 cars were generally nice to drive and gave their drivers a pleasant time. Looking back on all those Brabham races in the form of this AUTOCOURSE volume has therefore given me particular enjoyment. I have known the author Alan Henry since 1970, and while I have often disagreed with his opinions as a weekly motoring journalist, I think he has captured the flavour of Brabham's Grand Prix history in just the right vein.

Introduction and Acknowledgements

Twenty three years may not seem like a long time to serious motor racing enthusiasts, but in terms of Grand Prix racing it is an age. When Jack Brabham's first Formula 1 challenger emerged from the factory at New Haw, on the banks of the River Wey in Byfleet, probably the most pressing technical controversy preoccupying the racing world was whether a monocoque chassis was better than a spaceframe. Looking back on this relatively recent racing history from a vantage point in Motor Racing Developments's clinically efficient factory at Chessington, the contrast is so vivid it seems like comparing Stone Age with Space Age.

Crammed into those twenty three years has been a wealth of frantic racing activity carrying the Brabham marque name from the days of 1½-litre Coventry-Climax V8 engines, rebuilds in the paddock and relatively small budgets gleaned from motor industry sources, through to the present era of multi-million dollar budgets from television-oriented outside sponsors, carbon fibre composite chassis and turbocharged engines. The team has had its ups and downs but, generally, ever since Jack Brabham and Dan Gurney ran their first full season together in 1963, the team's name became synonymous with easy-to-drive, progressive-handling racings cars that were enjoyable to drive and gave their drivers a pleasant time.

The first nine years of the team's history centred round the efforts of Brabham himself and his long-time colleague Ron Tauranac. Both practical, straightforward individuals they forged a good working partnership at a time when Formula 1 racing was by no means the big money sport it was to become in the late 1970s. They believed that their Grand Prix cars should be as simple and easy to operate as the many customer cars for the junior formulae which poured out of the New Haw factory throughout the 1960s. The cars became a reflection of the men who designed and raced them.

Yet Brabham was shrewd, played his cards close to his chest and always seemed to have a pretty accurate idea of where he was going next. His deal with Repco for engines at the start of the 3-litre formula was typical. At a time when everybody was concentrating on complicated multi-cylinder engines in large, heavy monocoque chassis, it took a deal of confidence and nerve to opt for an updated 1½-litre spaceframe special powered by a production-based, single overhead camshaft V8. But although the Repco engine did not have much power compared to its rivals, Brabham accurately reasoned that anybody who was ready for the new formula, in a reasonably organized state, would be in a position to win from the word go. In fact, the uncomplicated Brabham-Repco partnership was good enough to win two World Championships before the Cosworth DFV became the state-of-the-art Grand Prix engine and everything else was eclipsed.

To many members of the press, Jack Brabham was something of an enigma; quiet, introspective, a self-possessed, private man. Denny Hulme admits that, when he was Brabham's team-mate, there was precious little in the way of idle conversation and Hulme never really knew what Jack's long-term plans encompassed. If he was quiet with his team-mate, the press had little chance . . .

On the other hand, he was loyal and staunchly devoted to those he chose to befriend. When one English journalist suffered a personal bereavement while at a

Brabham – slaking a victorious thirst.

French Grand Prix meeting in the late 1960s, Brabham flew him home after practice on the Saturday night and returned immediately to take part in the race. That is friendship in the true sense of the word. Generally, however, he kept himself very much to himself. Even in his official, personal biography, published more than a decade ago, Brabham only reveals so much about his *persona* – as much as he chose to and not a sliver more.

When Jack retired in 1970 at the age of 44, Ron Tauranac had already been in control of Motor Racing Developments, the Brabham team's "parent" company, for a year. Jack had anticipated retiring at the end of 1969, and to that end had sold out to Ron by the start of the 1970 season. He came back and raced for a final year when it became clear that the team was *not* going to be able to tempt the great Jochen Rindt back into the fold . . .

Tauranac without Brabham was like Flanagan without Allan, roast beef without gravy. They belonged to the same era, shared the same roots. Although Ron soldiered on to run the team alone throughout 1971, it is clear that his heart was no longer really fully committed to Formula 1 as the sport's emphasis changed and high-pressure commercialism really got into top gear. He sold out his business and, after staying on the fringes of the Grand Prix game for a couple more years, eventually founded Ralt Cars Ltd., continuing the Motor Racing Developments's tradition of building practical, easy-to-operate single seater racing cars on a volume basis for the junior formulae.

Ecclestone – centre of F1 attention.

The man into whose control the Brabham Grand Prix team then passed has since become the most powerful and influential single individual in professional motor racing. In the early 1970s some people recalled Bernard Ecclestone for his motorcycle and car racing involvements in the early post-war years, others for his shrewd, astute business management of the late Jochen Rindt. Perhaps fewer knew of his myriad business dealings, most of which had proved tremendously successful not only in the motorcycle and car sales areas but also in the high-flying world of industrial property. When Ecclestone took over Brabham, he was a rich man by the standards of most people involved in the sport. In the years that followed he would become richer still, while at the same time carrying Formula 1 racing as a whole through to a fresh era of popularity and world-wide television appeal.

Ecclestone will be judged a radical in historical motor racing terms. An autocrat and a workaholic with tremendous energy and perspicacity, he is quick-witted, sharp and bold in his approach to business. His critics say his initial foray into Formula 1 was something of an ego-booster, although if this was the case then it was an expensive exercise because 1972 proved a disaster for the Brabham team. More likely, he could see the business potential of the Formula 1 game. He organized the Formula 1 Constructors Association into the most powerful single lobby in the sport, steering it with a firm hand and almost dictatorial efficiency. Being a gambler at heart, Bernie quickly realized that his colleagues would be happy to leave him in the driving seat as long as he was successful in his task. He continues to be successful . . .

Yet, although Ecclestone retains an iron grip over all aspects of his racing team, he is shrewd enough to employ experts in key positions. Once Bernie is convinced he has recruited the right man for a particular post, he tends to leave him to get on with it. Gordon Murray has been with Ecclestone for 13 years and openly admits he has freedom of design action which is the envy of his Formula 1 rivals. Bernie only impinges on the team in terms of overall policy, leaving the operational details to his lieutenants. Again, his critics say that some of his major decisions have been dictated by commercial expediency rather than pure racing logic (the switch to Alfa Romeo engines in 1976, for example, or the change to hitherto uncompetitive Pirelli rubber in 1985). Others suggest that he has a burning desire to provide his team with a major performance advantage, a technical leg-up which is not available to his rivals. Perhaps it's a bit of both.

For the Brabham team, however, the racing record is there for all to see. World Champions in 1966 and 67 using the Australian Repco V8, and in 1981 and 83 the team provided the vehicles in which Nelson Piquet won his two World Championships, the former with Cosworth DFVs and the latter with BMW turbocharged engines. There has also been no shortage of leading drivers in the Grand Prix Brabhams over the years – apart, of course, from Jack himself. The names of Gurney, Hulme, Ickx, Rindt, Hill, Reutemann, Pace, Stuck, Lauda, Watson and Piquet represent a fair cross-section of top-class talent from the past two decades.

The more I investigated the subject of Brabham Grand Prix cars, the more absorbing the whole story seemed to become. In this respect I offer my thanks to Bernie Ecclestone and Gordon Murray for an enormous amount of good-humoured cooperation: their patient assistance with the post-1972 period in the marque's history was matched only by Ron Tauranac's equally time-consuming help over the previous ten years. All three provided photographs from their personal archives and checked manuscripts for facts, but not one of them ever suggested I alter any opinions or conclusions of my own. They remained hearteningly open-minded.

Of the dozens of others who helped, I would like to single out Dieter Stappert of BMW Motorsport and John Judd of Engine Developments. Particular thanks to Stappert for his remarkably candid account of the early problems surrounding the BMW Formula 1 engine project and to Judd for his pithy recollections of the Brabham-Repco era in which he was closely involved.

Thanks also to: Sir Jack Brabham himself, Dan Gurney, Rob Walker, Denny Hulme, John Watson, Niki Lauda, Ann Jones, Leo Mehl, Ralph Bellamy, Roy Billington, Ron Dennis, Uwe Mahle, Denis Jenkinson, Doug Nye, Tony Cleverley, Bob Dance, Herbie Blash, Nelson Piquet, Riccardo Patrese, Charlie Whiting, Frank Williams and Brian Hart, plus sincere apologies anybody I may have inadvertently forgotten.

Alan Henry,
Bradwell-on-Sea,
January 1985

Section 1: Jack's Brabham Years, 1962-70

Chapter 1
A fortuitous partnership

A youthful Jack Brabham tends to the engine of his "Redex Special" Cooper-Bristol during the 1953 season: the following year the Australian motorsport authorities decided to take a tough line on advertising and Jack lost this backing when the decals had to come off.

The circumstances which led John Arthur Brabham and Ronald Sidney Tauranac to cross each other's path early in their respective careers were unquestionably fortuitous, but not altogether surprising. They came from broadly similar backgrounds, had their family roots in Britain, both served in the Royal Australian Air Force at the tail end of the Second World War and both developed an early, as it was to turn out insatiable, enthusiasm for cars and motor racing. Men of few words, they were practical down-to-earth engineering types and, although privately ambitious, each developed individual talents which would complement the other quite admirably.

Jack Brabham's paternal grandfather was born in Bow, East London, in 1869 and emigrated to Australia at the age of 16. Grandfather Brabham clearly had a pretty idealistic notion of what Australia would be like. "He had expected to be met by bush rangers leading kangaroos on strings, or something . . . you can imagine how he felt when they reached the other side of the world only to see that it (Melbourne) was not much different from London or any other city. Just another dock in another town", recounts Jack in his memoirs.

Jack was born in Hurstville, about ten miles south of central Sydney, on April 2, 1926, an only child, the son of a greengrocer. Ron Tauranac was actually born in Gillingham, Kent, his family emigrating to Australia in 1928 when he was three and a half years old. They made their home in the rural community of Fassifern, between Sydney and Newcastle, and Ron recalls "we didn't wear shoes until we were 12. We were really out in the scrubs with a tiny village school. We spent our spare time riding and fishing . . . real backwood's kids . . ." It was not until 1941 that his family moved to the Sydney suburb of Bondi within the sprawling metropolis.

Jack's education embraced a course at technical college once his routine schooling was over, but he quickly decided to pass up his first job at a Sydney engineering shop for a career maintaining his father's trucks and cars at a local Hurstville garage. Needless to say, the young Brabham learned all about driving on his father's vehicles, this early experience imbuing him with a mechanical aptitude and resourcefulness which would reap repeated benefits in the years that followed.

At the age of 18, Brabham joined the RAAF and, although he dearly wanted to fly, at that stage in the war (1944) it seemed there was more demand for flight mechanics than for aircrew. Most of his time in the Air Force was spent working on Bristol Beaufighters until he was demobbed in 1947 and, in his own words, "looked round a bit vaguely for something to do."

With the assistance of a close friend, Brabham eventually started up a small engineering business of his own, but it wasn't long before the lure of motor sports caught his attention in a big way. He homed in on the then-fashionable midget car racing category, a highly popular class in which the events were staged on rutted, oval dirt tracks. Jack's first season saw him win the New South Wales championship after he had helped develop a JAP-engined special for established dirt track ace Johnny Schonberg, taking over the cockpit for the 1946-47 season after Schonberg retired from active racing due to pressure from his wife. It was in

Ron Tauranac with the original Ralt hillclimb special competing in a hillcimb at Newcastle, New South Wales, back in 1951. Already there is evidence of development work, the spoked rear bicycle wheels having been replaced by cast rims.

this close-fought dirt track environment that Brabham's distinctive oversteering, defensive driving style was initially developed: the technique would never leave him throughout his racing career . . .

When a broken connecting rod cost Jack the South Australian championship, he briefly opted to give this motor racing game a miss, entering the truck business with his father for a short time before changing his mind about retirement from racing after a particular truck deal fell through.

It was 1951 before that eventful meeting of the ways between Brabham and Tauranac took place. Ron's first job had been as a jig and tool draughtsman with the Commonwealth Air Corporation, but when war broke out he too joined the Royal Australian Air Force. He trained as a pilot on Harvards during a spell in Canada, converted to Wirraways back home in Australia, but was spared any involvement in the assault on Japan after it surrendered following the Hiroshima holocaust. After he was demobbed in 1945, Ron went to work for the CSR Chemical Company and became involved in the design of the first stainless steel plant for plastic manufacture in Australia. He acquired an Austin Seven and, out for a drive one day in 1946, heard some noises just off the road, went to have a look and discovered motor racing . . . the noise was coming from the Marsden Park air strip near Sydney and his interest was sparked.

In conjunction with his brother, Ron built a little 500cc Formula 3 machine, and deriving its name from a combination of Ron's initials with those of his brother, Austin Lewis Tauranac, the car was inevitably dubbed the Ralt. Ron confesses that this first Tauranac special was built mainly from his own ideas allied to technical knowledge culled from lengthy lunchtime sessions in the local library. "I had read somewhere that inter-leaf friction in leaf springing systems would provide sufficient shock absorbing for a light car, but when I up-ended the thing on my first competitive outing in a hillclimb at Hawkesbury, near Sydney, I had to revise my ideas". A total of 14 stitches in his face, the scars of which he bears to this day, convinced him that it would be worth "spending a tenner on a set of shock absorbers!"

Tauranac drastically modified the single cylinder Norton 500cc engine, so much so that eventually the only original parts of the 1932 unit were the oil pump and cylinder head. Considering the resources available to him, this Ralt special became remarkably advanced, featuring double wishbone suspension and low pivot swing axles at the rear – without knowing it, Tauranac had evolved a layout very similar to that which would be employed by Mercedes-Benz some years later.

In 1951 Ron and Austin called on Brabham's machine shop to see whether Jack would be interested in selling them one of his single-cylinder 500cc Velocette engines, but the future World Champion was more interested in "doing a deal" on the little Ford 10-engined Ralt sports car which the brothers had evolved. He liked the idea of fitting it with one of his dirt track engines in order to go road racing, but that sports car was not really a basis for a racer and Jack eventually got onto the tarmac with a Cooper Mk V powered by an 1150cc Vincent twin.

As Eoin Young wrote in the 1967 edition of *Autocourse*: "In the light of what happened a decade later, the results of the New South Wales hillclimb championships in 1953 and 1954 make interesting reading. Tauranac was second in 1953, and Brabham, was third with gear selection troubles on the Cooper-Vincent. Jack switched to a front-engined Cooper-Bristol the following year, but he was still dogged with gear selection troubles and Ron won the title with Brabham in second place."

Brabham aspired to a professional future in the sport and he was more than a bit upset when the essentially conservative Australian motor sporting authorities insisted he remove the extrovert *RedeX* sponsorship lettering from the flanks of his Cooper-Bristol. He continued to race it, *sans* sponsorship, throughout 1954 until an opportune meeting with the RAC's Dean Delamont and Dunlop's Dick Jeffrey at the New Zealand Grand Prix meeting convinced him that it was time to make tracks for England in 1955. This was to mark the start of a long, highly successful road for the 29-year-old Australian, Brabham consolidating a productive relationship with the Cooper company to win the World Championship in both 1959 and 1960. They were the first such titles to be won at the wheel of a rear-engined Grand Prix car.

As the partnership between the taciturn Brabham, grumpy old Charles Cooper and his genial, pipe-sucking son John really got into top gear, so Jack's correspondence with Ron Tauranac back home increased in volume. Although Cooper pioneered the rear-engined Formula 1 revolution, it was to be Colin Chapman's Lotuses which really capitalized on this exciting new dawn and, within two years of Brabham's second Championship, the team from Surbiton would be in decline.

Jack, of course, had a pretty shrewd engineering mind and was always interested to 'check up' on Cooper progress by bouncing technical suggestions off Tauranac during their correspondence. As often as not, Ron's replies would include interesting little sketches showing how to get round some problem or other, and the wily Brabham would discreetly feed the suggestion into the Cooper design system, such as it was.

With a view to setting up as a production racing car manufacturer, building cars for the junior formulae, Jack first asked Ron to come over to England late in 1959. "He originally asked me over to go into partnership with him on this," recalls Tauranac, "so I came over at the start of 1960, travelling via the US West Coast sports car series where I helped Jack to run his own Cooper-Monaco". By this time Brabham was exploiting his Grand Prix success and his garage business at Chessington was building up quite a profitable sideline in performance conversion work. This is where Ron worked to start with.

"I worked on installing Climax engines in Triumph Heralds during the day and drew the first racing car at home at night," he remembers, "We started the company, Motor Racing Developments, with Jack providing the capital and the shares split 60/40 in his favour." The first MRD, as the production Formula Junior car was called, was built in a tin shed at Esher and sold to Tasmanian Gavin Youl in the summer of 1961. Of course, Brabham had to treat the whole project quite tactfully from the word go, for this plan to build production racing cars for the junior formulae would inevitably cut across Cooper's business. After all, Cooper had been one of the cornerstones of the production racing car industry in Britain for more than a decade, so rivalry from a company headed by their very own World Champion was likely to produce a fairly muted reaction. It was unlikely that Charlie Cooper, for one, would see the funny side . . .

However, strong interest in the new MRD made it necessary for the firm to move to larger premises. The Repco company, which had been established before the war to market replacement car components in Australia, was in the process of establishing a market in England for its garage equipment and had space available in its workshop, in Victoria Road, Surbiton. Eventually, after some French colleagues pointed out to Jack that the initials MRD had unfortunate connotations when pronounced in their native tongue, it was decided that the cars should be known as 'Brabhams'. In fact, as a result of a very minor sponsorship deal with Repco, the production single seater racing cars were always officially dubbed Repco-Brabhams. It was, unwittingly, the portent of exciting developments to come – and not a small degree of confusion when it came to describing some of the team's later products.

By the end of the 1961 season, although Cooper had been first in line to use the new Coventry-Climax 1½-litre V8, Jack Brabham had finally decided it was time to move off to pastures new. There seemed little chance of long-term, imaginative progress being made by the Cooper organization and Jack did not wish to find himself left behind as the tempo of 1½-litre Formula 1 competition hotted up. He decided that he would not only go it alone in Formula 1 for 1962, but that Motor Racing Developments would build him a car. The first Formula 1 Brabham was on the way . . .

In the factory yard at New Haw, the very first Brabham Formula 1 car, stripped of its top bodywork, poses for the cameras. The outboard mounted coil spring/damper units would remain a Brabham Formula 1 trademark right through until the end of 1969.

Prior to its debut in the German Grand Prix at Nurburgring, the recently-finished BT3 is seen here during a break in testing at Brands Hatch, parked in the small lay-by at the top of Paddock Bend. As a helmeted Brabham prepares to climb aboard, Ron Tauranac (left) watches with a preoccupied expression on his face.

It was unrealistic to expect the new Tauranac-designed BT3 Formula 1 challenger to be ready until the summer: the business of designing, building and organizing a Grand Prix car was a daunting task. It was therefore decided that Jack would keep his hand in by acquiring a brand new Lotus 24 powered by a Climax V8 for the first part of the year. Unfortunately this customer car from Chapman's firm took some time to ready, so Jack found himself obliged to take yet another step backwards by starting the season in an out-dated four-cylinder Climax-engined Lotus 21. On April 14, 1962 the Brabham Racing Organization was scheduled to make its first Formula 1 appearance in the Lombank Trophy race at Snetterton . . .

"Unfortunately it didn't turn out that way," reflects Roy Billington who had just joined the fledgling team to work on Jack's car, "because his regular mechanic Tim Wall was stripping it down for a final check at the Repco premises in Surbiton when some fuel splashed in the undertray ignited and the whole thing went up. It was quite a drama with the fire brigade being called out, but Tim managed to get the thing pushed out of the workshop and the fire extinguished before too much damage had been done. Then it was a case of working round the clock to get it ready to race at Pau – my first race with the team."

Round the sinuous French street circuit, Brabham was clearly going to have a hard time with this underpowered contender. He qualified fourth behind Jim Clark's Team Lotus 24, Ricardo Rodriguez's Ferrari 156 and Jo Bonnier's Porsche, but retired after five laps with fading oil pressure. The race was won by Maurice Trintignant at the wheel of a Lotus 18/21 owned by Rob Walker – later to become an F1 Brabham customer!

A week later Jack retired his Lotus 21 from the Aintree 200 with gearbox trouble after five laps and it was confidently expected that his new Lotus 24 would be ready in time for the BRDC International Trophy at Silverstone on May 12. However,

Tim Wall and Roy Billington were busy assembling the new car right up until race morning, by which time Jack had been forced to use the old 21 to qualify in the middle of the fourth row. The race took place on a rain-slicked track surface culminating in Graham Hill's dramatic sprint round the outside of Jim Clark's works Lotus 24 at Woodcote on the last lap, giving his BRM victory by a nose. Brabham's 24 finished sixth behind Surtees's Bowmaker Lola-Climax, the UDT/Laystall entered works Ferrari 156 of Innes Ireland and Bruce McLaren's works Cooper.

Jim Clark slammed his brand new monocoque Lotus 25 round Zandvoort to grab third place on the grid for the Dutch Grand Prix, but Jack's 24 was only a tenth of a second behind in fourth place. Unfortunately what promised to be a reasonable showing for the former twice World Champion ended when the erratic Ricardo Rodriguez spun his Ferrari in the middle of the pack on lap five, Brabham collected him and retired to the pits with frontal damage. Clark was really getting into his stride at Monaco where the 100 lap, 195 mile contest was conducted under cloudy, overcast skies. Jack was more than a second off the Scot's pole-winning pace and by lap 77 "was looking very hot and bothered, and had been for many laps" according to *Motor Sport*'s reporter. He slid off onto the grass in Casino Square on that very lap and although he extricated the car he registered another retirement with bent suspension.

Back at the newly acquired MRD factory on the banks of the River Wey at New Haw, in Byfleet, the new BT3 was nearing completion but Jack still had to run a few more outings in the Lotus 24. He bagged a second to Surtees's Lola in the non-title Mallory Park 1000 Guineas, finished a lowly sixth, two laps behind, in the Belgian Grand Prix at Spa where he complained that the Lotus felt worryingly unstable at high speed, then produced an unlapped fourth place in the non-Championship Reims Grand Prix behind McLaren's Cooper, Graham Hill's BRM and Ireland's UDT/Laystall Lotus 24.

A week later came the French Grand Prix proper at *Rouen-les-Essarts* where Dan Gurney emerged triumphant in the flat-8 Porsche 804, but Jack's race ended when the Lotus suffered a rear suspension breakage and came limping into the pits with its rear end scraping along the ground. Now there was only the British Grand Prix at Aintree separating Jack from the debut of his new car and he rounded off his career in his own Lotus by finishing fifth, lapped by winner Jim Clark's dominant Lotus 25.

Although Colin Chapman was pointing the way forward with his new monocoque Grand Prix design, the Brabham BT3 was an essentially conservative Formula 1 concept by the standards of the day, relying on spaceframe construction from 18 gauge, predominantly 1in. diameter mild steel tubing. The Coventry-Climax V8 nestled so tightly in the engine bay, surrounded by tubing, that it seemed at first glance as if a hacksaw would be required to release it. However, two of the upper chassis members were detachable, enabling the V8 to be juggled out of position whenever necessary.

Outboard coil spring/damper units were employed all round, the front suspension having bottom wishbones the front pivot points of which were well ahead of the axle line and 'Y' shaped radius rods running back to the chassis frame, the branches of the 'Y' going to each end of the top transverse link. At the rear there was a top wishbone arrangement, with lower links and twin radius arms and cast elektron hub carriers. The front wheel rims were 13in. with 15in. rims at the rear.

A front mounted Serck water radiator was employed and the three tank fuel system had a total capacity of 28 gallons, supplying the Weber carburated Climax V8 which drove the rear wheels via a Colotti-Francis six-speed gearbox and articulated drive-shafts. The whole car was finished off in a striking shade of turquoise and the mechanics only put the final touches to Jack and Ron's new baby in the Nürburgring paddock prior to the 11.00am start of Friday practice in preparation for the German Grand Prix.

Unfortunately the Dunlop-shod BT3 did not open its competitive career on the most encouraging note. On Brabham's first timed practice lap the Climax V8 lost

its oil pressure and ran its bearings so the hard-pressed team had to cobble together a 'bitza' engine using additional parts from a Team Lotus V8 blown up by Trev Taylor. Jack did his first five laps very carefully, as the whole engine was sealed up with 'Holts Wonderweld', then speeded up slightly on his sixth only for the car to run out of fuel. He eventually qualified way back on the seventh row of 4-3-4 grid with a 10m 21.6s best, light years away from Gurney's Porsche pole of 8m 47.2s. A new Climax V8 was installed for the race and Jack ran midfield in the streaming rain before crawling in to retire with a deranged throttle linkage. Not an auspicious start . . .

Brabham missed the Italian Grand Prix at Monza after he was unable to agree starting money with the organizers, but the BT3 showed its long-term promise in the United States Grand Prix at Watkins Glen on October 6. Having revamped the car with bigger front brake discs and improved springing, Jack bagged fifth place on the grid only 1.1s away from Clark's pole position Lotus. He was fourth at the end of the first lap behind the magic Scot and the BRM's of Hill and Ginther, dropped back to fifth behind Gurney's Porsche, and then recovered to take back fourth at the flag, one lap down, behind Clark, Hill and McLaren.

Finally, Brabham rounded off his season by taking his new car to East London for the South African Grand Prix on December 29, that memorable event in which

Wearing a serious expression on his face, Brabham holds the BT3 on a tight line through Nürburgring's Karussell during the car's debut outing in the 1962 German Grand Prix. It proved to be a difficult weekend with engine problems in practice and retirement, owing to throttle linkage trouble, after nine laps of the race.

Jack glances in his mirrors to keep an eye on team-mate Dan Gurney's similar BT7 during their tussle in the 1963 French Grand Prix at Reims. Dan started from the front row behind Jim Clark's Lotus 25 and Graham Hill's BRM, but the two Brabhams could only finish 4-5, Jack ahead of the Californian, after both were delayed by brief pit visits.

Drama in the closing stages of the 1963 Italian Grand Prix at Monza as Brabham's BT7 stops for extra fuel to cure apparent pick-up problems after he had switched over to the small reserve supply. In the foreground a policeman holds a cloth over the front of the engine cover as Tim Wall tips the contents of a large churn into the tank and a tense, helmeted Brabham confers with Tauranac just ahead of them. On the left, a wistful Dan Gurney watches proceedings from a safe distance, his own BT7 having expired earlier, also with fuel-feed problems.

Graham Hill clinched the World Championship for BRM. He qualified third here behind title protagonists Clark and Hill, but made a slow start and eventually finished fourth behind the new World Champion and, perhaps ironically, the Coopers of McLaren and Tony Maggs.

Although the pilot Brabham Formula 1 programme was nominally handled by Brabham Racing Developments in 1963 (the name Motor Racing Developments would not officially be re-adopted until 1965), Jack decided that he would operate his Grand Prix team away from the production racing car business as from the start of 1963. Thus, while the cars continued to be built at the New Haw factory, Jack's Grand Prix machines were operated out of his new headquarters at Weyford House, Woodbridge Meadows, Guildford. That meant that Ron Tauranac had nothing to do with the operation of the Formula 1 cars right through until the end of the 1½-litre formula, concentrating his entire efforts on building up the production racing car business, a project he accomplished with outstanding results.

"That left the company in which I had an interest, BRD, designing and building the cars and then handing them over to BRO for £3000 per car," remembers Ron, "and if I then got some ideas to improve the design, then I made the necessary components and handed them over. They were never paid for as such, so BRD never earned anything out of that. It was a bit of a hiding to nothing in some ways, but we would run F/Juniors and later F2s, and Jack's contribution to those programmes were the trade contracts which provided us with the wherewithal to go racing. I did the design and ran the business . . ."

For 1963 Jack decided to field a pukka two car team and recruited the popular Dan Gurney to drive alongside him, the lanky Californian bringing an enormous amount of enthusiasm and additional experience to the programme. "At the end of 1962 I was caught by surprise when Porsche pulled out," admits Dan, "I liked the look of the Tauranac/Brabham partnership and I wanted to take the chance . . ." By this stage in his career Gurney had already been through the mill at both Ferrari and BRM before switching to Porsche and winning his first Grand Prix, the French at *Rouen-les-Essarts* for the German marque. The French track was lucky for him . . .

With most of the £10,000 budget for his season culled from traditional motor industry sources – which in this case meant the Esso petroleum company – Brabham opened the season using an updated version of his original BT3. For the first three British domestic races Brabham fielded a solo entry for himself with Gurney only joining the programme when the Championship contest got underway at Monaco on May 26.

Jack was classified seventh in the Glover Trophy at Goodwood after a lead became detached from the Lucas transistor ignition system while he was running a strong fourth, he non-started the Aintree 200 after a piston failure during practice (a shame, as he'd set second quickest time behind Jim Clark's Lotus 25) and he then made the outside of the front row for the Silverstone International Trophy meeting. He blew an engine during practice for this event as well, but this time a replacement was available and his mechanics worked throughout Saturday night in order to instal it.

Jack finished seventh in this race, using a special Hewland HD five-speed gearbox. Mike Hewland's small specialist factory at Maidenhead was at the dawn of its development into the biggest transmission manufacturer and supplier in professional motor racing. This was the second completely Hewland designed and built transmission incorporating a limited slip differential as standard equipment.

Tauranac: "When we built our first Formula 1 car there were no choices available in the gearbox department – there was only Colotti, so we put that type 34 Colotti in the first BT3. But Mike Hewland was then building his own VW-inspired unit for F/Junior and had the HD under development. Since we had contacts with him through the production car side, he eventually also made us a beefed-up version of his Mk 4 box for us. Later in the '63 season we also ran this at Zandvoort, but it tended to overheat. I suppose what we really needed was to dry-sump it, a task which seems pretty easy now, but when it started to run hot we decided that we would revert to the HD unit we had tried at Silverstone and we stuck with that thereafter . . ."

The World Championship chase started at Monaco on May 26 with Brabham still using his original BT3 while Gurney had the first of the new-spec, BT7s, this particular car offering slightly more in the way of cockpit room for the lanky Californian and the fuel tanks alongside the cockpit forming the body sides. Equipped with the Hewland five-speed gearbox, Gurney's new machine had the gear-change rod run along the top of the chassis with a diagonal rod over the gearbox casing from a right-hand gear-change in the cockpit, contrasting with the BT3's left-hand gear-change with a rod running beneath the engine to the Colotti six-speed gearbox. Both Brabhams were fitted with the latest specification Coventry Climax, short stroke, fuel injected V8 engines with Australian Lukey exhaust systems and megaphone tail pipes. The new car was broadly the same as the BT3, but included several minor improvements such as a re-designed front suspension layout with different top wishbones.

Unfortunately the weekend turned out to be a complete fiasco for Brabham whose BT3 suffered a major engine breakage during Thursday practice, a valve head breaking off and smashing a piston. He flew the damaged V8 back to England in his own private plane for repair work to be carried out, but when Jack returned to Monaco he found that Gurney's BT7 had suffered an almost identical failure just as Dan was geting into the swing of things during Saturday practice. The net result of this little drama was that there was only a single V8 for Gurney's use, Dan starting from sixth place with a 1m 35.8s behind Clark's pole position Lotus 25 (1m 34.3s), Hill's BRM (1m 35.0s), Ferrari new boy John Surtees and BRM's Richie Ginther (both sharing 1m 35.2s) and Innes Ireland's BRP Lotus 24-BRM (1m 35.5s). Dan completed the opening lap in seventh place and put in a promising mid-field performance until the crownwheel and pinion failed after 26 laps.

Brabham himself, without one of his own cars available, did a private deal with Colin Chapman to borrow the spare works Lotus 25-Climax V8, starting from the very back of the grid with the 1m 44.7s he had set in the BT3 prior to its mechanical demise. This Lotus was fitted with a ZF five-speed gearbox and Jack recalls it as "one of the most nerve-wracking races of my career because the gearchange gate was completely different to the Colotti layout on my own car. I drove the whole afternoon dreading that I might be about to select the wrong ratio." Jack had never so much as sat in this car prior to race morning and had a distinctly unproductive race, delayed by a pit stop and eventually finished eighth and last, 23 laps behind Graham Hill's victorious BRM.

On June 9 the Belgian Grand Prix took place at Spa-Francorchamps and Gurney was really getting into his stride now in the BT7, qualifying beautifully in second place with a 3m 55.0s to Hill's 3m 54.1s in the BRM. Brabham, again using the old faithful BT3, was inside row three behind Willy Mairesse's Ferrari 156, and the works Cooper-Climax V8s of Bruce McLaren and Tony Maggs. Jim Clark catapulted through from the third row to lead at the start in streaming rain, with both Jack's green and gold machines making very gentle getaways. Dan and Jack were no less than 15s behind Clark and Hill, in third and fourth places, at the end of the opening lap. Brabham's car suffered an intermittent short-circuit in the electric fuel pump system and he briefly stopped to try and get the problem fixed. Eventually he retired on lap 12 after a couple more abortive attempts to cure the car of its misfire. Towards the end of the race the circuit was almost flooded in truly diabolical conditions, but Clark kept control in what was soon to become acknowledged as typical fashion, winning from McLaren who passed Gurney's BT7 in the closing stages, leaving Dan third at the chequered flag.

Brabham's own new BT7, complete with Hewland five-speed gearbox, was ready for the 80 lap Dutch Grand Prix at Zandvoort on June 23, while Gurney's sister machine now sported new Australian-designed driveshafts incorporating sliding pot outer universal joints, thus doing away with the sliding splines on the shaft itself. At the start of practice Dan's BT7 suddenly stopped and refused to restart. The Brabham crew thought this was all most confusing, for the American's car had been thoroughly tested at Silverstone before this event, but it was discovered that the rear bearing on the tubular jack shaft which runs along the vee of the Climax engine's crankcase, from the timing gear to the distributor, had seized and the shaft had twisted through 180-degrees. As there was no spare shaft or engine available, Dan had to join the ranks of spectators while delivery of a fresh engine from Climax was arranged.

Practice on Friday afternoon saw Jack circulating in Dan's helmet as he had forgotten his own. Later, clad in his usual "battle bowler", he exploited the BT7's fine handling characteristics to do a 1m 32.4s for the inside of row two behind the inevitable Clark's Lotus (1m 31.6s), Hill's BRM (1m 32.2s) and McLaren's

Great battle! Brabham hit top form in the 1964 Aintree 200 and gave Jim Clark as good as he got during a splendid demonstration of close-fought Formula 1 racing. Here Jack's BT7 just hangs on ahead of Jim's brand new Lotus 33 which was eventually wrecked when Clark crashed heavily avoiding Andre Pilette's slow Scirocco-Climax at Melling Crossing.

Cooper (1m 32.7s). Dan's replacement engine did not arrive until after practice on Saturday, so it was just as well that he had borrowed Jack's car on Friday afternoon to do a 1m 36.2s which put him alongside Giancarlo Baghetti's ATS on row six.

Before the race Gurney's car had some modifications carried out to the fuel lines and exhaust pipe mountings as the only engine available from Climax was a new flat-plane crankshaft V8 with separate bunches of exhausts and low level tail-pipes, one on either side of the gearbox. The "Australian" style pot-type drive-shafts had been fitted to Brabham's car while Dan's still retained the normal Hardy-Spicer splined shafts.

At the start of the Grand Prix Gurney further compounded his own problems by changing from first to fourth as he accelerated off the grid, dropping right back to the tail of the field as his rivals engulfed him on all sides. At the end of lap one it was Clark, Hill and Brabham at the head of the pack, with Dan charging through the tail-enders with great determination. Hill's BRM began to overheat and the Englishman eased his pace slightly, allowing Jack to get through to second place, but Graham soon repassed him. Eventually Brabham found himself increasingly troubled by a sticking throttle and, after a huge, tyre-smoking moment going into Tarzan, stopped at the pits for a new throttle return spring to be fitted. But he eventually retired with a broken chassis on lap 69.

Gurney, meanwhile, certainly had his hands full. He was forced to make a quick pit stop when a strip steel bracing strut, tensioned diagonally beneath the chassis, broke one of its anchorage points. Although this in itself was not particularly serious, a fuel line was attached to it and this had to be wired up in place. Dan returned to the fray and wound up a magnificent second, a lap down on Clark.

For the French Grand Prix at Reims on June 30, both BT7s were prepared to the same specification, Jack's now appropriately strengthened after the chassis breakage in Holland. Gurney's was still using the flat-plane crank V8 and he qualified third on 1m 21.7s behind Clark (1m 20.2s) and Hill (1m 20.9s) while Jack was fifth on 1m 21.9, equalling Surtees's fourth-quickest time.

The start was chaotic with Hill stalling his BRM, but Dan held Jimmy's Lotus on the run away from the start and it looked as though the Brabhams might be in with a chance. At the end of the day, however, there was no way and the ultra-slim Lotus 25 rattled off another cracking victory. Gurney was delayed with a stop to replace a broken gear lever and Brabham got up to second place only to roll to a silent standstill at *Muizon* with an electrical lead adrift. He lost a lap sorting out that little malfunction, but fought back to fourth, behind Clark, Maggs and Hill, and ahead of team-mate Gurney.

Three weeks later came the British Grand Prix at Silverstone and the BT7s performed superbly in practice, Brabham being the only team to get both its cars on the front row of the 4-3-4 grid. Clark's pole position Lotus 25 turned a 1m 34.4s, ahead of Gurney (1m 34.6s), Hill's BRM (1m 34.8s) and Brabham (1m 35.0s). Jim was slow off the mark on this occasion and the crowd was thus treated to the impressive sight of Jack and Dan holding 1-2 formation during the opening laps.

Clark wasn't to be denied, of course, and was through into the lead by the end of lap four. The curious gremlin that always seemed to afflict a Climax V8 when installed in a Brabham chassis claimed Jack's BT7, its engine failing on lap 29, so Dan took over in second place and made a game attempt to erode Clark's advantage. Unfortunately the other BT7 was to share its stablemate's fate, and, running 17s behind Clark with 22 of the race's 82 laps left to run, Gurney's Climax V8 expired spectacularly on the Hangar Straight, coating the track surface with a swathe of oil as the Brabham coasted to a stop at Stowe.

The German Grand Prix was scheduled for the Nurburgring on August 3, so both BT7s were prepared for this event, but Brabham took time off to field the original, Colotti-gearbox BT3 in the 25 lap non-title Solitude Grand Prix on June 28. He qualified second only to Clark's Lotus and when Jim suffered drive-shaft failure on the grid, Jack was left in peace to lead the 285.425km contest from start to finish. Peter Arundell's Team Lotus 25 finished second ahead of Innes Ireland's BRP-BRM.

The Solitude winning engine was installed in Jack's BT7 for the following weekend's German Grand Prix, while Dan had to make use of an earlier spec. injected V8 as the only thing that could be salvaged from the Silverstone blow-up were the cylinder heads. Clark was on pole at the 'Ring in 8m 45.8s with Brabham on the inside of row three (9m 04.2s) and Gurney the middle of row four (9m 17.2s). After the promise of Silverstone and the success at Solitude, this was nothing short of a fiasco for the Brabham teamsters. Jack's car didn't leave the grid and was pushed straight to the pits with transistor box failure. This was duly replaced and Jack joined in long after the pack had disappeared out into the country and he had a lonely race thereafter to finish a distant seventh.

Gurney was in and out of the pits for most of the time with an engine that refused to run properly, despite having all its electrical ancillaries changed. He eventually packed it in on lap seven when a locking nut came adrift in the gearbox . . .

While all this Formula 1 groundwork was being carried out by Jack and Dan, the Brabham Formula Junior cars were making substantial inroads into the Lotus and Cooper domination of this cut-and-thrust category for wide-eyed Grand Prix aspirants. One of the new boys was gritty New Zealander Denny Hulme, a rough-hewn character whose father had won a VC at Anzio and who had clearly

inherited all his Dad's hard-nosed determination.

Denny, soon to be known as 'the Bear' because of his often abrupt, some would say *sudden*, manner with strangers (particularly the press), had come over from New Zealand after winning a "Driver to Europe" award in 1959. After campaigning a hand-to-mouth trail round the Continental Formula Junior events using a Cooper-Ford during 1961. He planned to update it for '62, but fate then took a hand in the proceedings and directed Denny's career towards the Brabham marque.

"I was working in Jack's garage, in Hook Road, Chessington," recalls Hulme, "when Gavin Youl wrecked the works F/Junior Brabham at Crystal Palace and broke his collarbone. So Jack came into the garage and said 'You'd better get yourself over to New Haw and build yourself a Junior Brabham for Boxing Day Brands Hatch'. From then on I worked at New Haw building the production racers and had a works car in F/Junior '63 and then F2 in '64."

Truth be told, Brabham himself was not too convinced about Denny's potential, and it took Jack's business manager Phil Kerr a fair deal of persuading before Hulme was offered his chance. Interestingly, Kerr had been studying accountancy in New Zealand when he first met Bruce McLaren and it was Bruce who pointed him in Brabham's direction in 1959, mentioning to Jack that Phil would be interested in some sort of motor racing management job. It was at about the time that Jack's business ambitions were extending beyond purely Cooper horizons, so Phil came over in 1959. An avid Hulme supporter, when Denny eventually left Brabhams at the end of 1967 to join McLaren Racing, it would not be long before Phil Kerr followed after him . . .

Somewhat unexpectedly, Hulme received a bonus – his first Formula 1 outing during the summer of 1963. On August 11, Jack and Denny contested the non-title *Kannonloppet* at the Swedish Karlskoga circuit, this two-heat affair seeing the

Commiserations! Dan Gurney (left) and Jim Clark share each other's apparent disappointment at failing to win the 1964 Belgian Grand Prix, both the Brabham and Lotus 25, on the exhaust pipes of which Clark is casually supporting himself, rolling to a halt out of fuel at Stavelot. Unbeknown to the Scot, however, when this picture was taken he had already won the race, the Scot having failed to see the chequered flag and remaining under the impression he had run out on the last lap. Sadly, that fate belonged to Dan, whose BT7 had totally dominated the race from the start . . .

22

Dan's day at last! For a change, everything went right for Gurney in the 1964 French Grand Prix at Rouen-les-Essarts. Clark had the trouble on this occasion, retiring with engine failure, to leave the Californian's Brabham BT7 a clear run through to victory. Here Gurney steers round the cobbled Nouveau Monde hairpin on his way to the marque's first Grand Prix success. Looking at that rollover bar related to Dan's height makes one realize just how attitudes towards car safety have changed in two decades! Inset on his way to victory, Gurney looked tense and concerned: perhaps not surprising after his disappointment at Spa.

Brabham twins ranged against the works Lotus 25s and a bunch of make-weight also-rans.

Clark and Trev Taylor buttoned up the first heat in 1-2 style and after Brabham hit trouble, they allowed him to win the second heat so he would pick up third place on aggregate. Jack used a BT7: Denny was allocated the old BT3 and finished fourth on his F1 debut. His only memory of the place is that "it hosed down with rain and they threw gravel on the track – which made things worse because you then couldn't tell the oil from the rain!"

A week after this Swedish outing, Jack fielded a lone BT7 entry for himself in the non-title *Gran Premio del Mediterraneo*, emerging a troubled 12th from the 60 lap slipstreaming blast round the sun-baked Enna-Pergusa circuit in central Sicily. Frenchman Jo Schlesser swelled the ranks at the wheel of a '63 F/Junior Brabham BT2, powered by a 1500cc Ford pushrod engine, and he was classified a similarly disappointing, troubled 11th.

On September 1 the rutted Zeltweg military aerodrome hosted another non-Championship Austrian Grand Prix in conditions almost as sweltering as those experienced in Sicily the previous weekend, offering a foretaste of the local ambiance to be enjoyed by those who would eventually attend the Osterreichring, yet to be built on a site nearby. Jack Brabham was the team's sole entry yet again, now using the Solitude-winning BT3 and qualifying second once more behind Clark's Lotus 25.

Brabham led from the start, pursued by Clark and Innes Ireland's BRP Lotus 24-BRM, and while Jimmy got through into the lead on lap four he held it only for another five tours before his engine expired. By this time Jack had reasserted himself ahead of Ireland after the Scot had first slipped ahead of the BT3 and then spun, but Innes quickly got things back under control again and the race developed into a dice between the two of them.

By lap 55 Jack was dropping away slightly from the pale green-liveried Lotus, heat from the front mounted radiator and the water and oil pipes making it so oppressively unpleasant in the cockpit that he was almost unable to so much as touch the brake pedal with his foot, let alone press it really hard. What's more, fuel vapourization was causing the engine to cut out intermittently and he dropped even further behind. By lap 63 it looked as though Innes had it in the bag, but next time round as he approached the starting line, the oil pressure fell and the Scot parked it. That bitter misfortune handed Jack his second non-title F1 victory of the season in a car bearing his own name – by the incredible margin of *five laps* over Tony Settember's Scirocco-BRM and Carel Godin de Beaufort's four-cylinder Porsche.

For the resumption of the Championship contest at Monza on September 8, Brabham continued to handle the BT3 with Gurney in his newer BT7. Practice for the Italian Grand Prix saw quite a healthy old row about the state of the banked sections of the Monza circuit, the bumps and vibrations taxing some of the British cars rather more than had been expected. Behind the scenes many of the teams began to drum up a petition to have the race restricted to the road circuit only, but the local police came to everybody's assistance and allowed both the organizers and the teams to save face. They said that the spectator protection round the lower edge of the banking was inadequate, so the race took place on the road circuit after all.

The scramble for grid positions saw one hell of a battle between Ferrari and BRM power, the Climax brigade being left a little breathless on this occasion. Dan's car was fitted with the latest Climax V8 and Hewland HD gearbox, qualifying on the inside of row three on 1m 39.25s as compared with Surtees's pole in the Ferrari V6 of 1m 37.3s followed by Hill's BRM (1m 38.5s), Clark's Lotus (1m 39.0s), and Ginther's BRM (1m 39.19s). Behind Dan was Bandini's Ferrari on 1m 40.1s and Jack's older BT3 on 1m 40.4s.

Surtees showed impressive form in the opening stages of the 86 lap, 307.28 mile thrash, leading strongly with Clark hanging on behind a small gap opening to Hill's BRM and Gurney. On lap 17 the Ferrari suffered engine failure, leaving

Jim's Lotus with a handy advantage, but deprived of the Italian car's slipstream, Clark fell back into the clutches of the pursuing BRM and Brabham. Dan took the lead on lap 21 as they lapped Trintignant's private BRM V8, Jim Hall's BRP Lotus 24-BRM, Phil Hill's ATS and Jo Siffert's Lotus 24-BRM and from that point onwards the leading trio swapped places unceasingly, so it was only a matter of time of waiting to see who would outfumble whom on the run in to the flag.

Hill dropped from the fray with clutch trouble, so it came down to a battle between Clark and Gurney, a contest finally resolved in Jim's favour when his rival brought the Brabham into the pits at the end of lap 63 suffering from fuel feed problems. Brabham was in third place at this stage, but his engine suddenly cut out and he fumbled to switch over to the small reserve supply, but still the V8 refused to pick up cleanly. He therefore made a quick pit visit to top up with extra fuel, dropping to fifth place behind the victorious Clark, Ginther, Bruce McLaren's Cooper-Climax and Innes Ireland's BRP-BRM. Although he was not running at the finish, Dan's BT7 was classified 14th.

Both Brabhams contested the Oulton Park Gold Cup on September 21, Jack finishing fourth behind Clark, Ginther and Hill while the perenially unlucky Gurney was left on the line thanks to a dud transistor box, started late and then eventually retired. The cars were then rushed back to Guildford where a busy time ensued preparing them for the United States and Mexican Grands Prix the following month.

During practice for the American race at Watkins Glen, where both drivers used their usual BT7s, Gurney's flat plane crank Climax V8 sprung an oil leak from one of its cylinder heads so it was decided to install the spare engine the team had brought along "just in case". Hill took the BRM round in 1m 13.4s for pole position from Jim Clark (1m 13.5s), Surtees's Ferrari (1m 13.7s), Ginther's BRM (1m 14.0s), Brabham (1m 14.2s) and Gurney (1m 14.5s). Clark was left on the line with fuel pump problems and eventually joined in a lap and a half in arrears and Gurney settled down to hold fourth place during the early sprint. He quickly worked his way through to second place behind Surtees's fast-vanishing Ferrari V6 and made a firm effort to catch the Italian car before succumbing to a cracked Brabham front wishbone mounting. Brabham himself finished the day fourth behind Hill, Ginther and the superb Clark who had made up miles on his rivals and would undoubtedly have won for Lotus had it not been for his earlier delays.

Mixture control problems abounded amongst the competitors when practice started for the Mexican Grand Prix, the *Magdalena Mixhuca* circuit situated some 7400ft above sea level in this Central American capital city. Jack and Dan used the same cars again, but the mechanics seemed unable to pinpoint and rectify a fuel feed problem which had slowed Gurney slightly during the race at the Glen. None the less, despite gearbox troubles in practice, Gurney qualified fourth behind Clark, Surtees and Hill and moved quickly through into second place once the race got underway. By lap 25 Dan was 25s behind Clark's Lotus, seemingly set for a safe second place, when it seems that a major misunderstanding, or straightforward "cock up", robbed him of his runner-up status!

It appears that Gurney forgot that the BT7's auxiliary fuel tank had not been fitted on this occasion, so when he turned the reserve tap on, the fuel gushed out all over his feet! He then found he couldn't close the tap and had to make a hurried pit stop for this to be rectified, eventually dropping to a distant sixth some three laps behind. Brabham thus ran out the race second to Clark, with Ginther, Hill and Jo Bonnier's Rob Walker Cooper T66-Climax splitting the two BT7s at the flag.

By now it was fairly clear that Ron Tauranac's Brabham chassis were pretty impressive propositions, the BT7s clearly as good-handling as anything apart from the monocoque Lotus 25. There were those, of course, who still maintained that the only real advantage that Lotus had on its side was Jimmy Clark, but that point of view devalued Chapman's part in the overall equation. None the less, Gurney was a flier: it only required the Brabham-Climax to hang together for the lanky, good-natured Californian to bring home the results.

As if to underline this point of view, Gurney's BT7 ran faultlessly in the final race

After the Brabham team's victory in the French Grand Prix, Gurney's fans flocked to Brands Hatch in their droves hoping that Dan would dish out a firm defeat to Clark on his home ground. Here at the start Clark's pole position Lotus 25 (No. 1, far left) accelerates cleanly into the lead from Gurney's BT7 (No. 6, right) and Graham Hill's sliding BRM (No. 3, centre). From the second row Surtees's Ferrari is looking for a way through while Jack's BT7 is lagging behind slightly. Jack finished fourth behind Clark, Hill and Surtees, but an early stop with ignition trouble scuppered Dan's chances.

of the season, the 85 lap South African Grand Prix at East London on December 28. Clark's Lotus bagged its inevitable pole position in 1m 28.9s, but Brabham (1m 29.0s) and Gurney (1m 29.1s) were alongside the Scot on the front row of the grid. Surtees briefly poked his Ferrari into second place behind the runaway Clark on the opening lap, but Gurney was soon through and held runner-up spot for the entire race. At the chequered flag, he was the only other runner to have completed the full distance. Jack over-revved his Climax V8 early in the race as he sought to get ahead of Surtees, losing about 700rpm from the top end. Later he spun at the Esses and finally retired with a split fuel tank. English amateur David Prophet fielded a '63 spec. BT6 F/Junior for this event, as he had in the Rand Grand Prix at Kyalami a fortnight earlier, but failed to finish in the final round of the Championship.

The success of those works Brabham Formula 1 entries naturally prompted a considerable degree of interest from amongst the privateers in Grand Prix racing, most of whom had relied on Lotus or Cooper products in an attempt to keep up over the previous couple of years. By the end of 1963, however, Cooper's level of competitiveness was questionable and Lotus sustained a clear and open policy of never allowing the customer to have equipment anywhere near as good as that available to the works drivers. Several private entrants had been more than a bit put out when Colin Chapman sold them Lotus 24s at the start of 1962, assuring his customers that they were being supplied the "1962 Lotus". He then equipped his works team with the monocoque 25s, saying they were the "1963 cars" under development.

Interestingly, if anything, Brabham was to adopt a totally opposite approach. Although the low-slung Brabham-Climax design hardly changed at all between 1963 and 65, a batch of customer cars, dubbed BT11, were laid down for the 1964 season and supplied to private customers before the factory team took over its own. These new BT11s were rather late being delivered to their new owners at the start of the '64 season, resulting in some non-starts in the British domestic non-Championship events which preceded the World Championship events, but there was *one* private Brabham which was ready for the start of the season. Jack's original BT3 was sold to Brighton garage owner Ian Raby and fitted with a BRM V8.

In depressingly familiar streaming wet conditions, the bleak airfield wastes of Snetterton saw the season open on March 14 with the *Daily Mirror Trophy* meeting, providing a lucky victory for Innes Ireland's new BRP-BRM. Jack appeared in a BT7 modified to take the latest 13in. tyres on Brabham cast wheel rims, but these new "podgy" Dunlops were not the trick in these appalling conditions and, after a spin which bent the exhaust pipes, Jack called it a day. Raby was also a non-finisher on this occasion.

On March 30 the *News of the World Trophy* at Goodwood saw Brabham out again in a different BT7 while Raby was the only other representative of the marque. Using revised suspension geometry to accommodate the bigger Dunlops, Jack sliced a second off the existing record to take pole position ahead of Clark's Lotus 25B and Hill's BRM P261. Graham boomed into the lead at the start and dominated the contest until a rotor arm broke in the closing stages, handing Clark's clutch-troubled Lotus a surprise win. Brabham's BT7 had second place in the bag until a rear wheel rim split, the tyre deflated and Jack found himself spinning off at Madgwick "just as he was counting the money."

Raby trailed his Brabham BT3 all the way to Sicily for eighth place in the Syracuse GP on April 12, but six days later Jack Brabham fielded his updated BT7 in the 67 lap, 201 mile Aintree 200. Hill took pole for BRM with a 1m 52.8s while Brabham was next 0.2s slower ahead of Pete Arundell's Lotus 25 and Clark's brand new 33. Graham led away from the line, but the race soon developed into a sensational contest between Brabham and Clark, the "Old Man" having the legs of his brilliant rival on this rare occasion. Jim got ahead on lap 26, but was unable to get away. On lap 42 Jack reversed the situation and, five laps later, the Lotus team leader tripped over André Pilette's slow Scirocco-Climax as they hurtled through Melling Crossing. The Lotus crashed heavily, Clark fortunately emerging unhurt, but Brabham was left to canter home to a well-earned victory. Hardly noticed by comparison with the attention focussed on his boss, Dan Gurney came through from the back of the grid to fifth place before retiring with a broken rubber driveshaft coupling.

By the time it came to the International Trophy meeting at Silverstone on May 2, two of the "customer" BT11s had been delivered. One, with a carburettor Climax V8 engine, was delivered to plucky former motorcycle ace Bob Anderson who had campaigned an ex-Bowmaker Lola-Climax throughout 1963, while the other went to that doyen of private team owners, Robert Ramsay Campbell Walker.

Operating from their racing shop adjacent to Pippbrook Garage in Dorking, Rob Walker's distinctive dark blue Formula 1 challengers with their white nose bands had sallied forth to do battle with the works teams for many years. One of motor racing's last real gentlemen in the true sense of the word, Rob Walker was, and is, none the less a shrewd businessman and a passionate racing enthusiast. However, since Stirling Moss's terrible accident at Goodwood two years earlier, the Walker team had not exactly enjoyed much in the way of success. Stirling's successors Maurice Trintignant and Jo Bonnier were worthy enough drivers, but mere journeymen compared with the brilliant Englishman.

Rob had opted for these steady performers after the deaths of both Ricardo Rodriguez and Gary Hocking at the wheel of his Lotus 24-BRMs at the end of the 1962 season. What's more, Walker's famous chief mechanic Alf Francis had slipped into a background consultancy role and the cars were now in the technical custody of John Chisman and Tony Cleverley. The BT11 was built up at New Haw by Walker's lads, which, recalls Cleverley, "involved three days and three nights hard at it only to see the thing go up in smoke not half-way round its first practice lap at Silverstone!"

Bonnier vacated the cockpit just in time to avoid his rump being singed and

Gurney really got to grips with the Nurburgring during the 1964 German Grand Prix, running in close company with Clark and Surtees until his BT7 began to overheat and he had to make a pit stop. An indication of the suspension loads involved in negotiating this banked corner can be gained from the contrasting angles of the front upper wishbones in this photograph.

although the foam-drenched Brabham looked a wreck at first glance, another intensive stint by the Walker mechanics saw it resuscitated in time for the Dutch Grand Prix.

The works team covered itself in glory during Silverstone practice, Gurney and Brabham qualifying first and second fastest ahead of Hill and Clark. They were slow off the mark, but Dan powered into the lead on lap seven and stayed there until loss of fluid from a rear brake seal caused his retirement 13 laps later. That left Brabham ahead, but Hill came back at him and it looked as though the BRM would just keep its advantage through to the end of the 52 lap race. However, Jack was not to be denied and, in a brilliant lunge round the outside of Woodcote on the very last lap, snatched victory by a nose. Both cars were credited with the same race time, but Jack bagged fastest lap at 112.58mph! Anderson retired his new mount with clutch trouble.

For the Monaco Grand Prix on May 10, Jack and Dan retained their '63 BT7s, Brabham's car appearing with new solid driveshafts incorporating rubber doughnuts, while Gurney's had the earlier Hardy Spicer shafts with sliding splines, although these were later changed to match his team mate's. Anderson had his private BT11 but Bonnier was in the Walker team's old Cooper T66 while his BT11 was being repaired.

A heated battle for pole saw Clark emerge in command with a 1m 34.0s ahead of Brabham (1m 34.1s), Hill and Surtees (sharing 1m 34.5s), then Gurney on 1m 34.7s. Clark put in a stupendous opening lap, but clipped the straw bales at the harbour front chicane, carrying on at unabated speed despite dislodging the rear anti-roll bar.

Brabham, Hill, Gurney, Surtees and Ginther led the pursuit with Dan scrambling through to second by lap 12, although he was unable to make more than the odd second here and then on Clark. Jack pulled up onto his team mate's tail before retiring on lap 29 with fuel injection problems and when Colin Chapman, fearful that Clark would be black-flagged by race officials, called his man in to have that trailing roll bar disconnected and removed, so Gurney surged into the lead. Was this going to be the Brabham team's first Grand Prix success? The question was answered very firmly in the negative on lap 53 when Hill forced the BRM through into the lead and, nine laps later, the BT7 broke its Hewland gearbox. Anderson, who had qualified 12th on 1m 38.0s, had an unlucky race, retiring on lap 91 when the bolts retaining the rear cover of his BT11's Hewland gearbox worked loose and let out all the oil. He was classified seventh, but would otherwise have been in the points . . .

After the first practice session for the Dutch Grand Prix at Zandvoort, Jack Brabham flew off to Indianapolis qualifying. He had returned a 1m 33.8s in his BT7 and that was good enough to retain him a third row starting place throughout the Saturday session. Gurney took pole with his BT7 on 1m 31.2s from Clark's Lotus 25, although most independent time keepers reckoned it should have been the other way round. Either way, Jim led from start to finish in Champion style, leaving Gurney to battle with Hill and Surtees for second place. On lap 22 Dan arrived in the pits complaining "something feels wrong with the rear suspension . . " The mechanics looked closely but could find nothing amiss, but they *did* notice a broken spoke on the BT7's steering wheel! Since there were still 56 laps left to run, and no replacement steering wheel available, that was the end of that . . .

Brabham climbed up to fifth and was closing on Peter Arundell's Team Lotus 25C when the distributor drive sheared and he was out as well. On the privateer front Bonnier's Walker BT11 was on hand again, taking eighth place, two laps behind the impressive Anderson who managed a fine sixth in his Climax-engined car. A late arrival on the scene was genial Swiss Jo Siffert's new BT11-BRM (with Colotti gearbox) which had been completed at New Haw by his mechanics Heini Mader and Jean-Pierre Oberson and rushed out to Holland just in time to compete. Siffert qualified last after only a few laps in his unsorted new mount and was classified a distant 13th after a troubled run.

All these minor, niggling little reliability problems were beginning to get on Dan Gurney's nerves because, inwardly, he felt certain he was one of the few people who could genuinely get on terms with Jim Clark's Lotus. However, what followed at the 1964 Belgian Grand Prix was an even more cruel disappointment: this was the fateful day on which Dan Gurney was the absolute class of the field, yet found himself deprived of a well-earned victory. His Brabham BT7 ran out of fuel . . .

Anybody who could drive competitively at the old Spa-Francorchamps circuit was, unquestionably, an ace of the first order. In practice for this particular race Gurney whistled round in 3m 50.9s which was over five seconds faster than anybody else could manage in the first session and, quite obviously, more than adequate for pole position. Hill eventually speeded up to 3m 52.7s and Brabham himself took the last place on the front row a mere tenth slower than the moustachiod Englishman, Jack later remarking laconically, "It must be our monocoque chassis and inboard front springs paying off on such a fast circuit!"

At the start of the 32 lap, 280.41 mile race Arundell briefly got the jump on his rivals, poking his Lotus 25 through from the second row to lead away up the hill beyond *Eau Rouge*, but Gurney was soon through to the front of the field. Surtees managed to scramble to the fore very briefly, only for his Ferrari V8 to go sick on him, and thereafter "Dan the Man" simply upped and disappeared from his rivals's sight.

Tauranac puts at least part of the effectiveness of those early Brabham-Climaxes on fast circuits down to some aerodynamic lessons learned from informal links with no less a Company than Jaguar. "I knew Malcolm Sayer, who had done the aerodynamics of the D-type, and we went to the MIRA wind tunnel under his auspices. From that we learned to run the nose of our cars as close to the track as possible in order to prevent too much air getting underneath and generate lift. I think this was the problem with the Lotus 24 which Jack had complained about at Spa in 1962 . . .

By lap five Gurney had 12s on the battle between Clark and Hill for second place, with McLaren's Cooper hanging on grimly in fourth spot. Surtees managed a 3m 52.4s before his retirement, but Dan came back with a 3m 52.3s and followed that up with lap record after lap record, finally settling the matter beyond question with a stunning 3m 49.2s on lap 27. That was an average speed of 137.60mph, a reasonable enough lap speed in the mid-1980s, but this was with a tiny little spaceframe Brabham powered by a 200bhp Climax 1½-litre V8 running on tyres narrower than those you nowadays find on a Porsche 928 road car!

On lap 28 Clark's overheating Lotus stopped to top up with water and then, horror of horrors, Gurney was slowing. On lap 30 Hill boomed past in the lead as Dan tore into the pits crying "fuel, fuel!" There was none immediately available, so rather than wait for churns to be humped in from behind the pits, Gurney resumed the chase, intent on coming in next time round. He had almost ground to a halt on the previous lap as the Brabham stuttered, low on fuel, but the mechanics were convinced he had sufficient to make it.

Thus, into the last lap the order was Hill, McLaren, Gurney and Clark, but Dan never made it to the finish, stopping before *Stavelot* with dry tanks. Hill ran out a few yards afterwards, leaving McLaren to stagger on towards the chequered flag, his Cooper misfiring ominously with a flattening battery. It looked as though Cooper was about to score an incredibly lucky outside win, but Clark came as if from nowhere and surged by Bruce within yards of the flag to take the unlikeliest win of his career. His Lotus ran out of fuel on the slowing-down lap and he coasted to a halt by Gurney's Brabham, not realizing he had won the race. The two men commiserated with each other until the truth was known . . .

An embarrassed Jack Brabham finished third behind McLaren, but, in reality, the 1964 Belgian Grand Prix highlighted the difference between Clark and Gurney. Both men were brilliant performers behind the wheel, but it was Clark who had the Midas touch, in whose direction the good fortune always ran. Gurney, who could never resist "fiddling" with his car at the last minute prior to the start of the race, never scaled the same heights, even though everybody knew he was as

Brabham privateers photographed during the 1965 British Grand Prix at Silverstone. In the foreground is Jo Bonnier's Rob Walker BT7-Climax, Jack Brabham's ex-works machine, while, running wide behind the bearded Swede, is the Willment-entered BT11-BRM handled by Aussie Frank Gardner. This machine was originally owned by the Walker team and took Graham Hill to victory in the two-heat, non-Championship Rand Grand Prix at Kyalami in December, 1964. Later it was used in the 3-litre F1 by John Taylor, equipped with a 2-litre BRM V8.

quick as the Scot.

Happily, Dan Gurney had only a fortnight to wait after his Spa disappointment before everything ran his way for a change. In the French Grand Prix at *Rouen-les-Essarts* Clark's Lotus started from pole, but was chased by Dan's BT7 from the word go, the Brabham now featuring a cockpit manual adjustment for the fuel injection mixture control, a system first seen on the Team Lotus cars the previous summer. This time it was Jim's turn to encounter bad luck, engine failure caused probably by gravel lodging in the unprotected fuel injectors bringing him to a halt on lap 29.

So it was Dan's day for Brabham at last, a long-awaited celebration for the little team from Guildford, and a justification for Jack Brabham's decision to go it alone after splitting with Cooper. Hill's BRM scrambled home second, but it wasn't for the want of trying on Jack's part, and the "Guv'nor" hounded him all the way to the line in a close third place. Further back, Bob Anderson's BT11 finished 11th but Siffert retired with engine trouble. The Rob Walker team did not attend this meeting after failing to agree starting money with the organisers.

After this French success, much was expected from the good-handling Brabham BT7s in the first British Grand Prix ever to be held at Brands Hatch on July 11. Clark, Hill and Gurney made a formidable trio lining up together on the front row, with Dan chasing the Scot hard for the first three laps. Then a communal groan from the crowd indicated that Gurney was in trouble, peeling off into the pits at the end of lap three with smoke pouring from the transistor ignition box.

Gurney lost five laps while replacement components were fitted, so there was no chance of catching up once he resumed the race. Clark held off Hill for another "routine" Lotus win while Surtees was third for Ferrari ahead of Brabham himself, delayed by a pit stop to change a deflated rear tyre. Bandini's Ferrari was fifth while Phil Hill's Cooper-Climax T73 was hard-pressed to hold off Bob Anderson's private DW Racing BT11 for sixth place. It was a sign of how times had changed . . . Siffert finished 10th, while a broken hub and a broken brake pipe claimed Raby's BT3-BRM and Bonnier's BT11-BRM respectively. Aussie Frank Gardner's Willment-entered Brabham-Ford BT10 FJ got tangled up in a startline shunt and failed to complete a single lap.

The busy summer schedule continued at Solitude the following weekend where the 20 lap, 141.78 mile non-Championship event was ruined by torrential rain with no fewer than seven cars, including Brabham's own BT7, skating off the circuit on the opening lap. Clark, predictably, got on with the job of winning from the plucky Surtees's Ferrari while Anderson profited from the indiscretions of his more senior colleagues to take a good third – even though he had to extricate his Brabham from a ditch at one point in the proceedings!

By this stage in the 1964 season, Surtees was spearheading a Ferrari renaissance and Clark was dislodged from pole position at the *Nurburgring* during practice for the German Grand Prix on August 2. *Il Grande John*, as he had been dubbed by his Italian supporters, slammed round fastest in his Ferrari 158 to record an 8m 38.4s best. Clark was 0.4s slower in second place followed by Gurney's BT7 (8m 39.3s) Bandini's Ferrari 156 (8m 42.6s), Hill's BRM (8m 43.8s) and Brabham (8m 46.6s). Siffert qualified 10th, Bonnier 12th and Anderson 15th. JoBo's Walker car retired on the opening lap with major electrical problems while Anderson stopped early on to top up with water, losing himself a lot of time.

Gurney loved the 'Ring and was determined to get in amongst the front-running bunch from the start. On lap three he was up to second place and got right up alongside Surtees as they braked for North Curve, going through into the lead a little further on when the Ferrari ran wide going into a corner "out in the country". The American finished lap four at the head of the field, but even then it was possible to see that paper debris was blocking up the Brabham's radiator intake . . .

Surtees led on lap five, but Dan was back in front on lap six and, although he briefly dropped away again as the Brabham began to overheat, Gurney threw caution to the wind and hauled back at the Ferrari, turning an 8m 42.9s to set a new lap record. Surtees responded with an 8m 39.0s, but Dan's challenge ended when he had to stop on lap 11 for attention. He resumed, but after yet another stop, Gurney could only gain 10th place at the finish.

Surtees won handsomely from Hill and Bandini, Brabham losing a good fourth when his crownwheel and pinion broke shortly before the finish. This allowed "Seppi" Siffert through a well-earned fourth, rewarding both his mechanics who had worked right through the previous night in order to install a fresh engine.

At last the works team allowed itself the "luxury" of a development BT11, Jack Brabham running this car for the first time in the first World Championship Austrian Grand Prix at Zeltweg on August 16. But by that time the BT11 had scored its first race victory thanks to Jo Siffert's spectacular efforts in the previous weekend's *Gran Premio de Mediterraneo* at Enna-Pergusa. Fighting off a challenge from Clark's works Lotus for the entire distance, Siffert came home the winner by less than a second. Twelve months later he would score an absolutely identical victory over the same exalted rival at precisely the same place!

Rob Walker; "He was absolutely *magnificent*. On several occasions he would come through the right-hander before the pits completely sideways and you could see Jimmy moving this way and that behind him, wondering which way Seppi was going to spin. But he didn't, and kept in front all the way . . ."

The new BT11 fielded by Brabham in Austria featured many detail improvements over the "production" cars, including smaller pannier tanks clad in glass fibre rather than themselves forming the outer skin of the cockpit side panels. The spaceframe tubing had been tidied up behind the cockpit, there was revised panelling around the engine and new tubular drive-shafts with Hardy Spicer joints outboard and flexible Layrub joints inboard. Gurney had his regular BT7, but possibly the most portentous development could be seen in the Walker camp.

In deference to the rather aloof Bonnier, who didn't seem to be able to get on with the "cammy" BRM engine, Rob purchased the ex-works BT7 hitherto used by Brabham himself, installing in it the Climax V8 and Colotti six-speed gearbox from the Walker team's old Cooper. This enabled the Brabham-BRM to be made available to a self-confident, some would say arrogant, Austrian with a boxer's nose and an abundance of obvious talent. It was Jochen Rindt . . .

Inevitably the bumpy track surface exacted its toll on the machinery, but Gurney quickly got into the swing of things in confident style, opposite-locking his way round the straw bales to qualify fourth, although he would probably have gone even faster had not the left front upright broken and the BT7 slithered to a halt on its belly.

Fortunately Jack Brabham thought very quickly, stopping for a consultation with Gurney and then driving on round to the pits. The team had no replacement suspension uprights with them, so Jack realized that he would have to get in touch with Ron Tauranac at New Haw as quickly as possible. He drove off round the circuit and pulled into the paddock, but, finding that the keys for his hire car were still in the pits, climbed back into his new BT11, motored back round the circuit to collect them and then promptly returned to the paddock!

Brabham then quickly hopped into his hire car, drove back to his hotel and phoned Tauranac at New Haw. By this time it was late on Saturday afternoon, but Ron loaded up a suitcase full of parts and embarked at Heathrow on a flight to Vienna, via Frankfurt, and the components duly arrived at Zeltweg in the small hours of Sunday morning, in time for Gurney's car to be prepared for that day's race. It was ironic that Gurney, who was well in command of the 105 lap contest, found himself forced into the pits when the BT7 began handling rather strangely. He managed another slow lap before stopping for good with a front lower radius arm pulling out of the chassis. Brabham had stopped at the end of the opening lap with fuel pressure problems, but was still touring round in ninth place at the finish, while Anderson covered himself with glory by taking a fine third place behind Bandini's winning Ferrari and Ginther's BRM. Siffert had spun out on lap 19, damaging the BT11's water radiator while Bonnier was unlucky to lose third in the closing stages when a sick engine dropped him back to sixth at the finish. Rindt retired with broken steering.

On September 6 it was back to Monza again for the 1964 Italian Grand Prix and John Surtees's Ferrari V8 proved even more impressive than the V6 had done the previous year. The Italian car bagged pole with a 1m 37.4s, 0.8s ahead of Gurney's Brabham BT7, then Hill, Clark and McLaren. Having failed to go for a really quick time on the first day, Brabham found his Saturday efforts rained out so he had to start from way down on the inside of the fifth row, slower even than Ronnie Bucknum's Honda.

Hill was left on the line when his BRM's clutch slipped out of business and McLaren ducked through to lead round the opening lap, although Gurney and Surtees were at the head of the pack as they came up past the pits for the first time. The race was the usual heart-stopping slipstream special with Gurney and Surtees left to slog it out relentlessly after Clark dropped out with a melted piston. Sadly, the "Gurney gremlins" struck yet again and his engine began to misfire owing to an overheating fuel pump. He stopped at the end of lap 68 for cool water to be poured over the offending component, but this was not the answer, so all Dan could do was stutter round to finish a cheerless 10th.

Jack retired on lap 59 with a broken connecting rod after an early pit stop to change a battery interrupted his battle for fourth place. Thus the best Brabham finisher was Siffert in seventh place, with Anderson 11th and Bonnier 12th. Neither Raby's BT3-BRM nor the Walker Brabham-BRM hired out to local F3 tyro Giacomo Russo (who raced under the pseudonym of "Geki") managed to qualify.

Brabham took his new BT11 to North America for the US and Mexican Grands Prix which rounded off the season, but Gurney still stuck to his trusty BT7 while Bob Anderson, alone amongst the independents, failed to make the trip.

At Watkins Glen, Hap Sharp was installed behind the wheel of the Walker Brabham BT7-BRM, the pleasant American retaining this car for the Mexico race as well, although he was never destined to be much of a threat. Gurney joined Clark and Surtees on the front row of the grid at the Glen on October 4, but made a poor start and came round seventh at the end of lap one. He pulled through to fourth, but retired at the end of lap 69 with oil leaking all over the Climax V8.

Jack retired with piston failure after 14 laps, but Siffert upheld the Brabham reputation splendidly, surviving to take third place behind Hill's BRM and Surtees's Ferrari. Sharp was still running, with 65 laps under his belt, but was far too many laps in arrears to be classified after a lengthy pit stop to sort out gear selection problems. Bonnier's BT11-Climax retired with a broken stub axle, so the whole affair was a bit of a disappointment for the marque as a whole.

Still, every cloud has its silver lining and Gurney's consolation prize for a generally disappointing season came in the Mexican Grand Prix on October 25. This was the race in which the three-way World Championship battle between Clark, Hill and Surtees would finally be resolved and Jim indeed took pole just ahead of Gurney, the two cars separated by 0.8s. Clark took the lead at the start with Dan in furious pursuit and, just as it they had in France, the cards fell in Gurney's direction again. Clark had the race, and the title, in his pocket until an oil leak robbed him of victory almost within sight of the chequered flag. As his Lotus ground to a halt, Gurney roared through to win with Surtees being waved past into second place by team-mate Bandini on the last lap in order to clinch the Championship. Bonnier and Siffert retired with a broken wishbone and fuel pump failure respectively, while Brabham's race was badly compromised by a rough-running engine which eventually succumbed to amplifier failure. Sharp was classified 13th, five laps behind the winner.

After the Mexican Grand Prix the next major commitment for the majority of Grand Prix teams was the South African Grand Prix at East London on New Year's Day 1965, the opening round of a new title chase. But December 12 saw the non-Championship Rand Grand Prix take place at Kyalami where Graham Hill was entered at the wheel of the ex-Rob Walker Brabham BT11-BRM which had recently been acquired by Twickenham-based Ford dealer John Willment. Bob Anderson supplemented the Brabham ranks with his private BT11-Climax and there were a couple of F/Junior BT10s on hand for Paul Hawkins and David Prophet.

The race was staged over two 25 lap heats for an aggregate result and, with Jim Clark out of action with a slipped disc incurred whilst snowball fighting, Jackie Stewart was assigned a place in the works Lotus team alongside Mike Spence. JYS qualified comfortably on pole 0.6s faster than his team mate, but broke a drive-shaft on the starting line which eliminated him from the overall equation. He managed to win the second heat in some style from the back of the grid, but meanwhile Graham Hill had done likewise in the first heat and took aggregate victory by following Stewart across the line, 10s adrift, in the second. It was just over a fortnight before Stewart joined Hill in the BRM line-up.

Dan Gurney had a brand new BT11 for East London, but, far more significantly, appeared in practice running Goodyear tyres. Jack stayed on Dunlops at this meeting. Gurney: "I knew Goodyear was not quite ready for top-line F1 competition, but I also realized that they intended to have a real go. So I decided to take the plunge and pull Jack in as well . . ." Once this little deal was finalized it added another £10,000 to the team's budget – small beer by the profligate standards of the mid-eighties, but big money 20 years earlier . . .

Jack qualified on 1m 28.3s to take the outside of row one behind Clark (1m 27.2s) and Surtees (1m 28.1s), but it was a disappointing start to the season for Gurney, the man who had chased Clark so hard at Mexico the previous October. The American was a lowly 13th at the end of the opening lap and trailed into the pits at the end of lap four in order to investigate electrical trouble. He was stationary for 45 minutes before the engine burst into life again, but after a few more laps he packed it in.

Jack held fourth place in with the leading bunch until a misfire caused by fluctuating fuel pressure forced him into the pits as well. A faulty rectifier was

Jo Siffert put in some tremendously courageous drives in Rob Walker's BRM-engined BT11 during 1965, notably at Syracuse (above) where the Swiss is seen splitting John Surtees's Ferrari 158 and Jim Clark's Lotus 33 during their spectacular three-way battle for the lead. Eventually "Seppi" got ahead of both the World Champions and opened out a slight lead when the BT11 jumped out of gear and over-revved its engine. Below, Siffert hung on ahead of Clark at Enna-Pergusa later that season to win his second straight Mediterranean Grand Prix from the Scot, the BRM V8's superior top-end power just enabling him to out-run the Climax-engined Lotus.

found to be the problem and he had to make another stop later in the race to fit a fresh battery: he finished eighth. Anderson, who qualified in the middle of row five, had brake problems and several resultant spins, slogging on to finish last, while Siffert's BT11-BRM (now adopted by the Rob Walker stable) wound up seventh. Hawkins's BT10 was ninth, Prophet 14th and Bonnier's Walker BT7-Climax retired on lap 42 with transmission problems. The Kyalami-winning Willment Brabham-BRM, now entrusted to regular driver Frank Gardner, was classified 12th after a stop for a fresh battery after the alternator drive belt broke.

On March 13, the first Race of Champions meeting at Brands Hatch allowed both Brabham works entries to demonstrate the quality of Goodyear's latest racing rubber. Dan's BT11 developed injection pump trouble whilst being warmed up in the paddock for practice, so it was whisked back to Woodbridge Meadows for attention and he did his grid time in Jack's car, managing only a lowly 1m 38.1s. for a place on the outside of row five. Brabham's 1m 36.5s got him onto the second row behind an on-form Bonnier in the Walker BT7-Climax which recorded an identical time. In the first 40 lap heat Gurney was an absolute sensation, rocketing through the field to finish second behind Jim Clark's Lotus 33. Starting the second heat from alongside the Scot on the front row, Dan then harried the Lotus remorselessly, to the point where Clark made a rare error of judgement under pressure and crashed heavily on Bottom Straight, thankfully without injury. Sadly, Dan was unable to capitalize on Jim's misfortune, for his engine almost immediately packed up, allowing Jack into the lead. Then an oil leak wrote the end to the team chief's chances, leaving the way open for Mike Spence to bag a lucky victory.

Bonnier took third on aggregate behind Stewart's BRM, with Gardner fourth, Siffert sixth and Ian Raby's original BT3-BRM a distant ninth. Anderson's BT11, now equipped with the Climax V8 updated to latest short stroke specification and running on fuel injection, had a fuel pump control rod break as he went into Clearways: the fuel mixture suddenly went on to full rich and the unsuspecting driver lurched into an uncontrollable spin.

After this race Bonnier got a bit short with Rob Walker. "He was always the one handing out orders," Rob remembers, "He told me that he might have won if I'd given him some proper pit signals. I told him 'look, I run this team . . . any more from you and you're out'." As a sequel to this, Walker also recalls the occasion he had to tell Bonnier that he was not going to be needed for 1966. "We were driving to a Swiss hillclimb at the end of '65 and I told him I was going to run just one driver the following year. Automatically he replied 'what are you going to do with Siffert?' I just told him 'I'm going to have him drive my car . . .' "

Dear old "Seppi" quickly became Rob's favourite and it's a matter of history how the genial Swiss would eventually win the 1968 British Grand Prix in Walker's Lotus 49B – the last true privateer's victory in a World Championship round for a "proprietory" racing car. But even in 1965 Siffert could occasionally show the class that indicated he was cut out for even better things . . .

On April 4, "Seppi" was the star of the 56 lap Syracuse Grand Prix in sun-soaked Sicily. Clark's Lotus took pole from Surtees, Bonnier and Siffert and while Jo Bo was left on the line when his BT7's clutch wouldn't bite, Siffert hurtled through to challenge for the lead from the start. There followed an absolutely blistering three-way confrontation between Siffert, Clark and Surtees, the two World Champions pulling every trick in the book to keep the moustachiod Swiss at bay, but there was no denying the blue Walker Brabham which clearly seemed to have the legs of its rivals.

Rob Walker: "I advised Seppi to adopt Stirling's policy of going like hell in the early stages to pull out as long a lead as possible and break the opposition's morale, so he was running ahead of Surtees's Ferrari and Jim's Lotus when he came up to lap Bonnier who had been delayed by that clutch problem earlier in the race. I signalled to Bonnier "SIFFERT-SURTEES-CLARK" and he knew exactly what to do. Going into the fast corner after the pits – which was *just* on flat out – he let Seppi through and then eased very slightly in front of the other two. That gave

Sampling 32-valve Climax V8 power for the first time, Jack Brabham's works BT11 sprints out of Tabac *during the 1965 Monaco Grand Prix ahead of Bruce McLaren's sliding Cooper T77-Climax and Dick Attwood's BRM-engined Parnell team Lotus 25. In the absence of Gurney at Indianapolis, Jack rose to the occasion magnificently, but the engine blew up after the rev. counter drive became undone. Judging gear change points accurately from memory round this tight street circuit was asking a bit too much . . .*

Seppi a two second lead which the others never pulled back. Eventually, though, he retired when the gearbox jumped out of fifth over a bump . . ."

Heini Mader was quoted at the time as saying "scrutineering is a bit lax down in Sicily, so we used an 1880cc engine!", referring not only to Syracuse but also to Seppi's two Enna triumphs over Jim Clark. He was grinning broadly when he proferred that explanation, though . . .

A fortnight after Syracuse Brabham came home third in the 42 lap, 100.8 mile *Sunday Mirror Trophy* at Goodwood with Bonnier fifth for Rob Walker and Gurney classified ninth after retiring five laps from the flag with fading oil pressure. The race was won convincingly by Clark, his Lotus 33 equipped with the latest 32 valve Climax FMW V8 an example of which would eventually be allocated to the Brabham team. These powerful prototype units were put out on loan by Coventry-Climax and ownership was always retained by the engine manufacturer during this final season under the 1½-litre regulations. These four-valves-per-cylinder V8s developed around 210 bhp at 10,500 rpm, an increment of about 10bhp over the regular units.

Dan Gurney missed the Silverstone International Trophy owing to Indianapolis qualifying and the classic Memorial Day event prevented him from running in the Monaco Grand Prix on May 30. His absence allowed Denny Hulme to partner Brabham on both occasions, but the New Zealander's outing at Silverstone ended as early as lap seven with an oil leak. Brabham led convincingly, only for the BT11 to suffer a seized Hewland gearbox which eliminated him with only 13 laps left.

At Monaco, Jack had his first taste of 32-valve Climax V8 power, Hulme had a "regular" V8 while Jo Siffert's BT11 had been built up round a new spaceframe after he clipped the chicane during the Goodwood meeting and almost bent his Walker car double against the wall on the opposite side of the circuit. He was still limping very slightly . . . In the absence of Jim Clark at Indy, Graham Hill was really fired up to score a Monaco hat-trick for BRM and the poker faced Englishman took pole on 1m 32.5s, a scant 0.3s ahead of the on-form Brabham. Hulme qualified on the outside of row four on 1m 34.8s.

Initially Hill and Stewart looked as though they would put on a BRM 1-2 demonstration run, but Hill was delayed by a trip up the escape road at the chicane as he sought to avoid Anderson's slowing BT11 and Stewart spun at *Ste. Devote*. This allowed Black Jack to get in amongst the Ferraris and he quickly ensconced himself at the head of the field, pulling away in confident style. Unfortunately a thin whisp of smoke from the rear of the works BT11 heralded Brabham's retirement. A bolt had worked loose from the rev. counter drive, allowing oil to seep out over the engine. More importantly, Jack was therefore left with an inoperative rev. counter and the task of trying to judge his changes correctly round this gruelling street circuit proved just too much for him. He over-revved the engine and that was that . . .

Denny was looking good for a finish in the points after a characteristically steady run, but two of the four wheel retaining studs sheared on one rear wheel hub, so he had to creep round very carefully for the last few laps to pick up eighth place. Siffert was sixth, Bonnier seventh and Anderson ninth while Gardner's Willment car retired with a broken engine mounting.

By June 13 both Clark and Gurney were back from Indianapolis – which had been won by the Scot at his third attempt – and prepared to do battle over 32 laps of *Spa-Francorchamps* in the Belgian Grand Prix. Clark's Lotus 33 had its 32-valve Climax V8, but the Brabham team's similar unit had blown up on the test bed in Coventry, so Jack and Dan had normal 16-valve V8s installed. Hill took pole on 3m 45.4s, 2.2s ahead of Clark, and managed to lead the first half lap, but the race belonged to Jimmy in stupendous style. Driving with virtuoso brilliance on a streaming wet surface he finished 45s ahead of Stewart's BRM, the only other runner to go the distance. The works Brabhams were literally at sea on their Goodyear wet weather rubber, Dan finishing two laps down in 10th spot after a pit stop, while Jack ran non-stop to a distant, lapped fourth.

A dispute amongst the private owners over qualifying procedure saw several of their number boycott Friday practice, but that worked against Bob Anderson who then had mechanical problems on the second day and failed to qualify. The best of the independent Brabham runners in the race turned out to be Siffert's Rob Walker entry which splashed home eighth. Bonnier and Gardner both retired with ignition problems.

Brabham himself had no racing experience at *Clermont-Ferrand*, venue for the 1965 French Grand Prix, so he took the unexpected decision to stand down from this race and allow Hulme to handle the second works entry. He later reflected "I still don't really understand why I did that," but at the time he was deeply involved with formulating plans for the new 3-litre formula which started in 1966 and toying, somewhat distantly, with the idea of retiring.

Jack's decision seemed fully justified as far as the French race was concerned when Denny emerged fastest during the first day's practice, dropping to sixth a mere 0.7s slower than Dan in the eventual reckoning which wasn't bad by any means as Gurney was using the 32-valver on this occasion. In the race Gurney was delayed with an early pit stop thanks to a duff sparking plug. He then got going quite quickly before the engine blew up. Hulme finished a solid fourth behind Clark, Stewart and Surtees while Siffert was sixth behind Hill.

Gurney: "After Jack blew up that 32-valver at Monaco, it never ran well from that day onwards, even though Climax tried hard to repair it. My best run with it was at Clermont, I suppose, where I set fastest race lap quite early on. Then the darn thing broke, as usual, and Jimmy went faster anyway . . ." One should add, as a significant rider, that Clark certainly went faster – at the wheel of his old faithful spare Lotus 25 with a normal spec. 16-valve V8 installed!

Any promise that Gurney's performances might have held for Brabham were to be cruelly dashed as the 1965 season continued, the Guildford-based team reeling from disappointment to disappointment. Jim Clark was running riot across the

16

Tough as old boots, Denny "the Bear" Hulme grits his teeth and presses on to fourth place in the 1965 French Grand Prix at Clermont-Ferrand, a race at which Brabham stood down and let this new lieutenant have a crack behind the wheel of the BT11. Denny had previously won at Clermont in F2 and didn't let his boss down: in the first session, he was fastest of all!

Grand Prix circuits of Europe in that superb Lotus 33, on his way to his second World Championbship, and there was absolutely nothing Brabham could do about it – certainly not with only a 16-valve Climax.

Hulme was fielded as a third entry in the British Grand Prix at Silverstone and, although all three works Brabhams practised with 16-valve engines, Gurney's 32-valve V8 was installed in the early hours of race morning. Dan tried it out briefly up and down one of the runways and felt confident he would be in for a good race. Sadly, it was not to be . . .

When Gurney came round to his place on the starting grid after the warm-up lap, it appeared that the engine had a duff sparking plug and Tim Wall immediately removed it, only to have the thread in the cylinder head itself strip. This suggested that the plug had been cross-threaded, but the explanation was more serious than that. A valve had broken and this was what had caused the damage to the plug thread, so there was nothing to it but for Dan to abandon his car on the grid.

Without a moment's hesitation, Jack Brabham handed his car to Gurney and took over a non-participating role, but his own car didn't fit Gurney at all well and it wasn't set up to the Californian's taste. The net result was a distant sixth place, Gurney finishing with a completely bald left front tyre which so worried him that he was lifting himself up in the cockpit from time to time over the last few laps to ensure that the inner casing was not starting to show. Hulme retired with a broken alternator belt while well-placed just behind the leading bunch. The whole business of driving these small V8-engined 1½-litre cars was clearly totally unmemorable as far as Denny was concerned – during his talks with the author he flatly refused to accept that he had driven *any* Grand Prix cars during 1965, thinking that he had made his serious debut the following year. Only after some very detailed probing did it start to come back to him!

After that Silverstone *débâcle*, the Brabham team had to do without its 32-valve V8 for the Dutch Grand Prix at Zandvoort. Detailed examination of the engine had revealed precisely what happened. A valve head had broken on one bank of the engine, somehow been ejected up one of the injection intake pipes, hit the wire cage which prevents stones from entering the inlets and somehow bounced down a pipe on the opposite bank, causing untold mechanical mayhem within the engine. It was the last time the team would have the use of that unit for a race.

At Zandvoort the grid had a well-ordered look with Hill on pole in 1m 30.7s from Clark, Richie Ginther's Honda and Surtees (all sharing 1m 31.0s) and Gurney (1m 31.2s). Hulme deputized for Brabham yet again, qualifying in the middle of row three on 1m 32.0s while Siffert was on row four (1m 32.9s), Gardner row five (1m 32.9s) and Bonnier row six (1m 33.8s). Bob Anderson was even further back on 1m 34.1s after running in a rebuilt engine following piston ring problems during the British Grand Prix.

The race turned out to be another convincing Clark-Stewart, Scottish 1-2 with Dan third, Denny fifth, Gardner 11th and Siffert 13th. Hulme was lucky to scramble home fifth after a late race pit stop to investigate a misfire: the exhaust manifold on one bank of cylinders was cracked, but he hurried back into the race once it was realized that little could be done at that particular moment. Of the independents, Gardner was 11th Siffert 13th, Anderson retired with overheating problems and Bonnier's mount succumbed to ignition and fuel feed gremlins.

For the German Grand Prix at Nurburgring on August 1, Brabham fielded himself, Gurney and Hulme in a trio of 90-degree crankshaft Climax-engined cars, all with the cross-over high level exhaust systems. Dan had not got the power to get on terms with Clark's 32 valve Climax-engined Lotus 33 and the American qualified on the inside of row two with an 8m 29.0s, as compared with the Scot's pole winning 8m 22.7s. Anderson badly bent his private BT11 during practice and non-started: the car would not be seen again until the advent of the 3-litre formula the following year. Hulme managed an 8m 42.3s with Brabham trailing badly on 8m 44.9s, slower even than both the Rob Walker entries.

Gurney performed stupendously throughout the 15 lap, 342.15km race although he was no match for Clark's victorious Lotus which led from start to finish, clinching the Scottish driver's second World Championship. Hill's BRM was second, but Dan had the Englishman in sight on the long straights and was closing strongly by the end of the race. Jo Bonnier was showing splendid form in the Walker BT7 until a sudden slide unnerved him slightly and he came into the pits for a quick inspection. Nothing was broken, so he continued to seventh place, mentally kicking himself for that over-cautious approach. The gearbox on the Willment BT11 packed up on the opening lap, thereby ending Gardner's race, Hulme stopped with a leaking fuel tank and Siffert's BRM engine failed on lap 10.

On August 15 Siffert scored that memorable second Enna victory over Jim Clark, while the last race for the 1½-litre Formula 1 in Europe took place at Monza on September 12. Jack stood down yet again, the AC Milano offering a particularly attractive deal to run Giancarlo Baghetti in the works car instead. Gurney demonstrated highly disappointing practice form and could only squeeze onto the inside of row four with a 1m 38.11s, a full 2.3 away from Clark's pole. As he was using the 32 valve Climax engine on this occasion it was reasonable to suppose that the problem was not with Dan, but with the engine. So it proved, a peak reading of only 180bhp being revealed when it was subsequently tested on the Coventry-Climax dyno.

Dan used a regular Climax V8 in the race to trail home third behind the Stewart-Hill BRM 1-2 with Bonnier the only other Brabham to finish, in seventh place at the chequered flag. Hulme suffered a suspension breakage, while the unimpressive Baghetti lasted only 13 laps before encountering engine failure.

That power reading hardly left Gurney particularly enamoured over the prospect of using the 32-valver unit at Watkins Glen for his home Grand Prix, although the unit was on hand, oozing oil from every seal and joint as was becoming usual. It was used in practice, but taken out prior to the start of the race which Gurney started from seventh place on the grid, a second away from Graham Hill's BRM pole time. In the event the 110 lap race, held in blustery conditions with the odd driving rain shower, proved quite rewarding for the works Brabhams.

Jack scrapped with Hill for the lead, briefly getting ahead of the BRM only to fall foul of a slippery track surface less than half a lap later and slide onto the grass. He dropped to third and never made up this lost ground, leaving Dan to hammer home second in the other works BT11. It was good, but not good enough to convince Gurney over the merits of staying with Brabham for 1966. Even when the Californian rounded off the season with a terrific, hard-fought second place in the Mexican Grand Prix at Mexico City, the fine-handling BT11 almost catching Richie Ginther's significantly more powerful Honda, Dan could not quite bring himself to sign for 1966.

For three years Dan Gurney and Brabham had promised great things, but, somehow, the partnership never seemed fully to flower. The Brabham-Climaxes were good-handling cars and there had been occasions when they proved as fast as anything that could be ranged against them from Lotus, BRM or Ferrari. There was no ignoring Dan's driving credentials either. But he was getting edgy for sustained success and, after lengthy talks with Goodyear and Esso, opted to go his own way to develop the All American Racers Eagle-Weslake. If only he had stayed with Brabham it might have been he, and not Black Jack, who won the 1966 World Championship. And Jack himself might well have retired from the cockpit five years earlier than he did . . .

Gurney admits that it was a difficult decision to split with Brabham: "I felt at home on the team and Jack had gradually come to rely on my driving as the strongest. However, I had the chance to do it with my own Eagle . . . that was too good a prospect to turn down, so I had to say goodbye with regrets.

"I always admired Jack and enjoyed working with Tim Wall and Roy Billington. We were a *very* small team, really, but we always seemed to be in the hunt. Jack was a very good engineer and a great man to fix things in the field, despite the fact that we might not have the proper tools or facilities.

"He was also tighter than a bull's ass in fly season! Those were the days . . ."

19

2

Section 1: Jack's Brabham years, 1962-70

Chapter 2
Champion on his own terms: the Brabham-Repcos, 1966-68

Former team-mates in their own cars. Jack's new Brabham BT26 brakes hard for* Tabac *during the 1968 Monaco Grand Prix with Dan Gurney's Eagle-Weslake hard on his tail. It was a bad day for the former Brabham teamsters on this occasion, Jack retiring the Repco 860-engined car with a suspension breakage while Gurney's creation stopped with engine failure.

Although Jack Brabham had done a deal with Repco for the use of those premises in Surbiton and brought the Australian company's name onto his racing cars for the first time via a relatively minor sponsorship arrangement, the first contact between the two parties had been as early as 1957. Then the Repco-owned Hardy Spicer (Australia) company manufactured some special universal joints and drive shafts for Cooper and he used them during his two successful onslaughts on the World Championship in both 1959 and 60. Geoffrey Russell had founded Replacement Parts Pty Ltd as a one-man engine reconditioning business in Melbourne during the early 1920s, also making components for imported cars when such spares were in short supply from the manufacturers' sources. Russell's business thrived and when it went public in 1937 adopted the "Repco" brand name, derived from "Replacement Parts," as its overall title.

By the early 1960s Repco's success had led it not only to be the largest manufacturer of automotive components in the Southern hemisphere, but it was also exporting to 85 other countries. What's more, not only had it developed into the largest outside supplier of components to the Australian vehicle manufacturing industry, making pistons, piston rings, bearings, ring gears, gaskets, clutches, drive shaft assemblies, drop forgings and brake components, it also had a thriving trade supplying hand and machine tools, dies for metal pressings, gauges and balancing machines.

It was to this well-financed, ambitious and prestige-minded Australian company that Jack Brabham would eventually beat a path to talk about racing engine manufacture and, from the little acorns of a 2.5-litre Tasman power unit, a Formula 1 engine would be spawned to carry Brabham cars to a couple of convincing World Championships.

In the early 1960s, the long-stroke, four-cylinder Coventry-Climax FPF was providing the life blood of the Tasman formula, Australasia's most prestigious single seater racing category, but it was clear that supplies of spares for these engines would not last for ever. Thus Repco's Chief Engineer Frank Hallam and Project Engineer Phil Irving were instructed to produce a new engine to fit into the existing Repco Brabham chassis. This they duly did, their answer being a new V8 which was based round the General Motors Oldsmobile F85 cylinder block rather than a totally new, purpose-made, competition engine. Abandoned by GM after initially being developed as part of a linerless aluminium engine programme for a projected 3½-litre ,Buick "compact", Repco picked up the pieces of this commercial *débâcle* and transformed a road car disaster into a motor racing dream.

Initially it was intended that the engine should exclusively be employed in the Tasman formula when the programme started in the early Spring of 1964. At that time there were two seasons of the 1½-litre Formula 1 still to run, but by the time another year had passed it was becoming clear that many teams were going to face a problem when the formula changed to 3-litres, unsupercharged, at the start of the 1966 season. Coventry-Climax was not going to continue its Formula 1 involvement into the era of these new regulations, so there was clearly going to be a

Assembling Repco Grand Prix engines at the Australian firm's base near Melbourne, summer 1966. In the foreground is a single-cam, outside exhaust type 620 V8 of the type which propelled Jack to his third World Championship title.

major scramble to find a suitable engine for the teams who intended to tackle the 3-litre formula.

Irving's development work on the F85 block led him to the conclusion that it could cope with engine dimensions within the range 2.5 to 4.4-litres, so its potential could encompass Tasman formula, Group 7 sports cars *and* Formula 1, should the decision be taken to capitalize on this capability. The block would need stiffening, so this was duly achieved by a steel tie-plate sandwiched between the crankcase and sump, and overhead camshafts on each head to replace the standard central camshaft within the vee which activated the overhead valves by long pushrods.

In order that the engine should be kept as narrow as possible to facilitate installation in the current Brabham chassis, Irving therefore opted for straightforward mirror heads for each cylinder bank, employing parallel valves in wedge-shaped combustion chambers, angled inwards at 10-degrees from the cylinder axis and operated by single overhead camshafts. All the unwanted holes and apertures now made redundant by the scrapping of the pushrod valve gear were plugged and filled while the engine's internals were all new. Laystall machined new crankshafts in England to run on five main Repco bearings, Repco's own pistons were cast in aluminium silicon alloy and two attractive magnesium castings rounded off the conversion. One was a Y-shaped cover for the camshaft drive chains, the other a 3¼in. deep ribbed sump which helped stiffen the crankcase even more to deal with the power increase it was now subjected to.

With a bore and stroke of 85 x 55mm, the 2.5-litre Repco V8 first burst into life on March 21, 1965 on the Repco test bed at Richmond, Victoria. It was to mark the start of a tremendously exciting Australian racing development which would take the stock block V8 much further than ever anticipated at the time Irving and Hallam first set out to produce it. By the time that first 2.5-litre unit was spluttering its way into hesitant action there were Formula 1 irons in the fire. Jack Brabham was pressing Repco hard to commit itself to a Grand Prix programme for

1966, so Phil Irving spent much of the 1965 summer over in England burning the midnight oil with Jack, sorting out the detailed specification of this proposed new variant. However, there were other problems in other areas to be surmounted before Jack could press the green light on his own 3-litre Formula 1 team plans.

Ron Tauranac made no bones about it, he was not really satisfied with the way in which Motor Racing Developments was involved in Formula 1. This business of simply building the cars and transferring them over to Jack's team for what seemed little more than a nominal payment was not a procedure calculated to suffuse him with enormous interest in the sport's most senior single seater category. When the formula changed at the end of 1965, Tauranac told his colleague quite candidly that he was not interested in continuing the existing arrangement.

"I told Jack at this point that I didn't really want to build any more Formula 1 cars," admits Tauranac, "because it was just a matter of a lot of effort for no real interest because I didn't go racing very much, so I figured I might as well get on with my main line business which was building production cars. So Jack went off and had a little think about that – I think he even tried to buy a Lotus – and then he came back and asked if we could do a deal. The main factor to get my interest was that MRD gradually took over the Formula 1 side from BRO, which is why I had a hell of a lot more interest in the 3-litre formula than I did before."

By the time all this was sorted out between Brabham and Tauranac there was only about a month to go prior to the start of the 3-litre formula, so the first type 620 Repco V8 Formula 1 engine had to be installed in an "interim" BT19 chassis originally manufactured to take the stillborn Coventry-Climax flat-16 in 1965. Running on Lucas fuel injection, the Grand Prix unit had a bore and stoke of 88.9 x 60.325mm for a total capacity of 2995.7cc, its claimed output being 315bhp at a leisurely 7250rpm.

The BT19 chassis was a typically practical Tauranac spaceframe design, its well-triangulated tubular frame unusual in that it used oval-section tubing round the cockpit: Ron found there was some oval tube available, so he employed it to give some extra beam strength adjacent to the cockpit, always the weak point in a racing design.

Suspension was undramatic, with unequal-length wishbones at the front, comprising a transverse link and trailing radius rod at the top and a one-piece tubular wishbone at the bottom. Suitably modified Alford and Alder uprights (from the Triumph Herald!) were employed, while the rear suspension employed single top links, reversed lower wishbones and twin radius rods which located specially cast uprights. Outboard spring/damper units were fitted all-round and Hewland's HD gearbox was originally employed to transmit the power to its rear Goodyear tyres, although this transmission really was not man enough for the job of handling 300bhp-plus and Jack subsequently commissioned Hewland to produce a heavier gearbox, dubbed the DG (for "different gearbox") which would eventually do the trick.

On the personnel side there were some interesting changes. With Dan Gurney moving on to plough his own furrow, Denny Hulme graduated to the Formula 1 team on a full-time basis as Jack's team-mate. Brabham had not exactly built up a reputation as a chatterbox and, since Hulme seemed almost mute, even by comparison with his boss, conversation and communication within the team hardly represented a *pot pourri* of extrovert witticisms!

Years later, grinning broadly, Denny admitted: "Jack was rather vague to most people. He knew precisely where he was going and what he was doing. He wasn't impossible to get along with, but he didn't communicate much – and since I *certainly* didn't communicate with many people in my whole career, there was never really a whole lot of talking going on!".

Tim Wall decided to follow Dan Gurney to All American Racers, but Roy Billington continued and was chief mechanic when the first Brabham-Repco V8 contested its debut race, the non-Championship 1966 South African Grand Prix, held over 60 laps of the 2.43 mile East London circuit on January 1. Jack's BT19 was the only truly new spec. F1 car to compete and would have won easily had it

That historic day. At the wheel of the "old nail" BT19, which was originally built to use the abortive 1½-litre Coventry-Climax flat-16, Brabham gallops across the plains of the Marne on his way to victory in the 1966 French Grand Prix at Reims.

not seized its fuel injection pump while well in command. Victory fell to Mike Spence's 2-litre Lotus-Climax 33 from Jo Siffert's 1½-litre Brabham-BRM BT11, Peter Arundell's Lotus 33 and Dave Charlton's 2.7 Brabham-Climax. Hulme's 2.75 Climax-engined BT22 failed to finish, Denny recalling that "it punched its gearbox in half and disengaged the crownwheel and pinion!"

After that South African disappointment Brabham continued on to the Tasman races for which the BT19 was fitted with a 2.5-litre Repco type 620 V8 to contest the Exide Cup at Sandown Park (where it retired) and the South Pacific Trophy at Longford, Tasmania (where Jack placed third). Meanwhile, a new face had popped up on the scene at New Haw in Jack's absence, a character who was destined to have a great deal of influence on the Repco V8 engine programme and, to this day, runs a racing engine development company in which Jack Brabham still has a stake. It was John Judd, now boss of the Rugby-based Engine Developments concern, but in those far-off days a young, inexperienced engineer fresh from his schooling at Coventry-Climax.

Judd: "I became an apprentice draughtsman at Climax when I left school in 57/58. I spent two years in the workshops and three years in the drawing office, the usual arrangement with apprenticeships in those days. I was interested in racing, which was one reason I was happy to join Climax, although I initially went there because I couldn't get in at Jaguar!

"After a year in the machine shop, I had a year building and testing 2½-litre FPFs for people like Jack and Moss, in a junior role, of course, because I was only about 18 at the time. Then during my three years in the drawing office I spent most of my time working on odd bits of racing engines which were the biggest part of the business in those days. Worked on the 1½-litre V8, even a little on the flat-16.

"Anyway, at the end of 1965 they stopped racing and gave me a job on fire pump development. At that time Jack Brabham had offered Harry Spears a job in his engine business which I think, at the time, also involved tuning kits on Japanese road cars he was planning to import. They must have been Hondas, surely? I told Harry that if he needed any help, then I'd be happy to come and join him there, but in the end he didn't take the job because his wife didn't want to move, so he put my name forward and Jack gave me the job. I received a phone message to get in touch with him and go for an interview, but I think he'd made the decision by then to give me the job anyway. It was February 1966 when I first walked into the place. Jack was in Australia and I was told to report to Phil Kerr, Jack's manager. He didn't know what to do with me – he'd obviously forgotten all about it – so he gave me a job for a couple of weeks in Ron's production car shop. When Jack got back he put me on a plane for Australia and I stayed there for four months working at Repco!"

Gamesmanship! "Old Man" Brabham, wearing a flowing beard and supporting himself with a "stick", ambles towards the starting grid at Zandvoort, 1966. Jack's extrovert demonstration showed a hitherto-hidden streak of dry humour in the dour Australian's character: at 40 years old, he certainly didn't feel over the top and wanted to get that message over to the press – very firmly!

On May 1, the BT19 made its second competition appearance in the 56 lap, non-title Syracuse Grand Prix, Hulme backing up Jack with the 2.75 FPF-engined BT22. Denny had won the previous day's Oulton Park Tourist Trophy in Sid Taylor's Lola-Chevy T70, while Jack's Brabham-Repco (BT8) sports car had been hampered by an oil leak, and the two men flew down to Sicily on Brabham's plane on the Saturday evening. After practising briefly on Sunday morning, they started side-by-side on the back row of the grid and Jack moved through to third before the engine died thanks to a metering unit malfunction. Then Hulme's BT22 blew a piston, as Bob Anderson's BT11 had done during practice, so the only Brabham to finish was Bonnier, fifth in the Siffert BT11 now fitted with a 2-litre V8 BRM.

Two weeks later came the turning point. Over 35 laps of Silverstone many of the pundits expected John Surtees's new Ferrari 312 V12 to administer a severe drubbing to Jack's BT19-Repco, but there was a major surprise in store. Now using square-shoulder 15in. rear Goodyears, Brabham started from pole and led all the way, posting fastest race lap and holding off *Il Grande John* by 7s. Bonnier's private Cooper-Maserati V12 was third ahead of Denny's BT22, Jochen Rindt's Cooper-Maserati, John Taylor's ex-Willment BT11, now owned by David Bridges and powered by a 2-litre BRM V8, and Anderson's 2.7 BT11.

Jack was under the weather at Monaco where the arrival of the works Brabhams was delayed by a British seaman's strike with the result that they missed first practice on Thursday. Clark's 2-litre Lotus-Climax 33 took pole on 1m 29.9s from Surtees's Ferrari (1m 30.1s), Stewart's BRM P261 (1m 30.3s), Hill's similar car (1m 30.4s), Bandini's Tasman Ferrari 246 (1m 30.5s) and Denny's BT22 (1m 31.1s). The below-par Brabham was way down on the inside of the sixth row on 1m 32.8s and although he climbed quickly through to fifth place once the race was underway, his new Hewland gearbox stuck in gear on lap 18 so he was able to retire to bed. Hulme retired from fourth place with a broken driveshaft coupling and a similar fault sidelined Anderson's private BT11.

The 1966 Belgian Grand Prix at *Spa-Francorchamps* will long be remembered for the cloudburst on the opening lap which sent half the field skating spectacularly off the circuit. Brabham, who had qualified his BT19 fourth behind Surtees's Ferrari, Rindt's Cooper-Maserati and Stewart's 2-litre BRM P261, got into the most heart-stopping slide imaginable, but just managed to retrieve the situation before the Brabham-Repco smote a house at around 150mph. Suitably chastened, he splashed home to fourth place behind Surtees, Rindt and Bandini, not aided by the reluctance of his Goodyear wet weather tyres to work up to temperature on the drying track surface.

Denny the Bear spun his BT22 at *Burnenville* on the opening lap, a feat likely to hold a driver's attention pretty sternly in itself. "I knew I was very late by the time I got re-started and I made for the pits, keeping an eye on the mirror all the time. Eventually I could see the lads coming up the other side of the valley, hell for leather in the rain, so I got out of the car at the side of the track and shinned up the bank out of the way as those idiots came by at a million miles an hour. Then I made my way round to the pits to retire because the car had been lightly damaged in the spin. The interesting thing was that, while I was out of the car up the bank, the Climax four was just idling quietly at the side of the road without any problem. Those FPFs were amazing like that. But I think that race put me off motor racing in the rain for the rest of my life . . .'

When it came to the French Grand Prix at Reims on July 3, a second, brand-new

VAK C

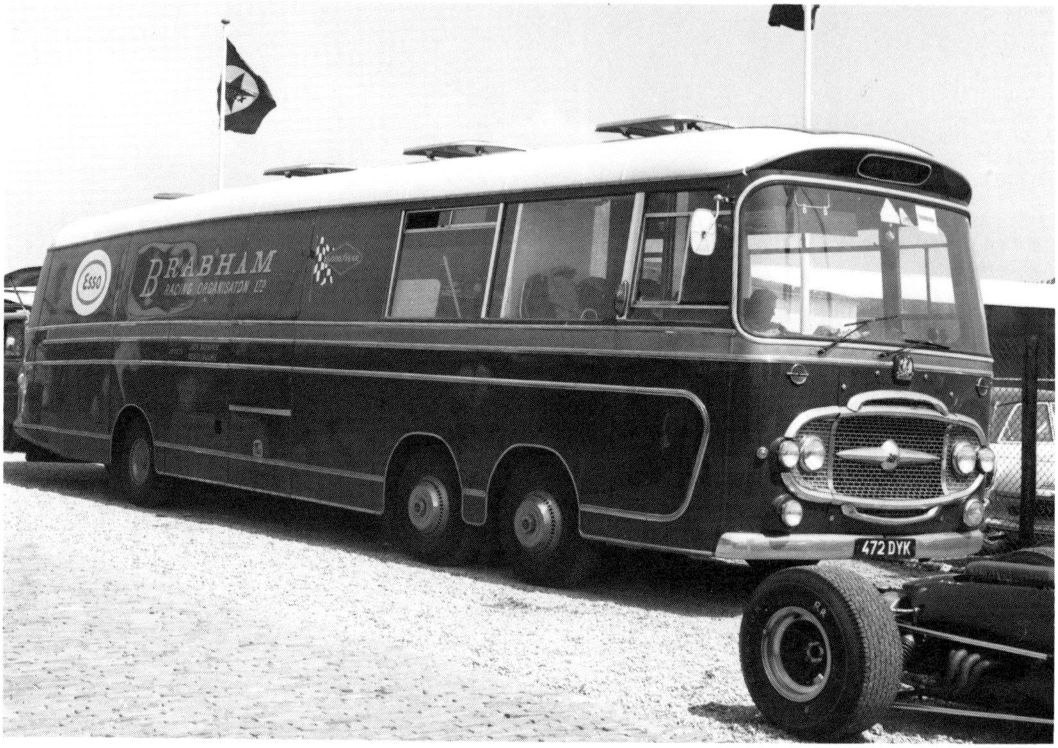
Esso
BRABHAM
RACING ORGANISATION LTD
472 DYK

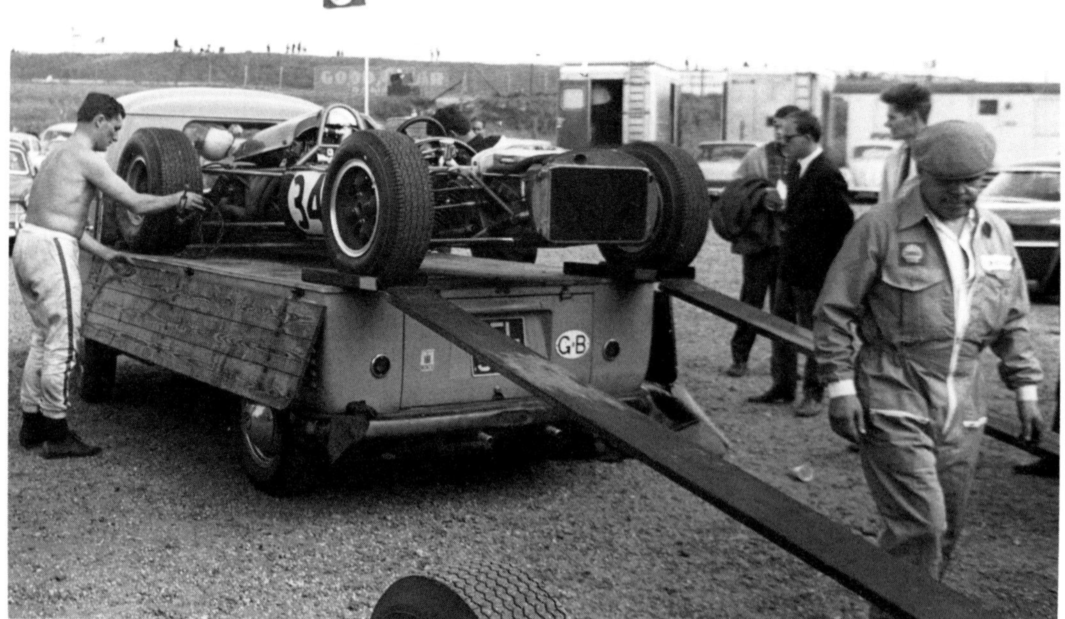

34
GB

Contrasting styles. Even as early as 1966 the Brabham works team's transporter was impressive by the standards of the day. Built on a six-wheeled Bedford coach chassis, the rig is seen here at the Dutch Grand Prix. At the other end of the scale, the resourceful Bob Anderson transported his ageing BT11-Climax FPF to the races on a tiny Volkswagen pick-up truck. Here, stripped to the waist, the determined owner/driver supervises its unloading at the very same race.

Repco-engined chassis was available for Hulme to drive, releasing the BT22 for hire to Jo Bonnier whose Cooper-Maserati was not yet repaired after crashing at Spa. The BT20 differed from the BT19 in that it used round-section tubing throughout its spaceframe, the main bottom chassis rails were revised and the cockpit area was double-braced with twin side tubes in place of the original car's oval members. The suspension was virtually identical to the BT19's although the geometry was revised to cater for 15in. wheels front *and* rear, allowing the BT20 to experiment with slightly larger 12in. diameter brake discs in its early races. The BT20 had slightly wider front and rear track, different engine covers and the exhaust piping wrapped round the upper rear radius arms rather than cramped inside it as on the BT19.

Denny's own car was not quite ready for first practice, so the New Zealander had a single flying lap in Jack's BT19 on Wednesday evening, but his BT20 was out on the circuit the following day. Once both the V8 cars had been tuned to their drivers's satisfaction, Hulme did a few laps checking out the BT22 before handing it over to Bonnier. On this super-fast circuit Bandini's Ferrari 312 qualified on pole with 2m 07.89s from new Cooper-Maserati recruit and Maranello refugee John Surtees, Mike Parkes in the second Ferrari and Brabham on 2m 10.2s. Hulme was on the inside of row four on 2m 13.3s with Anderson on row five, Taylor on row six and Bonnier slowest of all on 2m 23.5s.

In the opening stages of the race Bandini edged gently away from Brabham, the BT19-Repco almost able to hang on in the Italian car's slipstream. Driving sensibly, Bandini opened the gap to 2s after 12 laps and, after breaking the tow, pulled out a commanding 18s advantage before his Ferrari's throttle cable snapped. That handed Jack an historic victory from Parkes, Hulme's new BT20, Rindt, Gurney, Taylor and Anderson. With two laps to go, Hulme's car had rolled to a halt out on the back straight, its fuel pump apparently failing to deliver any more Esso to the fuel injection system. The Bear simply climbed out, lifted up the front of the car to get a pint or so through to the collector tank, climbed back in and proceeded to the finish. Even in the mid-1960s, Formula 1 could still be a downright leisurely pursuit!

Now Jack Brabham, the taciturn, shy and retiring Australian, suddenly became the focal point of the media. "The car that Jack built" attracted World-wide attention now that Brabham had become the first man ever to win a Grand Prix in a car bearing his own name, in contemporary times at least. What's more, having broken his duck at Reims, more victories followed!

On July 16, the 80 lap British Grand Prix at Brands Hatch fell convincingly to Brabham's BT19, his flag-to-flag victory run aided in some small way by the damp track conditions and the fact that Ferrari stayed at home and failed to send any cars. Formula 3 man-of-the-moment Chris Irwin was given a run in the Climax FPF-engined BT22 and this young Englishman, who had built his reputation behind the wheel of Brabham's F3 products, acquitted himself superbly to finish seventh, closely behind Bruce McLaren's McLaren-Serenissima.

However, if Brabham had it easy at Brands Hatch there was some far more stern competition awaiting him at Zandvoort in the Dutch Grand Prix eight days later. The team brought along its usual pair of Repco-engined cars with the BT22 as a spare and eventually Jack put the BT19 on pole from Hulme's BT20 and Jim Clark's 2-litre Lotus-Climax 33. On race morning there was a film making "free for all" session to cater for John Frankenheimer's MGM production *Grand Prix*, a celluloid epic which was being shot throughout the 1966 European Grand Prix season, and Hulme took full advantage of this in order to run in the spare Repco V8 which had been installed in his BT20 the previous evening.

Jack, who had turned 40 the previous April, had been increasingly irritated by oblique suggestions in some sectors of the press that he was past it. Intent on taking the rise out of those members of the Fourth Estate, he staged a most untypically extrovert demonstration just before the start of the 90 lap race. Wearing a theatrical beard and leaning on a jack handle as a makeshift walking stick, Brabham hobbled up to his car on the starting grid and went round shaking hands with his colleagues. It was an amazingly bold, tongue-in-cheek way of getting back at his "critics", but most people agreed that he would just *have* to win the Dutch Grand Prix after that little performance!

As the starter's flag fell, Jim Clark's 2-litre Lotus all but held the two Brabham-Repcos on the run down to *Tarzan*, Jack only hanging onto the lead as his BT19 arrived at the corner on the inside line. Jim split the Brabhams for three laps until Denny got by and there followed a tremendous chase with both Brabham drivers pulling every trick in the book in their efforts to keep the brilliant Scot behind them. On lap 17 the whole picture changed as Hulme pitted with ignition problems, these being traced to the distributor itself which was duly changed. That meant that Jack had to deal with Clark on his own, which was quite a different situation indeed, and as the two leading cars threaded their way through the backmarkers, Clark got ahead and began to pull away. Jack regained his rhythm and began to haul him back, but the Scot stayed ahead and it wasn't until the Lotus broke its crankshaft damper and debris from this fractured the Climax engine's water pump outlet, with resultant overheating, that Jack got back into the lead with 15 laps to go. Clark stopped for extra water, so he dropped to third at the chequered flag behind the triumphant Brabham, Hill's BRM and ahead of Stewart's BRM. Hulme eventually retired for good with ignition bothers while Anderson's BT11 dropped out with damaged suspension 17 laps from the finish.

On August 7 at the Nurburgring, Jack Brabham continued his inexorable Repco-propelled progress along the route to his third World Championship title. The 14 mile *Nordschleife* was at its rain-soaked, treacherous worst for the 15 lap German Grand Prix and Jack fought a skilful battle with John Surtees for most of the event. During practice Hulme had been obliged to do a few laps in the BT22 after his V8 had failed, while Jack also did some laps in Denny's BT20 after the BT19 suffered gearbox problems.

Clark took pole in the 2-litre Lotus-Climax 33 on 8m 16.5s, heading Surtees (8m 18.0s), Stewart (8m 18.8s), Scarfiotti's Ferrari 246 (8m 20.2s) and Brabham's BT19 (8m 20.8s). Hulme's BT20 was way back on the inside of row five with 8m 49.3s, behind Anderson's BT11, while John Taylor's Bridges-entered BT11-BRM was way down amongst the F2 runners on 9m 08.9s. Going down into the dip at *Quiddelbacher-Hohe* on the opening lap, Taylor's car tagged the rear of another competitor and crashed quite badly, catching fire before its dazed driver could be extricated. Sadly, the genial Taylor was to succumb to those burns several days later in a Koblenz hospital.

Surtees led for much of the opening lap, but Jack poked the BT19 ahead for the run across the line and he stayed there despite valiant efforts on the part of the Cooper-Maserati driver. Eventually Surtees's clutch went solid and the Cooper's handling seemed to deteriorate as the tyres started to wear: at the chequered flag he had fallen to 44.4s adrift the winning Brabham. Denny gradually got into his stride from that lowly grid position and moved up to fifth place before retiring with ignition problems after nine laps. Transmission failure claimed Anderson after 13 laps, so the winning BT19 was the only representative of the marque running at the end . . .

Jack had his own BT20 available for the 68 lap Italian Grand Prix at Monza on September 4 as well as the BT19 as spare: he tried both cars during practice, eventually opting to play safe and race the older chassis which he qualified on the inside of row three with a 1m 32.2s, Mike Parkes having turned a 1m 31.3s for pole in his Ferrari 312. Hulme's BT20 was on the outside of row four with 1m 32.84s, Anderson made the outside of row six in 1m 35.3s while Chris Amon, trying to qualify the ex-Siffert BT11-BRM which he had purchased after despairing of ever getting a second McLaren to drive, never had a chance of making the race on 1m 40.3s.

Once the race got underway, Brabham and Hulme hung on in amongst the warring Ferraris, Cooper-Maseratis and Richie Ginther's stupendously quick Honda V12, although the Repco-engined machines were unable to set the pace in the power race. At the end of lap six smoke was beginning to trail from the rear of

Jack's BT19 and two laps later he was in the pits: an inspection plate on the timing chain cover had worked loose, allowing much of the lubricant to seep away. It was only a short-term disappointment, though, for with Championship rivals Stewart and Surtees also failing to finish, Jack Brabham ended that afternoon at Monza as World Champion driver for the third time in his career. What's more, Denny Hulme really earned his spurs with a magnificent performance to finish third behind the more powerful Ferraris of Scarfiotti and Parkes, only losing out to the Englishman by a mere 0.3s.

While all this successful racing action had been going on in Europe, John Judd had spent a productive spell working with Repco in Australia in preparation for the 1967 season. Routine maintenance of the Repco V8s had initially been carried out in the New Haw factory, but by the middle of 1966 this task had been transferred to the team's racing base at Guildford. However, major technical changes and development were all carried out at Repco's Australian headquarters and Judd's time "down-under" had proved most instructive and enjoyable.

Judd: "Repco's engine department had been based at Russell Manufacturing, their piston manufacturing division of Richmond where they had a test bed, but by the time I arrived they were in the process of moving to a factory they'd just bought from Perfect Circle, the American piston ring corporation, on the other side of Melbourne at Foots Cray. By early March the 1966 race engines were being built and supplied to England, so we set up our drawing office in the canteen and started working on drawing stuff for the '67 engines. Because Phil was doing all the running around, I was given the job of doing the new cylinder heads for next season.

"We decided to make a vertical valve head rather than the original 10-degree angle with those wedge-shaped combustion chambers. They were obsessed with the fact that the original engine wasn't as efficient as the Cosworth SCA: in fact the whole Repco philosophy seemed to be based on the concept of a scaled-up SCA unit, but the original V8 never gave the output they were looking for. Looking back, I can now see that we didn't have the correct cams or trumpets or many other minor items . . . you could have tuned that original engine to produce 400bhp knowing what we know today!

"So my first task was to draw vertical valve positions more like the SCA, with the combustion chamber in the piston rather than in the head. I reckoned that would make it *really* go." Unfortunately for Judd, he had arrived at Repco just as a storm of a personality clash was beginning to brew up between Phil Irving and Frank Hallam. The young English engineer, keen and somewhat naïve by his own admission ("I was only 22 and didn't understand much about this sort of politics – at that age you don't give a damn about these things") found himself inadvertently embroiled in it all. There could hardly have been a more vivid contrast in styles than Hallam, the immaculately groomed middle-aged businessman, and Irving, the down-to-earth, essentially practical engineer recalled with affection by his colleagues as "Fag ash Phil" as he inevitably worked away with a cigarette dangling from his lips. A row cropped up, Irving obviously felt that Judd had been brought in to undermine his position, and the veteran engineer walked out of Repco one day, never to return . . .

The next thing in Judd's pipeline was a totally new cylinder block – "Repco wanted their very own block so that they could hold their head up high" – so John and Irving's successor, Norm Wilson, spent a weekend drawing the design for a new block which would be cast in aluminium alloy.

Judd originally drew the second generation cylinder heads retaining the original cross-flow characteristics with the outside exhausts, but mated to the new in-line valve/bowl-in-piston arrangement. At the time there was a school of thought which felt that with parallel valves, the gas had to make a pretty sharp turn as it left the cylinder and that it was immaterial to the gas which way it went. The fallacy of this argument was proved when some serious tests were run on these series-30 heads, but exhaust installation became a question of considerable importance with the new 1967 cars, Tauranac insisting on a central exhaust arrangement. So, after

Oversteer! Top, Denny Hulme powers his BT20 through Kyalami's Clubhouse corner whilst running away from the field in the '67 South African Grand Prix. Centre, Jack's BT20 adopts a similar stance ahead of Surtees's Honda on the way to victory in the 1967 Oulton Park Spring Cup. The car is using an interim, central exhaust type 640 Repco engine on this rare occasion. Bottom, Hulme's "computerized" BT20 sliding its way to victory in the same year's Monaco Grand Prix, Denny proving the point that this car was absurdly controllable!

Judd's return to England, Norm Wilson drew the series-40 heads and the resultant 740 engine would eventually do battle in defence of the Brabham-Repco's World Championship honours.

Reflecting on those first two seasons with the Brabham-Repcos, Tauranac makes the whole project sound disarmingly straightforward: "I don't think we were smart enough to reckon we could come up with the Constructors' Championship and the Drivers' Championship with what we had available at the start of 1966. It was really a matter of whether we were going to stay in racing or not. We really had to go 3-litre Formula 1 racing because it would have been so very difficult to re-enter F1 after leaving it. Once your sponsorship with fuel and tyres had passed onto somebody else it would have been difficult to get it back again. When we were originally weighing up the pros and cons of that 2½-litre Tasman Repco engine we thought that since some of the early races might possibly be won by a four-cylinder FPF Climax, then we must be better off with the V8. We thought we could possibly do reasonably well in the first few races of the 1966 season.

"Eventually we realized we had the measure of the opposition, so it was a little easier to sit back and plan for 1967, knowing how much power we needed for a down-to-weight car. A lot more effort was put into that '67 programme. The 1966 car just 'happened' in the time available, there was very little time spent on designing and it was more simply a kit of parts that we'd used over the years. In 1967 we started out to make a new car from scratch. With the same engine, the BT24 was 9mph faster than the previous year's BT20 because it was smaller and cleaner. What's more, if we went testing with the BT24 and the BT19, Jack would find himself about 500rpm quicker into every corner on a circuit such as Goodwood. That was largely due to the fact that the BT24 was 110lb lighter than its predecessor!"

To round off the 1966 season the only other victory scored by the Brabham-Repco was in the 40 lap Oulton Park Gold Cup on September 17. Jack and Denny fought an entertaining, but rather misleading battle with the H-16 BRMs of Stewart and Hill, cruising home to a 1-2 finish after the complex cars from Bourne failed to finish. The United States Grand Prix at the Glen saw both cars retire and the season finished with Surtees winning the Mexican Grand Prix in his Cooper-Maserati by 7s from Jack, with Denny taking third a lap adrift.

Once back at the team's Woodbridge Meadows, Guildford base at the end of his four month stint with Repco in Australia, John Judd kept in continual contact with Norm Wilson for the balance of the Brabham-Repco partnership right through until the end of the 1968 season. This voluminous correspondence file is still retained by Judd and if anything highlights the problems developing Grand Prix racing engines the opposite side of the world from the team that intends to use them, then it is this fascinating hotchpotch of airmail letters, frantic telegrams, hasty sketches and more detailed drawings. Much of this correspondence is fairly routine and it is quite obvious that, throughout 1966 and 67, the arrangement worked well as the Brabham-Repco V8s were still on the top of their job, but when the quad-cam Repco 860 V8 ran into non-stop technical problems during 1968 the tone of the communications changes from optimistic, through guardedly cautious to an ultimate air of resigned disappointment. One thing shines through it all, however, and that is the warm personal relationship which was built up between Judd and his colleagues at Repco; Frank Hallam, Norm Wilson and Lindsay Hooper.

By the end of 1966 Judd wrote to Wilson trying to allay the concern shown by Repco towards the V8 power outputs *vis-a-vis* the 1-litre Cosworth SCA Formula 2 engine. Whilst at the London Motor Show in October 1966, Judd bumped into Dick Atkins, Chief Development Engineer of the Tecalemit Petrol Injection project, who had accumulated considerable experience in running Cosworth SCA engines in connection with this work. He told Judd that it was Cosworth's practice to apply a humidity correction factor to the engine's power figure in addition to the normal air temperature and pressure correction factor. That meant, in Judd's

Keeping Amon at bay, Brabham storms through Becketts during the 1967 British Grand Prix at Silverstone in a BT24 which has vibrated away its rear-view mirrors, thus giving Jack even more of an excuse for his "defensive" driving style. It was all in vain, however, because Chris found a gap with a few laps to go and nipped through to take third behind Clark's Lotus 49 and Hulme's BT24.

estimation, that the so-called 140bhp output of the SCA was in truth nearer 123bhp, a detail which meant that the Repco engine really was not doing badly on power output after all, the series 740 V8 confidently expected to produce 330bhp at 8000rpm.

It was also particularly interesting to see the way in which Judd and his colleagues were attempting to establish cross-reference points on rival Formula 1 power units at the time. In view of Jack Brabham's productive partnership with Honda in Formula 2 throughout 1966, the advent of the new Honda V12 Grand Prix engine was awaited with great interest, although Judd wrote to Frank Hallam, "The new Honda engine weighs 230kg and is apparently very large. Jack feels that in its present form it will not be very competitive, but on the other hand they seem to be able to make the new engine in about six months, as they did with the Formula 2 unit.

"The Maserati (V12) engine which was at Climax (being tested on their brake) weighed in at about 500lbs and tested, as removed from the car, gave 310bhp at 8100rpm. The engine was later tested by Maseratis at 340bhp, but even so Jack was faster than John Surtees on the straight at Nurburgring!"

The general tenor of the correspondence at the time is significant because it underlines just how much stand was put by engine power in the early days of the 3-litre Formula 1, as opposed to other factors such as light weight and aerodynamic efficiency. Even if the Cooper-Maserati did indeed have 340bhp, as the Italian engine manufacturer claimed, it would not be difficult to imagine the Brabham BT19 being quicker on the straight using "only" 315bhp of Repco power. By comparison with the Brabham, the Cooper chassis was an overweight tank . . .

Propitiously, this particular letter written in the autumn of 1966, finished with Judd expressing the feeling that "it looks as though the V8 four-valve Cosworth will be the engine to beat next year, as it should be about the same weight and size as our own engine (the Repco 740), but with about 390bhp". How right he was!

With the tempo of 3-litre Grand Prix competition hotting up progressively throughout 1967, the Brabham-Repcos continued to be "there or thereabouts" near the front of the field, although the arrival of the Lotus-Cosworth 49 at Zandvoort virtually made every other Formula 1 power unit obsolete at a single stroke. But nobody *really* could have anticipated how good the DFV would be when the '67 Championship trail got underway with the 80 lap South African Grand Prix at Kyalami on January 2.

Jack and Denny appeared for this race in their BT20s, unaltered in specification since the end of the previous year. The two Brabham-Repcos ran smoothly throughout practice to qualify 1-2 with Brabham taking pole on 1m 28.3s, but Denny shot straight into the lead at the start, building up a comfortable lead while Jack had a big sideways moment at Crowthorne early on, was tagged by Surtees's Honda, and briefly dropped to fourth.

Hulme loved Kyalami: "It was a personal thing: I loved South Africa, Kyalami, that part of the World as a whole. That day the car seemed to do no wrong. I was gone. Then, suddenly, the brakes began to fail. I stopped at the pits, which was a big mistake, because they couldn't fix the problem. I think a line to the rear brakes must have been leaking, but, thinking back on it, I reckon I could have nursed it through to the finish because nobody was anywhere near me . . .' Hulme wound up fourth behind Pedro Rodriguez, a surprise winner in his plodding Cooper-Maserati, John Love's FPF Climax-engined Cooper and Surtees. Anderson's BT11 was fifth ahead of Brabham, delayed by a pit stop to check out a mysterious electrical problem.

On March 12 the BT20s performed disappointingly in the two heats/final Race of Champions at Brands Hatch, an event dominated by former Brabham teamster Dan Gurney in his Eagle-Weslake. Jack got well into his stride in the final and was closing on Dan until he had to pit with more electrical problems, while Denny never made the final after breaking a camshaft drive in the second 10-lap heat. Thus it was the eagle-eyed Hulme who spotted the trouble with Jack's car when he rolled into the pit lane. The ignition pick-up wires beneath the flywheel, connected by a special anti-vibration safety push-on clip, had fallen off . . .

A 1-2 Brabham-Hulme success in the Oulton Park Spring Cup was given added interest by the fact that Jack's BT20 used the latest interim engine, with the central exhaust series 40 heads on the 1966 type 600 cylinder block. But both cars were back to standard 620 engines for the Silverstone International Trophy where Denny slid off the road at Club and Jack chased Parkes's victorious Ferrari home a somewhat breathless second.

Jack returned to the cockpit of the original BT19 for the Monaco Grand Prix on March 7, but its debutant Repco 740 engine broke a connecting rod on the opening lap, the car spinnning at *Mirabeau* on its own oil. Amazingly, the unit kept running on seven cylinders, allowing Brabham to cruise back to the pits, coating the circuit with oil as he did so. Hulme, though, was at his brilliant best and led for most of the 100 laps to notch up his very first Grand Prix success in a race saddened by the death of Lorenzo Bandini who crashed his Ferrari pursuing the victorious Brabham-Repco.

Hulme: "That 3-litre Repco was *so* simple to drive: lazy, not cammy, but very smooth and progressive. And the BT20 was so easy in that race, it was unbelievable. It was as if on remote control, computerized. You could slow the thing up simply by throwing it sideways at the corner. I don't think Bandini was ever going to catch me – Stewart was the only one who gave me any trouble prior to his retirement."

Then came June 4, 1967, the occasion of the Cosworth DFV's momentous debut at Zandvoort. Brabham brought along four cars, two BT20s, the BT19 and a lone, brand new BT24 equipped with the latest 740 Repco V8 and a Hewland FT200 Formula 2 gearbox.

Tauranac regarded the BT24 as his first real Formula 1 design since the BT3: "We spent a lot of time going through the existing recipe from front to back, pruning everything to the minimum, using our own cast uprights and generally

Guy Ligier was a keen amateur who began his privately-financed Grand Prix career with a lumbering Cooper-Maserati and then switched to this ex-works BT20 which he conducted at a relaxed pace. He trailed home sixth in the 1967 German Grand Prix, but achieved little else during his time with the car and sold it to Silvio Moser for 1968.

designing just enough car to do the job. The amount of attention and detail which went into producing something as simple and light as the BT24 was considerable, possibly a lot more than if we'd attempted something more complex and ambitious."

The BT24s had the same wheelbase as the BT20s, but the front and rear track was slightly narrower and the suspension was very similar to the previous cars in general configuration apart from those new cast front uprights. The whole package was neat, clean and compact and the BT23(F2)-type front body section was cut in half so the nose section could be detached for ease of transportation. That FT200 box, however, just was not up to the job of dealing with 330bhp and was quickly replaced by the regular Hewland DG300 unit.

Jack qualified his BT19, fitted with the 740 engine, third behind Graham Hill's Lotus 49 and Gurney's Eagle, but Jimmy Clark came through in the 90 lap race to show everybody how it should be done with the other very new, almost untested, 49-Cosworth. Brabham survived to finish second with Denny's BT20 third, this car soon to be shipped to new owner John Love in South Africa. The writing was on the wall – Brabham needed more power!

The early unreliability of the Lotus-Cosworth combination none the less played right into the Brabham-Repco camp's hands. The Belgian Grand Prix at Spa, where the BT24 made its race debut, may well have been a disaster with both Jack's new machine and Denny's BT19 (running 15in. front rims, a BT20 nose section and a series 740 engine) retiring from the fray, but when both Lotus-Cosworths broke down in the French Grand Prix at the featureless Le Mans Bugatti circuit, Jack and Denny were sitting behind ready to take their new BT24s through to a 1-2 success.

For the remainder of the season it was left for the Brabham BT24s to sit behind those super-fast Lotus-Cosworths and simply wait for them to break. If they did not, then the Brabhams were merely placed: if they did fail, the Brabhams

Happy partnership. Jochen Rindt got on with the Brabham team like a house on fire and is remembered with affection by all who worked with him throughout 1968. Tauranac (left) recalls him as "an all-round good bloke" and it was mainly Colin Chapman's "telephone number" driving fee, underwritten by Firestone, which eventually caused him to move to Lotus in 1969 – and stay there rather than returning to Brabham in 1970.

invariably won. The British Grand Prix at Silverstone saw the fine-handling BT24s next in line behind Clark and Hill, Hulme storming home second to Jimmy after Graham's 49 retired. Brabham, his BT24 vibrating sufficiently to shed both its cockpit-mounted mirrors, fended off Amon's Ferrari 312 until the New Zealander found a gap with four laps left to run and squeezed through to take third.

Jack had a hair-raising moment in practice for the German Grand Prix at the Nurburgring when a bolt broke in his BT24's rear suspension, the suspension collapsed, the rear wheel twisted sideways and the tyre was punctured by the anti-roll bar, letting the car slide along on three wheels and the chassis frame. The car was duly repaired for the race and Clark took pole on 8m 04.1s from Hulme (8m 13.5s), Stewart's BRM H-16 (8m 15.2s), the Eagles of Gurney and McLaren, sharing 8m 17.7s, Surtees's Honda (8m 18.2s) and Brabham himself (8m 18.9s).

Clark and Hulme left the line together, but Jim immediately asserted his advantage and pulled out a 1.5s advantage on the first 14 mile lap. By the standards of the established Lotus Cosworth form, this did not seem to be anything to shout about, and it soon became clear that Clark was going to have difficulty building up his usual dominant lead. The problem was a soft rear Firestone and by lap four he had eased up sufficiently to allow Hulme and Gurney through, Dan quickly taking over the role of pace-setter at the head of the field.

Meanwhile, a short distance further back, a further Brabham Formula 1 team member was making his name at the wheel of a Tyrrell Formula 2 Matra, Jacky Ickx hauling his spectacular way up to fourth place overall before succumbing to broken suspension. Gurney, meanwhile, had consolidated a 46s advantage by the end of lap 12, but he never appeared again at the start/finish line, the Eagle rolling to a halt out on the circuit with a broken driveshaft universal joint. That allowed Denny to score his second convincing victory of the season with Jack fending off Amon for second in a re-run of their Silverstone battle.

REPCO —
BRABHAM

New combination for '68: the four-cam Repco 860 engine and the partly panelled spaceframe Brabham BT26. The chassis was just fine, but the engine . . .

Into sixth place, more than 14 miles behind the winner, came French amateur Guy Ligier in his ex-works BT20 which he had first used at Silverstone but which was now painted French blue. The thick-set, former rugby player would eventually build Grand Prix cars bearing his own name in the mid-1970s, but at this stage the Ligier was very new to the Formula 1 business. In practice at Nurburgring he had been bewildered by the reluctance of his Repco V8 to run properly – until it was explained to him that the ignition timing had been set to the wrong mark on the flywheel. It seems that nobody had told him that one of the two marks was no longer valid!

The next race on the calendar was the Canadian Grand Prix at Toronto's Mosport Park on August 27, but by the time the Formula 1 cars lined up again for that contest the Grand Prix fraternity was touched by an unexpected tragedy. Testing his aged, but still absolutely immaculate, BT11-Climax FPF at Silverstone in preparation for the trip to Canada, Bob Anderson aquaplaned into a marshals' post on the Club straight. It took some time before an ambulance could transport him to Northampton hospital, by which time the popular Englishman had succumbed to serious thoracic injuries. It was a stunning blow to his many colleagues and friends who admired the no-nonsense former motorcycle racer for his dogged enthusiasm and determination to continue as a private entrant in the increasingly unhelpful Formula 1 world of the late 1960s.

The 90 lap Canadian Grand Prix was held for much of its duration in pouring rain and Hulme, despite his avowed dislike of such conditions, put in a fine performance with Goodyear's latest "intermediate" tyres. If it had not been for a couple of stops, one for fresh goggles, the second for a bubble-type vizor, then Denny would certainly have won. As it was, he splashed home second behind Jack's BT24 to complete the season's third Brabham 1-2 finish.

At Monza Jack tried his new spare BT24/3 with an all-enveloping bubble top to the cockpit in an attempt to wring out every inch of straight line speed, but he suffered parallax problems with it fitted and ran regular BT24 bodywork in the race. The event turned out to be the customary slipstreaming special with Clark's Lotus 49 starting from pole, a mere 0.3s faster than Jack's BT24. At the start there was chaos after the official beckoning the field forward from the dummy grid used a green flag and Jack, reckoning it was time to be off, simply dropped the clutch and was away. Everybody else followed Brabham's example and the result was a shambolic getaway for the entire field!

Gurney moved the Eagle ahead at the end of the opening lap, and when Clark headed for the pits after 11 laps with a deflated tyre, it looked as though the road might be open for another Brabham-Repco success. Hulme was showing particularly determined form and forced his way up into the leading bunch, but he fell from the lead with head gasket failure after 30 laps, and Clark staged an absolutely historic recovery, extracting every ounce of performance from the 49 to haul back an entire lap and take the lead going into the final tour.

Sadly, the Lotus spluttered, low on fuel, during those last few miles, so Brabham's BT24 and Surtees's Honda came slamming down into *Parabolica* side-by-side for the lead on the last lap. The circuit was coated with oil from Hill's blown-up Lotus at this point and Surtees tricked Jack magnificently, leaving the door open for the BT24 to overtake going into the corner on the inside line. The Brabham hit the oil, slid wide on the exit and John ran the Honda back up the inside to re-take the lead on the sprint to the chequered flag, winning by less than a length. The crowd adored it all and went wild with vocal delight . . .

After Jack's BT24 won the Oulton Park Gold Cup, the Brabham works team went to North America for the last two races of the season with the destiny of the Championship to be settled between Jack and Denny. Clark and Hill finished 1-2 at Watkins Glen in the United States Grand Prix with Hulme, his BT24 down 500rpm, a lucky third and Brabham fifth. Jimmy won Mexico City to ram home the Lotus 49's superiority and although Jack was second, Denny's third place was sufficient to clinch him the World Championship instead of his employer!

Jack had been pressing Denny to renew his contract with the team for 1968, but

Typical pose: Rindt slamming on opposite lock in the BT26 during the 1968 British Grand Prix at Brands Hatch, one of many intensely forgettable outings for the previously successful Brabham-Repco partnership.

Hulme eventually did a deal to switch to Bruce McLaren's fledgeling Grand Prix organization which would be using the Cosworth DFV the following year. Summing up his relationship with Jack and his switch to McLaren Racing, Denny explained, "The best aspect of my career with Brabham's was learning how to set up chassis from Jack's experience. Ron was a very cost-conscious person, just like Jack: I mean, if a Zodiac front hub would fit on an F1 car, then that's the way it would be. Ron was essentially practical.

"By the time I graduated to Formula 1 with Brabham I was earning about £2000 from Esso and that raised itself to the giddy heights of about £7500 when I won the World Championship. Amazing, when you think what some guys in this business are earning now . . .'

Looking back on the '67 season, Hulme reckons Jack lost the Championship through his enthusiasm for experimentation with new, untested equipment. "He would always keep the good parts for himself – and in 1967 he was often in a position where the latest bits and pieces were not reliable, so it worked against him."

Tauranac confirms that line of thinking: "If I'd got a new idea for the chassis, Jack wouldn't let me rest in peace until I'd got it onto the car. But then I woke up and realized that you couldn't do that – you had to develop the component properly before it was used. So I stopped telling him my ideas until they were fully developed!'

With Hulme departing to forge a partnership with fellow Kiwi McLaren, the Brabham team embarked on a quite remarkable relationship with Jack's new team-mate in 1968. After three promising, but unproductive years with Cooper, Jochen Rindt was ready for a change of scene and readily agreed to join the Brabham-Repco line-up for the new season. As a racing season, what was to come would amount to an unmitigated disaster which would write *finis* to Repco's Grand Prix career, but Rindt's relationship with all members of the Brabham team is recalled with tremendous affection by everybody concerned. What's more, although Jochen then moved off to Lotus, it is clear that he disliked Colin Chapman and the Lotus environment pretty strongly, bending over backwards firstly to stay with Brabham in 1969, then to return to this team in 1970. Brabham team recollections of Rindt are particularly fascinating because many others remember him as a hard-nosed, uncompromising and arrogant young man. Not by those at Guildford, though . . .

Jack admits he was attracted to Rindt because he admired the press-on attitude he demonstrated in both the Cooper-Maseratis and the Formula 2 Brabham-Cosworths he had been driving for Winkelmann Racing. Jack could quite clearly see his own early style mirrored by the Austrian's extrovert driving approach

Tauranac: "Jochen was always very pro-us at Brabham. When he was offered the deal to go to Lotus he came to us, told us what Chapman was offering, and said that he would stay with us for a fraction of the price. We got on really famously. We were watching our costs in those days and we used to share a room together for much of that season. He was a good bloke."

For Jochen's part, he admired Jack Brabham enormously. Heinz Pruller, Rindt's biographer, explained, "Jochen put his trust totally in Jack. He wanted to be like him. He admired his attitude to motor racing, his dedicated professionalism. Because Jack drove the same car as his other driver, Jochen found driving for Jack reassuring. It was a relaxed, pleasant relationship."

When Jochen came across from Cooper he also brought with him his own personal mechanic Ron Dennis who was destined to stay on with the Brabham team through until the end of 1970, rising to the position of chief mechanic. Today he is Commercial Director of the Marlboro McLaren International team. However, while personal relationships were absolutely no problem, it was soon clear that Repco was going to encounter enormous difficulties with the four-cam type 860 V8 engine which was under development for the 1968 season.

There were two lines of development examined by Repco in order to boost the power output close to the 400bhp mark: one was for a short-stroke magnesium block engine and the other for an ambitious new cylinder head employing a radial valve configuration. In the end a combination of ideas was employed and the type 860 engine retained the original Repco engine dimensions, using aluminium short blocks with twin overhead camshaft, four-valve cylinder heads, but avoiding the radial valve layout or the short stroke.

Further development of the shelved series 30 cylinder heads had convinced Repco that there were significant power advantages to be obtained from cross-flow gas paths, so the 860 engines had their inlets within the vee and the exhaust pipes on the outside. The new engines were not ready for the start of the season, so Rindt and Brabham used regular '67 spec. BT24s for the South African Grand Prix at Kyalami, Jochen opening his Brabham F1 innings with an encouraging third place behind the Lotus 49s of Clark and Hill.

There were no works Brabham entries for the Race of Champions, but Silvio Moser appeared in Charles Voegele's old BT20, Peter Gethin tried a 2-litre BMW engine in his Frank Lythgoe Brabham BT21 and Tony Lanfranchi appeared in the ex-George Pitt BT23B-FPF entered by Climax engine specialists Racing Preparations.

Tauranac did another new chassis, dubbed BT26, to accommodate the new Repco 860 engine and it eventually made its abortive competition debut in the Spanish Grand Prix at Jarama on May 12. Tauranac: "We attempted to make a lighter, yet stronger, chassis frame by using alloy sheeting instead of tubular triangulation. This allowed us to use smaller-gauge tubing for the basic frame in the first place and, instead of making the bulkheads first and then joining them together in the jig, we laid down the bottom part of the frame on a flat bed, built the top deck immediately above it and then put the side members in between. We used main rails similar to the previous cars, but with five-eighths' inch 20-gauge square tubing carrying the stressed panelling on the floor, around the cockpit deck, the sides, behind the seat and in the instrument panel frame, around the driver's thighs. It worked quite well, but it might have been cheaper to build a monocoque in the long run." The BT26 was also significantly larger than the BT24, having a 1½in. longer wheelbase and 5in./5½in. extra front/rear track dimensions.

In spite of much work preparing the team's Indianapolis cars, the first BT26 was

Rindt splashes to third place in the rain-soaked 1968 German Grand Prix, his BT26 seen negotiating the Karussell during this rare trouble-free run for the Repco 860 engine. Inset, F2 star Kurt Ahrens slithered to a distant 12th place in the same race at the wheel of this works spare BT24 using one of the older and more reliable 740 engines. The rear wing support stay has broken, allowing the aerofoil to drop down at the rear – which must have made for interesting handling . . .

In the 1968 United States Grand Prix at Watkins Glen, both Brabham and Rindt (pictured here) ran their "bi-plane" BT26s 1000 rpm down in a desperate bid to keep the Repco 860 engines in one piece. It didn't work in either case, Rindt's throwing a rod and Jack's breaking a cam follower.

flown down to Jarama on a specially chartered aircraft in time for final practice. The mechanics's reward for all this effort was to see the Repco 860 explode on the main straight, destroying a piston, cylinder liner, cylinder head and a couple of valves. This was only the beginning . . .

John Judd: "I'd spent much of the 1967 season down in Australia doing that four-cam engine in conjunction with Norm Wilson. The power output was OK, but when it came to racing it we had a large number of quality control problems. Gudgeon pins, for example . . . We spent one weekend rushing around converting the engines to take gudgeon pins out of a Petter diesel engine. We also had problems with the valve seats. We went down to Jarama for that second race of '68 and Jack had that failure, caused by a valve seat falling out, so he had to scratch and Jochen started from the pit lane because we were all having tea in the transporter, not knowing quite when the race was due to start, and then we heard cars going out on the warming up lap . . .

"Jochen? No aggro with him at all, he was a bloody good sport. He got browned off with everything, of course, but he knew we were working bloody hard on that engine. Eventually we sussed out that Repco was making the valve seats out of the wrong material, and they were shrinking. So on the night prior to the Belgian

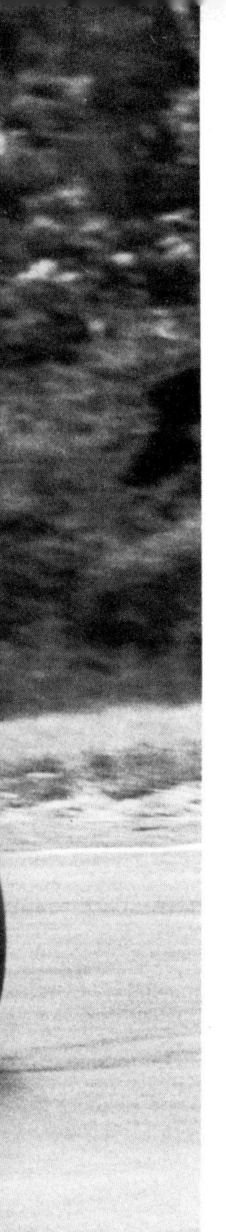

Grand Prix at Spa we tore down one of those 860 engines with the help of Roy Billington and Ron Cousins, who used to work at HRG and had subsequently joined Brabhams. It had shown the first signs of trouble during practice at Spa, so Jack flew it home after Saturday practice. We didn't have the right equipment, but Ron single-handedly drilled out the old valve seats on a radial drill, made new ones, put them in, cut them, the heads were cooked in Betty Brabham's domestic oven, she woke at about three o'clock in the morning and almost called the fire brigade because of the fumes in the house, the engine was reassembled and then flown out to Spa again sitting on the right-hand seat of Jack's Piper Twin Commanche!

"There was also the occasion that the cars had left for the Dutch Grand Prix at Zandvoort when we got a message through from Repco to say that the piston clearances on the most recently-delivered engine was incorrect, and if we started them up the pistons would make contact with the valves. Jack bought a chisel in a Guildford hardware store and we chiselled down the piston crowns when the cars got to Zandvoort. I didn't know enough, really. To be honest, I was a bloody virgin . . ."

The whole season degenerated into a total fiasco and the only time the four-cam BT26s finished a race intact was the rain-soaked German Grand Prix at Nurburgring with Jochen splashing home third, Brabham fifth. Yet there was no acrimony within the team, no bleating and complaining from any source whatsoever. The general feeling was that this was a communal problem which had to be solved for everybody's benefit.

John Judd: "As an indication of the atmosphere in the team that year, after all the problems in practice at Zandvoort, Jack, Jochen, Ron and myself took over the dodgems down in the town for half an hour to get away from it all. A great laugh! Can you imagine Bernie Ecclestone, Frank Williams or Ron Dennis on the dodgems? Neither can I . . ."

Notwithstanding all these problems, the BT26 was a fast car, Rindt slamming round to qualify on pole in both the French and Canadian Grands Prix. But he finished in neither race, a leaking fuel tank, caused perhaps by a venting problem, finishing his chances at Rouen, and brake problems and overheating forced him out at Ste. Jovite whilst chasing Amon's Ferrari. The enormity of the problems facing the Repco 860 engines were such that, realistically, there was little point in pursuing its long-term development when one could buy the virtually perfect Cosworth DFV "off the shelf". What's more, Cosworth in Northampton was somewhat nearer than Repco's base in Australia. Brabham even considered a swap to DFV power mid-way through 1968, but this was decided against out of loyalty to the Australian Company.

Throughout the latter half of the 1968 season it was becoming increasingly clear that the Repco F1 engine programme's salvation would depend on an almost unimaginable turn-round in technical reliability, but it was a false hope and there was no way in which the 12,000 mile supply route could sustain another season like this in 1969. Brabham took the essentially practical decision to switch to Cosworth DFVs for 1969, a move initiated as a short-term stop-gap but, in everybody's heart of hearts, could be seen as the Repco engine's death knell.

John Judd summed it up succinctly: "I think, given time, we could have sorted out the mechanical problems on the Repco 860, but by the end of the 1968 season we were facing more problems such as difficulties with those connecting rods and a tendency for the engine to wear out its cam follower on No. 3 cylinder – things which I could sort out easily today. But the DFV was a good package which could be used as a stressed member, and our engine couldn't, so although I think we could have done a reasonable job in 1969, at the end of the day the Cosworth DFV was far ahead in terms of design. So many things they did for the first time – and they did them right!"

Section 1: Jack's Brabham years, 1962-70

Chapter 3
First time round for the Cosworth DFV

In retaining the same overall dimensions after the switch to Cosworth DFV in 1969, the BT26 suddenly found itself with extra space behind the cockpit as the DFV was an inch or so shorter than the displaced Repco 860. Tauranac promptly filled it with the car's on-board fire extinguisher, as shown here.

The 1968 season may not have proved particularly competitive for the Brabham team's fortunes as a whole, but there was one area in which Ron Tauranac was right at the front of the field and that was the area of aerodynamic downthrust. As early as the 1967 Belgian Grand Prix the Brabham-Repcos had appeared running "trim tabs" on either side of the nose sections, presaging the aerodynamic revolution which really got off the ground some 12 months later. At the 1968 Belgian Grand Prix both Ferrari and Brabham appeared with strutted rear aerofoils and, as the year progressed, wings grew forth and multiplied to the point that, by the end of the season, many cars were running with front and rear mounted aerofoils, a trend which was carried forward to the 1969 season.

Adapting the BT26s to accommodate the Cosworth DFV engine was a pretty straightforward task, although the English V8 proved slightly shorter than its Australian predecessor with the result that there was a gap behind the cockpit into which the now-mandatory on-board fire extinguisher was slotted. Now that Rindt had finally taken the decision to leave, something he did with mixed feelings for he was rightly convinced that a Cosworth-engined BT26 would be a competitive proposition, former Ferrari driver Jacky Ickx was recruited to drive the second car. Enthusiastically involved with the JW-Gulf Ford GT40s in the international sports car arena, Ickx brought with him a couple of Cosworth engines from Ford and a measure of Gulf oil backing, all of whch helped the overall budget now that the days of free engines from Repco had come to an end.

Brabham's own bi-plane BT26 appeared for the South African Grand Prix at Kyalami powered by one of the latest '69 spec. DFVs, fitted with revised camshafts and modified timing gear covers, which could be wound round to 10,000rpm. He more than held everybody's attention by slamming round to take pole position, 0.2s faster than a thoughtful Jochen Rindt's Lotus 49 and 0.3s ahead of Denny Hulme's McLaren. Perhaps his former colleagues should not have been so hasty about leaving!

However, when it came to the 80 lap race Jackie Stewart's Tyrrell Matra MS10 led from start to finish, Brabham heading the chase for six laps until his rear aerofoil collapsed and he pulled in to have it dismantled, along, of course, with the front one. He rejoined, minus wings, but eventually decided to withdraw because he was so far behind and, in any case, the BT26 was over-revving badly on the straights without its aerodynamic appendages. Ickx, meanwhile, had also stopped for a collapsing wing to be dealt with, retiring when his Brabham refused to fire up again in the pit lane.

In addition to the two works entries, there was to be another Brabham BT26 contesting the World Championship in 1969, the immaculate, dark blue-liveried car fielded by enthusiastic private entrant Frank Williams. One of the leading lights in international Formula 2 for a couple of seasons, Frank had initially acquired an ex-works BT24 (the car which Gurney had driven at Zandvoort and Kurt Ahrens at the Nurburgring as third entries in 1968), equipped it with a 2.5-litre Cosworth DFW and dispatched it to the 68/69 Tasman Championship with Piers Courage driving. This impeccably prepared car did a fine job challenging the Lotus 49Ts and Ferrari Dino 246s, Courage actually winning the

With wings and without, the Brabham BT26 proved a highly competitive proposition once the Cosworth DFV replaced the Repco 860. Above, Jack qualified on pole for the 1969 South African Grand Prix at Kyalami, but eventually had to stop his bi-plane to be shorn of all its aerodynamic appendages as they started to collapse. He is seen here rushing into the Esses after that pit stop, eventually to retire rather than over-rev the new Cosworth engine on the long straight for no good reason or result. Below, at the 1969 Silverstone International Trophy, the "bi-plane" wing set-up remained intact for the duration of the race, Brabham just coasting home to win with dry tanks pursued by a fast-approaching Jochen Rindt's Lotus 49.

race at Teretonga to cement the plans in Frank's mind for a full-scale Grand Prix challenge that season.

Williams: "I then managed to acquire one of the ex-works BT26s from northern enthusiast David Bridges, who had purchased it with Formula 5000 in mind. That cost me £3500 and I paid Robin Herd another £500 to design a Cosworth installation which was duly carried out in the basement of a garage near Northampton owned by the father of Keith Leighton, later to become Ronnie Peterson's chief mechanic at Team Lotus."

There was a slight snag in that Frank's BT26 ran on Dunlop rubber, a factor which caused a touch of aggravation with Goodyear and the works team, particularly on the occasions where the always-improving Courage got on terms with Brabham and Ickx. Frank's programme was originally intended to start at Kyalami, but when it became clear that it would cost £6000 to ship the BT24 home via South Africa, this idea was shelved and the BT26 was readied for Courage to give it a first outing in the Race of Champions.

All three BT26s failed to finish this 50 lap non-title thrash, but on March 30

The absurdity of the spindly twin-wing developments in 1968/69 is amply demonstrated in this shot of the rear aerofoil on Ickx's BT26 collapsing during the 1969 Spanish Grand Prix at Barcelona. At the next Grand Prix, Monaco, the CSI ruled them illegal and they vanished overnight!

Brabham emerged from the Silverstone International Trophy a convincing winner in the pouring rain thanks largely to the superiority of Goodyear's latest G14 rain tyre. Thus equipped, Brabham was able to build up quite a commanding lead in the diabolical conditions, just as well as it turned out, because the BT26 spluttered out of fuel on the last lap and just managed to coast across the line 2.2s ahead of Jochen Rindt's fast-approaching Lotus 49. Stewart's Matra MS10 finished third ahead of Ickx's works BT26 and Courage in the Williams car.

The last race for the bi-plane wings turned out to be the Spanish Grand Prix at Barcelona's spectacular Montjuich Park on May 4, the works BT26s sporting several detail alterations including the fitting of a Hewland DG gearbox instead of the FG used hitherto, bearing in mind the strains which would be imposed on the transmission both in Spain and at Monaco. The combined water/oil radiator had been replaced by a full-width water radiator whilst a gearbox-mounted oil cooler was now fitted.

Brabham qualified fifth, 2.3s away from Rindt's stunning Lotus 49 pole position, with Ickx seventh and Courage 11th. Brabham retired with a major engine failure while Ickx succumbed to broken rear suspension after his twin aerofoil arrangement had started to fall apart earlier on. But the Brabham teamsters were relatively fortunate: both Team Lotus 49s were involved in spectacular accidents when their high-mounted rear aerofoils collapsed and the CSI became so concerned about the possibilities of a really serious accident, perhaps involving spectators, that the high wings were banned after first practice at the Monaco Grand Prix a couple of weeks later.

The sport's governing body would have dearly loved to pull a stunt like that in the years that followed, but the ban on these absurdly high aerofoils was met with grudging acceptance by most of the teams who could quite understand the potential for trouble if their development was not curtailed. However, it was generally agreed that the CSI should have taken this firm action long before practice actually started at Monaco, not mid-way through the meeting.

The works BT26s proved to be well-matched during practice, Ickx and Brabham sharing the fourth row a mere 0.1s apart. But once the race got going it was not the works entries, but Courage in the Williams car who really knuckled down to stage a quite stunning performance. Brabham's race came to a premature end when Surtees's BRM slowed suddenly immediately ahead of him with gearbox trouble and the two cars collided quite hard approaching the tunnel, while Ickx moved into second place and fended off Courage for many laps until the second works BT26 suffered a rear suspension failure and slid into the wall. That left Piers

The immaculate Frank Williams owned Brabham BT26-Cosworth on its way to a fine second place in the 1969 Monaco Grand Prix. Here Piers Courage barrels his Dunlop-shod mount confidently through Mirabeau *during a performance which seriously embarrassed the Goodyear-shod works cars.*

RACING DIVISION
CHAMPION

A testing accident at Silverstone in the early summer of 1969 meant that Brabham was unable to take part in the British Grand Prix at the same circuit. He attended, none the less, and is seen here easing himself out of the Champion sparking plug caravan in the paddock followed by a solicitous-looking Jo Bonnier. Outside, smoking the pipe, is Champion's Laurie Hands with* Autocar's *Peter Garnier standing behind him alongside the Jaguar XJ6 (very new and very smart at the time!) With a spare BT26 in the pit lane, Lotus organizational problems left Graham Hill (above right) with time to do a few laps in this Brabham-Cosworth. Here he prepares for his run as Ron Tauranac (right) watches mechanic Ron Dennis (with Goodyear decal on the back of his overalls) warm up the DFV and Roy Billington looks on from the left.

with an easy run home to second place behind Graham Hill's victorious Lotus, and the only Brabham runner to make the finish.

By the time everybody reassembled for the Dutch Grand Prix at Zandvoort, most of the teams were endeavouring, some subtly and others not so subtly, to find a way of correctly *interpreting* the latest CSI edicts on aerofoils to the effect that they "must now be fixed and part of the bodywork". The works BT26s appeared with an upswept aluminium frame supporting a rear aerofoil above the engine cover. It seemed as though this was quite acceptable and Ickx qualified fifth, 2s away from Rindt's pole position with Brabham eighth and Courage ninth. Silvio Moser also made the back of the grid again, with the ex-works/Williams Tasman BT24/3. In the race the works BT26s were not capable of running up at the front and while Stewart and the two Lotuses scrapped for the lead, Ickx and Brabham spent their race down amongst the second group, eventually finishing fifth and sixth. Courage retired his Williams BT26 when the clutch burnt out.

By the time the French Grand Prix took place at Clermont-Ferrand on July 6, Brabham had been injured in a tyre testing accident at Silverstone and only a single works entry was fielded for Ickx. Running on a near-empty circuit, Brabham was powering through Club Corner when BT26/2 suddenly snapped into a vicious understeer and charged into the earth bank on the outside of the circuit. The front left-hand corner was badly distorted and a dazed Brabham found himself trapped by his left ankle, initially unable to switch off the ignition and the fuel pump as the instrument panel had also been badly buckled in the impact. Jack recalls it seemingly took an age before help arrived and it was extremely off-putting to be trapped in that cockpit watching a tell-tale stain grow larger on the ground surrounding the wrecked BT26 as the contents of the fuel tanks began to seep out. It would have only needed a single spark . . .

With his left ankle in plaster and hobbling round on crutches, Brabham was obviously going to be out of the running for a few races, so Ickx now had to shoulder the burden of sole responsibility for the team's fortunes. Interestingly, the somewhat unpredictable Belgian rose to the occasion in superb fashion and seemed to be able to produce more impressive form when the effort was concentrated on him exclusively rather than being shared with the boss.

In the French Grand Prix he fought a tooth-and-nail battle with the Matra of Jean-Pierre Beltoise in the wake of Jackie Stewart's fast-disappearing sister car

Oulton Park seems to have been kind to Brabham F1 cars over the years! Here Jacky Ickx adds the 1969 Gold Cup to the team's tally of victories at the Cheshire circuit, a couple of weeks after his splendid triumph in the German Grand Prix.

Swiss privateer Silvio Moser hacked about his two year old BT24 to give it distinctively idiosyncratic lines by the time this photograph was taken at Monza in 1969. Whether he could see anything through those high-mounted mirrors on the cockpit sides is a matter of some doubt!

and, in a last lap scramble, only lost second place to the Frenchman by a matter of feet. The British Grand Prix at Silverstone was an historic, much-touted exclusive battle between Rindt's Lotus 49 and Stewart's Matra for overall supremacy, the Scot winning after the poker-faced Austrian hit trouble, as usual. But Ickx was the man to profit from Jochen's misfortune, slipping home a strong second in his BT26. At this stage of the season the entire Lotus camp was in a chaotic state of turmoil, the cars not being ready to run during first practice at Silverstone, so Graham Hill took time off to have a few laps in a brand new Brabham (BT26/4), clocking a time which was faster than Ickx managed in that particular session. Since the works Lotuses ran on Firestones and the Brabhams on Goodyears, Hill's action must have caused a fair deal of aggravation behind the scenes.

Rindt pipped Courage for fourth place on the very last lap, the Lotus driver recovering from a couple of pit stops, and Piers erupted from the cockpit to tell Frank Williams precisely what he thought of any pit strategy which would allow this to happen, insisting that he hadn't been tipped off about Jochen's approach. For a few moments there was an embarrassing scene in the pit lane as voices were raised, insults traded. In reality, it was by no means a bad result for Courage . . .

When it came to upholding Brabham's reputation at the Nurburgring, Ickx proved absolutely superb in the German Grand Prix on August 3. Practice saw Jacky's BT26 ranged against Stewart's Matra in a nerve-wracking tussle for pole

position, both men having previously established their class with brilliant performances on the circuit which threads its sinuous, demanding path through the Eifel mountains. Eventually Ickx emerged on pole with 7m 42.1s, a mere 0.3s faster than his arch-rival, remarkably evenly-matched performances when one considers that Rindt's Lotus 49B was almost 6s slower in third place on the grid!

Both Brabham and Matra got off the line cleanly at the start of the 14 lap thrash, but Stewart was away down into the tree-lined *Hatzenbach* section in the lead with Siffert's Walker Lotus 49B and Rindt's similar works car in hot pursuit. This was the order at the end of the opening lap with Ickx going like the wind in fourth place, Jacky disposed of Rindt second time round, completing that tour virtually alongside Siffert's blue Lotus and forcing a path through into second place mid-way round the third lap.

By the end of lap four Ickx was all over the leading Matra, but Stewart was not relinquishing his advantage without a fight and countered magnificently, fending off the Brabham as Ickx attempted to lunge through under braking for South Curve. Going into the sixth lap, Ickx briefly scrabbled past under braking for North Curve, but immediately slid wide across the Matra's bows and Stewart promptly nipped back ahead again. Ickx then glued himself to the Matra's gearbox for that entire sixth lap before finally outfumbling Stewart going into South Curve at the start of their seventh. By this time Stewart was suffering with gearbox trouble, the Matra occasionally not selecting third or fourth when he needed those ratios, but now Jackie was well and truly beaten by his Belgian namesake, so he eased his pace and stroked home a strong second ahead of Bruce McLaren's McLaren and Graham Hill's Lotus 49B, the only other F1 competitors to finish. Early in the race Piers Courage had landed heavily over a bump, his full-tanked Williams BT26 landing awkwardly and pitching him into a ditch, quite badly damaging its chassis, although Piers scrambled out unhurt.

Just under a fortnight later Ickx added yet another Gold Cup victory to the Brabham team's inventory of success, cruising to an easy non-title Oulton Park success after Stewart's Matra retired. Jack, feeling a bit stiff from that now-healed ankle fracture, was back in the cockpit for the Italian Grand Prix at Monza where he easily outqualified his youthful team-mate, the Belgian having an off weekend with a down-on-power engine to struggle home a disheartened tenth.

Ickx had arrived a day early at Monza to do some film work prior to practice and, during this session, had hit a pole which had been put across the track as a barrier, much to the detriment of the BT26's bodywork. That rather put him off his stroke and he had his mind more than occupied mulling over the terms of a deal for his return to Ferrari which he was close to finalizing. Tauranac recalls Jacky had a whole series of engine problems as well during official practice, but when offered a stint in Jack's car to get in some extra miles, rather took exception to the suggestion that, while he was out there, he might like to bed in some brake pads for the still below-par Brabham!

Ickx bounced back onto winning form in the Canadian Grand Prix at Mosport Park, shadowing Stewart's Matra almost from the start before pushing the indignant Scot off the circuit during an ill-advised stab at overtaking. It was a controversial victory, but Jacky publicly apologised to his rival after the race and feelings were smoothed over successfully. Just to prove that he was fully recovered, Jack stormed home in a strong second place, sharing the race's fastest lap with his victorious team-mate. Third was Rindt's Lotus 49B, ironically at a time when Jochen had been actively considering a return to Jack's team.

Rindt's long-awaited first Grand Prix victory came in the United States race at Watkins Glen, his Lotus 49B scooping a large bag of dollars which further sweetened this long-overdue success. A magnificent second place fell to Piers Courage's Williams BT26, the Englishman battling long and hard with Brabham's works car, cutting the corners and generally giving Jack a touch of his own treatment by showering him with stones and gravel. Piers had it easy over the last few laps as Brabham dropped to fourth after a late pit stop to top up after fuel starvation problems began to rear their ugly head, but Frank Williams recalls that

ell
SHELL
Sh

Wrong! On the very last corner of the 1970 Monaco Grand Prix Jack Brabham panics into an unbelievable error, locking his BT33's brakes in a sudden over-reaction to the apparent proximity of Jochen Rindt's pursuing Lotus 49C. Jack's car slid helplessly into the barrier in the foreground, allowing Rindt (in the next car) to nip through to a lucky victory. The third car in the picture is the de Tomaso of Piers Courage: Brabham had seen him in his right-hand mirror and panicked, not realising that Jochen was further over to the left of the circuit, close, but not really in with a chance of winning . . . until Jack lost his cool!

The two outstanding Cosworth-engined cars of 1970, Jochen Rindt's Lotus 72 and Jack's Brabham BT33, round Druids hairpin during the British Grand Prix, running in 1-2 formation. Brabham bided his time in Rindt's wake for many laps before surging through to lead, only to be deprived of victory when the BT33 spluttered, apparently out of fuel, on the very last lap and Jochen reasserted his place at the front.

Jack definitely was *not* amused at Courage's defensive driving. "He scattered the crowds on the road back up to the paddock garage with a great burst of revs, and he was wearing one of his really black looks, really scowling with annoyance . . ."

By this stage in the season Ickx had already agreed terms for a return to Ferrari and the plans for Rindt's return to the Brabham ranks had evaporated by the time Jacky and Jack rounded off the year with a 2-3 finish behind Hulme's McLaren at Mexico City. Brabham would have retired if Jochen had come back into the fold . . .

Rindt's business manager Bernie Ecclestone (of whom much more later) was stuck right in the middle of Jochen's dilemma over whether to stay with Lotus or return to Brabham. Bernie knew that the Austrian could be quite a sentimental soul in many ways and fully appreciated just how important it was for Jochen to be relaxed in his relationship with the team for which he drove, but he also understood that Chapman was prepared to bid the earth to keep him. Eventually Bernie got in touch with Goodyear in an attempt to put together a package which would enable Rindt to go back to Brabham, but Chapman eventually trumped the whole proposed deal with more money and the promise of a Formula 2 programme. That clinched it: Jack Brabham would have to drive for another year.

Goodyear's Leo Mehl recalls the dealings: "Jack was very interested in doing this deal because he would have liked to retire, and I had been quite a good friend of Jochen's and was very keen about the proposal, although I feared money would be the big problem. Jochen, Jack and I had talked about the deal, but nobody had really mentioned any hard figures. But Colin Chapman came up to me with a very serious look at one of the races and whispered, 'I don't care how much you are going to offer him because it won't be enough . . .' I was young and innocent and Colin was old and forceful, so I never pursued the matter any further with my management."

The necessity to enclose rubber fuel cells for 1970 steered Tauranac towards his first full monocoque Formula 1 design, the BT33, although this machine had been pencilled some time before and was originally intended to be ready mid-way through the 1969 season. The BT33 fell into line with the prevailing trend of using the Cosworth DFV engine as a stressed member, its straightforward "bathtub" monocoque constructed from NS4 aluminium alloy. The 40 gallon fuel load was carried in two side and seat tanks with a supplementary tank providing an additional five gallons when necessary. Front suspension included inboard mounted coil spring/damper units for the first time, operated by fabricated rocker arms, while the car initially appeared using the BT26 rear suspension layout with outboard mounted coil spring/dampers, lower wishbones, single top link and single radius rod.

New short front uprights carried Girling ventilated disc brakes buried deep inside the 13in diameter knock-on wheels, MRD rack and pinion steering was employed along with a front-mounted water radiator while the rear suspension was hung on a tubular yoke round the Hewland DG300 gearbox. A circular oil tank was also mounted at the rear of the car, as were the battery and the oil radiator. Tauranac remarked at the time, "I don't actually like hanging all that junk on the gearbox, but with the engine butting up close to the monocoque, there is not much space available for packaging these things." The overall impression of the car is unmistakably Brabham, retaining that typical big lower lip nose section on the two-piece body manufactured by Specialised Mouldings. The first car to appear was painted in a distinctive blue/green, not *quite* the flashy turquoise worn by the first Formula 1 Brabham of them all, but pretty close!

Jack's main commercial support continued to stem from Goodyear, but a second driver who could bring sponsorship with him had to be recruited and the choice fell on the bespectacled Rolf Stommelen, previously a respected member of the Porsche endurance team. Stommelen brought with him some backing from Ford Germany, including a couple of engines, and was entered under the aegis of the German magazine *Auto Motor and Sport.* This was the first time that the team had firmly nominated number one and two drivers.

From the word go, the Brabham BT33 proved to be a smooth handling and essentially forgiving car, reflecting traditional Tauranac qualities which had in no way been compromised by the switch from spaceframe to monocoque construction. Jack qualified third behind the March 701s of Stewart and Amon at Kyalami and survived a tangle with Rindt's Lotus at Crowthorne on the opening lap to pull back and challenge for the lead. By lap 20 Jack was ahead and the veteran 43-year-old spent the remaining 60 laps consolidating a convincing victory over Denny Hulme's McLaren and early leader Stewart. Stommelen's BT33 retired with engine trouble while local runner Pieter de Klerk finished a distant 11th in his old BT26, one of the many ex-works Brabhams to earn pensionable employment on the South African national championship scene.

A similarly dominant victory in the Brands Hatch Race of Champions was thwarted when the BT33's coil failed and had to be replaced during a hurried pit stop, dropping Brabham to fourth. It really was beginning to look as though Brabham might honestly have a very real chance of winning his *fourth* World Championship title in what was to be his final year in the cockpit.

The history books remind us that 1970 was the year of Jochen Rindt and the stupendous Lotus 72, but Chapman's trend-setting new car was far from the pace-setter it would eventually become and only a few quirks of ill-fortune and a couple of minor errors prevented Brabham from achieving his own remarkable personal goal.

The Lotus 72 had not been massaged into a state of competitiveness by the time Brabham planted the BT33 on pole for the Spanish Grand Prix at Jarama, lapping 0.2s quicker than Hulme's McLaren and Stewart's March which joined him on the front row. Jackie got the March ahead early on, but the BT33's chassis superiority told in the end and Jack hauled up onto the Scot's tail during the second part of the 90 lap race, harrying him consistently all the way round the undulating little track. Just as it seemed inevitable that Brabham must get through and win, the BT33's

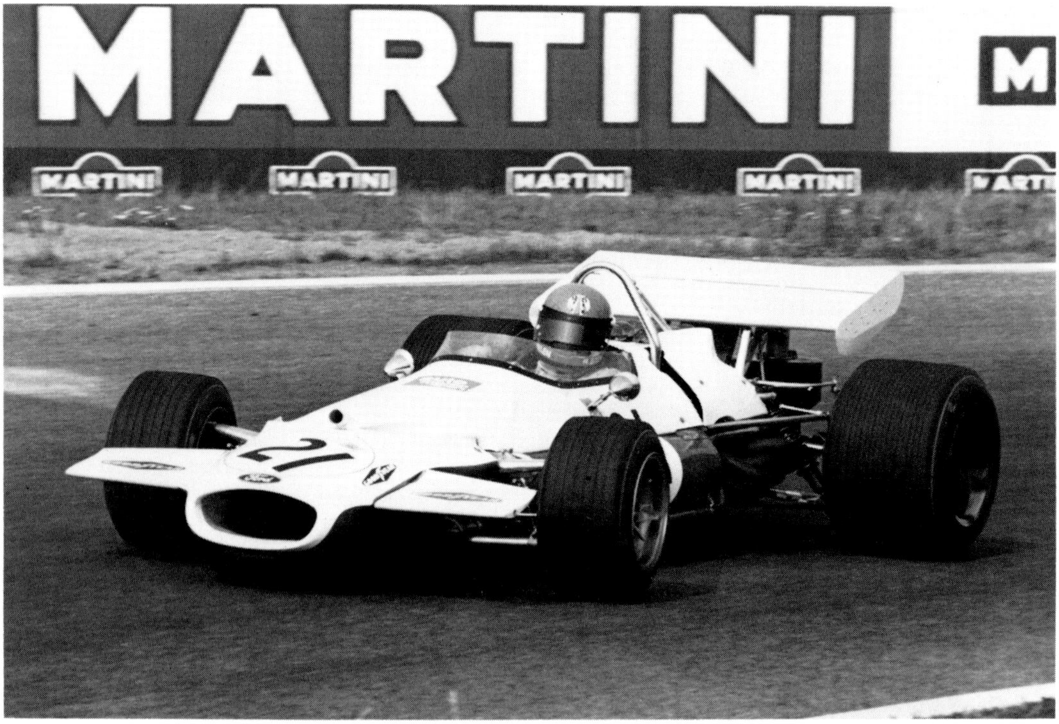
MARTINI
MARTINI
MARTINI
MARTINI
MARTINI
21

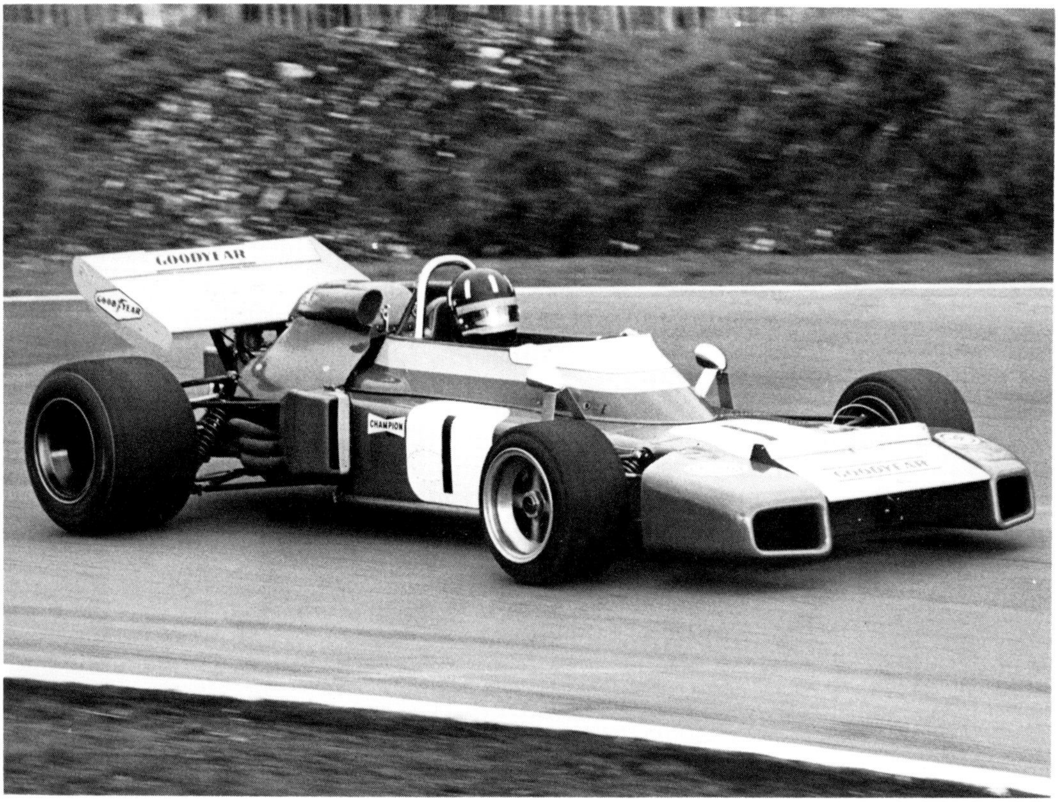
GOODYEAR
CHAMPION
1
GOODYEAR

The 1970 season was also the first year during which the Brabham team had a definite number one/number two driver arrangement. Jack's team-mate throughout the year was the genial bespectacled German Rolf Stommelen, seen here heading for fifth place in the German Grand Prix at Hockenheim.

Cosworth DFV abruptly expired, so that was that.

On April 26 Jack retired with engine trouble in the Silverstone International Trophy before "goofing" dramatically and losing victory in the Monaco Grand Prix thanks to the amazing last-corner error which saw the BT33 plough head-on into the straw bales, Jack erroneously thinking that Rindt's advancing Lotus 49 C was much closer than in fact it was. Jochen, who had shattered the lap record by almost two seconds in an amazing final spurt, nipped through to an unexpected victory, hardly noticing the turquoise BT33 as its owner reversed it gently, sheepishly, from the bales. Red faced, but grinning in self-critical admonishment, Brabham staggered across the line in second place with his car's nose cone frayed and rumpled. Silly boy . . .

Stommelen scored his first Championship points with fifth place in the Belgian Grand Prix at Spa-Francorchamps where Jack's BT33 succumbed to clutch trouble and the marque's ranks were swollen briefly by English F2 ace Derek Bell having a crack behind the wheel of Tom Wheatcroft's ex-works BT26 which he had driven initially in the Tasman series. Gear linkage problems sidelined this machine and it did not contest any more Grands Prix.

Private testing at Zandvoort prior to the Dutch Grand Prix saw Brabham upend Stommelen's regular BT33, rolling it up in a stretch of catch fencing in what could have been a very dangerous moment had there even been the smallest fire. Rolf's car was still being prepared in the paddock when practice began, so the whole team was off its stride and never really got going properly all weekend. Jack qualified down in the middle of the fifth row, finishing four laps behind in tenth place after stopping twice with punctured tyres. Stommelen failed to qualify.

Jack was right back on form in the French Grand Prix at Clermont-Ferrand, where he finished third, and he had the legs of Rindt's Lotus 72 in a memorable British Grand Prix at Brands Hatch where he started from the middle of the front row having equalled Jochen's pole time of 1m 24.8s.

The distinctive, one-off "lobster claw" Brabham BT34 showing promising form on its maiden outing in Graham Hill's hands, the 1971 Race of Champions at Brands Hatch. Graham later won the International Trophy at Silverstone in this car, but otherwise had a generally unimpressive time with it.

Once Ickx's Ferrari had retired early on with transmission failure, Brabham shadowed Rindt's Lotus from lap 7 to 65, making no attempt to get by, just sitting there and watching his former team-mate. It must have been most off-putting for the Lotus driver and when Rindt missed a gear-change, Brabham was through into the lead on 69, with only 11 left to run.

Brabham had the race in the bag, underlining that it *was* possible to defeat the Lotus 72 in a straight fight, even on a bumpy circuit like this one. Then, nightmare of nightmares, the BT33 ran out of fuel on the very last lap and Jochen swept by to win as Brabham stuttered those painful last few yards to the chequered flag. That was the second Grand Prix of the season down the pan for no good reason.

Tauranac: "I don't believe in bad luck, but things certainly weren't going for us through 1970. Jack started at Brands with 4-5 gallons in excess of the car's requirements and he wasn't *quite* out at the end, so it wasn't a case of the tank not scavenging. It's *possible* that all the fuel didn't go in, but the people concerned were very reliable and marked off their churns and so on. We could have used more fuel, this is possible because the car did appear to be running rich in the race, but the other possibility is that we had a leak. We did find a suspect bag which was wet when we pulled it out of its carrier after the race, although we haven't got any proof that it leaked.

"The BT33 was a good strong car, a fact which was underlined by Jack's accident when he rolled Rolf's car at Zandvoort and Rolf's own accident at Brands Hatch during practice which prevented him running in the British Grand Prix. When Jack rolled that car up in the fencing at Zandvoort, the impact just knocked off the suspension on one side and damaged the bodywork. The monocoque was untouched and the car was running again 30 hours later. When Rolf hit the bank at Clearways as he tried to go round Graham Hill, he was probably only doing 30mph when he impacted, but it grabbed the wheel, turned it square-on and we had one of these compression impacts where the monocoque collapses completely along one side. At that point in the season we almost had a spare BT33 ready, but

continued on page 114

The man who started it all, John Arthur Brabham, World Champion 1959 and 60 for Cooper, and 1966 for his own team.
Photo: Geoffrey Goddard Photography

Making do. After leaving Cooper at the end of 1961, Brabham had to wait until the following year's German Grand Prix before the first F1 car bearing his own name was ready to race. Early in 1962 he bought his own Lotus 24-Climax V8 to tide him over and Jack is seen here with it at Monaco, where he slid off the circuit into retirement.
Photo: Geoffrey Goddard Photography

Sweeping through Tabac chasing Jim Clark's Lotus during the early stages of the 1964 Monaco Grand Prix, Jack's BT7-Climax holds second place ahead of Graham Hill's BRM, Dan Gurney's BT7, John Surtees's Ferrari and Richie Ginther's BRM.
Photo: Geoffrey Goddard Photography

Jack in his BT7 on the starting grid prior to the 1964 Silverstone International Trophy, a race he would win in a dramatic lunge round the outside of Graham Hill's BRM on the very last corner. Roy Billington squats by the car on the left looking confident. (inset)
Photo: Geoffrey Goddard Photography

Gripping a handkerchief between clenched teeth to minimise the buffeting he was receiving in the cockpit that didn't fit him, an angry Dan Gurney presses on towards sixth place in the 1965 British Grand Prix at Silverstone. He is driving Jack Brabham's originally designated BT11, with 16-valve Climax V8, after his own similar car's powerful 32-valve V8 expired on the warming up lap and the team boss stood down without any hesitation.
Photo: Geoffrey Goddard Photography

Halcyon days for the Brabham-Repco partnership. Denny Hulme's BT24-Repco V8 leaps one of the Nürburgring's many jumps on its way to victory in the 1967 German Grand Prix, the rugged Kiwi's second victory of his Championship year.
Photo: Geoffrey Goddard Photography

22

ANTAR
5

5

7

2

HULM

REPCO
LR

FERODO
9
GOODYEAR
Esso
CHAMPION

GOODYEAR

Title clincher. A relaxed Denny Hulme locks over his BT24 into the hairpin at Mexico City during the 1967 Mexican Grand Prix in which he finished third behind Jim Clark's Lotus 49 and team leader Brabham. It was sufficient to ensure that the Championship title swapped hands between the two Brabham teamsters! Inset, Brabham tries the all-enveloping cockpit screen during practice at Monza, 1967. In this pit lane shot he is tended by Ron Tauranac (back to camera) and the ever-present Roy Billington.
Photo: LAT Photographic

Fast but fragile. The catastrophically unreliable four-cam Repco 860 V8 installed in one of the Brabham BT26s during the 1968 season. The failure of this, the most powerful version of the Repco V8 theme, spelled the end of Brabham's partnership with the enthusiastic Australian company.
Photo: Geoffrey Goddard Photography

Jacky Ickx's Cosworth DFV-engined, "bi-plane" BT26 splashing to third place in the rain-soaked 1968 International Trophy at Silverstone, a race won by the Guv'nor from Jochen Rindt's Lotus 49B.
Photo: Nigel Snowdon

The well-balanced lines of the Brabham-Cosworth BT33 are well shown in this shot of Jack speeding along Bottom Straight at Brands Hatch during 1970 Race of Champions meeting. In his last season, Jack won the South African Grand Prix with this machine – and only rotten luck prevented him adding the Spanish and Monaco GPs, and the Race of Champions, to this tally of success.
Photo: LAT Photographic

Shafts of late afternoon sunshine illuminate, somewhat appropriately, this pit lane conference between Graham Hill and Ron Tauranac during practice for the 1971 Spanish GP at Barcelona. The famous Englishman was approaching the evening of his competitive career, but the distinctive BT34 'lobster claw' was to help him score a surprise victory in the '71 International Trophy.
Photo: Geoffrey Goddard Photography

continued from page 95

once we'd used its suspension to repair Jack's Zandvoort shunt and the monocoque to rebuild Rolf's Brand Hatch wreck we didn't actually complete a third BT33, ready to roll, until after the Mexican Grand Prix at the end of the season."

Stommelen made up for his Brands Hatch disappointment by taking points in the next couple of races, bagging fifth at Hockenheim and third at the Osterreichring, Brabham himself hitting trouble in both these races. The Italian Grand Prix at Monza, saddened by Rindt's tragic death during practice, saw Jack's BT33 badly rumped against the guard rail when its engine cut out abruptly as he was exiting *Parabolica* and the boss went sliding off the circuit. Both cars retired from the Canadian Grand Prix at Ste. Jovite, trailed home near the back at Watkins Glen and rounded off the season with a couple of engine failures at Mexico City. But for Jack Brabham himself, it was a glorious way in which to round off his Formula 1 career: when his BT33 finally expired, the 44-year old triple World Champion was running strongly in third place, ahead of many of the new lads, the best-placed Cosworth runner headed only by a pair of considerably more powerful Ferrari flat-12s. There was life in the old dog yet right up until the final curtain.

If it was difficult for Jack to disentangle himself from the business of Grand Prix racing, his life for more than a decade, then it was perhaps doubly difficult for Ron Tauranac to continue without him in front-line international racing. The whole fabric of Formula 1 was changing relentlessly by the end of the 1960s and it was not to be long before the advent of the big commercial sponsor was going to require new qualities of PR diplomacy from many team chiefs, as well as the out-going, gregarious nature required to clinch those major backers in the first place. Tauranac's enthusiasm for Formula 1 was still that of an engineering purist and down-to-earth enthusiast: the commercial side held less appeal for him.

He none the less pressed on into 1971, though, and support from Esso enabled him to recruit Graham Hill as a "name" to lead the team with young Australian rising star Tim Schenken signed to drive as number two. Schenken had driven a semi-works Formula 2 Brabham BT30 for Rodney Bloor's Sports Motors (Manchester) team the previous year and was yearning to prove he had the talent of his F3 contemporaries Ronnie Peterson and Reine Wisell who were also now safely ensconced in Formula 1.

Tauranac's team fielded a pair of BT33s in the South African Grand Prix season opener at Kyalami, unchanged since 1970 apart from 13in. diameter rear tyres for the first time. Local star Dave Charlton handled the second entry on this occasion, easily out-qualifying Hill, much to the consternation of some onlookers. In the race Charlton ran confidently ahead of the team leader until engine failure stopped him after 31 laps, leaving Hill to trail home a distant ninth.

The only totally new Formula 1 car to emerge from the Brabham factory in 1971 was the distinctive "lobster claw" BT34 of which only a single example was constructed. The most visually obvious feature of this new Brabham was the way in which two separate water radiators were mounted ahead of the front wheels, leaving an adjustable full-width wing across the front of the monocoque. The idea behind this was that the air discharged from the radiators went into an area which would be turbulent in any case because of the disturbance caused to the airflow by the outboard spring/damper units, but that this discharge would cause less drag than would be occasioned by forcing the air upwards through the top of a conventional nose section. It also had the benefit of keeping hot air away from the cockpit.

The new monocoque had the steering rack positioned behind the hubs rather than in front of them, allowing the steering rack to be positioned above the driver's legs and him to be positioned some 3in. further forward than on the BT33. This also permitted the seat tank to carry 14 gallons of fuel which, with 16 gallons in each of the main tanks down either side of the monocoque, made a total capacity of 46 gallons. The rear end of the BT34 was much like the previous year's BT33 layout, although the lighter Hewland FG400 gearbox was employed on this new

Aussie Tim Schenken's BT33 storming round the Osterreichring on its way to a superb third place in the 1971 Austrian Grand Prix behind Jo Siffert's BRM P160 and Emerson Fittipaldi's Gold Leaf Lotus 72. The following year Schenken left to join Surtees, unconvinced that Ecclestone had the necessary savvy to run a competitive Grand Prix team. If only Tim could have his time over again . . .

machine.

Allocated to Graham Hill for his exclusive personal use, the lone BT34 flattered only to deceive in its first few races and the overall results tally for the Brabham team in 1971 makes pretty dismal reading by any standards. Hill drove the BT34 on its debut in the Race of Champions at Brands Hatch when it challenged Stewart's Tyrrell for second place before Graham missed a gear and took the edge off the engine. It managed fastest lap, true enough, but a 1m 26.7s was almost a second away from Jack's best at the wheel of the older BT33 in the previous year's British Grand Prix, so it was not too much to shout about.

Schenken managed to emerge fifth from the non-Championship Questor Grand Prix at California's Ontario Motor Speedway, but Hill retired with an oil leak. The BT34 retired with damaged steering in the Spanish Grand Prix at Barcelona and although Hill's twilight career enjoyed a fleeting Indian summer with a win in the Silverstone International Trophy, this was as nothing set alongside his embarrassment at Monaco. The hero with five Monaco Grand Prix wins to his credit bounced the BT34 off the wall at *Tabac* early in the race, climbing out of the wreckage and walking away into crestfallen retirement. Things were just *not* what they used to be . . .

Tauranac was not impressed with Hill's performances, the Australian designer

identifying and sympathizing more with Schenken as the season progressed. At the first French Grand Prix to be held at Paul Ricard few people really believed Hill's fifth-fastest qualifying time although when the race began quickly he stayed close to the leading bunch, eventually to spin on his own lubricant after an oil line became detached. But from then on Schenken consistently had the legs of him and Tim only missed out on a splendid third place in the British Grand Prix at Silverstone when his BT33's transmission packed up four laps from the chequered flag.

Schenken then picked up a sixth at the Nurburgring, and made the rostrum with third behind Siffert's BRM P160 and Emerson Fittipaldi's Gold Leaf Team Lotus 72 at the Osterreichring, but the Austrian race, where Hill produced a fine fifth place, was the last time the Brabhams would be in the points in 1971. The season petered out Hill finishing 11th at Monza and seventh at Watkins Glen, while Schenken netted a fifth in the tragic end-of-season Rothmans World Championship Victory Race at Brands Hatch which was stopped prematurely when Jo Siffert crashed fatally in his BRM.

Yet, as the Tauranac epoch in Brabham team Formula 1 fortunes came quietly to its end, the last few races produced one or two interesting little twists and turns which pointed the way for the future. Alain de Cadenet's Ecurie Evergreen acquired the ex-works BT33/2 which was entered for saloon ace Chris Craft in a few late season events, including the Oulton Park Gold Cup (where Craft finished fifth), the Canadian and United States Grands Prix. The engine from this BT33 would later go into the Duckhams Le Mans car, commissioned by de Cadenet in 1972 and designed on a freelance basis, by the youthful Gordon Murray when he was not slaving away over his Brabham drawing board at New Haw.

Finally, there was a third Brabham entry in that abortive non-title race at Brands Hatch. A second distinctively rebodied BT33 was driven to ninth place by Carlos Reutemann, a young man whose talent had attracted the Tauranac's interest during the final year of his regime, but whose full potential would be realized only after Ron had parted company with the organization he helped to found.

Brabham's retirement at the end of the 1970 had heralded the end of the old order, but it was Tauranac's departure, just over a year later, which finally guaranteed that the whole complexion of Motor Racing Developments would now change out of all recognition.

Ecurie Evergreen team manager Keith Greene bends over saloon ace Chris Craft in the cockpit of the ex-works BT33 acquired by the team at the end of 1971. This photograph was taken in the Oulton Park paddock prior to the Gold Cup meeting in which Craft finished fifth. The car later provided the bare bones of the Gordon Murray-designed Duckhams Le Mans car which Craft and Ecurie Evergreen patron Alain de Cadenet used at the Sarthe the following summer.

FILA
FILA
parmalat
parm

Section 2: The Ecclestone era

Chapter 1 The Brabham team in transition

The man who took both Brabham and Formula 1 into a completely new style of motor racing. Millionaire businessman Bernard Ecclestone, who made fortunes in car, motorcycle and property dealings before taking over the Brabham team at the start of 1972, seen here on the starting grid prior to the 1983 Grand Prix of Europe at Brands Hatch. He is standing alongside Riccardo Patrese's Brabham and talking to team engineer Don Halliday.

Notwithstanding Jack's decision to have one final stab at winning another Championship in 1970, the fact of the matter was that an era was coming to an end. Brabham had told his wife that he would be racing *only* for one more year and the seriousness with which he viewed the prospect of retirement was underlined by the fact that he sold his own shares in MRD to Ron Tauranac at the end of 1969. In effect, during 1970 the triple World Champion was just an employee of the company he had founded the best part of a decade earlier. True to his word, Brabham withdrew from active participation after the 1970 Mexican Grand Prix and Ron Tauranac was left on his own to preside over the Formula 1 programme in 1971.

Through those earlier dealings with Jochen Rindt, Ron had come to know Bernie Ecclestone quite well and the two men began talking on quite a casual basis about Jochen's former manager taking a stake in MRD. Bernie's interest in motor racing stretched back to the immediate post-war years when he was an active and enthusiastic participant, first on motorcycles and later at the wheel of a Formula 3 500cc Cooper, a Cooper-Bristol single seater and a Cooper-Jaguar sports car. A reflection of the man's fastidious and meticulous approach to life, his cars were always immaculately turned out, but the lure of business life provided a much greater stimulus to Ecclestone who retired from serious driving in 1954, although he briefly returned to the scene with a Formula Junior Elva at the start of the sixties.

Bernie had been a close friend of Stuart Lewis-Evans and, after the Connaught team went out of business in 1957, he acquired the cars and fielded them in the 1957/58 Tasman series for Stuart and Ivor Bueb. During 1958 they also appeared in some British domestic events and Bernie himself even had an unsuccessful crack at qualifying one for the Monaco Grand Prix! Ecclestone began to manage Stuart's affairs and a new team was planned for 1959 which would have used brand new Coopers with Lewis-Evans driving and Bernie organising: sadly the whole project never came to fruition after Stuart's sad death after an accident at the wheel of a Vanwall in the 1958 Morroccan Grand Prix.

Bernie dropped from the racing scene after Stuart's death to concentrate on his business interests. When he reappeared eight years later, taking up his connections with people like Roy Salvadori (then with Cooper) and Rindt, he was a successful and wealthy businessman with several strings to his bow. He had made a success of the motorcycle and car retailing business as well as some shrewd, timely property dealings. Distinguished bike racer John Surtees recalls being taken by his father to buy motorcycle parts from Bernie's family home in the early post-war years, the future Brabham boss apparently operating out of his mother's kitchen at the time! Although Bernie actually trained as a chemist, his true forte proved to be as a dealer, an entrepreneur: he was destined to travel a long way from his modest beginnings in the world of commerce!

His reputation as a clever, quick-thinking and mentally agile operator was about to be focussed on Formula 1, via, initially, the Brabham team. It is fair to say that neither has ever looked back . . .

"Ron had initially spoken to me as early as the 1971 Monaco Grand Prix about

Racing days. Above, a youthful Ecclestone poses in the cockpit of his F3 Cooper in the paddock at Boreham in 1951. Below, sitting on the tail of his ex-works Connaught which he, Bruce Kessler and Paul Emery all unsuccessfully attempted to qualify at Monaco in 1958.

the prospect of getting involved with him," reflects Ecclestone, "but negotiations were not completed until sometime that October. He initially asked me if I could give him some help on the business side, but later he said 'well, I think I want to sell, so do you want to buy half?' I told him that I didn't particularly want to buy half, but if he wanted to sell, then I'd buy the whole business. So he said that's what he would do.

"Initially it was intended that Ron would stay, although he wanted to move over onto the development side. I had just bought Colin Seeley's motorcycle business and Ron seemed quite enthusiastic about working with him on both the car and cycle developments we were planning at the time."

Observers watching on the touch lines had doubts as to whether Tauranac would be able to stay at MRD in his new capacity. He and Bernie were poles apart in terms of character and approach. Ron, by his own admission, missed the old days when he and Jack Brabham ran the business together. But the old days had gone for ever and Bernie planned a new, more expansive future for the organisation.

Tauranac recalls, "There was a change of emphasis. In the old days, I would stay at the circuit with Jack and the mechanics and we used to work on the cars, knock ideas about and discuss things . . . then we'd knock off and go back to the hotel and eat, perhaps a little bit before the mechanics, but still not very early. Then Jack retired and things were different. I didn't want particularly to stay up all night, but on the other hand I didn't want to leave the track early and go and eat by six o'clock. The fun had gone out of it and, by 1971, we were having a rather fraught time. As far as Graham was concerned, I think . . . well, whatever talent he may previously have had as a driver had drifted away and only his determination was left.

"I was no good at getting sponsorship and, although Goodyear was paying the lion's share of the budget in '71, it was still a £100,000 gamble every year and I was in no position to take that on, particularly as I was still paying back Jack the money he lent me to buy his shares. So I started talking to Bernie. It was originally mooted as a partnership, but I eventually sold out to him. There's no reason, in my view, why it couldn't have worked with me staying there, but Bernie was a bit of a loner and it didn't work out. But I've got no axe to grind, Bernie and I are still friends."

Looking back on the situation from a distance of 12 years, Ecclestone admits that it was a delicate situation, but says, "Ultimately, you couldn't really employ somebody who once owned the company. It wasn't good for him, it wasn't good for me." About Ron as a person, he is generous. "He was a very practical person, and because of the name 'Brabham' I think he managed to surround himself with a crowd of very good people. I think he missed Jack and, although he initially seemed happy to work with Colin Seeley, Ralph Bellamy and Gordon Murray, it didn't take the situation very long to come to a head. I think he honestly wanted us to make a go of it all on our own and be successful . . . but somehow he also tended to resent anyone making a success of the name Brabham without his being involved."

By the start of the 1972 season Ecclestone was in control and, while Colin Seeley turned his attentions to building up the production car side of the business, a task he was to perform with spectacular success, Bernie took over the helm of the Formula 1 team.

On the equipment side, the team had a BT33 and the distinctive lone BT34 on strength and Ron, prior to selling out, had originally anticipated that Carlos Reutemann would be paired with Tim Schenken for '72. Reutemann had previously shown impressive F2 form in a Formula 2 Brabham run by the Automovil Club Argentina and his team manager, the diminutive Hector Staffa, had originally been the one to talk about the prospect of Carlos driving Formula 1 in 1972. Ecclestone knew enough to appreciate Reutemann's promise . . .

"As far as I was concerned, Graham was out," says Tauranac flatly, "but Tim didn't want to drive for Bernie unless I was here." Feeling that Ecclestone was insufficiently experienced to run a worthwhile Formula 1 project, Schenken then

Business infancy. The smart premises of Compton and Ecclestone, motorcycle dealers, at 300, Broadway, Bexleyheath. Taken in the late 1950s, these photographs indicate just what a high level of orderly layout Ecclestone demanded in all his businesses from the word go. By the standards of the day these were very smart and well laid-out showrooms, as were those of the car sales business, James Spencer Ltd, which Bernie would later operate in the same South London suburb.

proceeded to sign for Surtees, a less than prescient assessment of the situation as things would turn out!

Basically, Schenken was unwilling to sign the two year deal which Bernie, quite reasonably, asked him to. Tim had initially confirmed that he would be staying with Brabham, but changed his mind after some quiet reflection. Ecclestone admits that annoyed him. "Ron had asked me if I would keep Tim on and I agreed, providing he did the two year deal. After all, if I was going to finance his Formula 1 racing and he turned out to be a star, then I wanted to make something out of him in his second year with us.

"It must have cost MRD about £60,000 to run Tim in 1971, so I thought it was a bit off when he asked me if he could have a contract with an option to leave if Ron left. I thought he saw my point of view, but eventually I had to ask him 'are you going to sign this contract or not:' We agreed to meet the following evening and sign, but he called me back the next morning and said that he had changed his mind.

"When I met Tim in Argentina at the start of the '72 season (when he was driving a Surtees), I asked him why he had rung up on the last possible morning to tell me he didn't want to sign. He replied, 'I thought you would ring back'. I told him that I wouldn't have phoned him back if he had been Jackie Stewart . . .

"Meanwhile Graham had desperately wanted a drive and I'd had to turn him down, while Carlos Pace and Wilson Fittipaldi had both offered sponsorship to take the seat alongside Reutemann. At the end of the day I ended up taking Graham and paying for it myself . . ."

Not only on the Brabham driver front was Ecclestone wielding what turned out to be a vigorous new broom. There were a lot of changes of personnel in other areas and, as many of them recall, the period of overlap between the pure-Tauranac and pure-Ecclestone eras was a little difficult, some would say downright embarrassing.

Former McLaren M19 designer Ralph Bellamy was recruited to join the design staff, fed up to the back teeth over seemingly endless rows with McLaren director Teddy Mayer, and he felt the situation was a little awkward. "Ron and I overlapped for a short while and it was very difficult and embarrassing for us both," he confessed, "but it was thankfully resolved when Ron left."

Two other well-known new faces on the Brabham payroll included experienced ex-Lotus and March mechanic Bob Dance and his more junior colleague Mike Blash, known universally by the soubriquet "Herbie" ever since his fledgling days with Rob Walker Racing where Rob's senior mechanic Tony Cleverley used to refer to him as "a right little 'erbert". Herbie had been Jochen Rindt's mechanic at Lotus and had got to know Bernie Ecclestone well after that fateful afternoon at Monza in September 1970 . . .

Dance had been encouraged to join Ecclestone's revitalized team on Herbie's suggestion, but things didn't exactly go right from day one as far as Blash was concerned!

"I'd got to know Herbie well from my days at Lotus when he used to be up there quite frequently working on Rob Walker's 49s," reflects Bob Dance, "and it was he who told me that Bernie was looking for new mechanics, so I went out to dinner with him along with Herbie, ex-Frank Williams wrench Kerry Adams (later to join Yardley McLaren) and we all agreed to join him.

"We all started one Monday morning shortly after the New Year in 1972 and had to get everything ready for Buenos Aires. Graham Hill was a good morale-booster to have on the driving strength and Bernie's team manager Keith Greene was a bright and breezy sort of chap, but on the first day Ron Tauranac came into the workshop telling us what to do."

He found Herbie fitting a bracket to the BT33's bodywork and told him quite bluntly, "we don't do things in that way at Brabham . . ." Herbie looked askance, mumbled something about "well, that's how we did it at bloody Lotus and it's the right way!" and the whole exchange got completely out of hand.

Bob Dance: "We all went down to the pub at lunchtime and Herbie told me, 'sorry, but I'm off, there's no way I can work with him'. I told him he must be bloody joking. He'd brought us here and he ought to try and stick it out with us. But Herbie kept saying 'there's no way I can work with Ron', and he went back to get his tool box and was away. We went off to South America and, meanwhile, Herbie got himself a job with Frank Williams. So who should arrive in South Africa as Frank's technical advisor? Ron Tauranac!"

Eventually Herbie came back to Brabham in 1973, initially as Wilson Fittipaldi's F2 mechanic, but he soon returned to the F1 team where he remains to this day as manager and Ecclestone's right-hand man. Some of the "old guard" chose to move on, including Roy Billington (who now via a circuitous route, is back at New Haw working for Ralt!), but others stayed on including the highly respected father-and-son panel shaping team of Fred and Pete Bedding, previously together at Cooper, and Ron Cousins of Repco improvization repute!

The new employees quickly came to read their new boss and what sort of a mood he was in. Dance, with a keen memory and an eye for detail, recalls "that you could always know what sort of a mood Bernie was in by the way he would drive his car down the track to the works. He would sometimes arrive in a bad mood and go away in a good one, or vice versa. One thing he was very particular about, though, was keeping the doors shut. We often used to work at New Haw with the doors open, but when we knew Bernie was on his way over from his base at Bexleyheath, we would all rush round shutting them before he arrived."

On a more general note, Dance, who stayed with Brabham until the end of 1976 when he returned to Lotus, acknowledges that Bernie's meticulous approach to things is largely responsible for the excellent working conditions enjoyed by F1 mechanics into the eighties. "Bernie was responsible for the enormous improvements in mechanics' working conditions. He has been responsible for the good garages we have at most tracks, the neat and tidy, organised paddock layouts. A reflection of his mentality, perhaps . . . everything just so. He was always *very* particular . . ."

The Brabham team continued to operate out of the New Haw premises which were still actually owned by Jack Brabham. Motor Racing Developments continued to lease the property from him until Bernie transferred the whole operation to far more modern, lavish premises of his own at Chessington some five years later. The team, along with FOCA's headquarters and Ecclestone's business base, remains there to this day, while the old New Haw factory has passed back into Ron Tauranac's hands and houses the Ralt factory where production racing cars for the junior single seater formulae continue to be built by the dozen . . .

Incidentally, Ecclestone has retained the team name Brabham and the 'BT-Brabham/Tauranac' type numbering sequence to this day, believing that this sort of continuity is worthwhile and sensible. When, several years ago, the author asked him why the cars were still called Brabhams, he replied, "Look, if you and I went into business together and bought Marks and Spencer, we wouldn't rename it Ecclestone and Henry, would we? Brabham is a good name with a good reputation." There's no answer to that . . .

For the opening race of the 1972 season, the Argentine Grand Prix at Buenos Aires on January 23, Ecclestone and Keith Greene presided over a two-car team. Carlos Reutemann was having his second Formula 1 outing on home soil at the wheel of the now-white liveried Brabham BT34 which had undergone some minor changes since the end of the previous season, incorporating a one-piece cockpit moulding and, more significantly, a slightly narrower rear track. Reutemann had finished third in the non-title '71 Argentine Grand Prix at the wheel of Jo Bonnier's old McLaren M7C and was anxious to impress once again in front of his madly enthusiastic home crowd. Cast in something of a supporting role was Graham Hill, the Englishman now relegated to handling the ex-Schenken BT33, updated with a new 16-gauge outer skin, strengthened bulkheads, the revised bodywork seen at the end of the previous year and new Girling four-pot brake calipers.

Reutemann was destined to start the revitalized Brabham team off on a heady note. Using Goodyear's soft G52 compound he whistled round the 2.121-mile *Circuito No. 9* in the Buenos Aires Autodrome to grasp pole position in a magnificent 1m 12.46s, edging out Jackie Stewart's Tyrrell 003 which shared the front row on 1m 12.68s. Hill qualified way down in 16th spot on the outside of row eight after a troubled time, grappling with a spin which lightly damaged the rear of the BT33 and a fuel leak from the metering unit.

The 95-lap, 201.50-mile race was run in predictably sweltering conditions, but the team none the less opted to run the same Goodyear compound as that on which Carlos had qualified. It was a mistake. Stewart eased immediately into the lead at the start and, running faultlessly on Goodyear's more conservative G31 compound, dominated the contest from start to finish. Reutemann hung on brilliantly in second place for the first eight laps before Emerson Fittipaldi's JPS Lotus 72D eased through and he drifted back to fourth place behind Denny Hulme's McLaren M19A before stopping for fresh rubber on lap 45. The BT34's left-hand tyres were replaced with a pair of G31 covers and Reutemann romped back to an eventual seventh place at the finish – an impressive drive even if it did have a disappointing outcome. Hill had a far less memorable time, retiring after 11 laps at the back of the field with a fuel pump malfunction and a deflated tyre.

The South African Grand Prix at Kyalami on March 4 brought little to encourage the team in the wake of Carlos's good showing in Buenos Aires. In practice Reutemann complained that the BT34's handling really was not very reassuring and, after he posted a 15th fastest 1m 18.2s the rear roll-bar was found to have seized in its mountings. Early in the race Carlos began to lose braking efficiency and the BT34 was sidelined on lap 27 when a fuel line to the metering unit fractured.

Graham Hill actually outqualified his team mate on this occasion, albeit by only a tenth of a second and a single place on the grid. The BT33 featured drilled brake discs for this race, but his brakes faded as well and to compensate, Graham spent most of the race pitching the car into oversteering slides as he approached braking areas for the various corners. A new transistor ignition unit had to be fitted minutes before the start, as a result of which the rev-limiter cut in at 9800rpm rather than the 10,500rpm it should have done. In the closing stages of the race Hill dealt out a very convincing driving lesson to a new boy in a works March 721 as he defended his sixth place with some vigour. The youngster was a buck-toothed Austrian, who many people thought, was wasting his time in Formula 1. Niki Lauda . . .

There was no Brazilian Grand Prix yet on the Championship calendar in 1972, but the explosion of Formula 1 interest in that country following in the wake of Emerson Fittipaldi's graduation to front-line international racing guaranteed that it wouldn't be long in coming. On Thursday March 30, 1972, the spectacular 4.95-mile Interlagos circuit in the suburbs of Sao Paulo hosted its preliminary non-championship thrash, attended, of course, by Fittipaldi's JPS Lotus and two MRD entries for Reutemann and Wilson Fittipaldi, Emerson's elder brother.

Unsurprisingly, Emerson was a full two seconds quicker than anyone else in practice, with Reutemann on the front row with him in the BT34 and Wilson F. lining up outside Ronnie Peterson's March 721 on row two. At the start Wilson catapulted Hill's regular BT33 up the inside to scramble into an immediate lead at the start and as he led younger brother Emerson in a family 1-2 up through the infield and out onto the main straight to complete the opening lap, the crowd went beserk with delight. The boys' father, Wilson Fittipaldi Snr, was commentating at that race and, according to those present, could well have fulfilled his task without the aid of a loudspeaker system, such was his vocal pride!

It looked like an easy win for Emerson, but on lap 31 of the 187.01-mile race the Lotus suddenly spun on the fast left-hander before the pits, crawling into retirement with a rear suspension breakage. That drama allowed Reutemann to stroke home to his first Formula 1 success, although by the time he took the chequered flag the grandstands were almost empty and the street lights already illuminating the onset of evening. Peterson's March was second with Wilson Fittipaldi bringing the BT33 home third.

Sponsorship from Bardahl ensured that Wilson was now in a position to take his place in the Brabham team for the remainder of the season, although Bernie Ecclestone would later recall, "really, it was only part-sponsorship when we look back and see how much we spent on his racing. Emerson asked me in the first place whether I would run his brother, but initially I was worried that there were too many problems involved in a three car team. But his behaviour throughout the year was perfect; I felt he was a very underestimated driver."

There was one other non-Championship race contested by the Brabham team before the European season got underway seriously, the GKN/*Daily Express* International Trophy at Silverstone. This marked the debut outing of the Ralph Bellamy-designed Brabham BT37 which was raced for the first time in the hands of Graham Hill.

Bellamy: "We were trying to rationalize things a bit and we needed a new car without going to the expense of a new monocoque, which would have meant new

19
BRABHAM

Graham Hill powers his Ecclestone white-liveried BT33 round Kyalami's Clubhouse corner during the 1972 South African GP mere inches ahead of fledgeling star Niki Lauda's March 721. Hill just hung on ahead of the Austrian to take sixth place at the finish. In the background, Reutemann's abandoned BT34 stands by the side of the circuit.

fuel tanks and whatever. The BT37 was only a BT34 with a front radiator and the new deformable structures to protect the fuel tanks which had become obligatory by the start of the European season in '73. I also had some doubt as to whether the full-width front wing on the BT34 really generated the downforce it was supposed to . . ."Dimensionally the BT37 was virtually the same as the BT34, although at 60.5in its front track was an inch-and-a-half narrower than its stablemate. Other alterations included new pick-up points for the top rear radius arms and a repositioned steering rack: it was also about 25lb lighter than the BT34. On its debut Graham Hill drove steadily to an unspectacular seventh place.

Just as the European season was about to get underway, Carlos Reutemann crashed his Formula 2 Brabham BT38 when a stub axle brake in practice for the Easter Monday meeting at Thruxton, hospitalizing himself with a broken ankle. That was very frustrating because it meant the team leader would miss both the Spanish Grand Prix at Jarama on May 1 and the Monaco Grand Prix a fortnight later, leaving Hill and Wilson Fittipaldi to sustain the Brabham reputation.

Wilson Fittipaldi completely overshadowed Hill at Jarama, qualifying the BT33 14th on 1m 20.83s while Graham was way down in 23rd slot on 1m 22.59s. On the opening lap of the 90 lap, 190.15-mile race the veteran Englishman found himself elbowed off the road in a jostling match at the first turn and he lost a lot of time restarting his engine, chasing home a distant and frustrated 10th. By contrast, Wilson did an excellent job and looked set to take sixth place at one point, but his Goodyears deteriorated towards the finish and he dropped to seventh at the end of the afternoon.

As far as the rain-soaked Monaco Grand Prix was concerned, Graham's famous reputation at this hallowed street circuit had long since dimmed and the Brabham team had a miserable time. Hill was more than five seconds away from Emerson Fittipaldi's Lotus 72D pole time after missing the first day's practice owing to a fuel pump failure, and Wilson was even slower. The misfire which plagued Hill's BT37 on the second day of practice was at least cured for the race and he trailed in a drenched, miserable and disappointed 12th at the flag. Wilson's BT33, fitted with a BT37 nose for the occasion, came ninth after a steady drive, eclipsing his more senior partner yet again.

Opening lap of the non-Championship 1972 Brazilian Grand Prix at Interlagos with a Fittipaldi 1-2 at the head of the field, Wilson's BT33 leading Emerson's JPS Lotus 72. Third is Reutemann's BT34, which inherited an easy win after Emerson dropped out, while Ronnie Peterson's March 721 completes the quartet on this photograph.

Although the team's morale was lifted with the news that Reutemann would be back on team strength for the Belgian Grand Prix at Nivelles-Baulers on June 4, there was more trouble in store for the somewhat taciturn Argentinian. At the previous weekend's Crystal Palace international Formula 2 meeting, where he'd driven his Motul/Rondel BT38 to third place on his return to the cockpit, he had also managed to sustain a broken finger when somebody contrived to shut a car door on his hand during the parade lap! As if that wasn't enough, Hill was still extremely sore after crashing his own private BT38 in the same meeting and was destined for an uncomfortable time throughout the Belgian weekend. Both the senior drivers ran BT37s for this race with Wilson Fittipaldi being rewarded for his early promise by taking over the BT34, now updated with the latest rear suspension geometry which could also be seen on Reutemann's BT37.

Increasingly, Emerson Fittipaldi's Lotus 72 pole time was becoming par for the Grand Prix course and Nivelles was no exception to that rule. Emerson managed a 1m 11.43s to head the front row and although Reutemann was a mere 1.1s slower this could only earn him a place on row four with Hill (1m 13.1s) and Wilson Fittipaldi (1m 13.2s) even further back.

The race turned out to be a right old shambles. Reutemann was in the pits at the end of the opening lap as the gear lever had come adrift in his hand. It was wired up and he resumed, only to make a later halt to have a misfire, due to a loose sparking plug, rectified. He finished 11th, two laps down on the victorious Fittipaldi (E) Lotus. Hill was holding a safe seventh place 11 laps from the end when a rear upright broke and Wilson, after suffering an engine failure in practice, retired after 28 laps with transmission failure, having raced without the use of third gear for many laps.

However, if Belgium was bad, then the French Grand Prix at Clermont-Ferrand

Unloved interim car. The BT37 was, in effect, a front-radiator BT34 cobbled together to carry the team through 1972. The first season of the Brabham team under Ecclestone's stewardship was a massive disappointment, both to its boss and to number one driver Carlos Reutemann seen (below) in the British Grand Prix at Brands Hatch. Progress in the right direction would be swift . . .

on July 4 had about it the nature of a recurring nightmare. New parallel link rear suspension had been evolved by Bellamy for use in conjunction with the new, lighter Hewland FL gearbox – but this was a long time in the pipeline so Ralph decided to kit out Reutemann's BT37 with the new arrangement adapted to the existing Hewland FG400 transmission.

Carlos suffered oil scavenge pump failure in first practice and his second day was ruined with gear selection problems. He qualified way down the back of the grid on 3m 0.7s, light years away from Chris Amon's 2m 53.4s pole time in the Matra MS120D. Thanks to a mix-up with pit signals he dropped behind Ickx's Ferrari in the closing laps and wound up a depressed 12th. Hill finished an equally disappointed 10th after turning a 3m 3.0s best in practice, fraught with trouble, while Wilson wound up eighth.

The summer of 1972 must have seemed like a lingering death for all those working at Brabhams: just when they thought things couldn't get any worse, they did just that! At Brands Hatch all three Brabhams were fitted with parallel link rear suspension, but the first day of practice was ruined by a dud batch of dampers and, before the race, Wilson F's BT34 was changed back to the original reversed wishbone rear suspension.

Reutemann was the only Brabham to be even remotely in the hunt at Brands. Despite tangling with Mike Hailwood's Surtees at the start, he hung on at the back of a big group of cars midfield and eventually got himself involved in a second collision with Carlos Pace's Williams March 711 during a territorial dispute at Druids. He stopped for the front wheels to be changed and continued to take eighth place at the finish.

Hill briefly stopped in the pits to investigate a chassis vibration – before moving over at Paddock to let the leaders lap him, sliding on the dirt and ending up against the bank in a heap. "From gentleman to twit in one-tenth of a second," he growled ruefully. The mechanics didn't see the funny side . . .

Wilson Fittipaldi completed the tale of woe when he retired after a radius rod mounting point pulled out of the chassis, in the very last moments of the race. He had been worried about bottoming and tyre vibration problems all afternoon.

On August 1 Carlos Reutemann gave the team a major boost with a magnificent performance over the bumps and ripples of the famous 14.18-mile Nurburgring, mastering the twists and turns with a deft brilliance to qualify only 5.4s away from Jacky Ickx's Ferrari B2 pole time. It was Reutemann's F1 debut outing at the Nurburgring and one of the few occasions during 1972 that the Brabham BT37 allowed him to unleash his unquestionable flair and talent. His white machine lined up on the third row behind the brilliant Belgian, Jackie Stewart's Tyrrell, Emerson Fittipaldi's Lotus 72D, Ronnie Peterson's March 721G and the Tyrrell of François Cevert. This was to become Carlos's *true* environment in the years that followed – ahead of such people as Regazzoni, Hulme, Pace . . . and even Lauda!

All three Brabhams sported new, wider wings for the German Grand Prix and a switch had been made to Koni dampers after the problems with Armstrongs at Brands Hatch. At the end of the opening lap Reutemann was a strong sixth, hanging on behind Ickx, Peterson, Regazzoni's Ferrari B2, Fittipaldi and Stewart. If he had been able to hold that position to the finish, all other things being equal, he would have wound up fourth because Regazzoni's second-place Ferrari shoved Stewart off the road on the last lap. As it was, the transmission failed on lap seven . . . Hill soldiered on to finish sixth while Wilson Fittipaldi followed him home seventh.

The Hewland FL gearbox made an appearance on Graham Hill's BT37 at the Austrian Grand Prix meeting at Osterreichring a couple of weeks later, although the production run of these units had been postponed until 1973 when it was found that the original castings had been made too small. However MRD decided to modify one of the rejected prototype units which had a stiffer casing than the customary FG400 box. Hill reckoned that the gear change was excellent, but again it was Reutemann's "conventional" BT37 which spearheaded the team's challenge.

The Brabham BT39 was an interesting experimental exercise built up round the Weslake Ford V12 power unit using components from the BT38 Formula 2 car. Unfortunately it proved very slow during its only test at Silverstone and was never raced in anger.

Starting from the inside of row three on 1m 37.15s, 1.3s off Emerson's pole time, Carlos occupied an early fifth place only for fuel pressure problems to end his race. Hill went out with similar problems while Wilson Fittipaldi had a dramatic time as a tired 10-series DFV had to be installed in the BT34 after he had experienced an engine failure during practice. By one of those unfortunate chances which crop up in a complex, high-pressure sport like motor racing, a mechanic had left a spanner in the footwell after a last-moment steering rack adjustment on the starting grid and Wilson had to make a pit stop so that it could be retrieved before it fouled the pedals. He got going again quite steadily before eventually succumbing to a split brake pipe.

By the time the team got to Monza for the Italian Grand Prix, fuel system problems were now haunting Reutemann and he had long since ceased to expect his car to finish a race. After a troubled practice he qualified 11th and retired from the 55-lap, 196.35 mile race with front suspension damage after clipping one of the absurdly tight chicanes. Hill, troubled by fading brakes, salvaged a worthwhile fifth, driving with a trace of his old grit and sparkle, while tyre vibrations on Wilson's BT34 resulted in a fractured rear suspension pick-up point.

The penultimate race of the season at least saw Reutemann gain some small recompense for his thoroughly miserable first season as a Grand Prix driver. He drove splendidly to hold Denny Hulme's McLaren at bay for much of the afternoon, and just as it looked as though he had third place in the bag, the Brabham stuttered out of fuel on the last lap and Hulme swept by to claim four Championship points. Carlos won the *Prix Rouge at Blanc Jo Siffert* (a contemporary 'fighting spirit' award), but Denny was grey and almost speechless with fury at what he saw as Reutemann's blocking tactics. Still, having tweaked the tail of the old Bear, Carlos was now not a man to be ignored . . .

Subsequent examination of the BT37's fuel system revealed that the control screw on the fuel metering unit had worked loose and the engine was running too rich. Hill finished a dogged eighth, while Wilson had a nasty moment when the BT34's throttle jammed open on the first lap, retiring eventually with gearbox problems after five laps.

Rounding off the Championship season, Reutemann was a splendid fifth fastest at Watkins Glen in practice for the United States Grand Prix, but his BT37's nose was savaged by Regazzoni's Ferrari on the opening lap and he lost a lot of time stopping for repairs. After resuming, Carlos found the handling deteriorating progressively and he eventually retired when the engine abruptly cut out. Hill finished 11th after a couple of spins while Wilson looked as though he was going to round off the season with a brilliant fifth place when the BT34's engine expired.

Finally, Reutemann and Hill appeared in the BT37s at the John Player Challenge Trophy staged over 40 laps of Brands Hatch on October 22, but the race was spoiled by rain. Carlos finished eighth, way out of contention, with Hill retiring after only eight laps with gear linkage problems.

Put politely, it had been an "exploratory" year – and a difficult one. "Twelve Cosworth DFVs, three World Championship placings and a deficit of around £80,000 at the end of it all," mused Ecclestone after the season had ended, "I think that underlines that if you want to be serious in Formula 1 it is a very expensive and extremely time-consuming business."

Of one thing, however, Bernie was confident: Carlos Reutemann had quite a future in Formula 1 and much of the early success that would follow was destined to be with the Brabham team. "Properly handled and looked after, I think Carlos is the quickest bloke around," said Bernie, "and that includes Emerson. He's rather inclined to listen to other people a bit too much and, being uncomplicated, tends to believe whatever they tell him. His talent is obvious. Fifth fastest at Nurburgring and Austria when he'd never been there before in a Formula 1 car. For his first year in Grand Prix racing he's done incredibly well. Really, I would be loath to swap anyone for Carlos . . ."

The financial burden of running the team without too much in the way of sponsorship might well have frightened off less single minded men. But Bernie Ecclestone had not come into Formula 1 just for a season: he had long-term plans for the Brabham team and an iron nerve when it came to business dealings. Far from being put off, the bleak disappointment of 1972 made him doubly determined to turn the whole project round.

One aspect of Ecclestone's approach to Formula 1 which was to characterize his attitude in the years to come was his tireless determination to gain the team a special technical advantage not available to its rivals. Later, when Cosworth DFVs were *de rigeur* for all the specialist British teams, he went out on a limb to do a deal with Alfa Romeo. He backed designer Gordon Murray up to the technical hilt on the development of the famous "fan car" in 1978, allowed him to explore surface cooling, supported a switch back to Cosworth in 1979 and did the deal with BMW for the supply of turbocharged engines. This trend was still continuing into 1985 when he concluded a deal with Pirelli for the supply of their hitherto unimpressive racing radials . . . Some gambles he lost, but some he won in style. He was nothing if not a gambler!

The first clear signs of this attitude could be seen in the summer of 1972 when he commissioned a one-off Formula 1 "special" to try the Weslake type 190 V12 which was also being tested in the JW/Gulf Mirage sports car. This 75.0 x 56.46mm, 2995cc 60-degree V12 was reputedly developing 455bhp at 10,500rpm which, if it had been true, would have put it well on a par with contemporary Cosworth DFV output.

Ralph Bellamy and Gordon Murray took a leaf out of March's book and cunningly adapted one of the Formula 2 BT38s to accept the new power unit at a time when March Formula 1 fortunes were enjoying something of a fleeting upswing thanks to the development of the F2-based 721G. The new Brabham was designated BT39, the F2 chassis being completely reskinned with bulbous side tanks to accommodate the 47-gallon fuel load required. Formula 1 uprights and hubs were employed, of course, and a special subframe built up to accept the British-built V12. The whole package was given a distinctly Brabham trademark with the adoption of the BT34 split-radiator nose treatment.

It was a waste of effort. Graham Hill drove it briefly in a Silverstone test session prior to the Italian Grand Prix and, although he reported himself impressed with the smoothness and free-revving qualities of the V12, it was clear that it simply did not have sufficient power. The car never raced, but it had seemed like a good idea at the time.

Section 2: The Ecclestone era

Chapter 2
The first Gordon Murray cars

Architect of the Brabham team's successes over the past decade, designer Gordon Murray photographed in the drawing office at Motor Racing Developments's Chessington factory during the summer of 1984.

Bernie Ecclestone often recalls with thinly-suppressed glee an apocryphal story of how Gordon Murray came to be Brabham's chief designer, a position he has occupied since the start of the 1973 season. "When I arrived, I found him under a drawing board," laughs Bernie, "Tauranac told me that I should get rid of him and keep everybody else . . . so I kept Gordon and got rid of everybody else!" It wasn't *quite* like that, of course, but innocent onlookers might have been forgiven for thinking it was if they surveyed the rather dejected state of the Brabham team at the end of 1972.

Ian Gordon Murray was born in Durban, South Africa on June 18, 1946 and studied engineering on a part-time basis at Natal Technical College from the age of 18 until 23 while working at the same time as a mechanical design draughtsman. His enthusiasm for cars and motor racing had been fired by his father Bill who originally raced motorcycles and later prepared racing cars for local Durban competitor Gordon Henderson. Some of Gordon's earliest racing memories are of events on Durban's Snell Parade road circuit.

During his time studying engineering, Murray built his own U2/Lotus 7-type club racer to compete in South Africa's national sports car championship in 1966 and 67. Dubbed the IGM – his initials – it incorporated his own engine, based on a re-worked Anglia 105E unit, and the whole package reflected a remarkable amount of initiative from its youthful creator. In his quiet, typically modest style Gordon recalls, "You couldn't buy any decent cars out there at the time, so if you wanted something fast, then you had to build it yourself."

Murray's IGM was designed, built and raced by its owner, "the special engine based round a 105E block and crankshaft, but with different connecting rods and pistons, the pistons home-made, plus different gudgeon pins, cylinder head, a Cosworth camshaft and two side-draught Webers . . . I did a lot of hillclimbs with it, won a couple and had a lot of shunts. It was all really very good experience."

Meet Gordon Murray today and you'll encounter a quiet, even-tempered, slightly distant individual who, outwardly at least, never seems to let the pressures of motor racing get him down. Tall and lean, with a slightly preoccupied expression on his face for most of the time, Murray operates in a technical world of his own without worrying too much about what is going on outside his own area of interest. Rock music and wine are his two main preoccupations away from racing cars! Knowing him thus, it is not too difficult to imagine him setting off for Britain during the December of 1969, not quite knowing what he was going to do – or even what weather conditions to expect when he arrived at the end of his journey!

"I had been writing to Lotus's Director of Vehicle Engineering about the chance of a job working on their road car programme," he recalls, "I didn't even think of applying for a job in racing as I didn't think I had the necessary experience. When I arrived in England it was in the middle of a freezing cold winter and I hadn't even bothered to bring a jumper with me. I don't know what I was thinking about. On my first day in England I went up to Norwich to see Lotus – by coach! I made the big mistake of thinking that coaches were quicker than trains, as they are in South Africa. But I had no luck there. Lotus had just been going through a bad patch, laying off people, and there was no chance for me.

TEAM AQUIL
A 6
GORDON MURR

Youthful enthusiasm! Gordon Murray seen at the wheel of his IGM Clubmans car in which he contested national level hillclimbs and races in his native South Africa.

"At the time I was living on the floor of a bedsitter in Hendon. It was an awful, bitterly cold winter. I didn't have any sort of job for six months . . ." None the less that didn't prevent Gordon's girlfriend Stella, Rhodesian born of a Canadian father, joining him a few months later. They were married in London in the summer of 1970.

Despite remaining unconvinced that he had the experience necessary to land a job with a Formula 1 team, Gordon "wandered into the Brabham works at New Haw on the off-chance and, luckily, they'd just lost three people from the drawing office.

"I think Tauranac actually mistook me for one of the formal applicants for the job who had already got an appointment, and he interviewed me on that basis. I've never really asked Ron about it, but knowing what a practical engineer he is, in retrospect, I feel it's likely that he gave me the job on the strength of the fact that I'd designed, built and raced my own car. There are a lot of people around with engineering qualifications, but I reckon that clinched it for me."

Murray arrived in the drawing office in the middle of Jack's final season behind the wheel, the year in which the team's first monocoque, the BT33, was proving a highly competitive proposition.

"In those days, of course, I was only given small detail design jobs to do on the Formula 1 cars," remembers Gordon, "minor jobs such as redesigning the front wishbones to save weight, modifying the rollover bars . . . but I did quite a lot of work on the F2 and F3 cars. I wasn't entrusted with a whole car until somebody came along and wanted a hillclimb special, so I got the job of stuffing a Repco V8 into an F2 chassis, the BT35X. It wasn't really a first design, of course, simply the adaptation of the existing chassis."

By the end of the 1971 season, Gordon frankly admits that he had decided to leave the Brabham organisation, accepting an invitation to design what became the Duckhams sports car for Alain de Cadenet's Le Mans programme.

"Frankly, I didn't like the way everything was heading," he admits, "so I decided that I would leave Brabhams and do the de Cadenet car. Then, through the grapevine, I heard that Bernie was about to take over the company, so I thought that I'd hang on thinking, well, maybe it's all going to get better, but it wasn't really looking too good.

"But I was still fully committed to designing the Duckhams. This was the first real car I'd designed apart from the IGM and four Mini-based road specials, called Mini-bugs, constructed on spaceframes with aluminium bodies and built in a wooden shed on the edge of Heathrow airport. One of these was my sole road car for two years and I did 35,000 miles in it!"

So Gordon stayed on throughout 1972. "Bernie got Ralph Bellamy in to do the BT37 and, although I didn't know Bernie at all, I thought that things might get better. I did the Duckhams in my spare time, finishing work at ten o'clock, going home and working on it until three or four in the morning, and then going back to work at eight the next morning. That carry on lasted for three months until I got that Le Mans car finished!"

As far as the Formula 1 programme was concerned, Bellamy's BT37 meant that the team was running three types of car at one point, the BT33, BT34 and the latest creation. "We did nothing, absolutely nothing," reflects Gordon, "it was an absolute, complete and utter mess the whole year. Carlos Reutemann was out for the best part of half a year with his broken ankle, I was learning . . . It was a time to forget."

At the end of 1972 Gordon received an offer to join the Tecno Formula 1 programme. "It was to do a totally new car for their flat-12 and I thought about it very seriously. It was for a lot of money, I could do my own thing and the whole project looked good. But that very same week Ralph had an offer to go to Lotus and Bernie called me into his office: he told me he wanted me to take over the drawing office and produce a totally new car for 1973. He didn't want to use any of the old components. I had a clean sheet of paper, a free hand to do what I wanted, so I stayed."

The Mini Bug special which Murray not only helped build, but which he used as his own personal transport during his early days with Brabham.

Gordon freely admits that he and Bellamy kicked around a number of design concepts during 1972 before Ecclestone ever gave the green light for a totally new car, so Ralph's contention that he suggested the distinctive "pyramid monocoque" concept which would eventually gell, in Murray's hands, into the striking new BT42, deserves recognition. However Gordon makes the point that several designs were talked about and nothing had been firmly decided before Ralph went on up to Hethel where he was to pencil the Lotus 76, supposed successor to the then ageing, classic type 72.

Talking about the BT42 concept, Murray reminds us that "at the time everybody had gangly, long ungainly cars, with coke bottle profiles, so all I could draw on was the best from my own limited experience. The first BT42 was absolutely tiny when compared with the BT37, its front and rear track about three inches narrower and its wheelbase two inches shorter."

It was a daunting task which faced Murray, designing and building a Grand Prix car from top to tail in about four months flat. The BT42 wasn't ready for the opening races of the season and the team, now consisting of Wilson Fittipaldi alongside Reutemann, was obliged to rely on the outclassed BT37s in the Argentine, Brazilian and South African Grands Prix.

Did Murray find the schedule which faced him in any way overwhelming. "No. Luckily, I didn't really have any time to stop and think. I didn't have anybody to help me with any of the drawings and in those days I was doing the job of factory and stores manager as well!

"Bernie would only come down from his base at Bexleyheath about once a week to see how we were getting on, so it was all bloody good grounding because I was thrown right in at the deep end. I started drawing the car in October 1972 and the first car made its race debut at the Brands Hatch Race of Champions the following March. Unfortunately John Watson crashed it there, but Reutemann would have won its first Grand Prix at Barcelona if it hadn't been for the failure of a rubber boot on a driveshaft constant velocity joint.

"The other thing that people had in those days were a lot of fabricated frames all over the cars. Gearboxes were crowded with frames and tubing reaching out to hold the suspension components in place. In the interests of less weight, increased strength, safety and reliability, I lunched all that and did a special casting for the rear of the Cosworth DFV cylinder head and mounted the spring and top link to the engine, and a machined aluminium bracket to take the lower parallel links beneath the gearbox."

Those first three races on the Championship trail simply continued the Brabham team's dismal 1972 vein. Reutemann's BT37 was almost two seconds away from Clay Regazzoni's BRM P160 pole position at Buenos Aires and he was out with gearbox trouble after only 16 of the race's 96 laps, leaving team mate

Wilson Fittipaldi to salvage sixth place, a lap down on brother Emerson's Lotus 72D. Two weeks later Carlos's chances at Interlagos were ruined in the first championship Brazilian Grand Prix when he made a pit stop after only five laps, losing almost two laps of the 4.946-mile circuit on the leaders while a fuel metering unit problem was rectified. He rejoined to finish a distant 11th, while Wilson Fittipaldi went out with engine trouble at the same time Carlos pulled in for attention.

At least Reutemann qualified reasonably well at Kyalami, making the outside of the third row on the South African GP grid with a 1m 16.94s, only 0.7s off Denny Hulme's pole time in the debutant McLaren M23. Carlos finished seventh in a depleted field while gear selector problems stymied *Wilsinho* with 52 laps under the Brazilian's belt.

The 1973 season also saw Ecclestone's team field a works Formula 2 car and this was entrusted to the modest, quiet John Watson, then 27-years old. This pleasant Ulsterman from Hollywood, near Belfast, had been brought up with motor racing in his blood and competed almost from the moment he was old enough to hold a driving licence. His father, Marshall, had been an enthusiastic amateur for many years and held the distinction of winning Ireland's first post-war (possibly first-ever!) saloon car race at the wheel of a most unlikely mount, a Citroen Light 15! Marshall Watson had supported his son's racing ambitions with tremendous enthusiasm and bought John a Brabham BT30 in which he contested the 1970 and 71 European Championship. His steady learning curve was marred only by a spectacular accident at Rouen when a tyre deflation pitched the BT30 into a guard rail and Watson sustained a broken arm and leg.

By the end of the '71 season professional motor racing was gripped firmly in the throes of a daunting cost spiral and there was no way Marshall Watson, although a successful and reasonably prosperous motor trader, could contemplate buying any more racing cars for his son. By that stage in his career John was at the "almost made it, but not quite" stage and he meandered through 1972 taking odd drives here and there when they were offered, continuing to make a good impression.

John's Formula 1 debut came at the John Player Victory race at Brands Hatch in October 1972 where he showed excellent form in the special bodied March 721 which had originally been styled by Lutz Colani for Heinz Henericci's Eifelland Caravans team. Originally driven by Rolf Stommellen, the "Eifelland" had now found its way into the hands of London wheeler dealer A. W. "Monkey" Brown. Watson used the car to good effect at Brands Hatch, finishing sixth after a promising spurt on the tail of the leading bunch. Clearly, the bearded Ulsterman had what it takes . . .

Not only did John get the works F2 Brabham drive for 1973, but he was also selected to give the Brabham BT42 its maiden outing in the 40 lap, 106-mile *Daily Mail* Race of Champions which was staged at Brands Hatch on March 18. The previous Monday "Wattie" put the car through a preliminary shake-down test at Goodwood and the distinctive, pyramid monocoque BT42 attracted a great deal of interested attention when it was wheeled into the Brands Hatch pit lane the following weekend.

The primary reason for the triangular monocoque shape was, as Murray explains, "to keep the stagnation point – the position where the airflow separates and goes either above or below the car – as low as possible." This guaranteed that the air flow would be used to generate the maximum possible downforce over the upper surface of the car rather than simply over the rear wing.

When it came down to it, there were no parts common to the BT42 and its BT37 forbear with the exception of the front hubs. The Cosworth DFV was employed as a stressed member and the latest Hewland FG gearbox was employed in conjunction with solid driveshafts. Front suspension was conventional, by means of double wishbones and outboard-mounted coil spring/damper units while similarly mounted spring/dampers were employed at the rear in conjunction with a top link, lower parallel links (picking up on the aforementioned casting beneath the gearbox) and twin radius rods. Brakes were inboard at the rear, outboard at

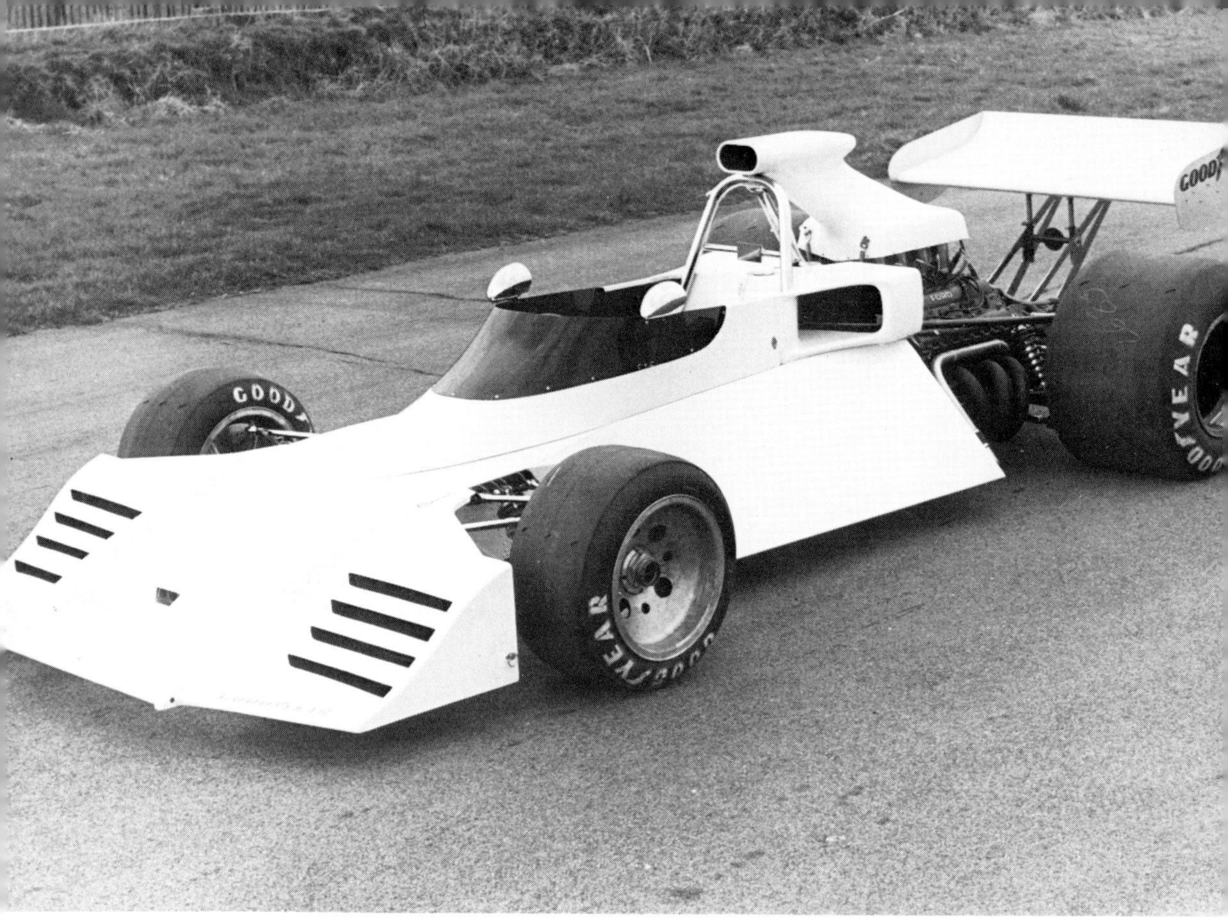
GOODYEAR

BRASIL
GOODYEAR
BARDAHL
CACIQUE
GOODYEAR
brabham

Murray's first full Formula 1 design was the stylish Brabham BT42, the prototype of which is seen (above) on its first appearance for official photographic purposes at Goodwood. This chassis BT42/1 was wrecked when John Watson crashed heavily in the 1973 Race of Champions at Brands Hatch. The lower photograph shows Wilson Fittipaldi three-wheeling round Monaco a couple of months later, by which time this example had attracted its full quota of sponsorship decals and the oil radiators had been moved from their initial position behind the driver's shoulders to a new home flanking the gearbox, although the original cowlings are still retained.

the front while the wheels and steering rack were brand new as well, cast to a specific MRD design. To comply with the safety regulations which were due to come into force from the 1973 Spanish Grand Prix, requiring all fuel tanks to be clad with "deformable structures", Murray had incorporated a glassfibre and polystyrene "sandwich" between the inner and outer monocoque skins.

Initially the oil cooler was mounted atop the car behind the rollover bar, but those early tests revealed that the temperatures were marginal, so the coolers were repositioned either side of the gearbox by the time Watson drove the BT42 at Brands. "But the ducting remained for several races," smiled Murray, "we were not quite so quick and organised in the business of making new bodywork in those days!"

Graham Hill made a fleeting reappearance in the Brabham team for the Race of Champions, being loaned an old BT37 since his new Shadow DN1 was not yet ready, but the whole meeting proved disastrous for Ecclestone's team. Hill was eliminated on the startline, the veteran Englishman getting into a lurid slide as he accelerated away from the grid and landing up against the barrier after being assisted on his way by another car.

Watson, managed only a modest 1m 26.5s in practice as compared with the 1m 21.1s pole position set by Jean-Pierre Beltoise's BRM P160 with the aid of some super-sticky Firestones. On lap eight of the race he crashed heavily at Stirlings, probably after the throttle stuck open, and the first BT42 was destroyed. John broke bones in both legs and was out of the cockpit for three months, effectively writing *finis* to his Formula 2 aspirations.

On April 29 the Spanish Grand Prix meeting took place at Barcelona's superb Montjuich Park circuit and MRD arrived not only with two brand new BT42s for Reutemann and Wilson Fittipaldi, but with Formula 1 racing's first articulated transporter. Converted from a Trust House Forte demonstration unit by mechanics Bob Dance and Gary Anderson, Ecclestone's team set a trend that would eventually be followed by all its rivals. "But at the time we were *very* proud of it," recollects Dance, "and it had a little office up at the front where Stella Murray used to cook us food at many of the races."

Wilson Fittipaldi's car had been tested at Goodwood prior to the Spanish race, but Reutemann's was brand new and suffered a variety of minor teething troubles in practice, explaining why the Brazilian out-qualified his team-mate with a 1m 24.5 to 1m 24.7s. Both men were absolutely delighted with the BT42's taut and agile handling, Reutemann flying in the race and coming close to a splendid debut victory.

After Ronnie Peterson's Lotus 72 retired with gearbox trouble it had looked as though Emerson Fittipaldi might pull it off for the JPS team but a deflating rear tyre slowed him to a crawl and, with 10 laps of the 75 lap event left to run, Reutemann was a mere three seconds adrift, simply gobbling up his advantage. It was in the bag . . . then that c/v joint gave trouble and Emerson was left to stagger home to a lucky win!

Wilson F wound up tenth after stops to deal with throttle cable problems, while one of the old BT37s was fielded for Andrea de Adamich with outside sponsorship from the Italian Ceramica Pagnossin tile concern. The bespectacled Italian had a massive accident on a fast right-hander just before the pits when a rear stub axle broke and the BT37 was wrecked against the guard rail at high speed. Happily, Andrea stepped out without a scratch.

The 1973 Belgian Grand Prix at Zolder will be recalled by most people for the enormous controversy over the diabolical state of the track surface. Practice was boycotted for a time by many of the drivers, the track was eventually resurfaced during the meeting and the race took place in an atmosphere of muted apprehension. Wilson Fittipaldi's BT42 appeared with its oil coolers back in their original position behind the rollover bar, but after a big practice engine blow-up replacement oil coolers were fitted at the rear once again (there were worries about metal fragments floating round in the lubrication system after the failure and the only replacement coolers were for the rear-mounted set-up).

GOODYEAR
brabham

Family snap of the 1974 Brabham team in the yard at New Haw on the occasion of the unveiling of the new BT44. From left to right, Nick Goozee (now with Penske) and works cat Bimbo, after whom Carlos Reutemann was nicknamed by some factory staff due to his feline gait; Gordon Murray, sporting a natty line in bell bottom trousers ('God, we thought we were trendy'); Derrick Walker, now Penske Indy car crew chief; Dave Lonoregan; Pete Bedding, still in charge of the fabrication shop in 1984; Bob Dance; Mike Bowron; veteran ex-Cooper master panel shaper, the late Fred Bedding (father of Pete) who was well into his eighties and still working at Chessington when he died; Ron Cousins, still in charge of the company machine shop; Tony Harvey; Herbie Blash, looking carefree and youthful; Paul Amond; Jenny, the secretary; the late Ian Hilton, who was killed when his car was hit by a train on a level crossing outside the LEC team's Bognor Regis base a few years later; Kathy Howell, in charge of accounts at New Haw and the mother of Penske Indy car mechanic Clive Howell; Harold Mendel and Ian, the storeman. In the background is the team's new articulated transporter, built up from a Trust House Forte demonstration unit.

Peterson's Lotus 72 took pole with 1m 22.46s with Reutemann on the inside of the fourth row after recording a 1m 23.34s. Wilson Fittipaldi was way down behind de Adamich's "replacement" BT37 after practice troubles and, in the event, only Andrea made it to the finish in fourth place, reflecting the high level of retirements on the treacherous track surface. Reutemann was out early with an oil leak while Wilson had engine and brake problems before packing it in.

The usual Monaco qualifying lottery saw all three Brabhams suffer engine failure in practice, Wilson Fittipaldi's BT42 qualifying as fastest of the trio with a place on the fifth row in 1m 28.9s. Reutemann was down at the back, slightly ahead of tail-ender de Adamich and the race produced yet more in the way of disappointment. Lying third with eight laps to go, Wilson's car retired with fuel feed problems, Reutemann succumbed to gearbox problems and de Adamich survived to seventh, three laps behind Stewart's winning Tyrrell.

As the summer of 1973 wore on, so the distinctive narrow-track Brabham BT42 gradually worked its way into regular contention on the tail of the established leading bunch, a select group made up at that time by the Lotus 72s of Emerson Fittipaldi and Peterson, Stewart and Cevert with their Tyrrells and the equally impressive McLaren M23s of Denny Hulme and, occasionally, Peter Revson. Reutemann was consistently qualifying in the top ten, making the third row of the grid during practice for the Swedish GP at Anderstorp, the French GP at Paul Ricard and the British GP at Silverstone. What's more, the team's overall standards of turnout continued to attract favourable comment. The cars were invariably gleaming in the spotless white livery and the mechanics always wore different colour shirts on each day of the meeting. Anybody trying to pass off a Brabham team practice colour photograph as a shot taken on race day was easily found out!

Wilson Fittipaldi ploughed off on the rough at Anderstorp during the opening lap of the Swedish race, damaging his BT42 quite badly, so his car was built up round a brand new monocoque in time for Paul Ricard. Reutemann came away from Sweden with a fine fourth place behind Hulme, Peterson and Cevert, Carlos overtaking a slowing Jackie Stewart in the closing stages of the race.

In the French Grand Prix, Wilson Fittipaldi lost seventh place shortly before the finish when the throttle mechanism somehow deranged itself and began sticking shut, while Reutemann again did well, this time with third place, again between Cevert and Stewart. Andrea de Adamich had missed the Anderstorp race, but returned to the scene in France only to retire his BT37 with a broken driveshaft after 28 laps.

There were no fewer than four BT42s on hand for the team at Silverstone where de Adamich was at last graduating to one of the latest machines, his surviving BT37 being sold to Hexagon of Highgate, the specialist sports car garage in North London whose enthusiastic owner Paul Michaels entered it at Silverstone for John Watson to make his Formula 1 Championship debut. Now painted in a rather drab chocolate brown livery, the Hexagon BT37 handled pretty badly over the bumps and ripples of the Northamptonshire track and Watson was also handicapped by an engine which was a few hundred revs. down on its intended maximum.

Reutemann's BT42 appeared with a distinctive, large "banana-shaped" rear aerofoil which Carlos insisted was one of the reasons he was slow on the long Silverstone straights. However, the '73 British Grand Prix was thrown into turmoil when Jody Scheckter's McLaren M23 ran wide out of Woodcote on the opening lap, triggering off a multiple collision involving about half the field. The race was stopped and the wreckage cleared: sadly, the sole serious casualty was de Adamich, trapped in his Pagnossin BT42 with a broken left leg and right ankle. Reutemann had made a stupendous start and was hard on the heels of Stewart and Peterson when the race was stopped in the wake of this enormous accident.

After de Adamich had been taken off to hospital, the track was cleared and the race restarted. At his second try, Carlos made a more gentle start and wound up sixth at the finish in a race highlighted by the battle between Peter Revson, Ronnie Peterson and James Hunt for the first three places. Wilson Fittipaldi successfully survived the carnage to take the restart in his BT42, but a leaking oil pipe led to his retirement after 44 of the race's 67 laps. A seized metering unit brought Watson's British Grand Prix to a premature end in the old BT37.

De Adamich's accident meant that there were only two MRD entries at Zandvoort for the Dutch Grand Prix, although a third BT42 was kept on hand as a spare for the two regular drivers. Peterson put his Lotus 72 on pole with 1m 19.47s, while Reutemann "closed the season's gap" by qualifying on the second row, just outside Denny Hulme's McLaren, on 1m 20.59s. In the race Carlos was going well until a front Goodyear threw its tread as he sped past the pits into the *Tarzan* braking area, the incident holding his attention fairly firmly as the Brabham skated to a standstill at the side of the track.

Wilson Fittipaldi spun off at Zandvoort, but the Brazilian more than made up for this error by scoring a magnificent fifth place in the German Grand Prix, held a week later over 14 laps of the famous 14.289-mile *Nordschleife*. Fittipaldi finished one place ahead of his younger brother, Emerson having a cautious race in his Lotus 72 after sustaining ankle injuries in a Dutch Grand Prix practice accident the previous weekend. Reutemann qualified on the third row (again!) and was holding a respectable position mid-field, only for his engine to expire at half distance.

At the Osterreichring, scene of his impressive practice performance 12 months earlier at the wheel of the old BT37, Carlos Reutemann scored a good fourth place from a third row start. Wilson Fittipaldi's status as number two driver was now being challenged by aimiable, bespectacled Rolf Stommelen who has been signed up by Ecclestone to handle the Ceramica Pagnossin BT42 from Nurburgring onwards. He qualified close behind Wilson in both Germany and Austria and then turned a few heads by out-qualifying both his team mates at Monza, albeit only beating Carlos by one-hundredth of a second. But the BT42s were still having bad luck and suffering from a succession of minor reliability problems which prevented them from being around at the finish. Stommelen retired in Austria with a seized rear wheel bearing, possibly the result of tyre vibration, while Fittipaldi had more problems with the fuel metering unit. At Monza Reutemann at least had a trouble-free run through to sixth place in this Championship-decider, Stommelen was a lapped 12th and Wilson succumbed to brake problems six laps into the race.

Reutemann qualified on the second row for the rain-ruined, chaotic 80-lap Canadian Grand Prix at Mosport Park: the whole affair degenerated into a miserable, sodden fiasco where the official lap charts became hopelessly confused and people still argue to this day precisely what happened. Peter Revson's McLaren M23 was ajudged the winner after detailed scrutiny of the official records and as many reliable, independent lap charts as could be made available. Reutemann was classified seventh with Wilson F and Stommelen 11th and 12th. Perhaps, if truth be told, they finished higher than that . . .

The final race of the season was, as usual, the United States Grand Prix held over 59-laps of the 3.337-mile Watkins Glen circuit in upper New York State, Carlos Reutemann finally came of age by qualifying his BT42 alongside Ronnie Peterson's pole-winning Lotus 72 on the front row of the grid, but practice at the Glen in that bright autumn sunshine of '73 was certainly not something to recall with pleasure. Francois Cevert, Jackie Stewart's nominated successor as Tyrrell team leader, was killed in a frightful, very violent practice accident and Ken's cars were withdrawn as a result. It must be said that while this perhaps had a bearing on the outcome of the race, it in no way diminished Carlos's achievement in earning a place on the front row. Up until the accident, neither Tyrrell driver had matched the Brabham team leader's quickest time . . .

The race turned into a demonstration run for Peterson's Lotus with Hunt's white Hesketh March worrying the black and gold car for the entire distance like a determined terrier, although there was never any chance of James getting by to win. Early in the race Reutemann settled down to a lonely drive which wound up being rewarded with third place, despite losing almost nine seconds on one single lap when an unwary Graham Hill baulked him disgracefully as he was lapped.

Wilson Fittipaldi was seven laps behind, running but not classified, while John Watson, given a chance in the third BT42, had all sorts of practice problems and eventually retired with engine failure after only seven laps.

The 1973 season had certainly proved that Ecclestone, Murray and Reutemann were all developing in the right direction together, but the revamped Brabham team's crucial breakthrough to its first victory was still to come. At the end of '73 Wilson Fittipaldi, reckoned by Murray as "bloody good fun and quite quick when he got it all together – but *much* too heavy", was dropped from the driving strength and returned home to Brazil where he started laying the foundations of the Copersucar Fittipaldi organisation which would arrive on the scene in 1975. Reutemann was obviously retained and Ecclestone signed up British Formula 3 exponent Richard Robarts to drive the second MRD entry at the start of 1974. Robarts brought with him a measure of sponsorship from his former Formula Ford racing partner and friend, estate agent Bruce Giddy, but wasn't destined to hold onto his position in the team for very long . . .

On the technical side, Gordon Murray had a long serious think about a new car which would capitalize on all the best points of the BT42, yet represent a worthwhile step forward in terms of overall competitiveness. Just before Christmas 1973, the wraps came off possibly the most attractive Cosworth DFV-engined Grand Prix car ever produced – the Brabham BT44.

Some of the BT44 design aspects stemmed from Gordon Murray's own personal desire to continue racing himself once he arrived in Britain. "One other thing I did in 1972 was to design a Formula 750 car because I wanted to go racing myself. I mean, I'd originally come to Britain with the idea that I might go racing, although when I found I couldn't initially get work and discovered how expensive racing in Europe was, I had to give all that up.

"Then I found this fantastic little formula where they had no chassis design restrictions, so I designed and began making my own F750 monocoque car. I spent about a month working on the suspension geometry, trying to keep the springs mounted inboard while at the same time holding the weight down as much as possible. At the time everybody was using heavy, flexing rocker arms, so I was messing about with all sorts of linkages to keep everything in tension and compression. It was during this period that I came up with the system I eventually used in the BT44. I spent a long time looking at different rising rate geometries until I finalized the lever/link system in conjunction with semi-inboard spring/dampers which was used on what started out as simply a re-hashed BT42. I just adapted all the work I'd done on the 750 design, strengthened up a couple of weak spots in the monocoque where the BT42 hadn't been stiff enough, revamped the fuel system and generally tidied the whole thing up."

Visually the most distinctive aspect of the BT44 was the way in which the cockpit section swept back to incorporate the engine cover and air box in one unbroken line. The twin radiator layout was retained at the front while the rear suspension initially remained the same as on the BT42, but the new semi-inboard front rising rate system was operated by means of pull rods running from the bottom of the coil spring/damper assembly and the outer end of the top wishbone.

Dimensionally, the BT44 was virtually identical to the BT42, factory records quoting its wheelbase as an inch longer (at 95in) while its front track was half an inch narrower (at 57in) and the rear track three inches wider (60in). It had the same 41 gallon fuel capacity and relied on Hewland's FG400 gearbox to transmit the DFV power to its rear Goodyears. "We did a lot of work on that gearbox," recalls Murray, "starting with our own dry-sumping system in 1974 which included a new rear casting with a pump built in. It collected all the lubricant, took it out of the box and re-pumped it through the gears. It made a big difference – the standard Hewland at that time only had splash lubrication . . ."

Ecclestone had yet to attract a major sponsor for his sleek white machines. He had Marlboro on the hook at the end of 1973, along with Emerson Fittipaldi, but McLaren's Teddy Mayer clinched the deal from under his nose. That didn't please him, but 1974 would produce as good an advertisement for the Brabham

organization as any team could hope for. From the word go Reutemann underlined that the BT44 was a winning proposition, even though diabolical luck was to deprive him of a sensational victory on the car's debut outing.

The 1974 Argentine Grand Prix took place on January 13 over 53 laps of the longer 3.709 mile *Circuito No. 15*, a total race distance of 196.55 miles. The track basked in the customary searing heat throughout the weekend and Reutemann hardly proved the threat in practice he was subsequently to be in the race. Niggling little problems kept him off the pace, including a spell when his BT44 was stranded out on the circuit after a fuel line came apart. Peterson's near-vintage Lotus 72 slammed round to take pole in 1m 50.78s, so Reutemann's 1m 51.55s, sixth fastest, didn't look too much to get excited about.

Pre-Grand Prix testing at Buenos Aires had seen Gordon Murray's innovative mind produce his first lightweight "qualifying car", the significance of which would only explode, centre stage, some years later. "It had no alternator, we took the crankshaft damper off the engine to reduce the inertia for better acceleration, and several other weight-saving changes," admits Murray, "subsequently DFVs often raced without their crankshaft dampers, even though Cosworth said 'no way' at the time . . ."

At the start Peterson bounded into the lead, but Reutemann took advantage of a

Almost a first time victory! Carlos Reutemann showing a clean pair of heels to the opposition in the 1974 Argentine Grand Prix at Buenos Aires. The new Brabham BT44 was the class of the field, but ran out of fuel in the closing stages . . .

Gordon Murray contemplates the front suspension of the BT44. Below, a close up of the semi-inboard pull-rod layout which Gordon originally had in mind for his own Formula 750 car!

first corner melée which eliminated the Shadows of Peter Revson and Jean-Pierre Jarier, slamming through into second place on the opening lap. Third time round and the crystal clear message was relayed to those in the Brabham pit by a thunderous roar from the huge crowd: Reutemann had nipped through into the lead and, from that point on, the opposition was just history.

The compact white Brabham simply motored off into the distance, pulling away at around a second a lap. The story of the race seemed over, the only attention focussing on the tussle for second place. Sadly, things eventually went badly wrong for Carlos. At around two-third distance the BT44's airbox began to come apart and Gordon Murray, watching from the infield, realized this would cost him about 200rpm on the straight. But worse was to follow . . .

During the race morning warm-up there had been a major panic to change a seized wheel bearing, with the result that the 'fuelling up' routine was not followed as scrupulously as usual. In the normal course of events the tank would be pumped out after the warm-up, then re-filled with the precise number of five gallon churns to make up the correct total. In the rush to change that wheel bearing the BT44 had simply been topped up by guesswork and, in the subsequent cold light of day, it seems that one five gallon churn was not tipped into the tank. Stuttering badly, Reutemann's mount was overtaken by Hulme's McLaren and Lauda's Ferrari on the penultimate lap, and then, within a mile-and-a-half of the chequered flag, finally rolled to a halt out of fuel.

"I worked out the consumption afterwards and, even taking account of the consumption if the engine's mixture control had slipped onto full-rich, the only realistic mathematical assumption pointed to that one churn of fuel being left out," reflects Gordon Murray with a pained expression. By any standards, it was a bitter, tragic end to a stupendous drive by a brilliant racing driver. Carlos Reutemann would never come so close to a home victory again in his entire career . . .

Robarts lost second and fifth gears, crucial at this circuit, and eventually retired, while John Watson was classified 12th, four laps behind, after his debut run in the Firestone-shod Hexagon Brabham BT42 at the wheel of which he was starting his first full Grand Prix season. This deal was arranged by Ecclestone, to whom Watson was still under contract, and Hexagon's BT42 was modified significantly by the team's Kiwi engineer Alan McCall.

Two weeks later the action moved to Interlagos for the Brazilian Grand Prix and Reutemann joined local hero Emerson Fittipaldi's McLaren M23 on the front row, only 0.3sec, away from the Brazilian's best time. Carlos exploded into the lead at the start, but his softish Goodyears began to blister after only four laps and he eventually had to concede his place at the head of the field. Rain prematurely stopped the 40 lap event with eight laps still to run, Fittipaldi taking a fine victory from Regazzoni's Ferrari. Reutemann, progressively hampered by deteriorating grip, dropped to seventh at the chequered flag. Robarts came home a distant 15th and Watson retired with clutch trouble.

While the majority of the Grand Prix circus headed back to Europe after the Interlagos event, the works BT44s stayed on to contest the *Grand Premio Presidente Medici* at the striking new Brasilia autodrome, Reutemann starting from pole position for this 40 lap non-title race. He led for several laps before a piston failed and made a right old mess of his Brabham's DFV, letting Emerson Fittipaldi through to score another comfortable home win. Robarts was not entered in the second car, Wilson Fittipaldi being tactfully nominated in his place. The elder of the two Brazilian brothers finished a lapped fifth.

Finally at Kyalami on March 30, Carlos Reutemann at last had everything go right for a change and he drove into the Formula 1 record books with a splendid victory in the South African Grand Prix. Niki Lauda's Ferrari B3 started from pole on 1m 16.58s with Reutemann fourth on 1m 16.80s, the two main contenders separated by Carlos Pace's Surtees TS16 and Arturo Merzario's Frank Williams-owned Iso-Marlboro! Some observers felt the timekeeping just a trifle suspect . . .

Lauda rocketed off into the lead at the start, but Reutemann's BT44 was more than a match for the Ferrari in terms of straight line speed and outbraked Niki into Crowthorne Corner at the start of lap ten. From that moment onwards the race belonged to the Brabham and, with Lauda retiring close to the finish, Reutemann completed the 78 lap, 198.90 mile race comfortably ahead of the BRM P201 driven by Jean-Pierre Beltoise. Robarts' BT44 was savaged by local ace Dave Charlton's McLaren M23 under braking for Leeukop, winding up 17th, while Watson's Hexagon BT42 dropped out with a broken fuel union. Incidentally, Reutemann's car wore a discreet Texaco sticker on its nose section, the result of a gin rummy game lost by Bernie Ecclestone to Texaco's John Goossens! Unusual for Bernie to lose . . .

Of course, the question on most people's minds was just how the BT44 could be so quick in a straight line and some of the more eagle-eyed observers noted that Gordon Murray was paying a great deal of attention to under-car aerodynamics, the long-term significance of which the Brabham designer admits he did not fully appreciate in 1974.

"It was a bloody good car, the BT44, very easy on tyres," reflects Murray with more than a passing degree of pleasure, "We were getting plenty of downforce from the triangular monocoque, so the car was like a moving air dam. The BT42 had taught us that we could exclude most of the air from going beneath the car, so when I did the BT44 I thought we ought to capitalize on that and proceed one step further down that road. I figured that the car never hit the ground in the middle, always at the back or front, so I put a 'V' shaped skirt beneath the monocoque in the centre to try and exclude more air. Of course what we were doing was to produce an area of low pressure under the car which meant that we could run with very little conventional rear wing, so we were quick in a straight line. It was the start of ground effect, of course, but we didn't really appreciate what we had found. We experimented with various skirt depths and did some tests with a manometer, something I'd learnt about from Ray Jessop, who'd worked as an aerodynamicist with us, to get some pressure readings from beneath the car.

"At that early stage were worked out that those V-shaped skirts were giving us around 150 pounds of downforce which confirmed that we could knock off loads of rear wing and still be competitive. Throughout the season we tried to keep it a big secret, although some people got close to understanding what we were up to, and after Kyalami we ran it at all high speed circuits quite regularly and it gave us a big bonus. Finally the game was up when a mechanic lifted the front of the car onto a stand in the pit lane at Osterreichring and Alistair Caldwell of McLaren took a good look, realized what we'd been doing . . . and it wasn't long before the M23s started appearing with those pieces of plastic all round the lower edge of the monocoques. It wasn't venturi ground effect in the way we would eventually come to know it, but we were on the way . . ."

Reutemann's outing in the Brands Hatch Race of Champions ended with him sliding the BT44 into the scenery at Druids hairpin, while Robarts also contested that race and the BRDC International Trophy at Silverstone, although, he was not to appear in any more Grands Prix. By the time the European season started at Jarama, the English novice had been replaced in the second BT44 by Rikky von Opel, one of the heirs to the German motor manufacturing dynasty. Von Opel had earlier financed the building of the first Formula 1 Ensign which he drove throughout the second half of 1973, but lack of development made it difficult for the German driver to see whether he was wasting his time in Grand Prix racing or not. He was destined to drive several Grands Prix that summer, his best result for Brabham being a ninth at Zandvoort. But following his failure to qualify for the French Grand Prix at Dijon-Prenois von Opel very honestly came to the conclusion he was wasting his time. He quit racing completely, retiring to the seclusion of distant Nepal where he kept in touch with his investments on the New York stock exchange by means of satellite telephone . . .

Reutemann started the Spanish Grand Prix in his "regular" third row spot, but spun off after 12 tricky laps in the rain-soaked conditions; at Nivelles, venue for the

Belgian Grand Prix a nightmare practice saw him qualify way down behind von Opel before retiring with a broken fuel line. He hit Peterson's spinning Lotus 72 and retired with deranged suspension at Monaco and went out with an oil leak in the Swedish Grand Prix at Anderstorp. He was 12th in the Dutch Grand Prix and retired with "impossible" handling in the French Grand Prix at Dijon-Prenois. The season's earlier momentum had not, it seemed, been sustained.

Meanwhile, there were several other independent Brabham BT42s now appearing on the scene, apart from John Watson's regular Hexagon car in which the Ulsterman managed to score the first Championship point of his career with sixth place at Monaco. The Finotto-Bretscher team acquired two of the '73 works cars and had intended to field diminutive Swiss Silvio Moser at Jarama, but the entry was withdrawn after he suffered what were to prove fatal injuries in a sports car accident at Monza a few days earlier. Former Matra ace Gerard Larrousse, later Renault and Ligier Competitions boss, tried a Bretscher BT42 to little effect at Nivelles where Teddy Pilette also popped up in the cockpit of a factory-entered BT42 spare.

Most significantly, the French Grand Prix saw Carlos Pace appear in a second BT42 run under the aegis of Hexagon, alongside John Watson. Pace, on the Surtees payroll for two years, had become increasingly apprehensive over what he considered to be the mechanical and structural unreliability of John's machines and a suspension failure at Anderstorp had been the last straw for the Brazilian. Surtees, never one to take criticism easily from any quarter, let alone from a *driver*, had suspended him from taking part in the Dutch Grand Prix – although by then Pace viewed that state of affairs with some relief.

After some behind-the-scenes dealing, it was agreed that Pace would take over in the works Brabham team following a try-out at Dijon, assuming that von Opel would retire as expected. Pace, a charismatic and tremendously popular Brazilian who had long been tipped to follow Emerson Fittipaldi to stardom, had a disappointing time with the BT42 at Dijon and failed to qualify. But he duly took his place in the second BT44 for the British Grand Prix at Brands Hatch on July 20. At last Ecclestone had homed in on a tremendously talented driver for his second car and Reutemann would no longer shoulder the responsibility for the team's chances on his own. The change was long overdue as the second BT44 had been totally wasted up until that point.

On a personal note, there is some doubt as to whether Reutemann fully approved of Pace's inclusion in the team. The Argentinian driver had a deep and serious approach to his motor racing which many teams, possibly Brabham, certainly Williams and Lotus, never quite understood. A brilliant driver on his day, he could be psyched out as much by internal tension as by his rivals' performance on the track. Ecclestone unquestionably rated him as one of the best, but his increasingly perfunctory attitude to racing drivers in general meant that the Brabham boss had little time to accommodate the subtleties of Reutemann's character and moods. He admired Reutemann, but he was to come to like Pace on a personal level much more. Perhaps the Brazilian had fewer obvious "hang ups" about racing, perhaps his uncomplicated and open character found more favour with Bernie. One way or another, Carlos Pace was one of only three or four racing drivers to become close personal friends with Bernie Ecclestone. "He was just my kind of guy," said the Brabham boss many years later.

Over the bumps of Brands Hatch, Reutemann found the BT44 was a real treat and the Kyalami winner was right up with the leaders again, qualifying fourth on 1m 20.2s behind Lauda's Ferrari and Peterson's Lotus (which both managed 1m 19.7s) and Scheckter's Tyrrell on 1m 20.1s. Pace's time with the team started on a spectacular note when he went spinning down Paddock Hill during his first practice session in the BT44, this tyre-smoking pirouette caused by a slower competitor who "slammed the door" in the Brazilian's face.

This little incident set the general tenor for Pace's British Grand Prix. He complained that his BT44 felt "very peculiar" and a few laps in the spare confirmed in his own mind that the problem was confined solely to his race car.

While the works team used BT44s throughout 1974, a handful of BT42s passed into private hands. By far the most successful was John Watson's Goldie/Hexagon example which is seen here storming to sixth place in the Monaco Grand Prix – the first Championship point of the Ulsterman's career!

Only after he had qualified way down at the back on 1m 21.7s did the mechanics discover that one of the front wishbones had virtually seized in a faulty pivot point . . .

Reutemann finished sixth at Brands Hatch with Pace ninth and John Watson 11th. The BT42 used by Pace at Dijon had been practised at Brands Hatch by Italian girl Lella Lombardi, then at the height of her achievement in the domestic Formula 5000 category, but the male chauvinists in Formula 1 were duly satisfied when she failed to qualify.

The German Grand Prix at the Nurburgring saw John Watson join the BT44 fold with the brand new Hexagon car on the scene for the first time, although it was originally intended that he should stick with the BT42 at this demanding circuit. However, when the older car suffered an engine failure during practice and filled its oil system with "gunge", the team policy was promptly changed and John was duly entrusted with the new machine.

Reutemann finished the 14-lap race in third place behind Regazzoni's winning Ferrari B3 and Scheckter's Tyrrell, the Brabham team leader having started from the third row of the grid *again*. His BT44's rear aerofoil started to disassemble itself on the last lap, but he still managed to hold his position to the flag, although Peterson and Ickx were on his tail. Pace was well down the grid after suffering continuing fuel pressure problems in his race car and the Brazilian swapped to the spare BT44, the handling of which he preferred, to take the start. He finished 12th. John Watson, his BT44 holding a splendid fifth place as the field climbed through the last right-hander before *Karusell* on the opening lap, found his new mount

snapping into an unexpected slide. Unfamiliar with the amount of adhesion afforded by his new car, he misjudged his corrective action and the brown Brabham glanced the guard rail, leaving the disappointed Ulsterman with nothing more to do than drive slowly back to the pits and retire with deranged suspension.

Although Niki Lauda planted his Ferrari B3 on pole position for the Austrian Grand Prix, the Osterreichring was undoubtedly a Brabham BT44 circuit, a fact which Reutemann emphasised by launching himself off second place on the front row to dominate the 94 lap, 198.34 mile race in Champion style. The BT44 outaccelerated the ostensibly more powerful Italian flat-12 from the start and Carlos held on brilliantly to win his second Grand Prix of the season. Pace, moving through to hold a strong second place after early scraps with Emerson Fittipaldi and Regazzoni, spoilt the symmetry of a Brabham 1-2 when a disconnected fuel line caused his retirement after 41 laps. Denny Hulme's McLaren M23 took an easy second thereafter with James Hunt's Hesketh and an on-form John Watson's BT44 coming through to take third and fourth, both after stops to change blistering Firestones.

Practice at Monza saw Reutemann, Pace and Watson boxing in Lauda's pole position Ferrari, the Ulsterman starting the race on this occasion at the wheel of the spare works BT44. After setting fourth quickest qualifying time, his Hexagon BT44 had been badly damaged when a wheel rim broke up and pitched it into the guard rail. Unfortunately the Italian Grand Prix turned out to be something of a fiasco for the Brabhams, Pace salvaging fifth place with fastest lap to his credit, while Watson struggled home seventh, grappling with snatching brakes. Reutemann retired on lap 11 when a gearbox bearing began to break up.

The Brabham team's see-sawing fortunes plunged again during the Canadian Grand Prix at Mosport Park, Pace and Reutemann emerging in a lowly eighth and ninth places, while Watson crashed his BT44 after a suspension failure, caused possibly by a brush with another car earlier in the race. Local hero Eppie Wietzes had a crack behind the wheel of a BT42 entered by Team Canada Formula 1 Racing, while Hexagon's old BT42 appeared in Ian Ashley's hand under the Chequered Flag/Richard Oaten banner. He failed to qualify, just as he would a week later in the United States Grand Prix at Watkins Glen.

James Hunt's Hesketh grabbed second spot on the grid at the Glen with a 1m 38.95s, the Englishman clearly out to improve on his previous year's second place finish behind Peterson, but Reutemann (1m 38.978s) was on pole and Pace (1m 39.284s) right behind James on the grid, in fourth place. Reutemann shot straight into the lead at flagfall, but Hunt wouldn't let him get more than a second ahead for the first ten laps or so, after which the Hesketh encountered fuel starvation problems, a repetition of the problems encountered during the morning warm-up.

Carlos Pace had made a slow start, but soon settled down to run in third place and although his car was not handling quite as crisply as he would have liked, his real problem was a somewhat unlikely personal one! Pace had recently been on a diet with the result that his hitherto glove-like BT44 seat no longer provided comfortable support. By the end of the race he almost had to be lifted from the car, such was the battering and bruising he'd received. But the spur of realizing he was catching Hunt forced him on to set the race's fastest lap just before pouncing on the brake-troubled Hesketh four laps from the end.

One little footnote to that splendid Brabham 1-2. Once Pace was into second place there was no question of showing him an 'EASY' sign and the gap to Reutemann was hung out for him all the way to the last lap. The Brabham policy was always that any race was a race to the finish, not a cosy party between team mates and that has not changed to this day.

On the technical side, the 1975 season saw Brabham relying on revamped versions of the existing cars, now dubbed BT44Bs. In fact three of the BT44s were stripped down and rebuilt into 'B' specification, incorporating a stiffened monocoque and losing some weight during the transformation. But although the BT44Bs were closely related to their forebears, featuring no changes in overall mechanical configuration, there was one overwhelming visual difference. Bernie

Ecclestone had concluded a sponsorship deal with the Martini and Rossi *aperitif* company and the BT44Bs were tastefully turned out bearing that organization's distinctive markings.

From the outset it was clear that the Brabham-Cosworths would pick up where they left off at the end of '74. In fact, if it had not been for a fluke performance by Jean-Pierre Jarier's Shadow DN5 in grabbing pole position for the Argentine Grand Prix at Buenos Aires on January 12, the BT44Bs would have been first and second on the grid. As it was, Pace qualified second only 0.4s away from the Shadow's pole while Reutemann lined up on the inside of row two another 0.2s slower than his team mate.

National rivalry plays a large part in any professional sport, but the competitive edge sustained between Brazilians and Argentinians is something that has to be seen to be believed. Initially the vocal Buenos Aires crowd roared its annoyance at the fact that Pace had out-qualified Reutemann, but there was an unexpected bonus in store for the local hero. Jarier's Shadow suffered transmission failure on the warm-up lap, with the result that the Frenchman was unable to take his place on pole position for the start of the 53 lap, 316.314km race. Reutemann thus had a clear track in front of him as he sat awaiting the starter's flag and surged into the lead the moment the battle began . . .

The two Martini Brabhams made a fine sight as they streaked across the start/finish line together at the end of the opening lap, Reutemann leading his colleague. Unfortunately this domination was not set to last for the entire race. Last-minute suspension adjustments to minimize rear tyre wear had left Reutemann with more understeer than he would have liked and, as the race progressed, so the problem gradually got worse. Pace nipped through into the lead on lap 14, but the Brazilian immediately spun on debris from Wilson Fittipaldi's crashed Copersucar-Fittipaldi and Reutemann got back ahead.

Eventually both James Hunt's Hesketh and Emerson Fittipaldi's Marlboro McLaren M23 displaced the understeering Brabham, the reigning World Champion winning after Hunt badly compromised his prospects with a quick spin. Reutemann finished third while Pace eventually succumbed to engine failure. The BT44Bs should have won that . . .

Jarier took pole for the Brazilian Grand Prix at Interlagos a fortnight later from Fittipaldi's McLaren, Reutemann, the Ferrari 312B3s of Lauda and Regazzoni, and Pace in the second BT44B. On this occasion the Shadow DN5 was the absolute class of the field, taking the lead from Reutemann on lap five, and striding away into the distance, building up a massive advantage until a seized fuel metering control arm sidelined him after 32 laps.

Reutemann had quickly come to the conclusion that his choice of a hard right front and three soft Goodyears was totally unsuitable and he started a gradual decline, dropping back through the field to finish a disappointed eighth. But Pace was going magnificently, actually making ground on the leading Shadow just before Jarier retired and surging through into the lead when he pulled up.

With 11 laps of the 4.9-mile Interlagos circuit left the crowd was going out of its mind with delight. Not only was "Moco" Pace in the lead, but Emerson Fittipaldi was working into a late-race sprint in an effort to catch the Brabham. Either way, the crowd was going to be delighted. With five laps to run Emerson was well wound up, catching Pace at about half a second a lap, but there was not sufficient time left and the delighted Brabham driver ran out the winner by just over 5s. It was to be the only Grand Prix victory of his career.

At Kyalami on March 1, the BT44Bs sustained their competitive challenge by buttoning up the front row of the two-by-two grid for the 78 lap South African Grand Prix, Reutemann out-qualifying Pace by a scant 0.07s. Reutemann was slow away and Jody Scheckter's Tyrrell 007 darted through to challenge Pace for the lead from the start, the determined South African easing through into first place as they went into Crowthorne on lap three.

From that point onwards the Brabhams found themselves outrun by the blue Tyrrell, Pace dropping away with progressively deteriorating brakes to leave

In command. The opening lap of the 1974 Austrian Grand Prix at the Osterreichring with Reutemann's BT44 leading past the pits from the Ferrari 312B3s of Niki Lauda and Clay Regazzoni, Pace's works BT44, James Hunt's Hesketh 308, Jody Scheckter's Tyrrell 007 and Emerson Fittipaldi's McLaren M23. Just above the 'Texaco' sign straddling the start/finish line can be seen Watson's new Goldie/Hexagon BT44. Reutemann led from start to finish, Pace retired and Watson finished fourth.

Reutemann in second place. Despite getting level with the Tyrrell's rear wheels on a couple of occasions he had to settle for second with Patrick Depailler bringing the other blue car from Ripley home third. Pace, pumping the brake pedal with his left foot on the straights in order to build up sufficient retardation for the corners, slumped to a disappointed fourth at the flag.

On April 13 Reutemann was the team's sole entry in the 27th International Trophy meeting at Silverstone, trailing home a miserable eighth after a dispiriting race grappling with a badly misifiring DFV. A fortnight later the European Grand Prix calendar opened with the Spanish Grand Prix at Barcelona's spectacular Montjuich Park road circuit where a major dispute over circuit safety led to a boycott of the first day's practice and threatened to see all the cars impounded by the Spanish authorities.

Eventually the whole affair was settled in time for Saturday practice to take place, but the whole problem had unsettled many of the competitors and the Brabham drivers produced a less-than-representative qualifying effort to line up 14th and 15th in the order Pace-Reutemann. The two Ferrari 312Ts were together on the front row, but they tangled with each other going down into the first corner and that opened the way for the rest of the pack.

It was a spectacular race with plenty of spins, minor collisions and irritating incidents during the opening stages. Eventually the race settled down with Mario Andretti's Parnelli VPJ4 running at the head of the field, but when broken suspension eliminated the American after 17 laps, Rolf Stommelen in Graham Hill's Cosworth-engined car assumed the lead with Pace's Brabham in close

Looking very smart in the team's new Martini livery, Carlos Pace presses on towards fourth place in the 1975 South African Grand Prix at Kyalami, shortly after his victory in the Brazilian Grand Prix. Look closely and you can see the 'vee shaped' skirt arrangement on the underside of the monocoque, pioneered at this circuit some 12 months earlier.

pursuit. The bespectacled German was driving at the peak of his form, but as the two cars went over the rise beyond the pits, the carbon fibre rear wing support on the Hill suddenly broke, pitching the car into an enormous accident. Pace clanged down the guard rails on the right as he successfully avoided the wayward Hill, but the Brazilian got away lightly. Stommelen's car had vaulted the guard rail, killing four onlookers and seriously injuring Rolf himself. This was no time to continue with the race, so the Spanish Grand Prix was flagged to a premature halt with Jochen Mass's McLaren M23 the winner from Jacky Ickx's Lotus 72 and Reutemann in the other BT44B.

The Brabhams were off the pace at Monaco as well, qualifying midfield with Pace again ahead of Reutemann and the Brazilian sprinting home a promising third behind Lauda and Fittipaldi in the rain-spoiled 75 lap (two hour) race. Reutemann trailed home a pathetic last, two laps behind, never seeming to get with it at all in the slippery conditions. Pace now asserted his psychological advantage, qualifying second only to Lauda for the Belgian Grand Prix at Zolder and rocketing into an immediate, if temporary, lead at the start. Unfortunately the Brazilian's tyre choice was not suited to the abrasive track surface and he gradually slipped back through the field to finish up a disappointed eighth. Reutemann, having started from the third row, warmed up nicely to produce a satisfying race performance and wind up third behind Lauda's Ferrari 312T and Scheckter's Tyrrell.

Earlier in the season Zolder had been the venue for a particularly memorable, if

rather off-beat, moment in the Brabham team's fortune. During a lull in tyre testing it was decided to try out some on-board camera equipment which Martini wished to use in order to shoot some footage for advertising purposes during practice at Monaco. The Belgian circuit was depressingly damp at the time and, with Reutemann reluctant to go out, it was decided that Herbie Blash should take the BT44B out for a couple of gentle laps.

Herbie: "I borrowed Emerson Fittipaldi's helmet and set off from the pits in a confident mood. I'd been kart racing the previous weekend and thought 'right, this is it . . .' Coming up behind the paddock I must have been doing 130mph, on slicks . . . on a damp track!

"Unfortunately, just before the chicane, there was a river running across the circuit. I backed off, the rear wheels locked and I shot straight through three layers of catch fencing into the guard rail – hard!

"I remember going back to the pits and explaining to Bernie that I'd bent a rear wing end plate . . . and then the wreck came back on the end of a crane: monocoque, all four corners, completely rooted. I'll never forget Bernie's reaction. He didn't lose his temper or shout and scream . . . he just stared at me. Sometimes, looking at my salary, I think I've been paying for that damage ever since!"

The most significant change in the Brabham camp at Anderstorp, venue for the Swedish Grand Prix, was a new, close-cropped haircut for Reutemann. He was also in a much more positive frame of mind than of late and qualified fourth, 0.8s away from that most unlikely of pole sitters, Vittorio Brambilla and the works March 751!

The constant-radius corners that abound at Anderstorp seemed to bring the best out of Reutemann's meticulous style and, after Brambilla and Jarier's Shadow DN5 dropped out of the contest, the Argentine driver inherited a comfortable lead over his team mate. But Niki Lauda and the Ferrari *trasversale* were to prove formidable adversaries. The cool Austrian pressured Pace into trying too hard, the Brazilian's BT44B spinning off as he went out onto the long main straight which doubles as an airfield runway: unfortunately his wayward Brabham collided with one of the landing lights which did the monocoque a power of no good!

With 25 of the race's 80 laps left to run it seemed as though stalemate had set in, Reutemann's BT44B steadying its advantage at 10s over Lauda. But gradually a build-up of dust and debris on Reutemann's rear Goodyears lost him the fine edge of the Brabham's adhesion and Niki relentlessly reeled him in. With ten laps to run the Ferrari picked him off and ran out a comfortable winner by 5.28s.

By this stage in the season an over-taxed Gordon Murray was hard at work pencilling the first of the Brabham-Alfa Romeos, so long-term development on the BT44Bs was shelved. This was a shame, because the Cosworth-engined challengers from the Ecclestone stable had proved they were capable of running at the front and now dropped back into an essentially supporting role. James Hunt's Hesketh defeated Lauda's in the damp Dutch Grand Prix at Zandvoort, so the Ferrari 312T was by no means invincible during 1975 and it would be a brave man who could argue that the Hesketh 308 was as good a chassis as Murray's Brabham at that time.

"We did nothing that summer but change gear ratios, set the chassis up for a particular circuit and then dispatch the cars off to the races," recalls Murray regretfully. "If ever there was a World Championship lost to us, then that was it!" Plotting the Brabham BT44B's gradually fading form in the latter half of the 1975 provides a depressing postscript to the career of one of the most attractive cars to spring from Murray's drawing board. There was one ray of promise, however, when Carlos Pace qualified on the front row of the grid at the Nurburgring and Reutemann, starting from row five a full 4s slower than his team mate, won the German Grand Prix.

However, this lone 1975 victory for the Argentine driver was but a pale reflection of his three dominant triumphs at the wheel of the BT44 the previous season. It took Lauda's Ferrari to be delayed by a puncture and Depailler's Tyrrell to break its suspension before Reutemann moved ahead at the start of the tenth of the race's

Twilight. Patrick Neve's RAM Brabham BT44B in action during the 1976 Belgian Grand Prix at Zolder. The potential of these highly competitive cars was squandered after the switch to Alfa Romeo power by the Brabham works team.

14 gruelling laps. For all that, Pace kept up his morale better than Reutemann did, the Brazilian also qualifying on the front row at Silverstone for the British Grand Prix where Fittipaldi emerged a fortunate victor after a thunderstorm drowned the circuit and brought proceedings to a premature halt!

By the time the team reached Monza, where Niki Lauda was to clinch his first World Championship title, the best a BT44B could qualify was seventh (Reutemann) on the inside of the fourth row. Carlos finished a distant fourth, out-classed not only by both Ferraris but also Fittipaldi's McLaren M23 – a car which the Brabhams had been comfortably able to deal with at the start of the year, but which had benefitted from a non-stop development programme ever since Emerson won in Buenos Aires.

Rounding off the season at Watkins Glen, the BT44Bs qualified third (Reutemann) and 16th (Pace), the Brazilian annoyed at having been jostled off the circuit over an unyielding chicane during practice by none other than his team-mate. Pace started the race in an irritated frame of mind and it was no surprise when he tangled with Depailler on lap three, both cars pirouetting into retirement. Six laps later Reutemann pulled off with a major engine failure, so the impressive 1-2 which the two South Americans had enacted here 12 months earlier was not going to be repeated!

As the Martini Brabham team scrambled to get its BT45-Alfas race ready for the '76 season, the delectable BT44Bs were sold off to English private entrant John MacDonald, a successful motor trader who was keen to establish a foothold in Formula 1. Almost nine years after embarking on this abortive programme, MacDonald still winces when he reflects on how naïve and inexperienced he was to tackle such an undertaking. With sponsorship from a variety of sources including Tissot watches (later to forge a more fruitful partnership with Team Lotus), the MacDonald Brabhams were handled initially by genial, under-rated Belgian Patrick Neve and the inexperienced Swiss Loris Kessel.

These private BT44Bs opened the season by contesting both the Brands Hatch Race of Champions and the Silverstone International Trophy (where Ulsterman Damien Magee drove a third car): Neve was the best placed runner in both races, seventh at Brands Hatch and 11th at Silverstone. Neve then stood down for Spanish Grand Prix at Jarama where Kessel was partnered by Emilio de Villota. They both failed to qualify. The prospects looked poor . . .

The Belgian Grand Prix saw both BT44Bs scrape in near the back, Neve acquitting himself moderately well, but only his team mate survived to run home a distant 11th. MacDonald did not bother wasting his time trying to qualify the cars at Monaco and after Kessel failed to qualify for the French Grand Prix, the team boss signed popular Englishman Bob Evans to drive alongside girl-of-the-moment Lella Lombardi at Brands Hatch for the British round of the Championship. Evans looked quite tidy, but by then trouble was looming as Kessel managed to get an injunction impounding the cars after practice at Nurburgring. That race was supposed to have seen Stommelen performing at the wheel of a BT44B, but when the legal eagles stepped in, Ecclestone slotted the available German into his third Brabham-Alfa.

Finally, after a reinstated Kessel had trailed round to qualify right at the back on the Austrian Grand Prix grid, the legal unpleasantness flared again and MacDonald found himself briefly arrested in the paddock at Zandvoort at the Swiss driver's instigation. That marked the end of Mac's hopes to make a mark with Brabham-Cosworths and they were not seen again in serious Formula 1 competition.

Two years earlier, the distinctive pyramid monocoque Brabham-Cosworths proved themselves capable of winning consistently in the hands of top drivers, so it was tragic to see these once impressive achievers spluttering round with the tail-end also-rans in 1976. Had Ecclestone kept them and run them for another year, had Gordon Murray been allowed to continue developing them, there can be no doubt at all that BT44B-derivatives would have been winning Grands Prix through 1976 and into 1977. Bear in mind that James Hunt won the '76 Championship in a McLaren M23, basically a three year old car – and one which the BT44s had beaten as a matter of course.

If Gordon Murray had not been shunted off down the Brabham-Alfa route, perhaps his Cosworth cars would have won a World Championship in 1975, 76 or 77. What's more, it is possible that he might have developed his ground effect theories quicker and more effectively. Perhaps he might even have beaten Colin Chapman to the "something for nothing" full under-car aerodynamic concept!

MARTINI RACING
MARTINI RACING
MARTINI RACING
MARTINI
7
MARTINI
BRABHAM
GOODYEAR

Section 2: The Ecclestone era

Chapter 3
The Brabham-Alfas, 1976-79

Gordon Murray in official pose with the BT46 surface cooled prototype – one of his few less-than-successful Brabham concepts.

Although by the end of 1974 the Brabham BT44s were established amongst the most competitive Cosworth-powered Formula 1 contenders, Ferrari had made it quite clear that his engineers were at last getting to grips with the 12-cylinder *boxer* engine which had proved potentially so dominant in the hands of Niki Lauda and Clay Regazzoni. With the new transverse gearbox Ferrari 312T all ready to go for the 1975 season there was no reason why this upswing in Maranello fortunes should not be sustained. The combination of Lauda and the Ferrari flat-12 pretty well set Grand Prix racing on its ear in 1975, winning the team its first Championship title for 11 years. It seemed as though Ferrari's engine configuration was signalling some sort of message . . .

At the start of 1975 Bernie Ecclestone became involved in lengthy, exhaustive discussions with Alfa Romeo about the prospect of using the 'other' Italian flat-12 engine in a Formula 1 application. Alfa Romeo's *boxer* had first seen the competitive light of day in one of the works 33TT12 sports cars during 1973, and although its competition performances to date had been spectacularly unimpressive against any worthwhile opposition, it managed to misfire its way to the World Manufacturer's Championship in 1975, having finished runner-up to Matra-Simca the previous year.

Undeniably, the engine looked a tantalizing Formula 1 proposition, for all its earlier shortcomings. With a bore and stroke of 77 x 53.6mm for 2995cc, the Alfa Romeo *boxer* employed Lucas or SPICA fuel injection, Marelli Dinoplex ignition and had a claimed power output of 510 bhp at 12,000rpm on an 11:1 compression ratio. It came under Ecclestone's critical eye at a time when a good Cosworth DFV produced about 465bhp, the BRM V12 a mere 447bhp and even the Ferrari 312 only a claimed 500bhp. As far as official figures were concerned, only the revitalized Matra MS73 V12, destined to power the new Ligier JS5, topped the Alfa's output with a claimed 520bhp. On the debit side, the Alfa flat-12 gobbled its fuel like an alcoholic on a day trip to a distillery, it was heavy and its reliability was questionable. However, Alfa Romeo seemed keen to get a feel of the Formula 1 water and an alliance with Ecclestone, even then probably the most powerful and influential single individual in Formula 1, seemed like a mutually profitable project. Bernie would get the engines supplied *gratis*, Martini and Rossi would increase its sponsorship while the Brabham team would be involved in the expense of building a whole new generation of cars to accommodate the Alfa Romeo power unit.

In the Brabham design office Gordon Murray was still working miracles on his own. Ecclestone has never been one to over-staff his business and it was not until the end of the 1976 season that Murray was joined by his invaluable assistant David North who had trained with BAC. Unfortunately he could have done with some extra assistance early in 1975 when the BT44B-Cosworths were at the absolute zenith of their development.

"The first cock-up came when we stopped development on the BT44B", reflects Gordon candidly, "I was on my own, the car looked like being invincible and we wound up getting over-confident as I had to turn my attentions to the BT45-Alfa design. I can tell you, that certainly gave me some big headaches, but it was a pleasant challenge to work with a brand new engine". Early in October 1975 the first Brabham-Alfa Romeo BT45 was unveiled at the Italian firm's Balocco test track and serious preliminary tests began shortly afterwards at Silverstone.

"It's not a lash up", Gordon Murray was quoted as saying on the car's launch, although it would have been hard to see how anybody could have come to this conclusion even after a cursory inspection of the smart Martini-liveried machine. However, what most observers probably *did not* know at the time was the only reason Murray had abandoned his triangular monocoque configuration was that he was unable to work out how thus to package the daunting 47 gallon fuel load which Alfa informed him he would need to provide if the engine was to run a full race distance. And even that assessment proved marginal!

In order to keep the centre of gravity as low as possible, the BT45 had a very wide monocoque which flared out to the absolute maximum width permitted under the 1976 regulations. As the engine could not be used as a fully stressed member like the Cosworth DFV, two pontoons extended rearwards either side of the flat-12 on the outer extremities of which tall, slender cold air boxes were mounted in such a manner as did not interfere with the air flow over the rear wing. There were no fewer than four separate fuel tanks – "a nightmare", recalls Murray – and a Hewland FG400 five-speed gearbox was fitted to the prototype. The distinctive Brabham full-width nose section with radiators on either side was retained, the semi-inboard rising rate front suspension was broadly similar to that on the BT44B and the rear suspension was by means of twin parallel lower links, single top links and radius rods.

The engine bay was so crowded that it was just impossible to change the sparking plugs with the engine *in situ*, a fact which Gordon Murray reluctantly came to terms with. "Initially I had thought of cutting apertures in the pontoons so that we could change the plugs, but that would have meant compromising the design too much. So I checked with Carlo Chiti who confidently told me 'Oh, don't worry, we never have to change sparking plugs'. I was sceptical to say the least, but he was right. The engine didn't need soft plugs to warm it up, then a switch to hard race plugs. I was amazed, I must admit, but it was quite a pleasant surprise!"

The BT45's public unveiling was carried out to the accompaniment of appropriately optimistic clucking from both parties involved in the Brabham-Alfa alliance, but very early on in the car's development it became clear that this was going to be no straightforward project to knock into competitive shape. To start with, at around 625kg, the car was appallingly overweight – almost 60lb heavier than its immediate predecessor. What's more, when Carlos Reutemann drove it for the first time, the usually dour Argentinian had his enthusiasm under very tight control indeed.

Bob Dance: "From the first time that Reutemann drove it at Silverstone, he said 'this car is an old lady', and, I think, from that point onwards he began to lose an element of support from the Brabham personnel. Pace was far more hopeful and optimistic and I feel he got more support as a result." Those initial tests were hampered by oil system problems, the Alfa flat-12 starting its Formula 1 career on a promising note by pumping out most of its lubricant! The Alfa engines had an oil scavenging problem which, at least in part, they were to sustain right through until 1979.

Although the motoring press spent much of the winter rumouring that Brabham might run Cosworth-engined cars until the BT45s were race ready, Ecclestone had no intention of the new project going off half-cock. If the team hedged its bets by retaining the BT44Bs they would never take the plunge with the BT45, so Bernie sold off the old cars to John MacDonald's independent team as previously recounted. This decision did not please Reutemann.

According to Carlos, Bernie said he would take a BT44B to South America for the early season races in 1976 if the BT45 could not lap Silverstone competitively. In Reutemann's view the Brabham-Alfa certainly was not competitive when it appeared at Interlagos for the Brazilian Grand Prix on January 25 – but there were no Cosworth cars to be seen. Ecclestone told the author quite firmly "Reutemann *knows* that wasn't the case", so the two men remain at odds over this particular situation. Unquestionably, however, Reutemann's interest and enthusiasm for the Brabham team waned quickly in 1976 and Bernie privately expressed the opinion that he thought Carlos might decide to quit. In the end he did decide to quit – but only the Brabham team. After a succession of generally disappointing performances with the BT45, he negotiated a release from his contract with Ecclestone after the Dutch Grand Prix and moved off to join Ferrari. Carlos had to pay for the privilege, unsurprisingly, but he reckoned it was money well spent . . .

Throughout the Brazilian Grand Prix meeting both BT45s suffered badly with misfires and the flat-12s proved reluctant to rev over 10,000rpm during the race. Pace qualified 10th on 2m 34.54s, a mere two seconds away from James Hunt's pole position McLaren M23 – on the face of it not far off the pace when you consider it is a 4.946 mile circuit we're talking about – but Reutemann was some way further back. In the race Pace managed to stagger home 10th, a lap behind Lauda's winning Ferrari, while Reutemann's miserable day came to a finish when his BT45 ran out of fuel with three laps to go.

At Kyalami on March 6, the cars were still mid-field runners, despite a concerted effort at lightening them during the interval since Brazil. Pace, incidentally, had been fielded at the wheel of a single BT45 in the non-Championship Brands Hatch Race of Champions and Silverstone Graham Hill International Trophy meetings and, although retiring with fuel injection gremlins in the first race, had managed to keep going for a lapped ninth place in the second event. Things didn't look promising.

The 78 lap, 198.90 mile South African Grand Prix saw Ferrari's flat-12 notch up another success in the hands of Niki Lauda, but the Brabham-Alfas could only run seventh and ninth at best. Eventually, having coated their pursuers with liberal quantities of oil, both Carloses pulled in when the loss of lubricant eventually showed up on the pressure gauges.

Despite handling problems during practice, Pace and Reutemann shared the sixth row of the starting grid for the Spanish Grand Prix at Jarama on May 2 and both managed to finish in the points, Argentinian ahead of Brazilian in fourth and sixth places sandwiching Chris Amon's Ensign.

So the summer of 1976 wore on with Gordon Murray learning all the time about the idiosyncracies of Alfa Romeo engineering, as well as exploring absolutely every avenue he could in the quest to pare more weight off the bulky BT45s. Gordon found that the logistics of working with an engine supplier at the other end of Europe really wasn't too bad. "The telecopier we had installed was very useful indeed," he acknowledges, "but the *real* problem was that all the engines were slightly different. Can you imagine that?

"The engine mountings would vary by up to about half an inch from one to another: mountings were different because they'd perhaps skimmed the heads or re-machined the castings, or whatever, so we found ourselves having to build in three dimensional adjustability. The engines were solidly mounted, of course, so we had eccentrics, holes, cams, spacers, plates and washers in all directions, so every time we changed an engine we had to 'set up' the pick-up points again for the replacement unit. Oh yes, and the exhaust pipes always seemed to be pointing in different directions! Eventually we got the hang of it, but it was bloody difficult . . ."

Both BT45s retired from the 70 lap, 185.38 mile Belgian Grand Prix at Zolder on May 16, Reutemann surviving 17 laps before the engine failed while Pace ran until 12 laps from the finish before terminal electrical troubles intervened. Experimentation with six-speed gearboxes and Lucas, as opposed to SPICA fuel injection, also characterized Brabham's somewhat desperate summer of '76 and the advent of a lightweight qualifying spare (hardly surprisingly) resulted in minute, but steady, performance increments. Monaco on May 30 saw Pace qualify 13th, Reutemann 20th and last. Pace drove in typically determined fashion but was rewarded only with ninth, two laps behind Lauda's winning Ferrari, while Reutemann got himself punted off under braking for the *Ste. Devote* chicane, a mere

Carlos Reutemann puts the prototype Brabham-Alfa Romeo BT45 through its paces at Silverstone, summer 1975. Bob Dance recalls him remarking "this car is an old lady" after his initial trial: thereafter Reutemann held his enthusiasm for the BT45 under tight rein. The predominantly white livery changed to red before the car was raced for the first time.

couple of hundred yards from the start, on the opening lap.

Reutemann's misery continued during the Swedish Grand Prix at Anderstorp on June 13, his BT45 suffering engine failure after two laps while Pace ran to the finish in eighth place. For the French Grand Prix at Paul Ricard Pace concentrated his efforts on the team's lightest chassis BT45/3 (*lightest* must be regarded as a relative term you understand!) Armed with minor front suspension geometry changes to promote better turn-in, slightly more power from the megaphone-exhaust equipped engine, deep skirting round the lower perimeter of the monocoque (touching on ground effect again) and slightly revised rear suspension, Pace raised the team's hopes by slamming through the speed trap on the main straight at 177.365mph, easily the fastest runner. He qualified well on the inside of row three with a 1m 48.75s best as compared with Hunt's pole winning 1m 47.89s and wound up a praiseworthy fourth on the road behind Hunt's McLaren, Depailler's six-wheeled Tyrrell P34 and the Penske PC4 of John Watson. A scrutineering kerfuffle later saw Pace briefly promoted to third when Watson was disqualified for a wing height infringement, but the Ulsterman was restored to the results on appeal. Reutemann was a disappointed 11th, lapped by the winner.

A fourth BT45 was ready for the British Grand Prix at Brands Hatch on July 18,

where the six-speed gearboxes were retained, although this new car only represented a reduction of about 5kg over its stablemates. Both cars were two seconds away from Lauda's pole position and Pace struggled home eighth after engine failure again claimed his team mate.

An air starter system made its appearance on the cars at Nurburgring for the fateful German Grand Prix on August 1 which would be marked by Niki Lauda's brush with death, but from the Brabham team's point of view the most interesting accessory was the addition of Dunlop carbon fibre brake discs. Pace tried them briefly in practice while they were run in the race by Rolf Stommelen who transferred into the Martini Brabham spare car for the race after the legal wrangling which meant he was unable to drive the RAM BT44B as originally planned.

Again Reutemann was out almost before he had started with engine failure on the opening lap, this run of failures hardening his determination to extricate himself from this particular mess before his reputation was totally ruined. But Pace and Stommelen performed well to finish fourth and sixth respectively: giving little indication of the development problems which were to bug the carbon fibre brake discs in the races to follow.

"We really did have horrendous problems with those brakes," recalled Gordon Murray, "what with astronomic temperatures, vibrations, inconsistency, wear, oxidation, fluid boiling, bolts snapping . . . Pace was almost killed in Austria during the '76 race when the discs expanded on the straight, touched the calipers, boiled the fluid and he arrived at the Glatzkurve at 180mph with no brakes . . . he mowed down a catch fencing pole which almost cut the monocoque in half. It was a lucky escape."

Pace agreed with that assessment, but his enthusiasm for the Brabham-Alfa was in no way compromised by this incident, although the ruthless campaign to produce a lightweight qualifying spare held no interest at all for Reutemann. The Argentinian had what might best be described as something approaching an *ethical* objection to qualifying cars and his enthusiasm for the entire Brabham-Alfa project had run out of steam. He personally harboured doubts as to whether the lightweight spare car was particularly safe, but he didn't have to worry about it beyond Zandvoort after which he moved off to Maranello.

Reutemann's Brabham career ended after 11 laps of the Dutch seaside circuit with a clutch fluid leak, and on this occasion Pace fared no better as an oil leak put paid to his chances.

The Italian Grand Prix at Monza on September 12 was obviously a particularly important event for the Brabham-Alfa partnership and Pace utilized all the lightweight accessories to qualify third a mere 0.2s behind Jacques Laffite's pole-winning Ligier-Matra. Sadly he made a slow start and a piston failure after four laps spelled the end of his efforts. After his promising performance at Nurburgring, Stommelen was drafted in to drive the second entry vacated by Reutemann, and he lasted until lap 21 when fuel system trouble caused his retirement.

For the last three races of the season bespectacled Australian Larry Perkins was recruited to drive the second Brabham-Alfa entry, this new boy having demonstrated his potential with some tidy drives at the wheel of an Ensign. When he had his first encounter with the Alfa flat-12, during practice for the Canadian Grand Prix at Mosport Park, he characterized its narrow power band quite neatly: "It feels a bit like a diesel, when you back off it all goes off and you find it takes a moment to come back when you put your foot down again." Perkins's car sported revised SPICA injection at the Canadian event while Pace had the fifth BT45 chassis to be built, yet again slightly lighter. Both cars were initially equipped with a new engine cover/airbox in which the air was channelled towards the injection system by means of two small ducts either side of the driver's shoulders. However, it was considered that this bodywork spoiled the air flow over the rear wing, so the injection trumpets were simply covered with gauze filtering and a smaller engine cover was fitted.

Pace qualified tenth, Perkins further back in 19th spot. Carlos went into the closing stages of the race battling for sixth place with Clay Regazzoni's Ferrari 312T2, the Brabham-Alfa pressing the Swiss driver pretty hard. With three laps to go, Regazzoni got into a big slide as he came through the rutted, bumpy uphill right-hander before the pits and Pace thought he saw his opportunity, steering the BT45 down to the right of Clay's car close to the pit wall.

Whether through petulance or misfortune, Regazzoni's car then shot back diagonally across the circuit and squeezed Pace out against the concrete pit wall! It was a quite horrifying manoeuvre which saw most pit crews hop smartly back a few feet as Pace and Regazzoni came careering past, virtually locked together, with sparks pouring from the Brabham's right-hand front wheel rim as it scraped along the concrete!

Regazzoni thus successfully defended his sixth place, but, in the author's opinion, it was a loutish and irresponsible piece of driving on Clay's part. The Brabham team protested, but the stewards rejected the protest after lengthy deliberation. Pace was trembling with fury as he confronted Regazzoni after the race. But with that sheepish, endearing innocence which Clay could project so brilliantly, he merely asked Pace why he had driven into his Ferrari! Carlos walked away, spluttering with rage, but it was a daft thing for Clay to do bearing in mind that he was under consideration for a Brabham drive in 1977. He wasn't very much longer . . .

Perkins had a spin on the opening lap, but thereafter drove sensibly to take a distant 17th place, two laps behind the winner in this Grand Prix which saw no fewer than 20 classified finishers. A week later the United States GP at Watkins Glen saw Pace eliminated in a collision with Jochen Mass's Marlboro McLaren M23 and Perkins retire with a damaged front suspension pick-up point. Finally, in the rain-soaked Japanese Grand Prix at Mount Fuji, the historic race in which James Hunt snatched his Championship title by a single point from Niki Lauda, both Brabham-Alfa drivers withdrew from the contest after a mere handful of laps on the diabolically slippery rain-soaked track surface.

By the start of the 1977 season the Brabham BT45s were weighing in at around 620kg, although the evolution of a 'B' version of the Alfa-engined car early in the season would cut another 5kg or so off this increasingly-impressive Grand Prix contender. A tremendous amount of development work had been carried out over the winter and when the cars appeared for the Argentine Grand Prix at Buenos Aires on January 9 the team was in an optimistic frame of mind. Alfa Romeo had now finalized the engine's specification using Lucas fuel injection and, with re-designed cylinder heads, the flat-12 was now delivering its 520bhp more smoothly and progressively. The bodywork had been slightly revised and the engine air intakes were now neatly faired in alongside the cockpit, level with the driver's shoulders.

The withdrawal of Roger Penske's Formula 1 team at the end of the previous season had left John Watson out of a drive, but that state of affairs was quickly rectified as Bernie Ecclestone snapped him up to partner Pace – thwarting Regazzoni's aspirations even as he was flying to England to discuss his own Brabham deal! Watson's first acquaintance with the Brabham-Alfa left him very impressed with the Italian engine's low speed torque and flexibility, so things had clearly improved dramatically over the winter. World Champion James Hunt grabbed pole position for this opening race of the season, but Watson was a mere 0.3s behind in second place on his Brabham debut outing, a heartening performance from the Ulsterman who had won his first Grand Prix in Austria the previous summer and was now imbued with a rare confidence. Pace was on the outside of the third row following practice troubles which included crashing the team's spare BT45 quite heavily.

As usual, the race was run in searing summer heat, but Watson catapulted into the lead from the word go and held on ahead for ten laps before Hunt's McLaren went through. James commanded the event with ease until a suspension failure sent him off the road at high speed on lap 32, allowing Watson to regain his first place. Unfortunately, by that stage John was seriously worried about the somewhat unpredictable and alarming handling quirks his BT45 had developed and he eventually pulled up after 41 laps, by which time team mate Carlos Pace had taken over at the front. It was just as well that Watson stopped when he did: pulling into the pits he reported that he was also having problems changing gear. A quick glance at the rear end of the BT45 revealed that the suspension mountings were pulling away from their anchorages on the gearbox casing . . . he retired, thoughtfully!

With only six of the 53 laps left to run, Pace had slumped in the oven-like Brabham cockpit to the point where he was driving on reflexes, near-unconscious in the broiling conditions. It was as much as he could do to keep going, but there was no way in which he could defend his advantage from the fast-rising challenge of Jody Scheckter's debutant Wolf WR1. As Pace's car weaved deliriously on the straights and slewed drunkenly under braking, Scheckter whistled through to take a lucky victory. The totally drained Brazilian just managed to hang on to second place in the face of an attack from Carlos Reutemann's Ferrari T2, and had to be lifted, almost unconscious, from the Brabham's cockpit at the end of the race.

Pace was determined to get into top physical shape for his home Grand Prix a fortnight later and went into training with one of the local Sao Paulo football teams for several days prior to the start of practice at Interlagos. As in previous Brazilian Grands Prix at this 4.946 mile circuit, qualifying times were amazingly close amongst the fastest runners, but although Pace was a mere 0.4s away from Hunt's pole position it meant that the Brazilian was consigned to the inside of row three with Watson lining up immediately behind him.

That disadvantage clearly didn't worry Pace once the field lined up on the starting grid and there were still a few seconds to go before flag fall when the Brabham-Alfa lit up its rear Goodyears and came catapulting through, shaving the pit wall, to indicate that the Brazilian Grand Prix was definitely under way! It had been a long-held view amongst other drivers that, in Brazil, you didn't watch for the starter's signal, merely Pace or Emerson Fittipaldi's rear wheels. Once they started spinning, the race was on – but this was ridiculous!

The enormous crowd, vocal as ever, was delighted and bellowed its support for the local hero as the red Brabham-Alfa number eight led the pack up through the twisty infield section and out onto the start/finish straight to complete the opening lap. Reutemann's Ferrari was on its tail to start with, but Hunt was through to second place by lap three and it was obviously only a matter of time before the Brabham-Alfa succumbed to McLaren pressure.

The issue was made dramatically more difficult by the fact that the track surface on one daunting downhill left hander was breaking up badly just off the line, demanding absolutely precise lines from the drivers if they were not to end up in the catch fencing. On lap seven Pace got the Brabham into a big slide at this point, but although he regained control, Hunt's McLaren nipped through and Carlos caught the BT45's left front radiator against the M23's right rear tyre. It was sufficient to damage the nose section (which then flew off) and puncture the radiator, so a bitterly disappointed Carlos was left to limp into the pits for attention. He subsequently resumed, only to spin off later at the same corner which also claimed team mate John Watson.

Prior to the South African Grand Prix at Kyalami on March 1, the customary bout of intensive tyre testing took place at the circuit near Johannesburg, during which John Watson produced a shattering 1m 15.2s at the wheel of the first BT45B, built up from the rumpled remains of chassis No. 1 which had been damaged by Pace in that Buenos Aires practice accident.

The BT45B had its flat-12 engine mounted an inch-and-a-half lower than the previous cars and reverted to parallel link rear suspension rather than the lower wishbone system which had been used on recent BT45s. It also had the first six-speed Brabham/Alfa/Hewland gearbox, the first major change in Brabham gearbox design since the team had evolved its own dry-sump system for the Hewland FG400 boxes on the BT44s back in 1974.

Engineering nightmare. The Alfa flat-12 engine installed in one of the 1977 specification Brabham BT45 chassis. The engine was suspended between the two pontoons, through which Gordon Murray once contemplated cutting individual access holes for the sparking plugs since they could not be changed with the unit* in situ. *No two engines were alike, varying in terms of pick-up points, exhaust pipes and other minor ancillaries, a factor which made life something of a nightmare for the Brabham mechanics in the early days of the partnership.

Gordon Murray: "When the Alfa deal came along and we realized they could do transmission work, we took things a stage further and designed our own gearbox casing. It was then cast by Alfa Romeo, fitted with Hewland gears, bearings, selectors and so on, with the result that we saved about 12lb from the overall weight of the package". Incidentally, while the Brabham team was occupied in South Africa, back home the factory was being moved from New Haw to Chessington.

Pace used the BT45B to qualify second behind Hunt's McLaren at Kyalami, but the Brazilian made a poor start and was slowed by an irritating degree of understeer as the race progressed. He eventually stopped for fresh front tyres and wound up 13th, two laps behind Lauda's victorious Ferrari 312T2, while Watson used an original '77-spec. BT45 to finish sixth right on the tail of Jochen Mass's Marlboro McLaren.

The 1977 South African GP will be remembered as a bitterly unhappy race owing to the death, in tragic and bizarre circumstances, of Shadow team leader Tom Pryce after a marshal ran across the track in front of him carrying a fire extinguisher. Both men died instantly. The accident cast an atmosphere of despair across the entire Formula 1 fraternity, but there was more bad news to follow.

John Watson took the lone Brabham BT45B to the Brands Hatch Race of Champions meeting and qualified on pole position ahead of Mario Andretti's Lotus 78 and James Hunt's McLaren M23 for this 40 lap race on March 20. The entire Brabham team was bubbling with enthusiasm and optimism in the wake of John's splendid showing, but this feeling of elation abruptly turned into bleak, stunned depression and horror by the end of the day. News came through from Brazil that Carlos Pace had been killed a couple of days earlier in a light aircraft crash. Elegant, stylish and courteous, every inch a racing driver in the story-book idiom, the 32-year-old Brazilian had been one of the team's most loyal and enduring supporters ever since he was recruited almost three years earlier. He had toiled hard with the Brabham-Alfa during its troubled infancy and now seemed on the verge of reaping the harvest of success sown by that early enthusiasm.

"He was a great driver – and a lovely bloke", said Bernie Ecclestone in rare and touching personal testimonial from a man not renowned for outgoing sentimentality. Years later, Ecclestone would endorse his opinion of Pace's ability in conversation with the author, remarking "if Pace had lived, I would not have needed Niki Lauda." It is difficult to imagine a more telling tribute.

Watson finished third in the Race of Champions and the problem now facing the team was who should be recruited to partner the Ulsterman. The choice eventually fell on the youthful, extrovert Hans-Joachim Stuck who was only too willing to disentangle himself from a commitment to drive a Penske PC4 for Gunther Schmid's ATS team, a move which hardly endeared himself to the German team owner.

Stuck made his debut in the second Brabham in the United States GP West at Long Beach on April 3, where all three of the team's cars were prepared to BT45B specification. Watson was eventually disqualified from this race after mechanics had come out to revive his car on the circuit after he had inadvertently knocked off the ignition cut-out switch. Earlier he had made a pit stop to change a deflating front tyre probably caused by a brush in the first corner *melée* which involved several other cars. At the end of the day, it probably didn't really matter because the Ulsterman had gear selection problems as well. Stuck's first Brabham outing ended with brake trouble.

The 1977 season will probably be remembered best for the fact that Colin Chapman's ground effect Lotus 78s served very firm notice of what could be expected from the innovative British designer for the following year. It turned out that although ground effect was a crucially significant straw in the wind, most of Chapman's rivals were amazingly tardy in getting the message: remarkably few designers twigged what was going on and it was not until 1979 that most teams followed Chapman's pioneering route. Gordon Murray, hamstrung by the very wide Alfa flat-12's dimensions, admits he did not fully appreciate what was

Reutemann sweeps up the **Rampa Pegaso** *at Jarama during the 1976 Spanish Grand Prix, his BT45 shadowed by Chris Amon's Ensign. Carlos finished fourth in this race with Pace sandwiching Amon in sixth place.*

happening until the start of 1978, although in 1977 the considerable power developed by the Alfa engine enabled the BT45s to drag huge conventional rear wings and still keep right at the front of the field.

In the wake of Pace's death, John Watson rose to shoulder the responsibility of Brabham team leadership in capable style. A fuel metering unit failure caused his retirement in the Spanish Grand Prix at Jarama, where Stuck finished sixth, but the Ulsterman really got his act together during practice at Monaco and planted the BT45B on pole position, an impressive 0.4s faster than Jody Scheckter's Wolf.

Scheckter led the race from start to finish, having got the jump on the heavier Brabham-Alfa at the start, but Watson kept the pressure on hard during the early stages as he sought to find a way through. Eventually this rough-and-tumble began to take its toll not only on the Brabham's brakes, but on its gearbox as well, and on lap 46 Watson went down the escape road at the chicane, dropping to third. Four laps later the transmission seized and he spun to a halt at *Ste. Devote*, but his had been a great effort while it lasted . . .

An electrical short-circuit caused a brief conflagration in the cockpit of Stuck's BT45B before it rolled to a silent halt, but the German had better luck in the Belgian Grand Prix at Zolder on June 5 where he survived the wet/dry conditions to finish sixth. Watson qualified second alongside Andretti for this race, splashed into the lead at the start and was then punted off by the American's Lotus mid-way

round the opening lap as they braked for the chicane behind the paddock. At least Mario was gracious enough to apologize . . .

The front row line-up was the same for the dry Swedish Grand Prix at Anderstorp where John again catapulted into the lead at the start and this time Andretti managed to duck through to the front on the second lap without hitting him. Watson held onto a marginal second place until Scheckter's Wolf gave him the "Andretti treatment" on lap 30, but although the South African was eliminated in the collision, a furious Watson tyre-smoked his BT45B through 180-degrees in a splendid demonstration of a Formula 1 "handbrake turn" and pounded off after his rivals once again. He finished fifth, but would have won, were it not for that spin, because Andretti ran short of fuel in the closing stages and made a pit stop which dropped him to sixth!

Watson's closest call came in the French Grand Prix, run over 80 laps of the 2.361 mile *Dijon-Prenois* circuit in absolutely sweltering conditions on July 3. Andretti and Hunt monopolized the front row with Watson alongside Gunnar Nilsson's Lotus 78 on row two. James bounded into the lead for the first four laps, but Watson had the Brabham-Alfa right with him and nipped through to first place on lap five, quickly easing out a couple of seconds' advantage. By lap 17 Andretti had the Lotus 78 through into second place ahead of Hunt and the serious business of the day really began.

Initially Mario just could not make any impression on Watson's five second advantage, but by lap 50 he had clawed his way up to only 3.3s away from the leading Brabham-Alfa and, with 20 laps left to run, John's cushion was a mere 1.8s. Lap after lap Watson clung on at the front of the field, the black and gold Lotus making no more ground. It looked like stalemate with the advantage to Watson and as the two cars went into their final lap, John was still confidently ahead. Then, tragedy of tragedies, the Brabham-Alfa's voracious thirst for fuel made itself felt less than a mile from the chequered flag: coming up off the "new loop", the BT45B stuttered and, in a flash, Mario was alongside, rubbing wheels with the race leader. The Brabham stuttered again, momentarily, then picked up cleanly. But it was too late: Mario was through to victory by a second-and-a-half over the bitterly disappointed Watson.

Mario: "Sure I feel sorry for John. He did a beautiful job today and never made any mistakes I saw. Obviously, I know how he feels because it happened to me two weeks ago in Sweden. What can I say?"

The doubters who thought, erroneously, that John had cracked under pressure,

After practising one of the RAM team's BT44Bs, Rolf Stommelen took over a third BT45 for the 1976 German Grand Prix at the Nürburgring. Here the bespectacled Rolf leads Jean-Pierre Jarier's Shadow DN5, John Watson's Penske PC4 and Emerson Fittipaldi's Fittipaldi through South Curve on his way to sixth place.

At the start of 1977, Motor Racing Developments moved from New Haw to these new premises at Chessington where the company has remained to this day. The office complex in the foreground also houses the administrative base of the Formula One Constructors' Association as well as Bernie Ecclestone's own business base.

were treated to yet another splendid demonstration of his ability with the Brabham-Alfa at Silverstone during the British Grand Prix on July 16. He qualified alongside Hunt on the front row, seized the lead at the start and held sway confidently for 49 of the race's 68 laps at the head of the field. Again, it was a fuel system malfunction which drove him into the pits for attention and, eventually, caused his retirement. As Peter Windsor remarked in the *Autocourse* seasonal review, "nobody since Chris Amon has gone through so much".

After the Silverstone race Gordon Murray was absolutely determined to get to the bottom of what caused John's fuel-feed trouble, but after removing the fuel system pumps from the car and running them on the bench for three hours, he admitted he was still "very puzzled" as to what caused the problem.

"I can only think that it was a speck of dirt in the line between the rear collector tank and the bendix pump," he reflected, "because nothing went wrong during that test. The BT45B has four fuel tanks, two on each side of the driver, and while the forward pair rely on a system of one-way valves to feed the collector tank, the rearward pair have pumps to bring the fuel forward. Dirt in the fuel lines has caused problems once before on these cars, but I can't be absolutely sure . . ."

Watson's fortunes spiralled downward after Silverstone. He made the front row of the grid at Hockenheim, but his German Grand Prix ended after a mere eight laps when the Alfa engine expired, leaving Stuck, off-the-pace in recent races, to coast home across the line third and out of fuel. John also picked up a viral infection in Germany which made him feel really unwell right through the Austrian Grand Prix weekend, so he was way off the pace at Osterreichring on August 14, finishing a lapped eighth. Stuck gave the Brabham team something of a fillip by holding off Reutemann's Ferrari to finish third.

By this stage in the year one could almost sense an air of desperation about Watson's driving. He dropped his BT45B over a kerb quite heavily at Zandvoort, moving out to make room for Andretti on the opening lap: the impact cracked the sump and he was out of the Dutch Grand Prix after only two laps. At Monza, in the Italian Grand Prix, he clouted a kerb and damaged both chassis and engine of his Brabham, retiring after three laps. Meanwhile, Stuck was seventh at Zandvoort and retired with engine failure at Monza.

In the United States Grand Prix, Hans Stuck went opposite-locking into an immediate lead on a saturated track surface and survived for 14 heart-stopping laps round Watkins Glen before crashing his BT45B quite comprehensively. The German had started the race on deep-grooved rain tyres, but, in an ill-judged bet-hedging exercise, Watson had started on slicks. By the time the track dried out he was so far behind that he could only claim 12th place at the finish. Watson rounded off the season by being eliminated from the Canadian Grand Prix after an early collision with Ronnie Peterson's Tyrrell P34 and engine failure stopped him in the Japanese Grand Prix at Fuji. All in all, it had been a disappointing year for the Brabham team, but there were exciting developments afoot for 1978 . . .

Mid-way through 1977, Gordon Murray had taken another long look at the Brabham-Alfa concept and, after re-thinking the whole concept very carefully, decided that he could, after all, package the fuel load into his favourite triangular monocoque configuration. But Murray decided that he would go several steps further. The result was an incredibly ambitious, extremely expensive, striking and elaborate racing car, the cost of which even rocked Ecclestone very slightly on his heels – the "surface cooled" Brabham BT46.

Murray had in mind a very advanced technical concept in order to obtain a long-term technical advantage, an improvement in the area of driver safety and a significant reduction in weight to compensate for that still-relatively heavy and thirsty flat-12 Alfa engine.

The triangular monocoque, with its impressively small frontal area, stamped a familiar Murray trademark on the BT46's appearance, but the concept of surface cooling was highly imaginative and, as it turned out, extremely complex.

The engine water and oil was cooled by passing through a surface cooling system comprising two water surface heat exchangers and two oil surface heat exchangers, these dip-brazed aluminium structures (manufactured by Marston), mounted integrally within the monocoque structure, thereby effecting a considerable weight saving. The liquid to be cooled flowed through a double-skinned channel which formed the outer wall, and then through another special, finned outer surface licked by the airstream.

Detailed attention was also given to cockpit strength, the monocoque extending upwards to shoulder height, while the front wing and nose assembly was in a separate monocoque structure incorporating foam filled compartments. A double-skinned panel led up to the instrument panel area and formed a support for the now-mandatory front rollover hoop. After an absence on the BT45B during 1977, Dunlop's carbon fibre disc brakes made a reappearance on the BT46, a lot of development having been carried out on this front in the previous twelve months.

Instrumentation was planned on a particularly elaborate level. Apart from a conventional rev. counter, it was intended to provide all the remaining driver information by means of electrically monitored and displayed details about engine pressures and temperatures. Oil pressure, oil temperature, water temperature and fuel pressure were to be monitored continuously by transmitters on the engine and this information relayed to a transducer switchbox mounted on the instrument panel. By using the switchbox, any one of these four functions could be called up by the driver and the information would then be displayed on a three digit electronic read-out. What's more, an automatic onboard timing system was envisaged by means of which the car would receive a signal once per lap and then automatically display the elapsed time from the previous lap, holding the display before eventually self-cancelling. Six years later progress would lead full-circle, with the BT53 featuring similar cockpit instruments activated by the same sort of switch.

As if this was not enough, the BT46 featured on-board air jacking system to facilitate quick tyre changes during practice and the race, activated by an external air bottle supply via a quick-release coupling. There were further weight-saving revisions to the six-speed Brabham-Alfa transaxle and it came almost as something of a disappointment after all that mouth-watering technical specification, to find that Murray's familiar suspension arrangement had been

MARTINI
GOODYEAR
8
MARTINI
RACING
FINA

MARTINI
GOODYEAR
MARTINI
RACING
MARTINI
FINA
CHAMPION
8
MARTINI
BRABHAM
alfa romeo
GOODYEAR

Carlos Pace in determined action at Interlagos (above) during the 1976 Brazilian Grand Prix in which he crashed his BT45 quite heavily. Below, his successor Hans Stuck slams on the opposite lock during wet practice at Monaco at the wheel of the later specification BT45B. You can judge from the size of this car's rear wing that Monaco is a much slower circuit than Interlagos!

retained both front and rear. It was originally anticipated that the BT46 would weigh in at an amazing 575kg, making it a veritable greyhound alongside that cart horse of a BT45B!

Exciting though it was, the BT46 was but part of a package which would focus more attention on Ecclestone's organization than probably any other team in 1978. Fed up with the absurd, bitchy politicking within the Ferrari team, the management of which seemed quite unimpressed by the fact he had returned to win another World Championship in 1977, Niki Lauda was joining Brabham. What's more, his personal sponsor, the Italian dairy food company Parmalat, would be coming with him to replace Martini and Rossi as the Brabham team's major sponsor.

Perhaps his years at Ferrari had spoiled Niki slightly, because his explanation of his decision to switch to Brabham was typically straightforward – almost naïvely so, as things turned out. And one of the things that clinched the deal was his first sight of the BT46!

Lauda admitted that he relished the prospect of a fresh challenge. "It's a brand new car, different engine, but Italian people. I understand them, I speak the language. One day I went over to England to negotiate with Bernie. We spent an afternoon talking: talking about how we'd get the money together, about my contract. Then he said 'Come out to the back, I've got something to show you.' And there it was, the BT46, all complete and ready to run. I was so excited that I knew I just had got to drive that car. If Bernie had said 'look, if you give me £10 then you can drive that car!' I'd have said 'here's the £10'. I had to think 'take it easy, be sensible.' But it was terrific. That's when I realized, so much, that I wanted to drive it.

"So I thought logically about Gordon Murray. All his cars have been fast from the word go. The BT42, BT44, BT44B, and BT45. He's not just good, he's fantastic. Each car has been an excellent machine. Normally a new car is difficult and you've got lots of work to do, but I reckon the BT46 must be as good as it looks. So then you say 'it's not reliable'. But what is reliability? It's the easiest thing in the world. Just *run* the car. Get the thing working, look at it logically. Take for example the brake pedal is going soft. There's no point in just accepting that. Make it work properly. Get some ducting, so it *works*.

"Is the BT46 too complicated? Yes, that's the whole point. Exactly, I like it. The more complicated it is, the more I like it. The more digital stuff, jacks, brakes and so-on: I love it. There's more for me to play around with, more to work on, more to make *work* . . ."

Whether the euphoria of his release from Maranello's political hot house had catapulted the normally unemotional Lauda into a rare state of irrational enthusiasm, or whether he truly had total faith in Gordon Murray's concept, is difficult to say in retrospect. One way or another, the surface cooling experiment turned out to be a fiasco: it simply did not work. The BT46 boiled its water after only a few laps at Donington and Silverstone in the depths of an English winter, so there was clearly no point in even speculating what might happen in Buenos Aires or Rio in the height of a South American summer.

"Not only that," reflects Murray with a somewhat fixed expression on his face, "but we found those dip-brazed panels expanded by about three-sixteenths-of-an-inch when they heated up – so we stripped them all off and re-mounted them on a Teflon back panel, secured on either side by some 270 tiny bolts attached with a special pneumatic tool, in order that they could slide along very slightly as they expanded. There were also all manner of production problems with the panels themselves, notably with 'hedgehogs' – huge bubbles appearing where the dip-brazing clearly hadn't taken properly. Interesting, though, the oil radiators mounted just ahead of the rear wheels seemed to work fine . . ."

As an interesting tailpiece to this particular development, Murray got fed up with the 'smart Alecs' who wrote to the motoring magazines stating with some authority that the heat-exchangers would have to be the size of a London bus to work effectively. "As an exercise, I calculated just how big the surface area covered

by those coolers was," smiled Gordon, "and it wasn't far off the size of a London bus . . ."

It was totally characteristic of the way in which the Brabham team operated that there were no recriminations at all in the wake of the surface cooling experiment. Ecclestone's policy is always to pick the right man for any important job and then, having made that decision, allow him to get on with it free from undue interference. Gordon Murray's design credentials had been proved beyond doubt with the Cosworth cars and the early Alfa-engined machines, so Bernie just shrugged the whole drama aside and waited for Murray to come up with a fresh solution. Dispassionate observers might also have concluded that since it was Ecclestone who saddled his team with the cumbersome Italian flat-12 in the first place, any criticism might have been muted for this very reason. On the other hand, he who pays the piper calls the tune, and Ecclestone never exactly had a reputation as a

The closest John Watson ever came to winning a Grand Prix for Brabham was the French race at Dijon-Prenois in 1977. For lap after lap the Ulsterman's BT45B fended off a stern challenge from Mario Andretti's Lotus 78 until the very last lap when the Alfa engine spluttered low on fuel and Andretti was through.

shrinking violet when it came to speaking his mind . . .

Clearly, there was no way in which the BT46 could be used in its existing form, so Murray rushed through another update on the BT45 theme. John Watson and new boy Lauda, tended by his personal former Ferrari mechanic Ermanno Cuoghi who had made the switch to Brabham with the Austrian, opened the '78 season at Buenos Aires on January 15 using distinctive BT45Cs fitted with slim full-width front water radiators.

Watson qualified fourth, Lauda fifth, John's appalling luck continuing in the race when a water leak caused his engine to fail while he was running ahead of Niki in second place. This retirement allowed his team mate to open his Brabham career with a confident second to Mario Andretti's Lotus 78.

The new BT45Cs proved significantly less effective when the team arrived at Rio for the Brazilian Grand Prix a fortnight later, Lauda complaining so emphatically

FINA
GOODYEAR
MARTINI
7
FINA
GOODYEAR

The old and new order. The original, Martini Racing-liveried surface cooling BT46 poses in the Silverstone pit lane along side one of the 1977 BT45Bs. The surface cooling concept was possibly Murray's only major failure in 12 years at the Brabham design helm.

Dunlop carbon fibre brake discs and (below) onboard air jacking systems were amongst the other imaginative features to be included in the original BT46 specification.

about oversteer that an original BT45B nose/radiator set-up was fitted to his car mid-way through practice. This proved just the trick, but the time wasted with it meant that Niki was still down on the fifth row with Watson a miserable 21st after being obliged to borrow Niki's revamped car as there was only a single BT45B nose section available in Brazil. Behind the scenes, however, Herbie Blash had been pulling out all the stops to get a second BT45B nose freighted out from Chessington in time for Watson to use in the Sunday race. It was a close call. Only on race morning did a welcome helicopter clatter down onto the pad behind the paddock, a scarlet Brabham nose section poking out of its door, much to Watson's thinly disguised relief!

In the Rio race Reutemann's Michelin-shod Ferrari T2 simply ran away and hid in the gruelling heat, but Lauda picked up a reasonable third place behind Emerson Fittipaldi's unusually competitive Copersucar-Fittipaldi. Niki was lucky, though: during a mid-race tussle with Hans Stuck's Shadow DN8, a lead wheel balance weight flew off the German's car, smashed the Brabham's windscreen, sliced through the air box and buried itself two inches into the leading edge of the BT45C rear wing with all the force of a bullet. It must have missed Niki's head by an inch . . .

Watson wound up eighth after a spin onto the sandy infield and a subsequent pit stop to clean up the nose section of his car. On the face of it, the Brabham team had made a technical step backwards, but Murray was learning all the time and had no intention of running the BT45Cs for the rest of the season. He was to revamp the BT46s, in relatively conventional form and with front-mounted water radiators, in time for the South African Grand Prix at Kyalami, but even that was a short-term answer in his own mind. He was touching on ground effect again and waiting, with considerable interest, to see what Chapman's yet-to-be-announced new Lotus was all about . . .

"What we didn't fully appreciate about the BT45C was that the full-width nose section was generating ground-effect downforce and that's why Niki was complaining about oversteer at Rio," reflects Murray, "the car was just pivoting round its front end. After Monaco, when I saw the first Lotus 79 it suddenly clicked with me as to what Chapman was doing. I went to Bernie and said 'look, we're finished. Unless . . .' "

Lauda qualified his front radiator BT46 on pole at Kyalami with a 1m 14.65s to Mario Andretti's 1m 14.90s, so things looked quite promising. Of course, to take such a view would have been a major over-simplification of the prevailing situation. In their haste to applaud the ex-Ferrari man over the apparent success of his switch to Bernie's team, what many observers overlooked was the fact that Lauda was in the latest Gordon Murray creation while Andretti still used the previous year's Lotus 78. Chapman had yet to play his 1978 hand.

At the start of the South African Grand Prix Lauda had the BT46 moving first when the starting signal was given, but he fumbled his first-to-second gear change and was swamped by Andretti and Jody Scheckter's Wolf on the run down to Crowthorne Corner. Niki held third place initially, then fourth, then third again. He seemed to be pacing himself and his Goodyear tyres perfectly and he was closing in on Patrick Depailler's second-placed Tyrrell 008 when the Alfa flat-12 expired abruptly on lap 53. Ronnie Peterson's Lotus 78 went on to win the race after a sensational last-lap battle with Depailler, while early leader Andretti first slowed with tyre trouble and then retired out of fuel. Watson came storming home third only five seconds behind the winning Lotus. Things didn't look so dusty.

The competition debut of the Lotus 79 came in the rain-soaked non-title International Trophy meeting at Silverstone only a fortnight after Kyalami. Lauda was the sole Brabham entrant, spinning off on the warming-up lap at the wheel of the BT45C and withdrawing from his place on the front row of the grid. The Lotus 79 was clearly going to be as good as it looked, so Murray put on his thinking cap and the front-radiator BT46s shouldered Brabham fortunes as the Championship trail continued in California.

Both the BT46s were well in play during qualifying at Long Beach, Niki qualifying third behind the Ferrari 312T3s of Reutemann and Villeneuve with Andretti (still in a 78) alongside him on the second row. John's BT46 was on the inside of row three and the Ulsterman launched one of the most ambitious assaults the author has ever seen as the pack tore off the grid down into the first hairpin about one quarter of a mile away. Watson aimed his BT46 up the inside, briefly holding the advantage as he fishtailed into the braking area far too quickly and losing his advantage as he ran wide on the exit, holding up both Lauda and Reutemann. Thus, the opening stages of the race saw Villeneuve, Watson, Lauda and Reutemann circulating in tight nose-to-tail formation at the head of the field, but while the Ferraris were destined to last the course, the Brabhams did not.

Watson briefly got alongside Villeneuve on one occasion when the Ferrari driver hooked the wrong gear, but he couldn't manoeuvre the Brabham ahead and John's race came to an end on lap 10 when he pulled up after hearing a large explosion from the rear of the car. Initial post-race examination suggested that John might have been hearing things, but it was initially suspected that an oil seal had collapsed under pressure and that was the reason for the "explosion".

Some cynics even suggested at the time that Watson had probably run over a Coca-Cola can, but John was clearly bothered by what *really* happened and was actually down at the Brabham factory to see the cars arrive back from North America.

Gordon Murray: "We looked over the whole car very carefully and couldn't find anything, but one of the mechanics suddenly noticed that the top of the oil tank seemed to be distorted. From there it wasn't a long job to diagnose what had happened. The exhaust pipes had set the oil pipe alight, burnt up it and ignited the contents of the tank: that was the explosion he heard. The oil tank was integral with the monocoque at that time."

Lauda's race ended with ignition failure on lap 28, so that was the end of the team's North American outing. Now it was back to Europe for the Monaco Grand Prix on May 7, where the BT46s showed tremendous form during practice round the tight Mediterranean street circuit, Watson and Lauda qualified second and third behind Reutemann's Ferrari T3 and it was John who burst into the lead at the start, making up for his performance the previous year when he started from pole only to lose the lead to Scheckter going into the first corner!

Depailler's Tyrrell got to *Ste. Devote* in second place with Reutemann and Lauda banging wheels quite hard as they went through the chicane almost side-by-side in third and fourth slots. The impact was sufficient to deflate one of the Ferrari's tyres, so Carlos trailed round into the pits at the end of the opening lap.

Initially it looked as though Watson might make a break, but he never quite managed to shake off the attentions of Depailler, although this leading twosome managed to make four seconds on Niki's third-paced BT46 in the opening sprint. Niki clawed that back gradually until, with 25 of the race's 75 lap, 154.35 mile distance completed, the order was Brabham-Tyrrell-Brabham in tight formation at the front of the field. Watson was driving magnificently, Depailler doggedly and Lauda tactically. Time and again the Austrian would pull out going into the braking area for a corner, have a long look down the inside, and then pull back into line again. It seemed like a matter of time . . .

At half distance, however, the picture began to change. Watson dropped to a distant third after taking to the chicane escape road on the harbour front: he had been grappling with progressively fading brakes for about 20 laps now, and there was just no way he could hang on ahead any longer. For five laps Niki sat right behind Depailler and then he vanished into the pit lane to have one of the BT46's rear tyres changed after sustaining a slow puncture. His climb back through the field from sixth place after this delay was one of the best drives of his illustrious career.

Watson briefly found himself back in second place, but those fading brakes sent him lightly into the tyre barrier at *Ste. Devote*, dropping him to third behind Scheckter's Wolf. Lauda slammed past him as they hurtled into *Ste. Devote* to start lap 67 and, as he closed in to polish off Scheckter a few laps later, the incredible

Niki set a new circuit record of 1m 28.65 (83.573 mph) which was an amazing three-tenths quicker than he managed in practice. And, of course, if he *had* done it in practice, he would probably *not* have had his brush with Reutemann going into the first chicane, *possibly* not sustained the puncture and *possibly*, therefore, led from start to finish. As it was, when the chequered flag came out, he was 22.5s behind Depailler and still going like the hammers of hell, with a disappointed Watson trailing home fourth behind Scheckter.

The Lotus 79 led its debut Grand Prix from start to finish in Belgium on May 21, Mario Andretti easily outpacing his opposition over 70 laps of Zolder, a distance of 185.38 miles. Reutemann's Ferrari was alongside Mario on the front row with Lauda on the inside of row two. Unfortunately Carlos missed a gear as he accelerated away at the start, and in the chaos behind him Niki wound up being punted straight off the circuit and out of the race almost before it had begun! Watson's BT46 was nudged from behind on the pace lap by Jean-Pierre Jabouille's Renault, so the Ulsterman started the race with his rear wing slightly askew . . . he wound up spinning over a kerb, damaging the Brabham monocoque and Alfa Romeo sump. With an oil leak and a rumpled car, he pulled off and retired after 18 laps.

The Spanish Grand Prix on June 4 saw Lauda and Watson struggling to keep up round the twists and turns of Jarama, Niki's engine expiring after 56 of the 75 laps while Watson finished fifth on the same lap as Mario's winning Lotus. Then came Gordon Murray's trump card.

After the failure of the surface cooling BT46, Murray had kicked around several ideas, not only to cool the Brabham-Alfas effectively, but also to come up with an answer to the increasingly competitive challenge posed by the super-competitive Lotus 79s. One of the options he considered was having the engine mounted immediately behind the cockpit with the fuel tank between the engine and gearbox, the input shaft actually running through a tube in the middle of the fuel cell. This concept would have permitted a progressively widening ground effect venturi towards the rear, visually not unlike the configuration employed for the upper surface on the rear platform of the McLaren MP4/2s some six years later. However, Gordon eventually decided that the handling changes would be too dramatic as the fuel load was consumed, so he turned his attentions to another concept altogether.

After reading the regulations very carefully, Murray and David North came up with one of the most imaginative, controversial and successful ideas one could have envisaged, the Brabham BT46B "fan car". In order to cool the BT45C's oil radiator sufficiently in South America, a small electric fan had been mounted on top of the engine beneath the horizontally mounted coolers. Although Murray had almost forgotten that little experiment when quizzed about it by the author six years later, it obviously indicated the way his thinking was going, even though he insists that short-term expediency was behind the use of the electric fan arrangement on the earlier car.

What Gordon Murray now had in mind was far more ambitious. The prototype BT46B was tested in conditions of some secrecy at Brands Hatch and then two such cars made their public debut in the paddock at Anderstorp at the Swedish Grand Prix meeting. After rejecting the idea of conventional radiator, fed by ducting, mounted atop the engine, Murray finalized a configuration which employed a large water radiator mounted horizontally on top of the engine, the whole engine/gearbox assembly sealed off from the outside air by means of flexible skirts and a large, gearbox-driven, extractor fan to suck out all the air from beneath the engine/gearbox bay. It took a lot of experimenting with skirts, fan speed and radiator sizes to come up with the ideal working arrangement, most of this work being carried out at Alfa's Balocco test circuit prior to the semi-public airing at Brands Hatch.

The striking BT46Bs attracted an overwhelming amount of attention at Anderstorp, particularly over the way that they sat down firmly on their skirts as the throttle was blipped, then rose slightly as the revs dropped away. Clearly,

parmalat
parmalat
parmalat
parmalat

The most technically interesting Formula 1 Brabham of all was the BT46B fan car which caused a storm of controversy when it appeared in practice for the 1978 Swedish Grand Prix at Anderstorp. Above, the car's water radiator is seen laid flat across the top of the 12-cylinder engine, while (below) the rear-mounted fan and the skirt system beneath the engine bay.

Murray was killing two birds with one particular stone here, and most of his rivals did not like it one bit. The "fan car" may well have been evolved on paper as a method of cooling the Alfa flat-12 engine and retaining the BT46's slim frontal profile, but it also stuck to the road like a leech thanks to that low pressure area beneath its engine and gearbox. Although Andretti's Lotus 79 claimed pole with 1m 22.058s at Anderstorp, the fan cars of Watson (1m 22.737s) and Lauda (1m 22.783s) were right behind and an explosive controversy had already erupted. What's more, at Ecclestone's insistence, the Brabhams practised on full tanks in order that aggravation over their potential should be minimised!

During practice the Brabham fan cars were visually quicker off most corners than their rivals, many of whom were complaining bitterly about all the muck, dust and debris they were allegedly sucking up off the track and shooting out behind them. But, aside from the emotional indignation from other drivers, designers from rival teams were thumbing through the CSI technical regulations. Under Article 1, item five, they read that an aerodynamic device is "Any part of the car whose *primary function* is to influence aerodynamic performance." Under Article 3, item 7, "Aerodynamic devices must comply with the rules relating to coachwork and *must be firmly fixed while the car is in motion.* It is permissible to bridge the gap between the coachwork and the ground by means of flexible structures subject to the coachwork measurements."

A total of five teams protested the Brabham's eligibility at one time or another over the Swedish Grand Prix weekend, their feeling being that the *primary* reason for the fan was to provide down load. Gordon Murray and Bernie Ecclestone stuck to their guns, insisting that its primary function was cooling. "Disconnect the fan and the car will immediately overheat," said Murray defensively.

In retrospect, of course, one must see the fan car as the absolutely legitimate use of a loophole in the technical regulations, and, years later, Murray would frankly acknowledge this to be the case. However, back in the summer of 1978, in the height of the gamesmanship in this matter, the situation was immeasurably complicated by two further aspects to the controversy. Firstly, the CSI was highly embarrassed by the whole business as it had given tacit approval to the fan car concept when Gordon Murray described the configuration to its representatives during a meeting in Madrid. Secondly, the Brabham BT46B won its debut race in convincing style!

Watson got off-line early on as he attempted to deal with Patrese after making a slow start, spinning off and filling his engine with sand and dirt. But Niki went after Andretti's Lotus in a big way.

Lauda recalls that fan car victory with relish: "I tell you, it was the easiest win I have ever scored. You could do *anything* with that car! I was pressing Mario really hard when one of the Tyrrells, Pironi I think it was, dropped oil all over the racing line and the track became very slippery. Mario's Lotus was sliding all over the place and my Brabham was just sitting there, like it was on rails. Then Andretti made a small mistake coming through a corner, I pulled over to the inside and just nailed him coming out . . . no problem at all.

"It was remarkable, but you had to alter your technique to drive it properly. I remember when we were testing at Brands Hatch, on the club circuit, when you came through Clearways you didn't back off to kill the understeer as you would on a normal car. You just booted it even *harder* – the thing just sat down firmly on the track, you were through the corner and away . . . it was great!" This was *precisely* the sort of advantage which appealed to Niki's rather dry sense of humour . . .

As far as Gordon Murray was concerned, however, the race was simply the culmination of several months' hectic design and development. The team was originally hoping to have the fan car ready for Monaco, but there were all sorts of problems to overcome with both the gearbox drive to the fan and the crucially important skirt system which "fenced off" that rectangular section beneath the engine bay.

"We got an independent consultant, David Cox, to do the sums as regards the number of fan blades we would need, their pitch and to calculate that it needed to

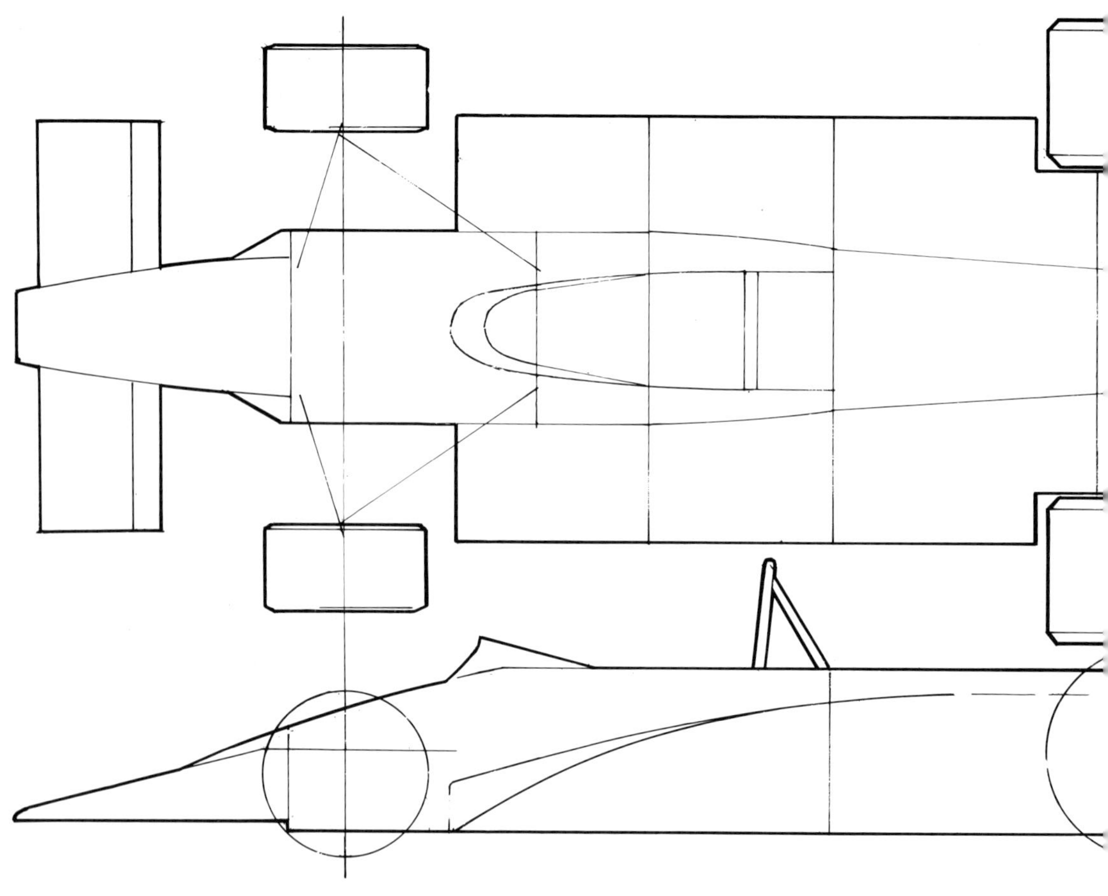

Gordon Murray's outline drawing for the 'second generation' fan car, the BT47 which was intended to take full advantage of a much larger skirted under-car area than the BT46. Some components for this stillborn Brabham were underway when the project was abandoned.

rotate at around 7000rpm," explained Murray, "but the actual business of developing the gearbox drive was amazingly complex.

"When we first devised the system we had to look at it from a practical point of view, anticipating all the problems we might encounter and designing the system to avoid them in advance. We took the fan drive off the bottom shaft of the gearbox, but if we had opted for a direct-drive system, the gearshaft would keep revolving due to the inertia of the fan whenever the driver depressed the clutch and we thought this would put an enormous strain on the gear train, making the change itself very stiff and slow as it would be difficult for the gear to mesh promptly. So we fitted a sprag clutch at the end of that bottom shaft so that the drive to the fan de-coupled when the driver depressed the clutch. We were concerned that leaving the fan running in the pits would be hazardous, so we built a control on the engine cover whereby the mechanics could manually disengage it while it was ticking over.

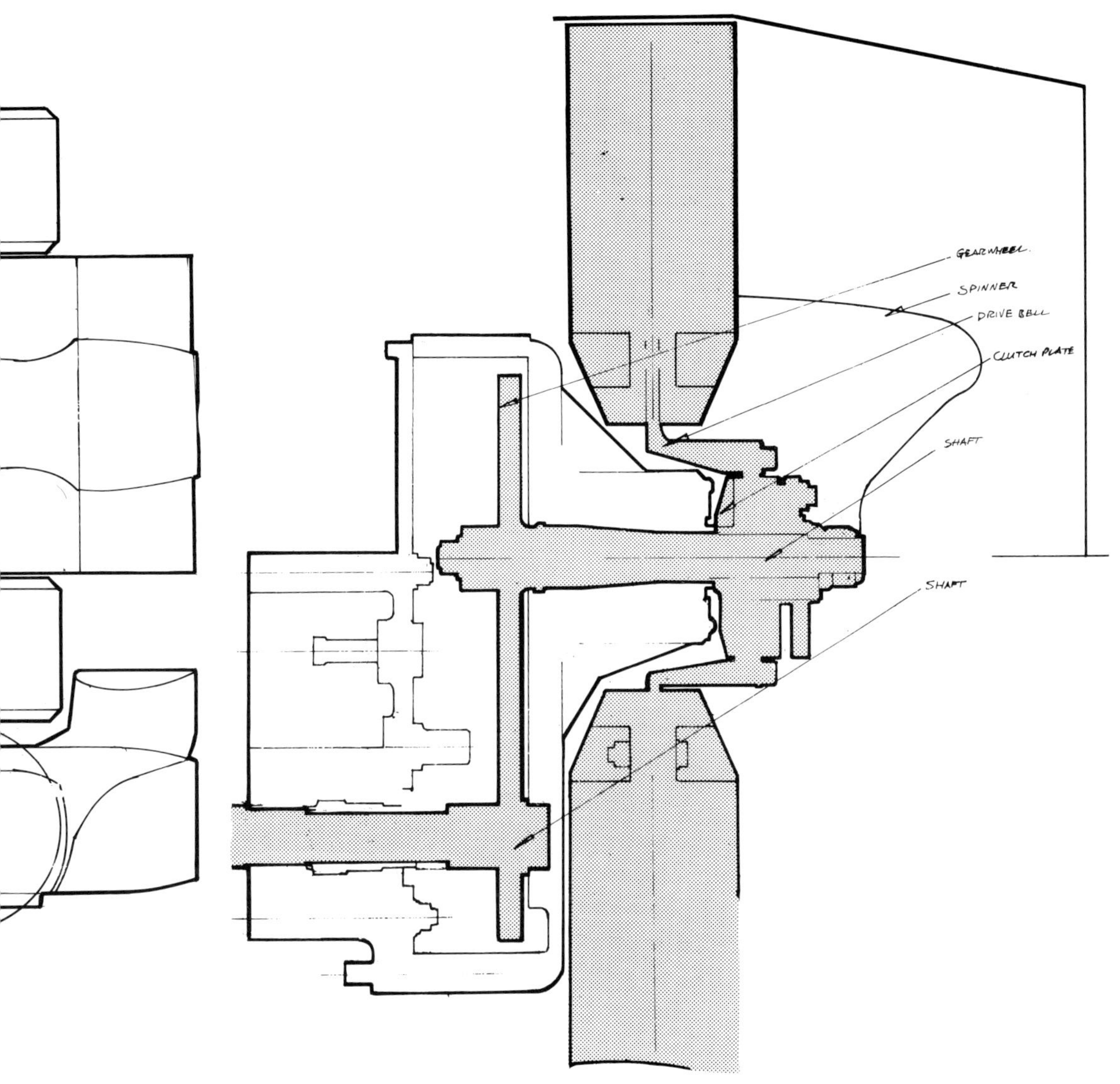

Early drawing of the gearbox-driven fan system for the BT46. In order not to raise any unwanted interest amongst component suppliers in the tight-knit motor racing industry, all Brabham drawings sent out to sub-contractors carried the legend 'automatic clutch' to throw any prying eyes off the scent!

"In order to employ a fan of suitable diameter we then had to use a system of spur gears to move the axis of the fan up to a point above the gearbox casing. The next thing was the problem of racing starts. If the driver dropped the clutch with the engine turning over at 12,000 rpm, we thought that the shock on the system would be far too much – asking the fan to accelerate to maximum speed instantaneously. So we put another friction plate clutch through the fan's hub assembly.

"We designed and built this whole complicated system and took it testing at Brands Hatch. The first thing we found was that it didn't cause the slightest problem with the fan running in the pits, so we got rid of the hand control. Then the sprag clutch welded itself solid and the gearchange remained just fine . . . don't ask me why, I just don't know!

"So, in effect, we had over-engineered the whole system and the direct drive was what we used when the cars went to Sweden! The next problem, though, was that

John Watson at speed during practice for the '78 Swedish Grand Prix, running with a full fuel load in order that the 'fan car' should not reveal its true potential in advance of the race. The Pitot tube on the nose section of the car is monitoring air speed beneath the car.

the fan blades flew apart: they were made out of plastic. So we revised the design and made glass fibre-filled fan blades. They bust too! Oh yes, and the hub was glass fibre, and that broke as well.

"So, with only a week to go prior to the Swedish race we set about casting magnesium fan blades and machining the hubs from the solid. We had sufficient made up for three fans, but no more. We just didn't have the time.

"Then, of course, there was the skirt system, by *far* the most complicated aspect of the fan car. We didn't have any experience at all at totally sealing off the underside of the car. The side skirts and the rear transverse skirt were not too much of a problem. We fitted a Pitot tube in the front of the car and an airspeed indicator in the cockpit: 60 knots' airspeed was the correct figure the drivers were looking for to indicate that adequate suction was being created. But we just *couldn't* make that leading transverse skirt work until David North solved the problem brilliantly by devising a system with two "sausage-like" bags mounted behind that transverse skirt. That prevented pressure variations from pushing the skirt up off the ground, but then we found, during practice at Anderstorp, that a particular bump on the circuit was wearing the skirt away. So we mounted a skid on its leading edge for the second day and it worked perfectly."

Lotus and Tyrrell immediately protested the BT46B after its win, but the race stewards decided not to adjudicate on the matter and the whole affair was eventually referred to the CSI via the Swedish national club. Meanwhile, the Formula 1 Constructors' Association came up with a remarkable contra-deal whereby Ecclestone's team could use the fan car until August 1 – i.e. through the

French, British and German Grands Prix – and then had to discard the idea. However, the CSI's special commission, which met on June 23, decided to reject this "consensus" approach and decreed that fans were banned from Formula 1 henceforth.

It should, of course, be emphasized quite categorically that the BT46B fan-car may have been outlawed *after* its victory at Anderstorp, but it was never declared illegal, nor was it disqualified from that Swedish Grand Prix success.

Interestingly, although the fan-car was banned by the CSI, a technical commission from the sport's governing body examined the BT46B and broadly agreed with Gordon Murray's contention that the fan was employed "about 70 per cent for cooling and 30 per cent for ground effect", but the system was still banned!

As Ecclestone remarked years later, "really, I suppose we had to get rid of it or we'd eventually have devised cars capable of climbing walls and running across the ceiling." Murray counters that jocular remark by reminding us that "it was a short-term expedient. It would never have developed the sort of downforce we would eventually see in the heyday of ground effect during the 1979 and 80 Grand Prix seasons."

Notwithstanding that point of view, Murray had finalized plans for a second generation fan car before the first machine had appeared in public. "Before Sweden I'd drawn the BT47 and reckoned we ought to get on with it as the BT46 wasn't built to the maximum permissible width. This proposed car would effectively have been a skirted box-shape with cockpit, engine and wheels. I'd completed the drawings, we'd ordered fuel tanks and planned to have it running in the last three races of the season. Chapman was going on about 'oh, we've been thinking about that and we'll have one within weeks', but I knew just how much we'd been through in the course of our car's development and I reckoned it would take them quite some time to catch up – by which point, in theory, we should have won the Championship!"

Murray clearly had to think things through again, but for the moment he was obliged to continue using the front-radiator BT46s. The French Grand Prix at Paul Ricard on July 2 turned out to be a race-long battle between the Lotus 79s of Andretti and Peterson, and Hunt's McLaren M26, but not until Watson had planted his Brabham-Alfa on pole, aided by a nicely-timed rain shower which slowed his rivals!

John faded to fourth in the race while Lauda's engine broke after ten laps. Two weeks later the British Grand Prix at Brands Hatch saw the Lotus 79s the class of the field yet again, but they broke down and Niki's BT46 looked set to take a well-judged win. Although Lauda was being steadily reeled in by Carlos Reutemann's Ferrari, it seemed as though the Brabham team leader would be able to keep his place at the front. Coming up to complete lap 60, Lauda and Reutemann flashed under the bridge into Clearways only to find Bruno Giacomelli's Marlboro McLaren M26 right on the fast line ahead of them.

Lauda went to run round the outside of Bruno, but the little Italian misunderstood and moved to the outside of the corner. Niki backed off momentarily and Reutemann seized his chance, slamming up on the inside with his right-hand wheels almost shaving the grass. He kept his foot down and hurtled past the Brabham-Alfa as they came up past the pits, easing confidently into the lead by the time they went into Paddock.

Niki seemed slightly flustered – certainly he was livid with Giacomelli – and took several laps before he regained his composure, by which time Reutemann had opened a four second advantage. But then Niki came back at the Ferrari with everything he could muster, shattering the lap record with a 1m 18.6s four laps from the finish, but failing by 1.3s to re-take the lead. Watson finished next up behind his team mate, so a second and third was not too bad a result on which to round off the British Grand Prix weekend.

Engine trouble claimed Lauda's BT46 in the German Grand Prix at Hockenheim, the reigning World Champion having started yet again from third spot on the grid behind the dominant Lotus 79s of Mario and Ronnie. Watson

parmalat
ALFA ROMEO

Tantalized by the prospect of driving the original BT46, Niki Lauda was lured away from Ferrari to join Brabham at the start of 1978. Here he is seen with Herbie Blash in the Brands Hatch pit lane during the '78 British Grand Prix meeting at Brands Hatch.

wound up seventh. Gordon Murray then came up with another Brabham-Alfa variant for the Austrian Grand Prix, the BT46C with its water radiators faired neatly into each side of the monocoque just behind the front wheels, thus enabling the original "needle nose" to be employed again.

Although the BT46C configuration produced better weight distribution, both Niki and John complained that the cars were short of revs and down on straight line speed, so the cars were changed back to front-radiator specification after the first day's practice. Niki's practice on home ground was spoiled when he had a nasty moment on Saturday when a rear wheel worked loose, and when he took over the team's spare car, its engine promptly expired. He therefore started from an uncharacteristic 12th on the grid, two places behind Watson.

A torrential cloudburst stopped the Osterreichring event after only seven laps, so the race was later restarted over the 47 lap balance remaining. Niki's race came to an end on lap 21 when he got off-line at the sweeping downhill *Rindtkurve* and bounced his Brabham-Alfa off the guard rails, trickling into the pits to retire after a most untypical mistake for the usually meticulous local hero. Again, Watson wound up seventh.

The Dutch Grand Prix at Zandvoort saw much the same story as usual. Niki qualified third behind the Lotus 79s and finished in that position after an impeccable race, while John brought the second BT46 home fourth after an energetic battle with Fittipaldi's on-form Copersucar-Fittipaldi. By this stage in the season Watson's future was now seriously in doubt as far as the Brabham team was concerned and Bernie Ecclestone had opened negotiations with the promising Brazilian Formula 3 star Nelson Piquet. The 23-year-old Brazilian who started racing under that name rather than his full title Nelson Piquet Sauto-Maior, in order to keep the fact that he was competing from the attention of disapproving parents, had made his name in the British Formula 3 arena with a succession of dominant performances that summer. At Hockenheim he made his Grand Prix debut at the wheel of an Ensign and was quickly drafted into a private McLaren M23 run by B. S. Fabrications for the balance of the European season. Ecclestone, and plenty of others, knew he was hot stuff, but Bernie was the one who got his signature on a contract first . . .

On September 10 the Italian Grand Prix took place at Monza. It was one of those cruel, bitter, eminently forgettable afternoons which motor racing can suddenly, abruptly produce as a telling reminder of just how dangerous a business this professional sport can be. It was the occasion of that horrifying multiple accident which cost the life of Ronnie Peterson and resulted in the race being stopped after only a single lap. At the restart, Andretti and Villeneuve were so keyed up together on the front row that they jumped the start, Lotus and Ferrari driver being rewarded with a minute's penalty which dropped them to sixth and seventh at the finish.

That small-minded penalty promoted Lauda and Watson to first and second places, Niki making a far better start than John although the Ulsterman was gobbling up his team mate's advantage in the closing stages. "And I'd have passed him!" said Watson firmly afterwards in response to any questions about team orders.

On October 1 the United States Grand Prix at Watkins Glen saw both Brabham-Alfas retire with engine problems, while for the final race of the season at Montreal's *Ile Notre Dame* circuit, Piquet was rewarded with an outing in a third Brabham entry. Ironically, on his farewell drive for the team, Watson comfortably out-qualified his two colleagues, but that was thanks to a chaotic wet/dry practice and a lot of irritating minor technical problems. The race, won by Villeneuve's Ferrari, proved to be a Brabham fiasco. Watson got involved in a collision with Andretti's Lotus as the American tried to force through at the tight hairpin before the pits. Lauda clipped a chicane kerb and deranged his steering, while Piquet managed to keep going to finish a lapped 11th.

Peterson's sad death provided an opening in the Marlboro McLaren line-up for Watson, a position he retained until his retirement from Formula 1 at the end of

The Brabham Formula 1 race shop at Chessington, summer 1978, with a couple of BT46s in the course of preparation in the two bays visible.

1983. Watson admits that he enjoyed himself at Brabham, but the arrival of Niki Lauda subtly changed his status with the team. Lauda was clearly much more Ecclestone's man in terms of personality.

"I had no problems at all with my relationship with either Niki or Bernie," John told the author at the end of the '78 season, "It was fantastic working with Niki and we had more laughs and fun with each other than either of us had with a team mate before. Bernie was no problem, but I felt he did seem to like people with a more aggressive nature than I'd got. I'm not aggressive as such and I think he tends to measure racing drivers outside the car against Jochen Rindt. He was tough and ambitious, like Niki. I'm no less ambitious when I'm behind the wheel of a racing car, but there's no way I'm as aggressive in normal life . . ." On leaving Brabham, John was so confident about the 1979 season that he bet Ecclestone he would finish ahead of Niki in the Championship points table at the end of the following year . . .

Gordon Murray, meanwhile, was focussing his attentions on what to do for 1979 on the technical side. It was quite clear that Brabham would require a proper ground effect car, but there was no way in which one could be properly adapted round the flat-12 engine configuration.

"I told Alfa Romeo that they'd better get on and build a V12 for 1979 if they wanted us to have any sort of a chance," he confessed candidly, "and, to my surprise, they agreed and just got on and did it. Alfa were always very good at getting jobs done in a hurry, but I have to say, by the end of 1978 I was pretty convinced that we might have won a couple of Championships if we'd stuck to the Cosworth DFV in 1976. On the other hand, if Chapman hadn't come up with his ground effect solution in 1978, I reckon we could have taken the Championship that year without too much trouble. Really, we had no real opposition apart from the Lotuses: take them out of the equation and we would have won a lot of races. The engines were quite powerful and we were finishing races regularly."

Alfa Romeo cracked on at an enthusiastic pace and produced its V12 Grand Prix engine by late autumn 1978, a few weeks before Gordon Murray's new ground effect chassis, the BT48, was ready to accept it. The new Alfa engine used many components from the superseded flat-12, was dubbed the type 1260 and had a bore and stroke of 78.5 x 51.5mm for a 2991cc capacity. On Lucas injection the engine was claimed to produce an impressive 525bhp at 12,300 rpm, utilizing modified versions of the flat-12 cylinder heads. It was hoped that the overall package would be substantially lighter than the BT46, but that did not turn out to be the case.

Although Murray did not put pen to paper on the BT48 until after the fan car was dead and buried in the summer, the first BT48 was rolled out of Brabham's Chessington factory a few days before Christmas. The V12 engine was installed as a stressed member on this occasion and Murray became the first designer to employ carbon fibre composite panels in a Formula 1 application on the BT48, in the panelling over the driver's legs, surrounding the fuel cell, a total of about 30 per cent content. The main monocoque structure itself continued to be constructed from aluminium alloy sheet while pull rod suspension was fitted all round in conjunction with double wishbones and now-totally inboard mounted coil spring/damper units.

At the time Ecclestone described it as "possibly the most expensive Grand Prix car ever built" and it certainly looked wickedly functional and competitive, its side pods leading straight through to a full-width "tail spoiler" mounted low down between large side plates. Six years afterwards, Murray simply rolled his eyes and said, "I was *amazed* when Alfa built that V12 in three months, but it was a *disaster*, My God, it was . . ."

Shaking his head despairingly, Murray recounts the *rationale* behind the BT48. "It was quite straightforward, really. I confidently expected everybody to make a giant leap forward in terms of ground effect design for the 1979 season after we'd all spent a season watching the Lotus 79. So I felt we should really make a big effort to catch up and, if anything, trying to leapfrog ahead of the others. Then we took the BT48 out to Argentina and everybody else turned up with copies of the Lotus 79 which represented very little in terms of progress. All through my time with Brabham we seem to have always over-estimated what our rivals would produce!

"So there we were out in Argentina, running a brand new sliding skirt ground effect car, with a brand new engine, virtually untested and trying to qualify for its first race. For a start we needed to revise the fuel system, but the big problem was the aerodynamics. David North and I figured that if you could really generate enough downforce from those side pods, then you could do away with a conventional rear wing.

"The trouble was that we didn't understand centres of pressure. We arrived in Buenos Aires with the rear wing mounted low down in its original position, the springs far too soft and the skirts sticking up. Any dynamic input of any sort – be it acceleration, braking or cornering – simply upset the whole thing and the centre of pressure went rocketing up and down the car two or three feet one way or the other!

"The car was awful and Niki actually felt the front wheels coming off the deck on the main straight at one point as it tried to 'rotate' like an aircraft. Niki qualified the BT46 just to get in the race and we built up a makeshift conventional rear wing for the second day to give the 48 some stability. Unbeknown to us Lotus were working on a similar configuration without a rear wing for the Lotus 80 and there were rumours going round to the effect that we'd got our hands on some of their drawings, which was rubbish of course. I really thought everybody else would have got 'second generation' ground effect cars by then, but they hadn't progressed and we wound up saddling ourselves with something we really didn't understand!"

This started a truly miserable season for the Brabham *equipe*. As Jacques Laffite's Ligier JS11 rocketed away to victory. Lauda's BT48 started from the penultimate row of the grid and crawled into retirement on lap eight with chronic fuel pressure trouble. Piquet, running an old BT46 for this first race of the season, unfortunately became embroiled in a first-corner multiple pile-up which resulted in the race being stopped and later restarted. His Brabham-Alfa demonstrated the

continued on page 210

Wilson Fittipaldi, elder brother of twice World Champion Emerson, was a popular addition to the Brabham team's driving strength in 1972. He took over the lone BT34, now sporting fresh white livery, and is seen here in action during the French Grand Prix at Clermont-Ferrand where he finished eighth.
Photo: Nigel Snowdon

The sleek lines of the attractive Brabham BT44 are shown off to good effect in this shot of Carlos Pace negotiating Druids hairpin at Brands Hatch during the 1974 British Grand Prix, his first outing for the works team. He was out of luck in this race, but quickly found his feet and was challenging team leader Carlos Reutemann by the end of the season.
Photo: Diana Burnett

Ready to go. A striking pit lane shot of Pace (foreground) and Reutemann, snug in the cockpits of their Brabham BT45s, waiting to start practice for the 1976 British Grand Prix at Brands Hatch.

A determined Carlos Pace hurls his Brabham BT45-Alfa into the banked *Karussell* corner at the Nürburgring on his way to a splendid fourth place in the 1976 German Grand Prix. Pace's dauntlessly enthusiastic approach to the complicated development of the Alfa engine programme was a vivid contrast to Reutemann's disinterest in the new car.
Photos: Nigel Snowdon

Photographed in distinctively Monegasque setting, John Watson's BT45B is seen braking for the Loews hairpin during the 1977 Monaco Grand Prix. John started the race from pole position, but Jody Scheckter's Wolf rocketed into the lead from the word go and, despite a furious chase, John never managed to displace the South African.
Watson at speed during practice for the 1978 Swedish Grand Prix at Anderstorp at the wheel of the BT46B fan car. The Ulsterman qualified on the front row, despite running full tanks throughout practice, but spun off early in the race leaving team-mate Lauda to score an historic, unique triumph.
Photos: Nigel Snowdon

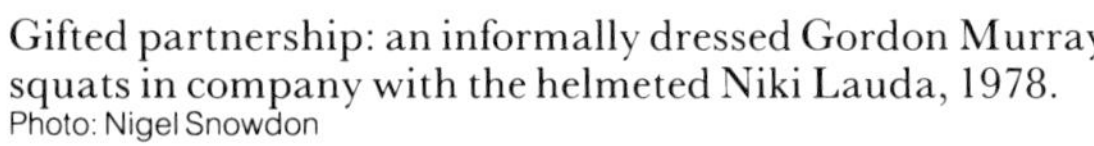

Gifted partnership: an informally dressed Gordon Murray squats in company with the helmeted Niki Lauda, 1978.
Photo: Nigel Snowdon

Bernard Ecclestone: former racing driver, property millionaire, financial wizard, enthusiastic collector of Oriental *objets d'art*, workaholic . . . and owner of the Brabham team since 1972.
Photo: Diana Burnett

Bustling pit scene. Piquet's BT49C-Cosworth is tended by Ecclestone and Murray in the pit lane at Monza, 1981. In the foreground stands Piquet's spare car, all ready with the correct race numbers.
Photo: Nigel Snowdon

BARDAHL
VARGA
BARDAHL
VARGA
10
BRABHAM
GOODYEAR
GOODYEAR

UCKHAM
8
CHAMPION

GOODYEAR
8

MARTINI
7
MARTINI
RACING
MARTINI

BRAHMA
MARTINI
FINA
CHAMPION
8
MARTINI
BRABHAM
GOODYEAR
CHAMPION
FINA
FINA

parmalat
parmalat
2
parmalat
parmalat
BRABHAM
ALFAROMEO
GOODYEAR
GOODYEAR

Rolling
Stones

TRIBUNA
arexons
Esso
PEMEX
parmalat
5
parmalat
BRABHAM
GOODYEAR
GOODYEAR

parmalat
5 parmal
PEMEX
parmalat
5
PEMEX
PEMEX
parmalat
BRABHAM

Santal

5
parmalat
FILA
Santal
MICHELIN

parmalat
parmalat
FILA
Santal
Santal
Castrol

DÉPART
Labatt

Shell Oils
Shell Oils
Shell Oils
Shell Oils
Shell Oils
Shell Oils
John Player
Shell Oils
Shell Oils
parmalat
Santal
MICHELIN
parmalat
parmalat

Nelson Piquet should have thrown the '81 Championship beyond reach in the Italian Grand Prix at Monza where he is seen at speed in his BT49C. Unfortunately, engine failure on the last lap left him lucky to scrape home with a single point for sixth place and his contest with Reutemann went all the way to Las Vegas.
Photo: Nigel Snowdon

Piquet's Brabham BT50-BMW leads René Arnoux's Renault just after the Brazilian had passed the French car in the early stages of the 1982 Canadian Grand Prix at Montreal. Nelson went on to score a timely first victory with BMW turbo power, a success which probably saved the Anglo-German partnership.

With its carbon fibre brake discs glowing brightly under maximum braking effort, Riccardo Patrese's BT49D heads for second place in the 1982 Canadian Grand Prix at Montreal.
Photos: LAT Photographic

Crucial victory. Piquet's BT52B, carrying its high downforce rear aerofoil, speeds towards victory in the 1983 European Grand Prix at Brands Hatch, a significant step towards his second World Championship title.
Photo: Nigel Snowdon

The striking lines of the sleek BT52 are shown perfectly in this shot of Nelson Piquet heading for second place in the 1983 Monaco Grand Prix.
Photo: Nigel Snowdon

Start of the 1984 Canadian Grand Prix with Alain Prost's McLaren MP4/2 briefly sprinting ahead of Piquet's victorious BT53. On the right of the picture is Derek Warwick's Renault RE50.
Photo: LAT Photographic

Pit lane debate. Ecclestone and Murray flank the cockpit of Piquet's BT53 in the pit lane at Brands Hatch during practice for the 1984 British Grand Prix. Nelson proved the only rival to stay with the McLarens in the race, but dropped back to seventh at the finish after loss of turbo boost pressure.
Photo: Geoffrey Goddard Photography

continued from page 191

strength of its monocoque when he tanked virtually head-on into an almost stationary rival, wrecking the BT46 but getting away with a sprained toe.

New skirts manufactured from a honeycomb material and a revised fuel system resulted in an upsurge of Brabham-Alfa fortunes at Interlagos a fortnight later, both drivers having BT48s at their disposal (with conventional rear wings), although Piquet was clearly in no position to go the race distance as his foot was still causing him considerable discomfort. From his position on the penultimate row of the grid, Piquet's BT48 was thus tanked up with considerably less fuel than would have been required for a full race distance and also started on soft qualifying tyres for a brief, crowd-pleasing sprint. To the delight of his fans he came smartly up through the tail-enders before getting a little over-ambitious trying to pass Clay Regazzoni's Williams FW06. The two cars collided and Nelson limped into the pits with deranged suspension to find his team mate already out of the picture with gear linkage problems.

In the South African Grand Prix at Kyalami Lauda really began to crank up the BT48 and managed to qualify fourth behind Jabouille's Renault turbo, benefiting from the altitude to take a rare pole on 1m 11.80s, and the Ferrari T4s of Scheckter (1m 12.04s) and Villeneuve (1m 12.07s). Piquet qualified on the outside of the sixth row and climbed through the field in fine style to tail his team mate in the closing stages. Niki was impressed. "Every time I looked in my mirrors, there was Nelson, so I tried really hard for a couple of laps, thinking to myself 'that'll get rid of him . . .' Then I looked again and he was still there, right behind . . ." The BT48s blared across the line sixth and seventh, lapped by Villeneuve's victorious Ferrari. Subsequent close examination revealed the rear wing mounting on Niki's car to have come slightly loose . . .

It was perhaps a bit too much to hope that the BT48s would shine round the tight confines of Long Beach, Lauda and Piquet sharing the sixth row of the grid almost a second and a half away from Villeneuve's pole time. Tambay's Marlboro McLaren M28 savaged Niki's BT48 from behind going into the first corner, eliminating the Austrian on the spot, while Piquet kept going to finish eighth, two laps behind Gilles' winning Ferrari.

On April 15, Lauda slammed round Brands Hatch in 1m 17.76s to take pole position for the 40-lap Race of Champions, qualifying ahead of Andretti, Piquet and Villeneuve who was using an older Ferrari T3 on this non-title occasion. Using optimistically soft Goodyears, Niki went sprinting away from the pack after the start, but wound up stopping for fresh tyres and finished a lapped fifth. Villeneuve won from Piquet, the Brazilian trading lap records with his Brabham team mate and eventually settling the matter with a 1m 17.46s to his credit on lap 15.

For the Brabham-Alfa teamsters, the summer of 1979 was a long, frustrating haul with only a few promising moments to puncture the seemingly endless disappointment. Lauda was steadily getting fed up with the whole Brabham-Alfa business and secret talks were going on behind the scenes to get him into a Marlboro McLaren-BMW turbo. Piquet was happy to be showing so well against a driver of Niki's established calibre, yet the novice Brazilian was privately relieved that the BT48s seldom lasted a race distance as he was short on physical stamina. Gordon Murray was similarly browned off with the whole affair, Ecclestone was annoyed with Alfa Romeo and the Italian marque bewildered as to why they did not seem to be enjoying any success since they'd obliged with the construction of that V12 engine in double-quick time.

Gordon Murray: "Those V12s varied alarmingly engine to engine. They could vary as much as 600rpm on full song and, at one point, I was beginning to believe that there was something wrong with my chassis, but we eventually pinpointed the problem to oil scavenging. Some engines worked fine, others simply drowned the crankcase. There was no rhyme or reason to it."

Nelson Piquet: "There were times that I was quicker than Niki in practice and just came in and watched him. He would be out there pounding round and round, trying as hard as he could, but I knew there was no way he would be able to match

my times. If you had a bad engine, you were uncompetitive. It was as straightforward as that!"

In the Spanish Grand Prix at Jarama Lauda went out with a water leak while fuel metering unit failure sidelined the Brazilian. The Belgian Grand Prix at Zolder saw Nelson turn a few heads with a second row start, but both his and Niki's engines blew up in the race. Monaco saw Niki valiantly trying to hold up the third place queue long enough for the Alfa to burn off some of its fuel, but Didier Pironi duplicated Tambay's Long Beach attack as they went into Mirabeau and drove over the top of the BT48, eliminating both cars. Nelson went out when a driveshaft broke. And so it went on, and on, and on . . .

The French Grand Prix saw Niki spin on a fast corner and was unable to restart the hot Alfa V12, while Piquet crashed after showing well in company with Alan Jones's Williams FW07. Pre-Grand Prix testing at Silverstone at least let a select few observers see Lauda go howling through Stowe without lifting in sixth gear on one sensational lap, the otherwise almost empty circuit lit up by the joyful wail of the Italian V12. Trouble was, it did little else but make a nice noise, but the BT48 part of the equation clearly worked well on a fast circuit where the drivers could build up a rhythm.

Piquet and Lauda qualified third and sixth for the 68 lap, 199.38 mile British Grand Prix, Niki being treated to the amusing sight of his team mate spinning off right in front of him at Woodcote at the end of the second lap! The Rat made himself singularly unpopular by chopping rivals ruthlessly right left and centre as

After the surface cooling system failed and the 'fan car' was outlawed, the BT46 raced for the balance of 1978 in this twin front radiator form. Here John Watson negotiates Druids hairpin on his way to third place in the British Grand Prix at Brands Hatch.

The first Brabham-Alfa V12 BT48 photographed at Chessington on its completion just before Christmas 1978. Murray's first ground effect design, its development proved a nightmare and the wide variation between the performance of the individual Alfa V12 engines contributed to the problems it would experience throughout 1979.

he slipped helplessly back through the field, his brakes overheating and losing their edge. Lauda started in his spare car without brake cooling ducts fitted, an unusual oversight. After 12 laps the fluid had boiled and he was out.

Earlier in the season Alfa Romeo had signalled its long-term intentions by fielding a flat-12 engined machine in the Belgian Grand Prix off its own bat with Vittorio Brambilla in the cockpit. It was clear to Ecclestone that the factory was toying with the idea of running its own Formula 1 operation and, mid-season, he became totally convinced and there was no future for the Brabham/Alfa Romeo partnership.

There was an element of bluff and counter-bluff throughout the discussions between the two parties, but Bernie got quite hot under the collar at one point during a debate with Alfa President Ettore Massacesi. "He told me that the problems were with the Brabham part of the equation, not with Alfa Romeo's engines," explained Ecclestone, "so I told him, right, let's have a divorce. Let's split up now. We'll stop the whole Brabham-Alfa project here and now if you want to. He was rather taken aback and back-tracked slightly because he knew that he wanted Alfa to be well represented in the Italian Grand Prix, so he wanted our cars there. But I knew we were coming to the end of the road, so I went back to the factory and we began sorting out our plans for the new Cosworth-engined cars."

Now sporting a conventional rear wing, Niki Lauda's BT48 exits Casino Square during the 1979 Monaco Grand Prix shadowed by Didier Pironi's Tyrrell 009 and Alan Jones's Williams FW07. At the bottom of the hill, Pironi's impatience to pass the tardy Brabham resulted in the Tyrrell flying over the rear of Niki's machine, eliminating them both from the race.

Apart from Piquet coming home an amazed fourth in the Dutch Grand Prix at Zandvoort, surviving to score three World Championship points as all around seemed to drop off the circuit or retire with mechanical maladies, the Brabham-Alfa BT48 saga seemed to be coasting to an unspectacular conclusion. On September 7, Alfa Romeo fielded its own works type 179 in the Italian Grand Prix at Monza, powered by the 1260 V12 engine and driven by Bruno Giacomelli. It qualified respectably 1.8s slower than Lauda's BT48 and was hauling in Niki during the race before Bruno spun off. Herbie Blash grinned broadly: "Niki was playing with him and Bruno didn't realise. He lured him into thinking he could get on terms with the Brabham, then he sped up slightly and Giacomelli went off . . ."

Piquet's Italian Grand Prix came to an end at *Curva Grande* on the second lap, his BT48 touching Regazzoni's Williams before richochetting from barrier to barrier, its engine tearing off the back of the monocoque in the ensuing impact. When all the dust settled, Nelson was still safely strapped into the cockpit section on one side of the circuit while the engine, gearbox and rear wheels were deposited over the guard rail on the opposite! He was a very lucky boy indeed. Niki, having dispensed with the works Alfa challenge, ran home a heartening fourth behind the Ferraris of Scheckter and Villeneuve plus Regazzoni's Williams.

It was too late to have any bearing on the imminent demise of the Brabham-Alfa Romeos, although Lauda wrote a quite astonishing postcript to the BT48's Championship career a mere week after its Monza *finale*. The *Gran Premio Dino Ferrari* held at Imola's refurbished autodrome the following week saw the Austrian embroiled in a frantic scrap for the lead with Villeneuve's Ferrari, resolved in the Brabham's favour when Gilles damaged the T4's nose wing against one of the BT48's rear wheels at the height of their jousting. For once the V12 Alfa ran like a precision watch and Niki came home winner of the 40 lap race ahead of Carlos Reutemann's Lotus 79 and Scheckter's Ferrari T4.

As the next chapter will confirm, not only was this the end of the Brabham-Alfa Romeo's career, but it also looked like the end of Niki Lauda's Grand Prix innings. The partnership between the Italian motor manufacturer and the small specialist British team may not have been the most productive in terms of hard results, but it spawned some fascinating, innovative cars from Gordon Murray's drawing board and must be recalled as possibly the most interesting, varied era in the 23 year history of Brabham's Grand Prix cars.

MICHELOB.
MICHELOB
Convention
Center
PSA
Marlboro
Marlboro
parmalat
5
22
23
9
4
15
RENAULT elf
elf
16

Section 2: The Ecclestone era

Chapter 4
A return to the Cosworth route

Scrambling into the first hairpin at the start of the 1980 United States Grand Prix West at Long Beach, Nelson Piquet's BT49 grasps a lead it was never to lose throughout the race, René Arnoux's Renault RE20 takes a wide line in second place while Patrick Depailler's Marlboro Alfa Romeo is just ahead of Alan Jones's Williams and Jan Lammer's ATS.

The switch to Alfa Romeo power at the start of 1976 had been made in order to gain a straightforward performance advantage over the team's Cosworth-engined rivals, but the days during which pure power was the main criterion had temporarily vanished by the start of 1979. As Gordon Murray feared, Colin Chapman's ground effect technology breakthrough gained momentum at a pace which surprised many people, and even though Alfa Romeo reacted with commendable speed to build the new V12, the endless technical problems it encountered throughout 1979 indicated that it was not really the answer. If the onus was now on a designer to produce the most efficient ground effect package, there was really no point basing it round a troublesome and unreliable power unit, particularly when the use of that engine dramatically increased the weight of the car in racing trim. Therefore, with the benefit of hindsight, the Brabham team's return to the Cosworth route at the end of that season was supremely logical in every way, disregarding the problems that the team was beginning to experience with Alfa Romeo.

"Going back to the Cosworth route was like having a holiday," beams Gordon Murray reflectively, "OK, so the first BT49s were based round sawn-down BT48 monocoques, but we designed and built two of them in six weeks. It was an absolute doddle compared with the Alfas . . ." Of course by this time, Alfa Romeo's own plans for fielding a team of works Formula 1 cars were well advanced and Ecclestone was not about to stand in line behind them when it came to obtaining competitive engines.

Murray privately acknowledges that, towards the end of the Brabham-Alfa partnership, Autodelta was effectively pumping him for information to help it with its own Grand Prix programme, so it can be seen that there were several incentives to prompt a change of technical route. Once the decision was made to change back to Cosworth power, the Brabham factory staff responded in its usual magnificent fashion and no fewer than three BT49-Cosworths were produced in six weeks, enabling the team to field a totally new range of cars for the Canadian Grand Prix at Montreal's *Ile Notre Dame* circuit on September 30.

Piquet briefly tried the first of the cars in a Silverstone test session before they were shipped to Canada and was instantly impressed: "I was always led to believe that the DFV was quite a rough, coarse engine, but it felt quite the opposite to me. After those Alfa V12s it felt smooth and willing to rev . . ."

Two of the converted BT48s and one brand new BT49 were on hand for Niki Lauda to experiment with in Montreal, the Cosworth car visually very similar to its Alfa-engined predecessor. But everything behind the cockpit was totally new, as were the aerodynamic side pods and rear aerofoils. As on the BT48 the fuel tank was an integral part of the monocoque structure, but the oil tank was now fitted between the engine and the Brabham/Alfa/Hewland gearbox which was retained on the BT49. The water and oil radiators, in the left and right-hand side-pods respectively, were mounted at a slight angle rather than lying flat as they had done in the Alfa-engined car, and the brakes were mounted outboard all round with single four-pot calipers on each disc. Front and rear suspension was largely unchanged, with double wishbones employed in conjunction with semi-inboard

Thank you and good night! Niki Lauda lapping Montreal's Ile Notre Dame circuit at the wheel of one of the first Brabham-Cosworth BT49s during the first practice session for the 1979 Canadian Grand Prix. Within the hour the Austrian had announced his retirement from racing . . .

spring/damper units activated by pull-rods. The rear anti-roll bar was controlled from the cockpit by means of a flexible cable, but the BT48 arrangement was retained at the front with a mechanical linkage of rods and bell-crank levers. With a wheelbase of 107in, the BT49 was, rather surprisingly, an inch longer than that of the BT48, but with a front track of 67in and a rear track of 62¾in, it was identical to its predecessor in these respects. Of course the Cosworth car's fuel tankage was reduced to 38 gallons maximum, seven gallons less than the capacity of the BT48, a reduction of about 17½ per cent! Most crucially, at 580kg, the BT49 was 15kg (33lb) lighter than the car it replaced.

The debut of the BT49 was awaited with enormous enthusiasm and sense of anticipation by the hard-working Brabham personnel, but first practice at Montreal brought with it an unexpected surprise in the form of Niki Lauda's sudden retirement. After completing ten laps during the untimed session in the new BT49, the Austrian pulled into the pits and told Bernie Ecclestone of his decision. Rather than try to persuade him to "think about it", Ecclestone acted decisively and said "OK, if you want to go, then I agree it's best to go now." Later, although not best pleased with the abruptness of Niki's decision, Ecclestone explained, "there was no point in trying to debate the matter with him. If I had changed his mind and he had then been involved in an accident, you can imagine how I would have felt. No, I don't think he was trying to be seduced into staying, into changing his mind. I think, more likely, he wanted somebody to confirm to

him that he was doing the right thing. He really wanted to retire, so I wasn't going to stand in his way."

Lauda later explained that it simply came to him that he "was no longer getting any pleasure from driving round and round in circles. I feel I have better things to do with my life . . ." Within hours, he had returned to his hotel and jetted off to California to pursue business for his burgeoning airline on which he would focus the lion's share of his attention in the two years that followed.

Some people have speculated that Niki Lauda was getting bored because he was losing his touch and knew full-well that Nelson Piquet was now capable of running rings round him. More likely, once the enigmatic McLaren-BMW project fell-through earlier that summer (you can read about that in the following chapter!), Niki's disillusionment with the Brabham-Alfa project became complete. There are those, including 1980 World Champion Alan Jones, who felt that Lauda decided to retire once he realized that Brabham was returning to the Cosworth route, putting forward the theory that without a very powerful 12-cylinder engine, back in a Cosworth car like the rest of them, Niki probably thought it was simply going to be too hard, too difficult.

As an important aside, I feel that it should be emphasized just what an ill-judged, absurd contention this was. If you analyze Niki's progress with the Brabham BT48 through 1979, there is no question that the man still had talent and, although Piquet was clearly developing into a *quicker* driver, the suggestion that he was daunted by the prospect of a return to Cosworth power is quite ridiculous. Unfortunately for Jones and others who supported this outlandish hypothesis, Lauda's retirement proved temporary: in 1982 he came back at the wheel of a McLaren and proved, with Cosworth DFV power, that he was still one of the most shrewdly talented drivers of all . . .

Lauda's place in the team was immediately taken by Argentine Formula 2 graduate Riccardo Zunino, who had just happened to be on the scene and available, but it was Piquet who closed the season for the Brabham on a promisingly high note. The 1979 Canadian Grand Prix might well be recalled primarily for the great Alan Jones/Gilles Villeneuve battle, but it should be recalled that Piquet qualified fourth a mere 0.9s away from Jones's pole time with the Williams FW07. Early in the race Piquet stormed ahead of Clay Regazzoni's Williams FW07 to take third place and kept station there until the BT49's gearbox broke with 11 of the race's 72 lap, 197.28 mile distance left to run. Zunino qualified some way down the field but handled his Grand Prix debut with commendable verve and confidence, slicing through to finish seventh, two laps down on the winner.

The following weekend saw Piquet qualify second alongside Jones's Williams for the United States Grand Prix at Watkins Glen, but when the circuit was doused with a rain shower shortly before the start, the Brazilian had to start on slicks when the Brabham lads were unable to get their air gun equipment working in time on the grid in order to fit wet weather tyres before the off! Nelson dropped to the tail of the field in the wet conditions, but gradually began to make up places as the circuit dried out and wound up setting the fastest lap in 1m 40.054s (121.25 mph) before his BT49 rolled to a halt with driveshaft failure six laps from the chequered flag. Looking most uncomfortable and out of his depth, Zunino had spun off after only 25 precarious laps.

Clearly, the Brabham BT49 had proved itself a promising machine and the whole team was absolutely delighted with the way Nelson Piquet had shouldered the responsibilities that come with number one status.

Gordon Murray: "Technically, I think that by the end of 1979 Nelson was improving tremendously and there's no doubt that he learned a great deal from Niki. He wasn't afraid to make intelligent suggestions and he quickly found out what *I* wanted to know from *him*. He had progressed to the point where he always provided me with intelligent, accurate and relevant information. He appreciated precisely what I needed to know to make progress in setting up the cars and didn't waste any time with superfluous information."

Nelson himself confirms just how much he owed to Lauda's help, advice and guidance. "He was an honest, open and sincere man to deal with. If he thought you were a fool, or had done something stupid, then he would tell you, openly and to your face. There was no messing around with Niki. He had a keen sense of humour and I learned a great deal about testing from him. Not merely how to drive the car, but how to be selective about the information collected during a test session."

Throughout the 1980 season, Nelson Piquet's stature continued to grow within the Formula 1 fraternity. This was the heyday of ground effect, where sliding skirts, 2000lb springs and critical centres of pressure beneath the crucially sculptured aerodynamic side pods were the most important aspect of the competitive picture for any Formula 1 car. You might have power in abundance, but unless you were in a position to make your car stick, leech-like, to the tarmac, then you would find yourself consigned to the outer darkness as a perpetual also-ran . . .

History relates that Patrick Head's Williams FW07 was the most effective car of this season, enabling the brave Alan Jones to clinch the World Championship title with a total of five wins to his credit. But, while *Autocourse* rated Jones as number one its top ten assessment at the end of the season, editor Maurice Hamilton wrote the following prescient words about rated number two, Nelson Piquet:

"Second in the World Championship; nine finishes in the top five places. The results speak for themselves as Nelson Piquet, a driver of exceptional ability, lived up to the promise shown at the end of 1979 . . . Winning the Championship would have been a bonus in 1980. Given the continuing support of the equally talented Gordon Murray, it may be a mere formality in 1981".

Measured up against Jones and the Williams, Piquet found himself faced with a hard nut to crack, but it was a worthwhile barometer against which to measure his own progress. In the scorching conditions of an Argentinian summer, Nelson qualified his BT49 fourth behind Jones and the Ligiers of Laffite and Pironi in practice for the opening race at Buenos Aires on January 13. Despite a pit stop to attend the overheating, Jones emerged a brilliant victor on the crumbling track surface, but Piquet did well to keep everything pointing in the right direction to finish an equally impressive second. It was a good start.

Two weeks later at Interlagos Jean-Pierre Jabouille qualified his Renault turbo on pole and Nelson was well down after tyre problems during practice: in the race he quickly nipped up to sixth before a rear tyre failed and he had to limp a considerable distance in order to get his BT49 back to the pits. A fresh wheel and tyre were fitted, but Nelson crashed heavily when the over-strained suspension eventually broke. Thankfully, he emerged unhurt.

René Arnoux won for Renault in Brazil and was destined to repeat this success at the high-altitude Kyalami circuit, venue for the South African Grand Prix on March 1. Piquet was third on the grid for this race, a full 1.87s slower than Jabouille's pole position Renault, but severe understeer dropped him to fourth place at the chequered flag behind a French threesome comprising Arnoux, and the Ligiers of Laffite and Pironi.

Prior to the United States Grand Prix West at Long Beach on March 30, 1980, Indy 500 winner Rick Mears spent a day at Riverside at the wheel of a BT49, both the American driver and Ecclestone toying with the idea that he might like to run in the Californian race. Mears showed up quite competitively alongside Piquet, who was also present for the test, but FISA bureaucracy concerning the nomination of additional drivers left insufficient time for him to be accepted as an extra runner at Long Beach. There was also the question of sponsorship. Mears, as a man used to being paid handsomely for his motor racing, didn't quite understand the financial mechanics of Formula 1 whereby *he* would have had to find some dollars. Most people on the inside of Indy car racing felt that the financial aspect of a Mears/Ecclestone deal might have been irreconcilable, even if FISA had allowed him to run.

Mears's loss, however, was unquestionably Nelson Piquet's gain. The tight street circuit and the Brabham BT49 seemed made for each other. Nelson slammed round to qualify on pole by more than a second from Arnoux's Renault, prior to leading the 80½ lap, 161.61 mile race from start to finish. Patrick Depailler's Marlboro Alfa Romeo held off Jones's challenge in second place for the first 18 laps, by which time Piquet had vanished into the distance. The Australian's Williams was eventually eliminated in a tangle with Giacomelli's Alfa, so Piquet ran out unchallenged to the finish with only Riccardo Patrese's Arrows A3 and Emerson Fittipaldi's plodding Fittipaldi F7 on the same lap.

On the technical front, Long Beach was also a significant race for Brabham as it marked the first public appearance of the new gearbox/final drive unit developed by American specialist Pete Weissmann, who had plenty of experience of transmission work in the Indy car and Can-Am arenas. The new gearbox, which could be fitted with either five or six speeds, was mounted with the gear shafts running transversely across the car, this being part of Gordon Murray's desire to produce the "ultimate" ground effect layout and therefore keeping the underside of the Brabham as uncluttered as possible. The directional change from the crank axis to the gear shafts was by low friction, straight-cut bevel gears and on the right-hand side of the casing was a detachable plate through which the gear cluster could be withdrawn for easy ratio changing. This layout was used in conjunction with inboard mounted vertical spring/damper units mounted vertically behind the ultra-slim transmission package and activated by rocker arms. The oil tank was mounted within the bellhousing, there being a common lubrication system shared by engine and gearbox.

"The whole package was neat, light and rigid," Murray recalls, "but we really needed more facilities and personnel to develop it. Ideally we would have needed a separate factory with about a dozen technicians to get the ultimate out of the whole project. Gearbox development is a very time-consuming business". Perhaps the precision, specialist work that goes on at Hewland's Maidenhead factory is often underestimated!

Piquet's inexperience showed up during the Belgian Grand Prix where he made an error of judgement, spinning off the road in his BT49. In the early stages of the 72 lap race at Zolder he had been plagued by a high wear rate on his front tyres and managed to lock up the rears as he juggled with the cockpit brake balance control in an attempt to effect an improvement. He blamed nobody but himself as he strolled back to the pits . . .

At Monaco Nelson kept control on a rain-licked track surface to finish third behind Carlos Reutemann's Williams and Jacques Laffite's Ligier. The non-Championship Spanish Grand Prix saw him retire with gearbox trouble while the French Grand Prix at Paul Ricard had the BT49 chase home Jones's Williams and the Ligier duo, Pironi and Laffite. The British race at Brands Hatch saw Gordon Murray take an early bath – literally! After Nelson complained about lack of grip on Friday, the Brabham designer went home for a long soak in order to mull over the problem: clearly it worked, for Nelson was right on the pace on Saturday, bagging fifth on the grid a scant 0.6s away from Didier Pironi's Ligier pole time. Both the Ligiers led, but fell by the wayside, so Piquet scrambled home a worthy second, the meat in a Williams sandwich with Jones and Reutemann first and third.

By the middle of the 1980 season the tremendously high cornering speeds being achieved by the ground effect breed of Grand Prix cars were worrying everybody in the business, from drivers to designers, from sponsors to spectators. If anything went wrong there was little chance of retrieving the situation at high speed, a fact dramatically underlined to the Formula 1 world when Patrick Depailler's Alfa Romeo crashed at the dauntingly fast *Ostkurve* during pre-Grand Prix testing at Hockenheim and the popular Frenchman was killed instantly. When it came to the German Grand Prix, Piquet cooked his clutch on the starting grid and limped away at the back of the field, eventually fighting back to take a splendid fourth at the finish.

After emerging from the Austrian Grand Prix with fifth place to his credit, following a crash at the *Boschkurve* during practice and clutch trouble again in the

Indy car front-runner Rick Mears tried this BT49 in tests at Riverside just prior to the 1980 Long Beach race, but no deal for a drive was struck and, in any case, FISA regulations would not have permitted him to run at Long Beach as a late entry.

race, Piquet helped himself to a couple of very impressive victories in both the Dutch and Italian Grands Prix. At Zandvoort Piquet capitalized on a mistake by Jones, the Australian destroying his Williams's sliding skirts after momentary inattention caused him to veer out over a kerb as he started his second lap. Nelson then confidently dealt with René Arnoux's Renault to score the second Grand Prix win of his career, following this up with an equally well-judged run in the first World Championship round to be held at Imola's *Autodromo Dino Ferrari*, a totally new chassis for that particular race proving ideally suited to the circuit. By lap four, having dealt with an early challenge from the two Renaults, Nelson had moved through into a lead he would never lose . . .

Piquet's success at Imola meant that he was still in with an outside chance of winning the World Championship: in fact, he went off to the final two races in North America nursing a one point lead over favourite Alan Jones. A sensational practice battle between these two leading contenders saw Nelson grab pole in Canada with a 1m 27.328s lap round the *Ile Notre Dame* circuit, edging out Jones's Williams to the tune of eight-tenths of a second. The prospects looked good for Piquet, but the start of the race exploded into chaos when Williams and Brabham touched going through the first ess-bend immediately after the start, triggering off a violent multi-car pile-up which caused the race to be stopped at the end of the opening lap.

Jones's Williams needed only a fresh engine cover and a replacement right rear wheel, but Piquet's BT49 had sustained a damaged steering arm in the *fracas*, so Nelson, who had banged his arm quite painfully against the side of the cockpit, was obliged to take over the spare car fitted with a demon development engine.

At the restart Jones and Didier Pironi's Ligier both got the jump on Piquet (the Frenchman rather too effectively, as it turned out, for he was docked a minute for a jumped start!), but the Brabham simply whistled past them both and was pulling away comfortably in the lead by the end of lap three. In the wake of Nelson's astounding performance at the head of the pack there were all manner of dark rumours about the Brabham's high-compression practice engine running on some specially brewed fuel or other, but on lap 25 Piquet's DFV suffered a major piston failure and that was the end of his Championship aspirations. Jones won the race and clinched the title, rounding off his season with another victory at Watkins Glen a week later where Piquet, running too hard a Goodyear compound, spun into the catch fencing whilst defending his second place from the advances of Carlos Reutemann's Williams. It was a disappointing end to the season for the talented Brazilian.

As he walked away from his blown-up Brabham at Montreal, Piquet put a brave face on his disappointment, making the very shrewd observation that winning the Championship would have been nice but it would not have made one penny piece of difference to the amount of money he could have squeezed out of Bernie Ecclestone in the form of a retainer for 1981. Never one to see a good deal slip through his fingers, the canny Ecclestone had obtained Nelson's signature on a three year contract at the start of the 1979 season, paying him what could only be seriously regarded as a "nominal" 50,000 dollars a year for the privilege. Of course, this was by no means the sum total of Nelson's income: prize money, bonuses, additional support from Parmalat and a good few thousand dollars for winning the much-touted Procar Championship at the wheel of a BMW M1 ensured that he didn't go hungry. "But if I win the Championship next year . . ." grinned Piquet with a sense of confident anticipation.

Hector Rebaque's arrival in the Brabham team had brought with it a co-sponsorship deal from Pemex, the Mexican national petroleum corporation, and so his inclusion in the team for 1981 was guaranteed. Hector's early Formula 1 outings had been at the wheel of an uncompetitive Hesketh 308E and he later graduated to privately-run Lotus 78s and 79s before he commissioned his own Cosworth-engined "79 lookalike" at the end of 1979. Most of the financial impetus behind his career came from his father, a wealthy Mexican businessman, but it was not until the summer of 1980 that the Pemex deal resulted in Hector replacing Zunino in that second BT49. Curiously, perhaps, once Ecclestone had ensured Piquet's continued future with the team he never seemed unduly anxious to obtain the services of a top-line driver for his second car, a trait he continued through until the end of 1981. He then had two years with Riccardo Patrese on the team before apparently reverting to his earlier philosophy for 1984 season. Without doubt, in 1981, the failure to provide Piquet with adequate support was to cost Brabham the Constructor's Championship.

However, by the end of the 1980 season, Ecclestone had more than enough to keep him busy in motor racing away from the day-to-day worries of running the Brabham team. After a couple of years' increasing tension, the problems which had been slowly fermenting between the sport's governing body (FISA) and the commercially influential Formula 1 Constructors' Association (FOCA) finally came exploding to the surface in a devastating volcano of acrimony and bitterness which briefly threatened to tear asunder the whole fabric of international Grand Prix racing.

The election of Jean-Marie Balestre to the FISA Presidency at the end of 1978 was partly responsible for triggering off this state of affairs. Balestre, a self-made French businessman, wealthy, with plenty of time on his hands, reckoned that FOCA had helped itself to a dangerously excessive amount of power in motor racing as a whole. He intended to ensure that "the sporting power" returned to Paris and FISA's base, where he reckoned it belonged. The FOCA fraternity, which flourished during a period when the sport's governing body subsided into little more than a figurehead organisation, rubber-stamping anything FOCA put in front of it, railed at the prospect of uninformed interference in what it considered a comfortable *status quo*. Balestre decided to fight first on the question of reducing lap speeds and cornering capabilities. That effectively meant legislating against ground effect, a move which would deprive the innovative British teams, reliant on clever chassis design and aerodynamics to make up for the Cosworth DFV's power deficiency, of their technical advantages.

In February 1980 an Extraordinary Meeting of the FISA Technical Committee banned skirts on Formula 1 cars as from the end of the season, citing "safety grounds" as the reason for this decision. FOCA, meanwhile, was arguing the case for a change of chassis dimensions and a limitation on turbocharged engines to be introduced from the start of 1981. The drivers, in the main, supported a ban on sliding skirts, although it has to be said that this was hardly an opinion which left them in agreement with their individual (FOCA) teams!

Finally, when several drivers failed to appear at the now-mandatory pre-race briefings at Zolder and Monaco, FISA suspended their licences until the resultant fines were paid. It became clear that many of the drivers had no intention at all of paying those fines and FOCA announced that, unless the fines were quashed, its members would not take part in the Spanish Grand Prix at Jarama in June 1. Worried sick that it would not have a race, the *Real Automovil Club de Espana* decided to go ahead with a race run under FIA, not FISA, regulations and so the event duly took place. This exercise in semantics was destined to fail. The major motor manufacturing teams (Alfa Romeo, Renault and Ferrari) clearly decided that they could not compromise their positions by participating in what was clearly a "pirate" event and withdrew their cars. The race went ahead, was won by Jones's Williams and, in due course, was retrospectively confirmed as *not* counting for the Championship.

By the end of the year the FOCA-aligned teams were supporting the idea of a 1981 World Championship run outside FISA rules by the enigmatically-titled "World Federation of Motor Sport", a so-called independent organisation set up to promote an 18 race series "which has the support of FOCA". By this stage in the proceedings, long-time tyre suppliers Goodyear had decided that it could no longer be involved and, at the end of the 1980 season, withdrew from Formula 1 and left Michelin a monopoly.

It was only ten days or so prior to the opening round of the 1981 World Championship that "peace" broke out between FISA and FOCA, by which time the FOCA-aligned teams had already run a non-Championship South African race at Kyalami to full 1980 sliding skirt rules. Nelson Piquet qualified in pole with a BT49, just ahead of Carlos Reutemann's Williams, but the roles were reversed in the race and the Argentinian cantered home a comfortable winner.

Gordon Murray had initially drawn the revised BT49C, a lighter, tidied-up version of the original car using more in the way of carbon fibre composite panels in its monocoque construction, as a sliding skirt car. But after Kyalami he had to revamp the design to accommodate fixed side skirts and the farcical 6cm ground clearance rule which was demanded by the new technical regulations. Many designers focussed their minds on this complex and irritating problem, but Murray and David North unquestionably came up with the best idea: it was also the one which caused a storm of protest and indignation amongst his rival designers . . .

They employed a system of soft air-springs which the aerodynamic load compressed as speed built up, dropping the BT49C down to a ground effective stance, and as the speed dropped away again as the car arrived in the pits, so the car would automatically rise up again to conform with the 6cm ground clearance rule. Nelson Piquet tested the system at Willow Springs shortly before the Long Beach race which opened the official 1981 Championship season, but the system still needed some development and he had to sit back in a lonely third place and watch another Jones-Reutemann Williams 1-2 in the United States Grand Prix West.

Murray got the system working properly in time for the Brazilian Grand Prix at Rio where Piquet rocketed round to take pole position with a 1m 35.079s ahead of Reutemann (1m 35.390s) and Jones (1m 36.377s). Amazingly, the Brabham team sluiced its chances down the drain when the incredible decision was taken to run Nelson on slicks in the pouring rain – believing that he would be in good shape if the weather dried out. It was a totally incomprehensible judgement which left Piquet floundering in 12th place, two laps behind Reutemann's winning Williams, at the chequered flag.

However, notwithstanding this disappointment, the Brabham team moved centre stage two weeks later for the Argentine Grand Prix at Buenos Aires. Nelson qualified on pole once again quite easily, his 1m 42.665s best for the 3.709 mile *Circuito No. 15* easing out Alain Prost's Renault turbo by 0.3s with Jones, Reutemann, René Arnoux's Renault RE20 and Hector Rebaque in the second BT49C next up in line.

Piquet ran away and hid when the race started, the outcome of the 53 lap contest never looking the slightest bit in doubt. But what really angered the opposition was the way in which Rebaque swept through to second place on lap 15, contemptuously despatching Carlos Reutemann's Williams in the process. That started the tongue-wagging in a big way! No chance, said the critics, that Hector Rebaque was in the same league as Carlos Reutemann. The Brabham must have been illegal. Rebaque's race came to an end with a distributor rotor arm failure on lap 33, so Reutemann was able to regain second place at the chequered flag. But there was no catching Piquet.

During practice Frank Williams had whipped up support for a protest against the Brabham, his contention at the time being that it was not so much the fact the Brabhams were running a clever hydro-pneumatic suspension system, but they were running *flexible* skirts, albeit not *sliding* skirts. In Williams' view these were specifically banned by the regulations. Gordon Murray retorted that he reckoned the Williams team was "simply being a bad loser", but the acrimony continued and would eventually get out of hand as the teams returned from South America for the start of the European season.

When the Brabhams ran in Buenos Aires they ran 3cm plastic skirts with a thicker block of the same material on the bottom edge for an additional degree of abrade resistance. This led many rival teams into experiments with a variety of other skirt materials, but, in truth, everybody was thrashing around in the dark until FISA produced one of its famous "rule clarifications" in which it insisted on the use of a single material throughout the "rigidly attached" skirt which could be no more than 6cm deep and have a uniform thickness of between 5cm and 6cm.

Although at the time Williams was extremely indignant about the Brabham team's performance at Buenos Aires, he has subsequently declined to publicly reiterate his feelings on a race result which, at the end of the day, cost Carlos Reutemann the World Championship for Drivers. Gordon Murray, however, has a lot to say on the matter and was absolutely incensed when, at the Belgian Grand Prix meeting, the FISA officials figuratively threw their hands in the air and allowed in cockpit switches in order to raise the lower the cars, his indignation reached fresh heights.

"I missed that race because of mumps . . .", he reflects on the Zolder "rule change", "and I reckon we were well stitched up by everybody who put a switch on their car. We threw away several races early in '81 while we spent a great deal of time developing our hydro-pneumatic system. There were tiny little valves in the hydraulic fluid system which often got blocked and, just as it was working properly, they said 'right, you can have a switch'. This aspect of Formula 1 designing drives me crackers . . . I mean, it's so frustrating when you've come up with a really good idea.

"When our system first appeared everybody said we had something illegal in the suspension. The next mob to come along said we had a hidden switch to pump it up: I think Ducarouge was leading that little lot. So I said, 'OK, come into the garage and inspect the car. Show me where this switch is'. But they wouldn't accept the invitation. Then bloody Zolder and the switches were allowed. Up until then there had been some hilarious test sessions with Williams and other people, with cars coming through the corners with either their back or front ends stuck up in the air as they tried to do it legally, just as we had done.

"Finally at Imola, after Williams had said that their skirts were rigid and ours

PEMEX
PEMEX
PEMEX
PEMEX
PEMEX
PEMEX
parmalat
Week

Back at Long Beach twelve months after his first Grand Prix victory, Nelson Piquet had to work hard at the wheel of the BT49C to finish third behind the Williams FW07Cs of Alan Jones and Carlos Reutemann.

were too flexible, everybody ganged up on us again and they sent the scrutineers round. They went 'flop, flop' with the skirts and said, 'yes, they're too flexible', so we said 'OK, you go and get us some material and we'll make skirts out of it'. They did that – I think they got it from Osella or somebody – we made the skirts, put them on the car and Nelson went out and won the race. I enjoyed that!"

The Belgian Grand Prix of 1981 will be recalled with sadness by most people who took part. Winner Carlos Reutemann was involved in a totally inadvertent pit lane accident which cost the life of an Osella mechanic during practice and a messed-up startline procedure saw Arrows chief mechanic Dave Luckett badly injured when he was savaged by Sigi Stohr's car as he attempted to start Riccardo Patrese's sister A3 on the grid. Piquet qualified his BT49C second between Reutemann and Didier Pironi's Ferrari 126 CK and then he was mixing it in with the leading bunch when, in his view, Alan Jones elbowed him off the road and out of the race.

This episode really fired up the Brazilian. "What the bloody hell did he think he was doing?" asked Nelson quizzically, "I don't see why he couldn't have come and apologized for that. If he comes near me again then, I can tell you, he's going to be off the track and that's all there is to it . . ." The needle match between the slightly built Piquet, not physically the fittest of men, and the hefty Jones with his ox-like physique, was set to rage for the remainder of the season.

The Monaco Grand Prix on May 31 saw Piquet's BT49C start once again from pole position alongside the brilliant Gilles Villeneuve's Ferrari 126CK, but the Brabham team again found itself enveloped in the swirling mists of controversy. This time its much-vexed question of lightweight – correction *underweight* – qualifying cars which was at issue. Brabham, along with several other teams had for several years been employing lightweight cars, stripped of all unnecessary ancillaries and often running with a tiny fuel tank, for qualifying purposes, but there were now strong rumours to the effect that Piquet's BT49Cs had been well *below* the minimum weight limit throughout 1981. It was well known that many Cosworth-engined cars were carrying ballast to sustain them above the minimum weight limit during the races, but this allegation was something altogether more serious.

At the end of the day it was the normally placid, easy-going Jacques Laffite who went off the deep end on the subject in an interview carried by the French sporting magazine *L'Equipe* during the Monaco Grand Prix weekend. Laffite contended, "Piquet has two cars, one ultra-light which he uses in practice, and then his race car which is to normal weight. A regular Brabham is already on the weight limit. Good for them. But the practice car has carbon fibre brake discs which save 12 kilos, and I'm told that the car also has a tiny fuel tank, much lighter than the normal one. The car should be weighed as soon as Piquet stops, before the mechanics can touch it. But no, no one will do anything because it's a Brabham, owned by Ecclestone. Nobody can touch him. Everybody is frightened of him."

Strong stuff, but treated with a fair degree of lofty disdain by the Brabham team as a whole and Gordon Murray in particular. "They checked our cars on the scales more often than anybody else in 1981," recalls Gordon, "It was supposed to be a lottery but we were checked so regularly that it was a standing joke amongst the mechanics that only cars number five and six were entered in that lottery, by the officials, in the first place."

None of this stopped the gossips, of course: in typical Formula 1 style, the rumours spread like wildfire. There were, wagged the tongues, three BT49C cockpit tops leaning up against the pit counter when a gust of wind sprang up: two of them (presumably the 'regular' ones) fell over, but one (presumably the 'weighted' one)stayed upright. The mechanics were said to have mounted a lead-filled rear wing onto the car before it was weighed . . . and so it went on. All good rip-roaring stuff, but none of it proven. Perhaps Ecclestone's colleagues were indeed afraid of him. Perhaps his success on the commercial side of Grand Prix racing had made them so rich and comfortable that they were prepared to mouth complaints without following them up with formal protests – which might upset

Piquet scratches round Jarama during the 1981 Spanish Grand Prix, a race which saw the Brazilian first collide with Mario Andretti's Alfa Romeo and then slide off the road into retirement.

the lucrative gravy train. Perhaps they couldn't prove it or perhaps, as Ecclestone rather thoughtfully remarked to the author in 1984, "people in glasshouses are not in a position to throw stones."

When the Monaco starting signal was finally given, Piquet was off like a jack rabbit in his race car, settling down ahead of the brilliant Villeneuve who was wrestling his ungainly Ferrari through the confined streets with typically deft brilliance. Eventually Alan Jones came scything through to challenge Piquet for the lead, harrying Nelson remorselessly into an error which saw the BT49C slide off into a guard rail. Jones managed to keep his laughter under control only to realize that, perhaps, he was not going to win Monaco after all. Fuel feed trouble intervened, he made a quick pit stop, the trouble persisted and Gilles picked him off cleanly with four laps to go to score a popular victory.

The Spanish Grand Prix at Jarama saw Piquet ram Mario Andretti's Alfa Romeo in a rather rash and ill-judged passing manoeuvre, both cars continuing until Nelson later flew off the road at a corner which had earlier claimed Alan Jones's Williams. For the French Grand Prix at Dijon-Prenois, both Williams and Brabham swapped back from Michelin to Goodyear now that Akron's senior management had undergone a change of heart. As far as the BT49C was concerned, the change involved Murray and Piquet in a fair deal of work to get the best out of the crossply Goodyears after spending the season thus-far on the French radials. Piquet did a good job qualifying fourth overall, but Arnoux, John Watson and Prost ahead of him were all on Michelins.

Problems with the starting lights caused some chaos on the grid, with nobody quite sure when they should be moving, but at the first hint of a "green", Piquet buried his right foot in the Brabham's front bulkhead and eased into a lead he

didn't look likely to lose. As the much-fancied Renaults were outdistanced, Piquet increasingly seemed to have the race in the bag – until, that is, a sudden downpour flooded the circuit and the red flag was shown at the end of lap 59.

This was where Piquet lost the race. The remaining scheduled 22 laps, making an 80 lap total, would be run when the weather settled down once again and Renault was then able to play its ace card. In 1980 Goodyear had enthusiastically subscribed to a "no qualifying tyre" regulation and, since the American firm's temporary retirement from Formula 1, the regrettable practice of using these super-soft covers had returned. Thus Michelin was able to slap soft tyres on Prost's Renault for the sprint to the chequered flag, confident that the RE30 wouldn't blister them on a light fuel load, while Piquet's Brabham had no such Goodyear luxury at hand. The practice of permitting cars to change tyres "between heats" rather than obliging them to do it during the race itself was ridiculous, yet legal, and changed the whole outcome of the '81 French Grand Prix. Prost was handed a lucky victory on a plate from Watson's similarly Michelin-shod McLaren MP4 while Piquet was left to trail home a disappointed third.

Hector Rebaque, meanwhile, had been enjoying an unspectacular season in the second BT49C, rarely looking any better than a midfield runner and never, since Buenos Aires, looking even remotely in Piquet's class. That trend continued throughout the British Grand Prix meeting at Silverstone on the weekend of July 16/18, a race at which the Brabham team might well have lost – or certainly seriously damaged – its number one driver, had it not been for the constructional integrity of the BT49C monocoque and a healthy slice of good fortune.

Hampered again by the lack of a super-soft Goodyear qualifier to match Michelin's best, Nelson none the less qualified brilliantly in third place behind the more powerful Renault turbos, a mere 0.9s off Arnoux's pole time. After the hectic early laps saw Gilles Villeneuve's famous spin out of the Woodcote chicane, and the resultant carnage that triggered off amongst the front runners, Nelson was left in second place, apparently the only contender who could keep tabs on Prost and Arnoux.

Problems with Goodyear rubber were destined to let Nelson down again in a big way. As he went into lap 12, he was still holding third place but had made up his mind that he would stop for fresh rubber at the end of the lap, the front tyres already losing some grip. But as he went through the fast left-hander Maggots Curve into the braking area for Becketts, the left front Goodyear literally flew apart and the BT49C spun into the barrier of vertical sleepers on the outside of the circuit. Nelson escaped with no more than a severe bruising to his left foot and subsequent examination of the BT49C monocoque revealed the inner walls to have remained undistorted by the impact. Even the team's most bitter rivals acknowledged that it was a good advertisement for Brabham . . .

Hector Rebaque underlined that simply by finishing one could pick up a worthwhile result, the Mexican bagging fifth place at Silverstone and then managing fourth at Hockenheim a fortnight later, a race won by his team leader. Turbo power was the crucial factor in qualifying with Prost taking pole position on 1m 47.50s, ahead of Arnoux, Reutemann, Jones, Pironi's Ferrari and Piquet (1m 49.03s). This was a race in which Piquet was to have lucky break after lucky break, although perhaps it didn't *seem* like that to Nelson at the time!

In the first corner scramble, Nelson damaged his left front nose wing against the right rear Michelin on Arnoux's Renault and the damaged lower surface of that wing flew back, partially blocking the oil cooler. This obstruction luckily became dislodged just as Nelson was thinking about a pit stop for attention and later the Brabham's left skirt was slightly damaged by some debris it hit on the track surface. Throughout all this apparent drama, grappling with unwanted understeer for much of the way, Nelson came through to score a more-than-fortunate triumph after both Williams had failed and Prost's Renault faded in second place. Carlos Reutemann now led the Championship with 43 pts to his credit, but Nelson, always on the pace, was beginning to feel lucky now that he had 35pts in the bag after Hockenheim.

Jones's bad luck at Monaco and Hockenheim, plus his driving error at Jarama, had robbed him of three convincing victories and his German disappointment now virtually wrote the reigning title holder out of the '81 Championship equation. From this point onwards the battle was between Reutemann and Piquet, a battle which would eventually be lost, at least in part, by the Argentinian psyching himself out when he should have capitalized on his points advantage and held Piquet at bay.

The Austrian Grand Prix saw Jacques Laffite pick up a popular win in his Michelin-shod Ligier-Matra and, with Piquet coming home third behind Arnoux and Reutemann fifth behind Jones, Nelson managed to narrow the gap yet again. At Zandvoort Piquet qualified third behind the Renaults and, by dint of looking after his Goodyears sympathetically, was in a position to grasp second place from Jones's Williams with four laps to go. Reutemann, in an amazingly unrealistic "inside dive" beneath Laffite's Ligier going into Tarzan, managed to eliminate both the Frenchman and his own Williams in one inexplicable moment.

With 45pts apiece, Piquet and Reutemann went into the Italian Grand Prix at Monza on September 13 in a determined frame of mind. The Williams driver managed to qualify alongside Prost's Renault RE30 on the front row with a stunning 1m 34.240s, leaving Nelson back on the third row on 1m 35.449s, flanked by Jones. Nelson had to make do with his Friday time after a nasty moment in the T-car on Saturday when the brake pedal went right down to the bulkhead as he slowed for the Ascari chicane. In sheer panic, Nelson came off the brakes and then slammed the pedal back down again: this time the rear tyres locked up and pirouetted the BT49C to a halt in the sandy run-off area. Detailed examination revealed that a small stone had found its way through a front brake cooling duct and jammed between the brake caliper and the wheel rim – whereupon it had cut through the wheel rim like a knife through butter!

In the 52 lap, 187.403 mile Grand Prix, Reutemann faded briefly to eighth during a mid-race rain shower, but came back to challenge Piquet from fourth place only for Nelson's engine to explode on the last lap! Reutemann thus picked up a helpful third place while Piquet was eventually classified sixth, taking a crucial Championship point despite his disappointment.

Two Grands Prix were now left to run: the Canadian at Montreal's *Ile Notre Dame* circuit, and the new Caesars Palace event at Las Vegas. Carlos had three points' advantage over Nelson at the start of the Canadian Grand Prix, during practice for which Nelson found himself ruthlessly "brake tested" by Arnoux's Renault. Furious, he demanded a partly-used rear from one of Rebaque's marked sets in order that he could go out and exact his revenge on the Frenchman. By that time, thankfully, Nelson had pole position in the bag, which was just as well under the circumstances. An eagle-eyed Reutemann had, not surprisingly perhaps, drawn officials' attention to the fact that car number five was using one marked tyre from car number six and Piquet's subsequent times were disallowed thanks to that little irregularity!

Streaming rain on race day spelled Michelin domination and it was Jacques Laffite's torquey Ligier-Matra V12 which emerged the victor, the Frenchman also making a late, though mathematically unlikely, challenge for the Championship title. Watson's McLaren was second ahead of Gilles Villeneuve's frayed Ferrari 126CK, Bruno Giacomelli's Alfa Romeo 179C and Piquet, the best of the Goodyear runners. Reutemann was floundering now, way out of contention in tenth place, three laps behind the winner.

Gordon Murray is emphatic that Nelson drove with true brilliance in that race, a fact which should be never underestimated. "He was sensational. Goodyear's race tyre compound was too hard, but Nelson finished fifth. I've never seen him so tired: I mean, there were burst blood vessels in his eyes, he'd been concentrating that much. And all this, I might remind you, in a race where Alan Jones gave up and Carlos Reutemann just went backwards down through the field from the word go. Hector came in no fewer than three times to tell me that it was slippery out there. I was getting a bit browned off with this by the time he stopped for the third

Three sleek BT49Cs ready for action in the spacious pit lane garage at Imola prior to the 1981 San Marino Grand Prix. Having manufactured new skirts from material provided by the organizers on the night before the race, Gordon Murray then derived enormous satisfaction from seeing Piquet go out and win convincingly. "I liked that", smiled the Brabham designer.

time and finally told him that if he couldn't race then at least he could go out and get in the way! But, really, Nelson was terrific . . . that race put him in the mood for Las Vegas . . ."

The convoluted 2.268 mile car park circuit behind the World-famous Caesars Palace hotel complex in arid Las Vegas might seem an unlikely venue at which to decide the outcome of a Grand Prix World Championship, but there is no underestimating the commercial idiosyncracies of this multi-million dollar sport which is motor racing! The blistering and unstinting heat gave rise to familiar, Buenos Aires-like conditions for Carlos Reutemann and the Argentinian stunned everybody's senses by taking pole position in 1m 17.821s, fractionally quicker than team mate Jones, with Villeneuve third and Piquet fourth. It was clearly going to be a dramatic title-clincher, but the race itself was something of an anti-climax. Jones walked away convincingly, writing *finis* to a glowing Grand Prix career – or so we thought at the time. Reutemann, puzzled by an apparent handling imbalance on the warm-up lap, drove with astonishing docility and, in the words of an amazed Nelson Piquet, "braked early to let me pass when I came up behind him. He made it so easy for me I couldn't believe it . . ."

Disheartened and off-the-pace, Reutemann dropped to a pathetic eighth while Piquet, suffering increasingly from heat exhaustion in the closing stages of the race, found himself driving on reflexes, in a heady daze, for the last few miles. Completely consumed by the sweltering conditions and on the verge of collapse, he just managed to survive long enough to bring the BT49C across the line in fifth place. Those two crucial points were enough to tip the Championship contest in his

parmalat
parmalat
5
parmalat
BRABHAM

In what Gordon Murray rates as one of Nelson Piquet's great drives, the Brazilian splashes towards a crucially important fifth place in the 1981 Canadian Grand Prix at Montreal to keep his Championship hopes very much alive. His Brabham's Goodyear wet weather tyres were no match for his Michelin-shod rivals in these diabolical conditions, but Piquet was the first Goodyear car to finish on this occasion, totally exhausted with the effort and concentration involved. Here he surfs through the murk ahead of one of the Renault RE30s.

direction by a single point. But he had to be lifted, semi-conscious, from the Brabham's cockpit when it was all over.

Nelson acknowledged that there was still a question mark over his physical fitness at the end of the 1981 season: "I admit I don't train, but I don't smoke or drink and I get lots of sleep." Perhaps, in the age of rock-hard suspension systems, that did not add up to sufficient self-discipline on the part of the new World Champion.

Gordon Murray was more generous. "In the last few races of the '81 season he became more relaxed and confident than I'd ever seen him before. At Zandvoort he played it cool, really looking after his tyres. At Monza he went hard in the rain shower, knowing that Reutemann would ease up, and he was brilliant at Montreal. Finally, at Las Vegas, he did *precisely* what was required of him. In terms of talent and promise, I think he'll go on and on improving, peaking out in about two year's time. And by then, he'll be very, very good."

Although Brabham propelled Piquet to that first World Championship with Cosworth DFV power, the days of normally aspirated engines were fast disappearing in the Formula 1 firmament. The prototype Brabham BT50-BMW had taken everybody's breath away with its straight line speed during a fleeting public appearance during practice for the '81 British Grand Prix at Silverstone and, as you can read in the next chapter, most of the new World Champion's time over the winter '81/'82 was concentrated on the painstaking development of this new concept. But, as events were to prove, there was life in the old BT49 yet . . .

The 1982 season opened on January 23 with the South African Grand Prix at Kyalami where a much-publicised drivers' strike took the edge off proceedings in a big way. The Brabham BT50-BMWs made their race debut at this event, hoping to capitalize on the high altitude which had worked to the Renault's turbo advantage quite regularly in the past. The race was a fiasco for Brabham, as will be recounted later, and the team fielded its latest BT49 variants for the Brazilian Grand Prix at Rio on March 21.

Further lightened, employing carbon fibre brake discs and one-piece bodywork, the BT49Ds were now well under the 580kg minimum weight limit in un-ballasted form, a distinction they shared with several other Cosworth-engined cars from rival top teams. The addition of water-cooled braking systems, with a large water tank, brought the cars up to the weight limit again – when that tank was full. During the course of the race, it was accepted that the weight fell below the 580kg limit, but, when topped up after the race, the cars would be legal. Gordon Murray and his fellow designers of like-mind considered this to be a perfectly legitimate interpretation of Article 1, section 8, of the Definitions of Single Seater Racing Cars which stated: "Weight: Is the weight of the car in running order with its normal quantity of lubricants and coolants but without any fuel or driver on board".

Quite naturally, Ferrari and Renault saw this as a means of circumventing the rules. They contended this water was nothing more than ballast and doubted whether any of the reservoirs were intended to be full at the start of the race. Murray and his colleagues pointed out that it had been standard practice to top up oil tanks after the race in order that cars should top the minimum weight, so why, if that was acceptable, did they object to this procedure? Because, replied Renault and Ferrari, it is the blatant misuse of a rule the meaning of which we all understand. "You could say that about turbocharged engines," replied the water tank faction. And so the debate continued.

After the nonsensical farce of the 6cm ground clearance regulation in 1981, the technical rules permitted fixed side skirts for 1982, but in order to make them work as effectively as possible, a by-product proved to be the development of rock-hard suspensions which transformed the current breed of Formula 1 car into a high-powered, excruciatingly uncomfortable, difficult-to-control go kart.

Despite all the controversy over the Cosworth cars' water tanks, turbo power buttoned up the front row at Rio with Alain Prost's Renault RE30B snatching pole with a 1m 28.808s ahead of Gilles Villeneuve's Ferrari C2 (1m 29.173s). On the second row was Keke Rosberg's Williams FW07C ahead of René Arnoux's

Renault RE30B (1m 30.121s), Niki Lauda's McLaren MP4 (1m 30.152s), Carlos Reutemann's Williams FW07C (1m 30.183s) and Piquet's Brabham BT49D (1m 30.281s). Nelson had initially been troubled by lack of downforce, and consequent low tyre temperatures, but Gordon Murray had sorted out that problem before retiring to bed on Sunday morning with a touch of the "Aztec two-step" following a helping of rather suspect Brazilian mushrooms the previous night!

At the start Villeneuve accelerated straight into an immediate lead with the Ferrari C2, and the dogged French Canadian driver settled down in command at the head of the field, fending off a succession of attacks from different rivals. Eventually, as both Renaults faded, the battle for the lead of the Brazilian Grand Prix turned into a three-way contest between the Ferrari, Piquet's Brabham and Rosberg's Williams, the Finn relishing his new-found competitiveness since his switch to the FW07C's cockpit at the start of the year. Rosberg briefly showed in second place, but as the race eased towards the halfway mark, it was becoming clear that Piquet's efforts were holding the bulk of Villeneuve's attentions.

In reality, Gilles was fighting a losing battle, his incredible reflexes and masterly touch holding the heavy Ferrari turbo ahead of the feather-weight Brabham. Mid-way round lap 30 Nelson was closer than ever as they ran round the fast right-hander which immediately precedes the left-hand hairpin out onto Rio's long back straight. Gilles ran wide, got onto the marbles and the blue and white Brabham edged level with his Ferrari. Braking later than ever, Gilles simply couldn't hold it, slithered spinning across Nelson's bows and went punting off backwards into the guard rail.

That left Nelson an apparently clear run to an easy victory, but things were not to be quite as clear-cut as that. Exhausted by the torrid conditions, even with 30 laps to run, Piquet's head could be seen lolling to one side in the cockpit, the Brazilian pummelled into submission by the stiff, unyielding suspension and the airless heat. On lap 34 team mate Riccardo Patrese spun his BT49D, waltzing drunkenly back into the circuit in another half loop: he crawled round to the pits and gave up. He was shattered, completely done in. Helped from the car, the Italian slumped in the back of the Brabham garage, unable to move . . .

With Rosberg's tyres past their best, Nelson was able to ease home to a relatively unchallenged victory, but he was to collapse on the winner's rostrum after it was all over. Meanwhile, as Gordon Murray staggered to the airport to catch his Concorde back to Europe, still nursing a dangerously volatile digestive system, Ferrari and Renault protested the first two cars home. The stewards rejected the protest, but a FISA appeals tribunal, sitting on April 19, upheld their appeal, decreeing that at all times during the race the cars should conform to the 580kg minimum weight ruling. From that point onwards, all hell would let loose . . .

The 75.5 lap, 160.81 mile Long Beach race on April 4 saw Patrese damage his BT49D beyond immediate repair during practice, ripping a front wishbone out of the monocoque in an impact with one of the concrete walls which surround the circuit. Riccardo was thus obliged to use the team's spare BT49C in which he hurried home fourth on the road after a spin, then third following the disqualification of Villeneuve's Ferrari for a rear aerofoil dimension infringement. Piquet hit the wall on lap 22, so that was the end of the World Champion's business.

The first European round of the Championship was scheduled to take place at Imola on April 25, but, in the wake of a crushing FIA Appeal Tribunal decision *not* to allow the water tank principle, the FOCA-aligned teams held a meeting in London on the Wednesday preceding the race where they voted not to attend. This decision by the FIA lost the FOCA teams their weight-saving loophole in the regulations and was a major factor in ushering in the era of the turbocharged Formula 1 engine, even quicker than it would have otherwise arrived.

Even to this day, Gordon Murray smarts under the penalty of disqualification at Rio in 1982. "There are some things you accept, some things you just smile over, but that is one race which we at Brabham rightly count as a totally justified victory. They used the rule clarification excuse to *change* a rule and make a new one." This

Wasted effort. Nelson Piquet's determined efforts to win the 1982 Brazilian Grand Prix at the wheel of his BT49D (above) were initially almost ruined by heat exhaustion which caused him to collapse on the podium after beating Keke Rosberg and Alain Prost into second and third places. The lower sequence of photographs show his two rivals first supporting him, then helping him back to his feet. His efforts were all in vain, as were Rosberg's, as the Brabham and Williams were subsequently disqualified in the famous water tank controversy, leaving victory to Prost's Renault.

Valvoline
malat

AIR FRANCE
cargo
Beba
3

Beba
Coca-Cola
AIR FRANCE
cargo
1

Mexican Hector Rebaque supplanted Riccardo Zunino as Piquet's number two for the second half of 1980 and the entire 1981 season. He brought along sponsorship from the Mexican national petrol consortium Pemex, but was never a match for his Brazilian colleague. Here he presses on towards fifth place in the 1981 British Grand Prix at Silverstone.

Imola boycott, however, was a major trial of strength between the sport's governing body and the influential FOCA lobby, the cause of which was tirelessly championed by Ecclestone. Irrespective of the rights and wrongs of the situation, FOCA lost and some people argue that the organisation has never been as powerful and influential again. However, Bernie's decision to align his team with BMW put him in a "heads-I-win, tails-you-lose" situation. The prevailing straws in the wind indicated an irrevocable trend towards turbo power and, as we will see in the following chapter, Brabham was in a very strong position indeed.

After the Kyalami *débâcle* BMW started to get a bit het up over Ecclestone's apparent reluctance to run the turbos, threatening him with a big stick that he ought to get on and run them in line with the terms of their agreement. Thus, for the Belgian Grand Prix at Zolder, Ecclestone demurred with little debate: anybody who saw him in the Brabham garage mid-way through Zolder practice, his face a picture of resigned disbelief, amidst what looked like a couple of dozen BMW turbos in varying stages of disassembly all over the floor, might well have questioned the wisdom of BMW's insistence!

In a weekend overshadowed by the tragic death of Gilles Villeneuve during practice, and the resultant withdrawal of the Ferrari team, Piquet struggled home sixth after a spin with the BT50. Patrese, also in a BMW-engined car, spun off for good after 52 laps. It was not an auspicious performance and one which definitely lent credence to those who argued that the BMW engine was not yet ready for battle . . .

One of those who never doubted that the BMW route was the correct one to take was Nelson Piquet, but even the World Champion must have thought twice when he saw team mate Patrese plant the Cosworth-engined BT49D on the front row of the grid at Monaco, half a second behind René Arnoux's pole-winning Renault.

Piquet languished in 12th place with the temperamental BT50, retiring in the race after 50 laps with gearbox problems.

Patrese, meanwhile, was never out of the top four, and when a gentle rain shower tipped Alain Prost's leading Renault into a spectacular accident coming out of the harbour front chicane with only four of the race's 76 laps left to run, it seemed certain that Riccardo would cruise home to his first Grand Prix triumph. Yet, with a lap-and-a-half to go, the BT49D spun on the now-glistening track surface going into the Loews hairpin – and Didier Pironi's Ferrari C2 slithered past, now apparently set for a fine victory. Patrese's impetuosity, yet again, had robbed him of success . . .

After being pushed out of the line of fire by marshals, the Italian trickled downhill and bump-started the Brabham without any further outside assistance, mercifully for him, as it turned out. Pironi's Ferrari gasped to a halt with electrical trouble on the very last lap, so Patrese was given a rare, second bite of the cherry, carefully negotiating the last mile or so to win the most action-packed, remarkable Monaco Grand Prix in recent memory.

That, effectively, marked the end of the BT49 series competition history, this unexpected victory almost, but not-quite, closing its list of achievements in the Brabham record book. Yet to come was a stupid accident at Detroit, Patrese nosing his BT49D into the tyre barriers after a quite absurd overtaking manoeuvre early in the race. Red hot brake discs briefly set fire to their cooling ducts, the marshals stampeding into a violent over-reaction, thinking the car was about to explode in flames, and race was red-flagged. Not that a second start would have helped Nelson Piquet – he failed to qualify in the BT50-BMW!

Finally, with little more than the glow of the BT49D's carbon fibre brake discs lighting up a dark Montreal evening as Patrese hurtled into the braking area for the pits hairpin at the newly-titled *Circuit Gilles Villeneuve*, the Brabham-Cosworth DFV story finally came to an end a week later. Ricardo drove with tremendous verve to finish second in the Canadian Grand Prix, even closing slightly on the winner towards the end, but it was not a performance guaranteed to win a further reprieve for the last of the Brabham-Cosworths.

Because, you see, the winner was that hitherto-troublesome Brabham BT50. *With* its BMW engine. *Without* missing a beat!

parmalat

Section 2: The Ecclestone era

Chapter 5
The Brabham-BMW turbos

BMW breakthrough: Nelson's BT50 on its way to victory in the 1982 Canadian Grand Prix, seen here against the backdrop of the Montreal skyline.

It was two o'clock in the morning of Monday, June 14, 1982 when BMW Sales Director Hans-Erdmann Schoenbeck awoke to the tinkle of the telephone at his home in one of Munich's smart suburbs. Fumbling for the receiver, he eventually lifted it to his ear, somewhat irritated at having been woken at this unsocial hour. Recognising the voice at the end of the line he listened quietly for a few seconds before sitting bolt upright with a mixture of sudden surprise and elation.

"Say that again slowly," he intoned. More than three thousand miles away in Montreal, he heard BMW Motorsport Competitions boss Dieter Stappert's excited chatter. "Herr Schoenbeck! Our engine has just won the Canadian Grand Prix!"

This was a motor racing milestone of incalculable significance not only to the German engine manufacturer, but also Ecclestone's Brabham team which had nailed its colours to the BMW mast almost two years earlier. What's more, it was realized by only a few onlookers close to both Brabham and BMW that the marriage between Munich and Chessington had been no bed of roses by any stretch of the imagination. There had been times over the previous year when divorce seemed to be staring both firms in the face and the bespectacled Stappert, a gentle, pleasant man who had abandoned a career as one of Europe's most influential and informed motoring journalists to join BMW's Competitions Department some five years earlier, appeared to be under constant pressure from both parties to the engine supply agreement. There were times, frankly, when he looked like the meat in an uncompromising sandwich with a sometimes cynical, sarcastic Ecclestone and a bemused BMW board providing the bread which squeezed him hard from both directions.

The Brabham-BMW Grand Prix partnership represented the culmination of the German firm's sporting renaissance which had originally got under way in the late sixties and early seventies. In the late 1950s, BMW had almost sunk without trace as a car manufacturing company, tottering back from the financial brink with a range of square-cut four-cylinder saloons starting with the 1500. That machine's early racing activities spawned a generation of high-powered competition saloons which projected the blue and white BMW aircraft propellor *motif* to the forefront of European Touring Car Championship success, transforming the marque's image and aiding its hard slog back to profitability.

By 1969 the four-cylinder 1500 c.c. engine had grown to 2-litres and, running on fuel injection, was approaching the 100bhp-per-litre level. By this time the firm's chief of power unit development, veteran silver-haired Alex von Falkenhausen, was pushing hard for an expansion of the BMW competitions programme. He had no intention of resting on the laurels already gathered in and his enthusiasm was heightened when his strikingly attractive daughter, Juliane, married Austrian touring car ace Dieter Quester. The Viennese had won the 1968 European Touring Car Championship at the wheel of a fuel-injected 2002, the first of four such titles he would take in the cars from Munich – the last being as late as 1983, when, at the age of 44 years, he took the title in a Schnitzer-prepared 635CSi.

Incidentally, it should be explained that Falkenhausen had already been involved in one Brabham-BMW partnership, albeit informally, long before

Ecclestone bought Motor Racing Developments or Stappert even began his career with the Swiss magazine *Powerslide*. The ex-works BT11 which Dan Gurney had driven, with Climax V8 power, to the marque's first Grand Prix victory at Rouen back in 1964 was acquired, less engine, by BMW after the 1½-litre Formula 1 expired at the end of the 1965 season.

Fitted with a 310bhp carburettor version of the 2-litre BMW engine, equipped with a radially disposed four-valves per cylinder head developed for the company by freelance designer Ludwig Apfelbeck, this Brabham-BMW was used extensively for test and development work. It was also taken to Hockenheim on September 22, 1966, for a successful assault on the half-mile and 500 metres World records, von Falkenhausen hunched in the cockpit for this particular performance!

Returning, however, to the contemporary Brabham-BMW alliance, Stappert recalls in vivid detail how the whole project originally started – and how it was almost lost for good in a proposed sale to Talbot!

"I joined BMW on July 13, 1977," grins Stappert reflectively, "I remember this date very well. Everything of real significance always seemed to happen on the 13th of the month. I joined on the 13th, we ran our Formula 1 engine for the first time on October 13, 1980, which happened to be my birthday, and we won that first race in Montreal on June 13, 1982.

"I originally joined BMW as Jochen Neerpasch's personal assistant. I was having huge problems as a journalist and had got really fed up. In 1975 I'd received an offer to join BMW, but I'd chosen to hang in there with the paper. Then my son was born prematurely and only just survived. That made me think that I must change my life style. I was only writing to be finished . . . I could never bring myself to read my own stuff. Neerpasch told me to keep in touch and, when I was ill in hospital on one occasion, I decided 'right, this is it.' I rang him and told him that I was available if he wanted me. So I joined BMW as his assistant working, at least partly, with the BMW 'Junior team'. I joined the day after the big Norisring shunt when Surer took off Heyer and lost his licence for two months.

"This was a quite incredible week, because after what happened at Norisring, Neerpasch wouldn't allow the juniors to race the following weekend, so we produced the BMW 'Gentlemans' team' for the race at Diepholz, entering Hans Stuck, Ronnie Peterson and David Hobbs. But they turned out to be far worse than the youngsters and the weekend ended up with bent motor cars, all the drivers shouting at each other, but Neerpasch couldn't really say very much because we won the race."

In 1979 Stappert was heavily involved in the Pro-Car series, where BMW M1 coupes were used in a programme of supporting events at several prestigious European Grands Prix. But, away from the rough and tumble excitement of this particular programme, other developments were simmering away behind the scenes.

"In the 2-litre class of the German championship, you needed a 1.4-litre turbo if you were going to be truly competitive. Schnitzer produced his own 1.4-litre turbo which was quick and competitive for as long as it stayed together, running against the factory's 2-litre-engined 320s. Neerpasch wanted to do something similar at the works, but we didn't have the capacity at BMW Motorsport. But McLaren Engines in Livonia, near Detroit, were running our IMSA programme with 2.1-litre turbocharged 320s. So, one day, Neerpasch said, well why don't we do a 1.4-litre for development purposes? So we did . . . and then we did a 1.5-litre which looked even better. And all this was happening around the time that Renault won its first Grand Prix with a turbo . . ."

At this point, an amazing sequence of events unfolded about which, even today, Stappert is unwilling to elaborate. A deal was done that McLaren should run a Marlboro-backed, BMW turbo-engine car for Lauda in 1980. Browned off by the wide performance disparity amongst the Alfa Romeo V12s, and a little concerned that Nelson Piquet was starting to get the better of him on a regular basis, Niki wanted to leave Ecclestone's team. But the McLaren-BMW deal never got off the ground, so the rumours said at the time. Or did it?

The reality was quite different. The team was fixed up, the driver was fixed up and the deal all ready to be activated. All that was needed was the approval of the BMW board for a McLaren-BMW to be racing throughout the 1980 World Championship season. But Neerpasch had bitten off a bit more than he could chew and the BMW board became wary of his approach. He had already been to see Lauda, got his provisional agreement for the deal and then, with misjudged optimism, attempted to present the whole project to the Board as a *fait accompli*.

Neerpasch, by this stage, already had a few directors gunning for him because of the expense of the BMW racing programmes as a whole. He had enemies at board room level. Neerpasch had put them into a position where they could only say 'yes' or 'no' to his proposed Grand Prix plans. With no apparent room to manoeuvre, the Board had no choice but to reject his suggestion. His policy of engineering such situations from which it was difficult to back out had blown up in his face. The BMW Board felt obliged to get the point home to Neerpasch that *they* were the people who decide, not him. It was one of the darkest days of his life and, arguably, the beginning of the end of his BMW career.

This would, unquestionably, have been a project to hold Niki Lauda's interest. Without it, he soon retired, abruptly leaving the Brabham team mid-way through that memorable Montreal practice session. But there was a fascinating tailpiece to this whole espisode. Lauda appeared shortly afterwards with Stappert on German television and made what amounted to a thinly-veiled plea to BMW, tempting them to think again. But there was no way; it was the end of the marque's Formula 1 plans. For the moment, at least . . .

By the end of November 1979, Stappert began to suspect that Neerpasch might be making plans to move on. "I was looking for a new flat at the time," Dieter recalls, "and Jochen knew this very well. One day I met him at the competitions department and he asked me 'have you found a new flat?' I told him I had, adding 'why? Don't you think I'll need it?' But he wouldn't say a thing. He told me he would tell me what was on his mind the following day. I said 'no way, you tell me *now*', so we went up to his office and told me he was leaving BMW to join Talbot. He asked me whether I would come along with him as his assistant or, if I wanted to stay with BMW, he would propose me to take over his job as Competitions Manager."

Stappert asked him for a day to think it over. "But I didn't have to think about it for very long. I couldn't really see myself working in France, not knowing the language, but to take over Neerpasch's position would be an incredible challenge.

"The next day I was in the BMW head office building where I knew Neerpasch was talking to Schoenbeck. I was down on the ground floor when Schoenbeck's secretary rang through and asked me to come up to his office. I went up immediately, curious to hear what was going to happen. Neerpasch greeted me and explained 'I have to tell you now that I'm leaving to go to Talbot and Herr Schoenbeck has accepted my suggestion that you take over my post since you've told me you would rather stay here at BMW.' "

Then Neerpasch dropped a bombshell into the conversation with a revelation which almost made Stappert rock on his heels. "I'm going off to Talbot and taking the Formula 1 engine with me . . ." Stappert, aghast, replied "*what* Formula 1 engine?" Neerpasch continued, "Yes, BMW is going to develop a Formula 1 engine for Talbot." Stappert almost forgot himself. "*No way;*" he replied with tremendous forcefulness.

Stappert was resolutely opposed to the idea of selling any proposed BMW Formula 1 engine project to anybody and moved into top gear in his efforts to retrieve the situation. "It was explained to me that the deal was already done between BMW and Talbot, but I investigated this further and tried to discover what the basic arrangement really was. Eventually I found out that, although they had started talking and negotiating the contractual terms, there was not even as much as a letter of intent on the files. The engine wasn't built by this stage, so I hurriedly got involved in consultations with our engineer, Paul Rosche, and tried to persuade the board not to sell it to Talbot. I wanted the company to keep the

The first Brabham-BMW! Alex von Falkenhausen easing out to the circuit at Hockenheim prior to setting two new World records on September 22, 1966. The car is the BT7 used by Dan Gurney to win the 1964 French Grand Prix at Rouen, the engine a 2-litre unit developed by Ludwig Apfelbeck.

engine design, develop it properly and find a partner with whom to enter Grand Prix racing. It was a major problem persuading the board that BMW, a large motor manufacturer, should enter Grand Prix racing. We debated it, argued, and finally persuaded them that we should be identified in a top-line international sport such as this."

On April 24, 1980, the decision was announced that BMW would be building and supplying engines for Formula 1. Stappert's long battle had been won at last, although there would be plenty more aggravation waiting down the road before the German company's Grand Prix engine would eventually vindicate itself in terms of hard results. Interestingly, Stappert says that BMW "didn't even consider international rallying. Even by then you could see that, long term, you would need a specialized car with four-wheel-drive and a turbocharged engine and that was clearly going to be very expensive and difficult." Later, during the summer of 1984, Stappert would express his view to the author that BMW's Grand Prix programme had cost significantly *less* than Audi's Quattro rally programme – and that the Munich company had reaped a more worthwhile return on its investment. Cynics would doubtless observe that he was hardly likely to take any other point of view!

The marriage between Brabham and BMW, forged during the summer of 1980, could hardly have been more mutually convenient. Notwithstanding the fierce, almost passionate, rearguard action being fought by the FOCA-aligned teams to protect the outdated Cosworth DFV's pre-eminence, there was no stemming the irresistible turbo tide. Renault had breached the DFV's defences with that historic first win in the 1979 French Grand Prix and Ferrari was all ready with a brand new engine. In fact, anybody who couldn't see the turbo writing on the wall was not really thinking straight.

Bernie Ecclestone, from the FOCA driving seat, could see quite clearly *precisely* how things were likely to develop. He did the deal with BMW in order to have a turbocharged contender in his team's armoury, although both he and Gordon Murray were happy to play every card in the Cosworth deck before giving up the normally aspirated route. In the summer of 1980 there was a *lot* of life left in the BT49-Cosworth recipe. But it was just as well to have the BMW project gently simmering away in the background.

As for Stappert, his enthusiasm for a link with Brabham was based on very straightforward and practical grounds. "Firstly, it was clearly a well-financed, high-technology team. Secondly, Gordon Murray is one of the very best designers. Thirdly, Nelson Piquet is one of the very best drivers and I had already built up a good relationship with him during the Pro-Car days in 1979. Nelson and Niki Lauda were the only drivers who would be present with their overalls and helmets, all ready to go, when Pro-Car practice was scheduled to start. They were the only people I didn't have to chase all round the paddock . . ."

Stappert then added thoughtfully, "Of course, then there was Bernie! FOCA generally didn't like turbocharged engines, so by going with Bernie we were clearly going to be in good shape . . . signalling, perhaps, that after a certain amount of time, we might be in a position to make the engines available to other teams."

The man behind the development of BMW's four-cylinder, turbocharged Grand Prix engine was a big, beaming Bavarian who had first joined the company back in 1957. Paul Rosche initially worked as a designer in the BMW engine development department on road cars, although it didn't take long for him to get involved in the increasing amount of competition work which mushroomed in the late 1960s. Later, he was to become better known as the technical architect behind the great BMW victories in Formula 2 throughout the 1970s, when the four-cylinder engines from Munich powered Jean-Pierre Jarier, Patrick Depailler, Jacques Laffite, Bruno Giacomelli and Marc Surer to a succession of European championship titles.

Rosche became General Manager of BMW Motorsport, at Neerpasch's invitation, in 1975 and he has presided over the competition engine development ever since. Stappert makes it clear that there was never any question of the BMW Formula 1 engine ever being anything else but a production-based in-line four-cylinder unit. "It had to be that from the word go. We never thought about anything else, bearing in mind all the experience we had accumulated with the various four-cylinder engines up to that time." It was also very important, from the promotional point of view, that BMW's Grand Prix involvement was seen to stem from an essentially production-based engine.

All the development work carried out by McLaren Engines, plus the experience BMW had amassed from turbocharged touring car engines on this side of the Atlantic, gave Rosche an enormous amount of data and accumulated expertise on which to draw. He was thus able to take the first confident steps forward on the Grand Prix engine project during 1980, the unit designated M12/13, indicating that it was the 13th version of the original M12 engine design.

It did not take long for the BMW Motorsport engineers to discover that the standard production blocks performed at their best when they were two or three years old, perhaps with as much as 100,000 road kilometres to their credit. Apparently the mileage and ageing helped remove inherent tensions and stresses from the blocks, but apart from the fact that about 5kg of superfluous metal was machined away (such as stiffening ribs and water channels on the inlet side), they remained unmodified blocks.

The twin overhead camshaft, four valves-per-cylinder engine had a bore and stroke of 89.2 x 60mm, officially rated at 1499cc by BMW. The steel crankshaft ran in five main bearings and short, forged alloy Mahle pistons with very rugged titanium connecting rods were employed to withstand the much higher loadings to which they would be subjected. With a 6.7:1 compression ratio, the M12/13 output was originally claimed as 557 bhp at 9500rpm, forced induction being supplied by a single KKK (Kùhlne, Kopp and Kausch) turbocharger mounted low on the left-hand side of the engine. The injection system employed a Bosch electric high-pressure pump for starting and then a Lucas mechanical pump, mounted on the inlet camshaft and driven directly by the camshaft gear. The fuel metering unit is based on a Kugelfischer design, developed by Bosch to be adapted for use with

Winning trio. Nelson Piquet sits strapped in the BT50 cockpit during practice at Kyalami in 1982, flanked by Gordon Murray (with John Lennon spectacles) and a prosperous looking Paul Rosche, BMW Motorsport's engine development wizard.

digital electronics.

In order that the new BMW Formula 1 engine could be tested, Gordon Murray had a BT49 chassis hacked about to accommodate the turbocharger intercooler in a left-hand side-pod (the water radiator balancing it up on the opposite side of the car) and this "BT49T" test car was used throughout the winter of 1980/81 in a long, sometimes troubled series of development runs. By the start of the 1981 season there was still no word as to when the BMW-engined car would make its competition debut, but eventually Murray finalized his BT50 design and the car appeared in public during practice for the 1981 British Grand Prix at Silverstone.

Bearing a continuing family resemblance to Murray's contemporary Cosworth-engined cars, the BT50 shared basically the same monocoque as the successful BT49C, employing double wishbone suspension all round with pullrod activation of the semi-inboard coil spring/damper units. Its most distinctive difference was a tall fuel cell, containing 48 gallons rather than the BT49C's maximum 38, shrouded with gently curving rear bodywork. At 108 in, the BT50's wheelbase was a mere inch longer than its stablemate, but it retained the same 68in/64in front/rear track dimensions. At 590kg, officially it was only 10kg heavier than the BT49C, although everybody knew full-well by that stage that the Cosworth car was capable of being prepared in much lighter trim than the minimum weight limit of 580kg.

Although only used briefly by Piquet, the BT50's straight-line speed was recorded at just over 190mph, even though its overall lap time was quite modest – a 1m 12.60s as compared with Piquet's 1m 11.952s best in the BT49C. For some of the time it was out on the circuit, the BT50 circulated with a tall aerial extending from just behind its rollover bar. The engine was fitted with a telemetry system which sent radio signals to an unobtrusive little Mercedes-Benz van which was situated behind the Brabham pit. Inside the van BMW engineers were monitoring charge air and engine temperatures, turbocharger boost pressure and the functioning of the electronic ignition and fuel injection systems. The Brabham-BMW race debut might well have been the best part of six months away, but the Munich company was gathering as much data as it possibly could to ensure that the M12/13 would acquit itself respectably when the time finally came.

However, developing a reliable and competitive turbocharged Formula 1 engine was a long, involved and often painful task. Over the winter of 1981/82, Stappert recalls a demoralizing two weeks spent in the bleak, lonely surroundings of Paul Ricard, during which BMW engines were popping left right and centre like Christmas crackers. The programme was even getting on the normally even-tempered Gordon Murray's nerves, but the one person who never wavered in his commitment to the new engine was Nelson Piquet. Newly crowned as World Champion, the Brazilian could appreciate that the turbocharged route was the *only* route forward, so, no matter how much short-term frustration awaited the team, it was something that simply had to be endured for the long-term good.

This attitude made a big impression on Stappert and strengthened the personal friendship between the two men, for BMW's Motorsport chief was clearly under a fair deal of pressure from his Board of Directors. It was often difficult to explain the day-to-day technical problems of Grand Prix racing to the smart-suited, essentially conservative businessmen on the upper floors of the distinctive, cylindrical BMW headquarters building in Munich. Stappert needed all the moral support he could get!

Dieter recalls that test session vividly. "We were down there at Paul Ricard and Patrese had just been signed up from Arrows. He was going round and round in the BT49C-Cosworth, setting new lap records all the time, followed by dozens of Italian press men who were trumpeting about renaming the circuit 'Paul Riccardo', all that sort of hysterical stuff. But Nelson, who had just won the Championship, never once thought about getting into the Cosworth car even though there was one standing in the next garage. He wasn't interested. He was always optimistic about the turbo and never wavered in his support . . . even though, at one point, Paul Rosche and I felt like going down to Marseilles harbour, climbing aboard a sailing boat and vanishing for good!"

Notwithstanding these technical problems, Brabham and BMW agreed that the BT50s should make their competition debut in the South African Grand Prix, opening round of the 1982 World Championship series held at Kyalami on January 23. The trio of BMW-engined cars were broadly similar to the prototype BT50 which had appeared at Silverstone the previous summer, although they had generally been tidied up and looked functionally menacing in appearance. During pre-race testing Piquet had brushed the 200mph mark on the headlong plunge down the hill beyond the pits, so hopes were for their performance in the race. Unfortunately, this was to be a weekend when off-track politics totally overshadowed efforts on the circuit.

A major row blew up between the drivers and FISA over the terms of the super-licence application forms. The drivers boycotted first practice, locking themselves away in a Johannesburg hotel from where their leaders negotiated with the race organizers and the sport's governing body. Bernie Ecclestone, in particular, was absolutely outraged, although he did his level best to conceal his irritation. Here he was, FOCA's President and working all hours to promote the sport on a world-wide basis only for the drivers to do a pretty good job of flushing the whole credibility of Grand Prix racing down the pan in one outlandish demonstration. He suppressed his fury, the storm blew over (predictably) and the sheepish drivers appeared at the track for the second day's practice on Friday.

In front of the Brabham pit were three BT50s – each carrying Patrese's number two! Some team bosses may well be scared of their drivers, but Ecclestone certainly has never been: determined to teach Nelson Piquet a lesson for being involved in this disruptive wildcat action, Bernie refused to let him take part in first practice. "He's been up all night and I feel he should be examined by a doctor before he goes out on the track", explained the Brabham boss. Piquet got the message, even encountering severe hostility from his beloved mechanics, men whom he rightly

"Hissing Sid", as the latest team decal is affectionately known amongst the Brabham team personnel. This menacing combination of snake and scorpion has adorned Ecclestone's cars since the start of the 1982 season!

regarded as friends and had entertained on his power boat down in the sunny Mediterranean a matter of weeks before. It was a sobering experience for the Brazilian, but, once allowed into a Brabham cockpit again, he slammed round in 1m 6.625s to grab second place on the front row alongside René Arnoux's pole position Renault RE30B.

The 77 lap, 196.35 mile race turned out to be a disaster for the Brabham-BMWs. Piquet bogged down at the start, being passed on all sides. He completed the first lap in 13th position and then spun off under braking for Crowthorne as he went into lap four. He scrambled out unhurt, but the car was slightly rumpled. Patrese ran fourth for a while, but eventually succumbed to turbo bearing failure. It was a dark day for the Brabham-BMW partnership, as well as for tensions within the team. Ecclestone had made a very firm point which Nelson would remember for a long time. It was perhaps an appropriate meeting for the Brabhams to appear decked out with a distinctive new team logo – a menacing Oriental cross between a snake and a scorpion, scowling at the world from its lookout point on the nose cones. "If it's provoked, a scorpion will sting!", explained Ecclestone to the author. I knew there was a moral to this little tale somewhere, but none the less asked the inevitable question. "Like you perhaps?", I enquired. "You could be right," he smiled weakly.

In Brazil and Long Beach the Brabham team fielded Cosworth-engined cars and, after missing the controversial San Marino event in line with the FOCA boycott, had it in mind to run the BT49Ds yet again in the Belgian Grand Prix. The twists and turns of the tight Zolder circuit seemed the last place that turbo would feel at home and, in any case, neither Ecclestone nor Murray really felt that the German engine was race ready. The whole affair looked suspiciously political at the time, because Brabham had been at the sharp end of the Cosworth water tank battle and, to the FOCA teams, "turbo" was something of a dirty word. However, Ecclestone insists his reluctance to run was purely because of technical reservations (which were, in honesty, quite justified) but the whole matter was sorted out when BMW came wading in waving a big stick.

On April 28, 1982, just over a week prior to the Belgian Grand Prix, BMW issued this terse statement which also alluded to the recent boycott of the San Marino race:

"BMW has threatened to 'terminate its co-operation' with the Brabham Formula 1 team if the two Brabham-BMW cars do not race at the Belgian Grand Prix at Zolder on May 9.

"The warning comes in a letter sent today to Mr. Bernie Ecclestone, chief of the Brabham team and President of the Formula One Constructors Association, whose members boycotted Sunday's San Marino Grand Prix in a row over minimum weight regulations.

"World Champion Nelson Piquet and team-mate Riccardo Patrese did not race their BMW turbo engined Brabhams because of the boycott and the letter to Mr. Ecclestone demands 'that Brabham adheres to the agreement between the two companies and races two Brabham-BMW cars in the Belgian Grand Prix', adding that should this requirement not be met by Mr. Ecclestone, BMW will terminate its co-operation with Brabham."

Frankly, on the face of it, this looked like no sort of threat at all – unless BMW *really* was going to pull the plug on the whole project. That seemed unlikely at the time and it has to be said that, although Ecclestone complied with the request, he did not appear unduly worried about it. Indeed, when I taxed him on it two-and-a-half years later, he shrugged and said, "I don't really recall all the details. I suppose I must have received a communication from them, but I don't recall the details." The BMW Board was getting a little jumpy for success to come the way of its engine, but there was even more aggravation and brinkmanship yet to be served up on this particular menu!

At Zolder the Brabham BT50s hardly shone in practice, Piquet and Patrese qualifying eighth and ninth, some 1.5s away from Prost's pole position Renault. In the 70 lap 185.38 mile race, Patrese spun off but Nelson managed to come home fifth, three laps down on John Watson's winning Marlboro McLaren-Cosworth. It had been a fraught race for the World Champion: at one stage the BT50 jammed in fourth gear, so he swung into the pit lane for attention, whereupon the gear freed itself, so he drove straight past his bewildered mechanics and back into the race. Later he had a spin on the same corner that claimed his team-mate, but gathered everything up and took the chequered flag without any more alarms.

As previously recounted, Patrese took a BT49D-Cosworth to a lucky victory at Monaco where gearbox problems sidelined Piquet's BT50, but the absolute *nadir* of the team's fortunes was reached in Detroit where the inaugural Grand Prix was held on June 6. Reigning World Champion Piquet failed to qualify in the Brabham-BMW. In the first session one car blew its engine after six laps and the T-car steadfastly refused to pick up properly from low revs – not the sort of handicap a driver needed round a tight street circuit. The following day saw qualifying effectively rained out, so Nelson was reduced to the role of spectator.

Dieter Stappert: "Things looked very bleak after that performance at Detroit, and when the team flew in another BT49 monocoque for the following weekend's Canadian Grand Prix it looked to me as though they were only going to prepare a single BMW and a spare Cosworth car for Piquet. I told Gordon frankly that if he didn't prepare two BMW cars then we would be finished. I told him this when I arrived at the Hyatt Regency Hotel in Montreal. He thought for a moment and said 'OK, so that's it'. So I said, 'Look, drive to the circuit and think about it. Don't make your decision now.' I was really concerned because Bernie and Paul Rosche were not around, so Gordon, Herbie and myself would have to sort the whole problem out.

"I told Gordon that if he was only going to prepare a single BMW then I would get straight onto the plane and be back in Munich in time for the Rolling Stones concert at the weekend. But Herbie phoned me from reception after breakfast and said 'for heaven's sake hang on, don't do anything . . .' Later that day I came out of my room to find Patrese and Parmalat's PR man, Sante Ghedini, having a right old shouting match in the corridor. I heard the words 'spare car', but they suddenly shut up when they saw me. I said 'Everything OK?' and they said 'no problem'. So I went off out to the circuit."

When Stappert arrived on the pit wall, his heart sank. Sure enough there were just two number ones lined up in front of the Brabham pit – a Cosworth and a BMW. He just stood on the pit wall for a moment, watching and wondering. Gordon caught his eye and grinned broadly. Then he beckoned on the mechanics and they pushed away Brabham-Cosworth number one, replacing it with a *second* Brabham-BMW sporting the same number. Stappert breathed again.

"I can't tell you how much I appreciated what Gordon had done," he reflected, "In Germany we say 'he jumped over his own shadow' – which means that he had done something which he wasn't totally convinced was the correct course of action. Then, would you believe, Nelson came in after two laps' practice with a misfire. I nearly died. Then he took the other car and it never missed a beat all weekend . . ."

"Those early days with the turbo were like the Brabham-Alfa nightmares – only worse," insists Gordon Murray, "The lowest point was Detroit, of course, where I honestly began to think we were banging our heads against a brick wall. But BMW made what was really a very simple alteration to the mixture control and it was transformed. I just can't over-emphasize the importance of that change: it went from totally undriveable, in Nelson's view, to behaving just like a Cosworth DFV. It was very nearly the end of the road for the whole deal and such a big decision was hanging on such a minor alteration to the engine. Amazing when you look back on it, but it was just one of those things . . ."

Didier Pironi's Ferrari 126C2 qualified for pole at Montreal on 1m 27.509s closely followed by the Renaults of Arnoux (1m 27.895s) and Prost (1m 28.563s) with Nelson's BT50 fourth on 1m 28.663s. Unfortunately Didier stalled at the start as he dipped the clutch to prevent his Ferrari creeping forward and the stationary C2 was rammed from behind by Riccardo Paletti's Osella. The bespectacled Italian novice was fatally injured in the accident and the race red-flagged to a halt

For the 1982 Belgian Grand Prix, Brabham was obliged to run the BT50s before they were really race ready in the wake of strong threats from BMW. Here Riccardo Patrese leads team-mate Nelson Piquet, eventual winner John Watson's Marlboro McLaren MP4 and Elio de Angelis's Lotus 92 during the early stages of the race. Piquet finished fifth, but Patrese left the road . . .

after only a single lap. It would be six o'clock in the evening, with dusk falling and a biting wind blowing off the St. Lawrence river, before the grid lined up for the restart.

Pironi, now using his spare Ferrari, managed to scramble round the opening lap of the fresh race in the lead, but Arnoux and Piquet were soon through into first and second places. Rene did his utmost to hang on at the head of the field, but the Renault V6 was no match for the flame-spurting BMW straight-4 in the cool evening air, Nelson slamming through into the lead on lap nine. From that moment onwards Piquet and his Brabham-BMW dominated the Canadian Grand Prix, heading towards a memorable and truly gratifying victory as the evening shadows lengthened.

Bernie Ecclestone, sentimentalist that he is, reckoned his most pressing priority was checking in for the night flight to London, so the Brabham boss made tracks for Montreal's Mirabel airport. Left in command was Herbie Blash, with Dieter Stappert timing the leader's advantage. Eventually Patrese hove into sight in second place and, for a few fleeting laps, the Brabham pit crew agonized as their Cosworth-engined BT49D began to close in on the leading BT50. But Nelson was fully in command of the situation, easing open his advantage to 14s at the chequered flag. Stappert, not sure how precisely he ought to be checking the winner's advantage, was consoled by an anonymous Brabham mechanic who

remarked "to the nearest second or two will be sufficient – it's as close as Bernie usually gets . . ."

Suddenly, it was all over and Piquet cruised round on his slowing down lap, totally satisfied that all the heartache had been worthwhile. It was a great day for both Brabham and BMW but, in honesty, it had been a close-run thing.

Three weeks passed before the Dutch Grand Prix took place at Zandvoort, during practice for which Piquet was caught out by the recently installed cockpit boost control knob, spinning wildly during first practice when he felt down to adjust the boost and twisted the brake balance control instead! Locking up its rear tyres, the BT50 pirouetted down the track under braking for *Tarzan* and Nelson crept slowly round to the pits where he confessed his error.

Nelson qualified third behind the two Renaults, his best lap of 1m 14.723s being a mere 0.5s away from Prost's pole winner. But when the 72 lap, 190.228 mile race got underway it was Didier Pironi's Ferrari C2 which took command, pulling confidently away to score a fine victory for Maranello. Both Renaults retired from the contest, so Nelson came home a strong second, using just enough turbo power to stay a couple of lengths ahead of Keke Rosberg's Williams FW08 at the chequered flag.

By the time the British Grand Prix at Brands Hatch came round, the pit lane was buzzing with rumour and speculation as to the Brabham team's plans, particularly when the BT50s appeared equipped with two quick release couplings on their fuel tanks – one clearly for quick filling, the other for venting the tank. Murray had done his homework, made his calculations, he and Herbie Blash taking a trip to the Indy 500 to study form – and concluded that pit stops for fuel and fresh rubber would be advantageous. The idea was to run softer rubber than usual with a reduced fuel load from the start of the race: this, in theory, would allow the Brabham-BMWs to build up a significant advantage which would allow them to make the stop for fuel and tyres around half distance. They would still be in a competitive position when they rejoined the race and, with new tyres, were hoped to be in a position to press home their advantage and win.

Gordon Murray: "It's perhaps a bit difficult to believe, but it had been a joke we'd been banding round the office for some months– 'why don't we start light and make a pit stop?'. It was a fairly easy sum to do, working out whether the idea was worthwhile, because we knew how long a fresh set would be effective and, indeed, how much time you lost by keeping going on a worn set.

"What wasn't so simple to judge, with no acceleration or braking figures, was how much time you would lose in the three laps involved – that's to say, one lap slowing down, the time in the pits, and the lap speeding up again. So, in the middle of the season, we equipped one of the BT50s with all the necessary gear, including the air jacking system, and went to Donington to test in secret. We timed those and came to the conclusion that we had to do the whole slowing-down, speeding-up process, including the stop itself, in under forty seconds. The first time we practised it, with Nelson coming into the pits *very* slowly indeed, we lost only twenty six seconds, so we knew we were OK. With more training we were obviously going to do it a lot quicker than that."

With coloured tape leading down the pit lane to the Brabham pits, both BT50s went to the starting line at Brands Hatch amidst overwhelming media attention, excited comparisons being made to Indianapolis etc., etc. The reality turned out to be a stark disappointment, but Murray recalls with pleasure the looks of disbelief on the faces of rival team personnel as all the refuelling paraphernalia was unloaded in the Brands Hatch pit lane.

Rosberg qualified his Williams FW08 on pole with a magnificent 1m 9.540s, followed by Patrese (1m 9.627s) and Piquet (1m 10.060s) but when the Finn was unable to get his Williams started for the parade lap, Riccardo effectively took premier position on the grid. When the starting signal was given the Italian underlined just how difficult it was to get the BMW engine, with its narrow power band, off the line. He stalled, was savaged from behind by Arnoux's Renault and the pair of them were out on the spot. Piquet galloped into an early lead, but was

The installation of the BMW M12/13 four-cylinder engine in the BT50 chassis: note the upswept ground effect side pod which cramps the amount of room available. The intercooler was mounted in the left-hand side pod.

not pulling away from Niki Lauda's second-place McLaren MP4 sufficiently quickly to allow the pit stop mathematics to make sense. The whole question was academic, though, for the BMW engine's stuttered to a halt after a fuel metering unit drive pulley came loose.

The super-fast *Mistral* straight at Paul Ricard was surely guaranteed to produce some sensational turbocharged Formula 1 battles when the circus arrived for the French Grand Prix on the weekend July 23/25. Quite frankly, though, it was truly frightening to see turbocharged ground effect cars slamming into the *Signes* right-hander at the end of that long back straight, their drivers scarcely lifting from the throttle, if at all. Most of the turbo brigade was running close to the 200mph mark, and, indeed, the Ferraris were breaching that psychologically crucial barrier. Media attention was exploding against the tremendously fast turbos, prompted as much as anything by a tangle between Jochen Mass's March and Mauro Baldi's Arrows early in the race, resulting in the German's car cartwheeling into a spectator debris fence against which enthusiasts were tightly packed. It was a miracle that nobody was killed, but the irony of this whole situation was that neither of these cars were turbos!

None the less, the combination of tremendously high straight line speed and phenomenal cornering capacity underlined the enormous concern felt in many

quarters that something would soon have to be done about these spiralling lap speeds, and the pace at which the fight for the lead was waged during the early laps of the race was truly awesome.

Problems with a weak fuel mixture had played havoc with the BMW turbos during practice with the result that the BT50s spent much of the time in the pit lane with their engine covers removed, Patrese and Piquet qualifying fourth and sixth while the Renaults of Arnoux and Prost buttoned up the front row. René tried to make a break at the start, but the Brabham-BMWs were a match for all their rivals once the Grand Prix got under way, swooping into contention down the *Mistral* straight until, at the end of lap five, they held first and second positions with Riccardo leading Nelson.

Longevity, yet again, proved to be the BT50's Achilles Heel. On lap eight Patrese dropped from the lead, blazing rear bodywork heralding another major engine failure. Nelson held his advantage until mid-way round lap 24, when a less spectacular, but no less terminal, engine malfunction wound up his further involvement in the proceedings. Still we had to see a Brabham pit stop . . .

Practice for the German Grand Prix at Hockenheim was saddened by Didier Pironi's practice accident, invaliding the Frenchman out of the sport and depriving Formula 1 of a worthy World Championship contender. Prost and Arnoux again qualified first and second for Renault, Piquet and Patrese lining up third and fifth in the BT50s. Arnoux briefly showed at the front once the green light was given, but Piquet's light fuel load and soft tyres enabled him to gallop ahead on lap two, the Brazilian quickly pulling away from the pack. The mathematics looked pretty promising on this occasion.

Going into lap 19 Piquet was 24s ahead, bang on target for the pit stop which was due in another couple of laps. Going into the first chicane he came up behind Chilean driver Eliseo Salazar struggling along in his ATS and the World Champion lined up to pass this backmarker as he aimed his Brabham into the next chicane just before the *Ostkurve*. Unfortunately Salazar misjudged the speed at which the turbo BMW-engined Brabham was overhauling his Cosworth-powered ATS. The Chilean moved off-line to the left, allowing Nelson to draw alongside on his right. This gave Piquet the correct line for the chicane, but by know Salazar was on the marbles and, as the two cars braked hard, the ATS punted the Brabham into the tyre barrier on the outside of the chicane with all the slick efficiency of a Championship snooker player potting the black!

The two cars shuddered to a halt, stalled but only lightly damaged. A furious Piquet erupted from the cockpit and demanded an explanation of Salazar, although he was clearly in no mood to be reasonable. Eliseo tried to explain, but his remonstrations fell on deaf ears as the World Champion lashed out with his arms and feet at the luckless also-ran. Unfortunately Nelson's fiery outburst was caught by the television cameras and transmitted World-wide: not a terribly good advertisement for Grand Prix racing.

Anyway, that was the end of the Brabham team effort for yet another race as engine failure had claimed Patrese's BT50 on lap 14. It had been a particularly disappointing display on BMW's home ground, but Piquet had nobody but himself to blame for his accident. It would have done him no harm to wait a few seconds until he was through the *Ostkurve* chicane and then flatten Salazar with his superior turbo power on the following straight. But the split-second demands of the impending pit stop had him keyed up to an intensely high pitch of competitiveness and he made that slight error of judgement as a result.

The Austrian Grand Prix at the Osterreichring gave the Brabham team its long-awaited opportunity. Piquet and Patrese ran through practice with remarkably few mechanical troubles, qualified first and second and really got going once the race started. Brushing aside an initial challenge from Prost's Renault, the two blue and white BT50s disappeared into the distance, Riccardo taking over at the head of the field on the second lap. Unfortunately Piquet had blistered a tyre early in the race and was having difficulty keeping up with his team mate so, on lap 16, he signalled that he would be coming in for fresh rubber.

Piquet's BT50 has just passed René Arnoux's Renault RE30 and is now heading for a long-awaited victory in the restarted 1982 Canadian Grand Prix at Montreal. A week earlier he had failed to qualify at Detroit, so relations between Brabham and BMW had been strained almost to breaking point immediately prior to the Canadian event. Below, Piquet looks almost bewildered as he waves to the crowd from the victory rostrum while team-mate Patrese, who stormed through to second place in a BT49D-Cosworth, looks a bit miffed to say the least.

The car that never raced. Looking for all the world like a BT49C, this is the ground effect pit stop BT51 prototype which Murray and his colleagues produced towards the end of 1982, accepting Ecclestone's assurances that ground effect aerodynamics would still be permitted in 1983. Then came FISA's rule change which demanded flat bottoms for 1983 – so Murray just scrapped this concept and started all over again to build the BT52 . . .

Unfortunately the pit crew misunderstood his signals because his scheduled pit stop was not due for several more laps. The mechanics were thus caught completely off their guard when the World Champion rolled to a halt in front of them at the end of lap 17. Fresh pre-heated tyres had to be rushed from the oven at the back of the pits and the carefully drilled routine went by the board as they scrambled about trying to get Nelson back into the fray. This little circus act lost the Brabham team leader the best part of a minute, so he resumed in fourth place. But Patrese was still running round imperiously at the head of the field.

On lap 24 it was time for Riccardo's routine stop. All eyes were on the pit lane as Brabham number two rolled to a stop in precisely the correct position. The air line was connected to activate the triple jack system, the BT50 raised up a few inches and the two men-per-wheel slammed on a set of harder compound Goodyears in place of the softer ones which had already blistered on Nelson's car. Through the filler on the right-hand side of the fuel cell, one helmeted mechanic replenished the car with 24 gallons of fuel while a similarly bedecked colleague vented the tank through the aperture on top. Just 15.6s from the time the BT50 stopped in the pit lane, Patrese engaged first gear and roared off back into the race – in the lead. The mechanics grinned and slapped each other on the back: the long-practised technique had worked to perfection!

Sadly, the whole exercise came to nought a mere three laps later. Having settled down into the rhythm of the race once more, adapted himself to the rather twitchy feel of his new Goodyears, Patrese suddenly found himself pitched into a lurid spin on a fast downhill left-hander. A gudgeon pin had broken, the engine locked solid and the BT50 careered off backwards across the greensward, its wayward progress arrested only by a rather solid earth bank up which it rode. For a few agonizing seconds it seemed as though the car might flip over, but it remained the right way up and a bitterly disappointed Patrese stepped out into retirement. Three laps later Piquet rolled to a halt just beyond the pits with a broken camshaft drive. That victory at Montreal was beginning to look like a mid-summer fluke . . .

The balance of the 1982 season produced nothing more to speak of for the Brabham team. The BMW engines ran reliably through the Swiss Grand Prix at Dijon-Prenois on August 29, but the BT50s were twitchy and unpredictable on this undulating circuit. Opting for a Goodyear compound which was far too hard negated any advantage to be gained by the pit stop routine and Piquet was lucky to scramble home fourth ahead of team-mate Patrese who had run non-stop in the other BT50. Clutch problems eliminated both cars from the Italian Grand Prix at Monza within a few laps of the start and Gordon Murray's iron-willed refusal to return to the tinsel of Las Vegas meant that the BT50s were totally at sea with handling problems round the acrobatic car park circuit behind Caesars Palace. Patrese encountered clutch trouble again while a broken sparking plug electrode badly damaged Nelson's BMW engine, so there were no Brabhams around at the finish. Times change: only a year earlier Nelson had clinched his first World Championship here . . .

It had been a troubled season, BMW struggling to deal with ignition and injection problems which were behind many of the engine failures, while Brabham had done its absolute best to accommodate the German engine manufacturer. Gordon Murray and his colleagues had learned just how difficult turbocharged engines were to work with as compared with the "screw in and fire up" Cosworth V8 philosophy. But, perhaps more importantly, BMW had come to appreciate just how intense the pressure could be working in the rarified air of Grand Prix competition.

Dieter Stappert remains totally convinced that the only way for an engine manufacturer to be involved in Formula 1 is with a small specialist British team. "I am certain that a Brabham-BMW, McLaren-Porsche or Williams-Honda combination will always be better than a major manufacturer, such as Renault, doing it on their own. The thing that a big manufacturer has to get used to is the *tempo* of the whole Formula 1 business.

"It surprised us and I'll give you an example. I think Paul Rosche developed a new camshaft design for the engine and Nelson tried it at a mid-season test. He came in after a few laps and said 'it's much better'. So Gordon Murray said to Paul 'when do you plan on having a batch of these ready for racing?' Paul replied 'well, next season actually'. Murray just fixed him with a stare. 'Next week' he said firmly. That sort of thing happened quite frequently. Gordon would ask Paul 'how long?' when it came to the supply of a new component. Paul would give his answer and Gordon would say, flatly, 'no way'. We learned a great deal from Brabham in this respect about the speed at which you had to operate in order to be competitive in Formula 1."

On the political scene, meanwhile, a major debate raged as to what should be done about Formula 1 technical regulations in 1983. The predominantly British FOCA-aligned teams had honed under-car aerodynamics to their current levels of sophistication and were clearly anxious that they should not have this advantage legislated away. However, FISA was adamant that ground effect would have to be ruled out for 1983 and the Formula 1 Commission meeting on November 3, 1982 outlawed skirts once and for all as well as insisting on a flat-bottom rule to kill under-car aerodynamics. Frankly the cars were now too fast for the circuits (Piquet's pole time at Osterreichring amounted to an *average* speed of over 151 mph) and this unilateral action had to be taken in the interests of safety. There was also the distant, horrifying spectre of a third-party insurance claim should a car catapult into the crowd, like the March and Arrows had come so close to doing at Paul Ricard. In America, heaven forbid . . .

Gordon Murray was now going to find that working for the most powerful single individual in Grand Prix racing did not always work out to the Brabham team's advantage. Over the previous few seasons there had been an increasing number of knowing nods and winks in the Formula 1 paddocks, the general feeling being that Murray always had prior notice of any technical rule change thanks to his proximity to Bernie. This has always been strenuously denied by Ecclestone who says, "because of my position I have always made absolutely sure that my team is not favoured. In fact, because I've gone out of my way to do this they've often ended up by being handicapped." His rivals do not always accept this, but it was certainly the case when Murray came to finalize his proposed 1983 chassis design.

Notwithstanding the prevailing trend of opinion against ground effect, Ecclestone remained convinced that it would not be outlawed for '83. Consequently, when Murray asked for guidance, he received the green light to go ahead and produce another skirted ground effect design.

Murray decided on a neat little 'half tank' pit stop car, visually much like the Cosworth-engined BT49. The first prototype, the BT50B, was built up using the familiar Brabham-Alfa gearbox, but by now Murray felt this development was getting close to the end of its potential and initiated the production of a brand new trans-axle which would be fitted to the finalized version of the car, dubbed BT51.

"The whole transmission was designed, the patterns were under way – and then we lost the skirts," shrugged Gordon, "so it was back to the drawing board in a big way. The transmission had to be thrown away because it was all wrong for what I had in mind as a flat bottom car, so we started again on that using the same concept."

What followed next was a quite remarkable demonstration of team spirit and loyalty, the sort of commitment that is difficult for the average nine-to-five man in the street to understand, but which has a routine part of professional motor racing for many decades. It was now mid-November and the first race of the season was on March 13 at Rio de Janeiro. A totally new car had to be built from the ground up and the entire Brabham workforce knuckled down to do just that.

As Gordon Murray reflected, "I got BMW to alter the exhaust system, turbo position and other ancillaries on the engine, so there was no argument about it, we *had* to get the BT52 ready in time. There was no question of wheeling out the BT50s, because the revised BMW engines wouldn't fit into them. We had some of our fabricators and glass fibre specialists kipping down on the floor in sleeping bags for weeks at a time, snatching a few hours' sleep and then getting back on the job. I was working non-stop for three months as well, of course, staying awake on pills for most of the time. It was certainly the hardest winter I've ever experienced."

A quite astonishing level of commitment pervades the whole Brabham organization, spawned, I suspect, by tremendous affection for Nelson Piquet and Gordon Murray on the part of workers who feel that they're toiling for the best designer and driver in the business. And if Bernie Ecclestone is not the softest sentimentalist in the Grand Prix game, his employees' respect for him is founded on the knowledge that he always wants the best for his racing team, whether in terms of equipment or personnel. Knowing that, it is obviously quite easy to put up with the occasional 'blitzes' Bernie makes on the factory, his over-riding obsession with tidiness and order preoccupying his mind on these spectacular occasions!

Ecclestone has surrounded himself with a clique of hard-working associates whose loyalty is beyond question, notwithstanding the punishing schedule which seems a day-to-day feature of the Brabham team's modus operandi. That is not to say there is not the occasional threatened resignation or vociferous outburst, of course. Bernie's personal secretary Ann Jones, a veteran of 24 years working for his companies, admits, "the number of times I've put my coat on and walked out . . . well, I just can't begin to tell you. But he's always managed to talk me round. The great thing about working here is the interest and variety – plus the fact that Bernie trusted me from very early on . . ."

The sensational result of these endeavours, the BT52, was shown in public at a BMW press conference in Munich shortly before the start of the 1982 season, although, heavily camouflaged, it had briefly run at Brands Hatch the previous week. Owing nothing to the long line of Brabham monocoques extending back to the original BT48, not only was the BT52 totally new, its appearance was strikingly and distinctively different.

With ground effect requirements out of the window, the BT52 had no side pods, so the cockpit looked dramatically slim, almost vulnerable. The monocoque was made in two sections: the lower half from L72 aluminium panelling, the upper section from moulded carbon fibre composite. At the front of the monocoque a magnesium casting had been machined to carry the inboard mounted

spring/damper units, activated by a double wishbone/pushrod system. The front anti-roll bar was mounted across the front end of the chassis casting, connecting to the magnesium rockers on which the inner end of the pushrod was mounted. Machined magnesium uprights provided the mounting points for the steering arms and brakes, the discs themselves being of carbon fibre with Girling calipers.

The rear end included the new Brabham-developed gearbox, employing Hewland internals and offering either five or six forward speeds. The bellhousing was integral with the gearbox casing and doubled as the engine oil tank as well as containing the hydraulic clutch mechanism. The rear carbon fibre disc brakes were mounted outboard and the one-piece rear wing formed from honeycomb and carbon fibre laminate with the side plates bolted directly to it.

The BMW engine installation was by means of a steel frame and an aluminium anodised front plate bolted to the rear of the monocoque. On the right-hand side of the engine bay was a large Behr oil/water radiator and, on the left, a large Behr air-to-air intercooler mounted ahead of the single KKK turbocharger. The flat underside of the BT52 extended rearwards beneath the engine bay thanks to a carbon fibre/honeycomb laminate under tray. With a fuel capacity of 42 gallons, the BT52 was designed from the outset as a 'pit stop car' and was unlikely to be capable of a non-stop run except in the shortest races on the calendar.

Gordon Murray: "Three of the biggest changes with the BT52 were the heavily rearward weight bias, the way in which the driver's position had been shifted back and the fact that it was a relatively non-adjustable car. It didn't have a rear anti-roll bar, you couldn't adjust the rear wings. The whole idea was to keep it simple and to save weight, also there was no cockpit adjustment for the front anti-roll bar. We had found that the turbo bearings were suffering badly, seriously

Nelson Piquet on his way to a first-time win with the striking new BT52 in the 1983 Brazilian Grand Prix at Rio. The cooling duct on the rear bodywork is to prevent the left rear shock absorber from overheating, a problem which had contributed to a mysterious handling imbalance during practice.

The much neater installation of the BMW engine in the rear of the Brabham BT52 contrasting with the photograph on page 250. The rearward weight bias of the car is enhanced by positioning of intercoolers and oil/water radiators just ahead of the front wheels.

overheating, during even the briefest of pit stops. Thus we rigged up cooling system for them from a connection on the air jacking system, blowing cool air over the turbo as long as the car was stationary with the air jacking system activated."

There were minor technical problems at the first race, but nothing terribly serious. The rear mounted water radiators overheated the spring/damper units on one side, but this was quickly sorted out by some hastily-added ducting and Nelson qualified fourth on 1m 35.114s, behind Keke Rosberg's pole position Williams FW08C (1m 34.526s), Alain Prost's Renault RE30C (1m 34.672s) and Patrick Tambay's Ferrari 126C2B (1m 34.758s). Riccardo Patrese was seventh on 1m 35.958s.

This was the second season of the Brabham-BMW partnership and people were beginning to ask why the German car manufacturer did not have more identification on the cars, bearing in mind the engines were being supplied free of charge. Dieter Stappert simply explained "It was agreed in the first contract it should be like that", his tone suggesting very strongly that it was a matter he did not wish to pursue.

The facts of the case are, however, that when the initial deal was done, some BMW directors were cautious of being identified in Formula 1 just in case the

whole project turned into a fiasco. Once it was obvious that things were going just fine, pressure was applied for a little more identification, even though it was not specified in the contract with the Brabham team. Those who studied practice at Rio in 1983 closely would have seen a brief, fleeting "difference of opinion" between Stappert and the Brabham team management which almost resulted in Paul Rosche taking the Bosch-BMW electronic control components out of the car unless a BMW badge was stuck on it. The matter was resolved to everybody's satisfaction, but it looked a close call at the time . . .

Gordon Murray was amazed that only Williams, out of all the other teams, had organized itself with the facilities to make a routine fuel stop and this strategy paid off comfortably for Rosberg who shot straight into the lead at the start, holding on at the front of the field for six laps before Piquet picked his way past. From then on it was plain sailing for the brand-new Brabham-BMW, even the routine stop at the end of lap 40 failing to deprive Nelson of the lead. The Brabham team was keeping its fingers crossed that the new gearbox would stand the strain, but everything worked fine and Piquet ended the day with a gratifying, worthwhile debut victory. At one point a BT52 1-2 looked on the cards, for Patrese worked his way up to third place before a broken exhaust, and consequent loss of turbo boost pressure, resulted in his retirement after 19 laps.

It seemed impossible that the Brabham BT52s could be relegated to the role of also-ran in a matter of a fortnight, but that is precisely what happened when the teams began practising for the United States Grand Prix at Long Beach. Over the bumps and ripples of the makeshift Californian road circuit both Piquet and Patrese were in big trouble as they tried to get the Michelins to heat up to a reasonable working temperature. "I think we've changed more springs on the first day here than we did throughout the entire '82 season," remarked one exasperated mechanic during practice.

The whole affair turned out to be a nightmare, and while Tambay qualified his Ferrari with a 1m 26.117s to take pole round this tight 2.035 mile track, Patrese was an indifferent 11th on 1m 28.958s with Piquet a truly hopeless 20th on 1m 30.034s. This 75 lap race was highlighted by McLaren turning practice form on its ear, Watson and Lauda sailing through the depleted field to finish 1-2 after starting 22nd and 23rd. The Brabhams, intending to run non-stop, had a disappointing race. Piquet's throttle linkage was awry from the start and he struggled into midfield before the throttle stuck open and he retired. Patrese survived a quick spin and was holding third place with five laps to go when the distributor broke and that was the end of his race.

Before the Championship circus assembled again for the French Grand Prix at Paul Ricard, Brands Hatch staged its non-title Race of Champions 40 lapper which attracted a quite reasonable field on April 10. Unable to enter either of the team's regular drivers, Ecclestone got a flea in his ear from the press corps when he produced Hector Rebaque in a lone BT52-BMW. The car wasn't too good over the Brands Hatch bumps, but the genial Mexican was certainly not the sort of world-class driver one would have liked to see as a stand-in – nor was he a promising new boy with a reputation to consolidate. The mechanics must have wished they'd all stayed at home when this embarrassing fiasco ended with the Brabham damaging its suspension during a tyre stop when the air jacks were lowered before the replacement wheels had been properly fitted. Bernie described Rebaque as "one of the world's most under-rated drivers." Not by me, he wasn't . . .

Renault, Ferrari and Alfa Romeo joined the pit stop ploy for the French Grand Prix at Paul Ricard on April 17, Alain Prost throwing down another strong challenge for the World Championship by leading the lion's share of the 54 lap, 194.95 mile race. He catapulted the new Renault RE40 into an immediate lead at the start, losing it only briefly to Piquet's understeering BT52 through a fumbled pit stop, but regaining the advantage when Nelson made his own stop for fuel and tyres. At the end of the race Prost had almost half a minute on the Brabham with Eddie Cheever's Renault sandwiching Nelson in third place. Patrese again failed

Marlboro British Grand Prix
parmalat
parmalat
FILA

Pit stop perfection. Nelson Piquet's BT52B receives fuel and fresh tyres during a 14s stop in the 1983 British Grand Prix at Silverstone. The Brabham team initiated the return to scheduled pit stops and their well-organized drill was invariably one of the best and most efficient.

to finish, retiring this time with overheating.

The San Marino Grand Prix at Imola on May 1 saw both Brabham drivers make elementary errors of the first order. Nelson qualified second only to René Arnoux's Ferrari C2B – and then fluffed his start, stalling the BMW engine and being left on the line. He climbed through the field in splendid style once he got going again, but retired after 36 laps with a broken valve whilst holding fifth place. Despite stopping in the wrong position for his pit stop, which took over 20s as a result, Riccardo Patrese was in a strong position as the race went into its closing phase. The Brabham-BMW was gobbling up Patrick Tambay's leading advantage and the Italian sliced past into the lead on lap 55 . . .

With Patrick worried about marginal fuel consumption, notwithstanding his stop to replenish the tank, Patrese had it in the bag. Yet at the *Acque Minerale* chicane he got onto the marbles and threw it all away with a head-on impact into the protective tyre barrier on the outside of the corner. It was an incomprehensible, unforgivable lapse of the sort which has characterized Riccardo's career from day one.

When it came to the Monaco Grand Prix meeting it looked as though the Brabham team might be hard hit by the Principality's long-standing rule which banned the storage of petrol in the pit lane. Fortunately this little hiccup was sorted out by Mr. Ecclestone and Piquet did a reasonably good job in practice, bearing in

Riccardo Patrese heading for third place in the 1983 German Grand Prix at Hockenheim showing off the "reversed" dark blue and white colour scheme adopted on the BT52B. The revised car also featured different aerodynamics, altered top bodywork and several other minor improvements.

mind the problems faced by the BT52s at Long Beach, qualifying fifth 1.9s away from René Arnoux's pole position.

Race day brought with it the gamble of wet or dry tyres. The track surface was still slippery after a recent shower, but the rain had stopped by the time the race was scheduled to start. Keke Rosberg and the Williams team gambled on conditions drying out, the FW08C ran on slicks and led from start to finish in splendid style. Piquet started on wets, stopped for slicks at the end of lap four and then pounded through to a strong second place, setting the fastest lap as he did so. Patrese had electrical problems which caused his BMW engine to cut out, the Italian glancing a wall as he struggled vainly with the cockpit switches, hoping to coax the machine back into life.

Prost's domination of the Belgian Grand Prix at the newly revamped Spa-Francorchamps circuit on May 22 heightened the confidence of those who predicted a Renault-mounted driver would, at last, win the World Championship. Piquet, who had a troubled practice and qualified fourth, held second place from lap 26 to lap 33, before dropping back to finish an eventual fourth, hampered by gear selection problems and eventually losing fifth gear altogether. This gearbox was proving marginal, but Pete Weissmann would help beef it up into a reliable survivor.

Arnoux and Piquet appeared again on the front row of the grid for the Detroit Grand Prix on June 5, Nelson leading initially, but then letting René run ahead of him, the Brabham team leader not worried about the prospect of a pit stop as he was running straight through this short 50 lap, 150 mile event. In the event Piquet was handed the race on a plate when Arnoux's engine quit with electrical trouble a couple of laps after scrambling back into the race with a couple of seconds' advantage over Nelson after the Ferrari pit stop.

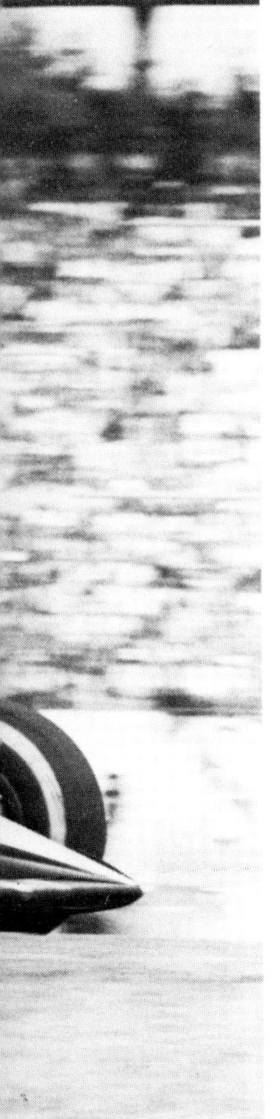

It looked as though the BT52's second win of the season was in the bag, but going into lap 51, Nelson suddenly felt the car go loose at the rear end. He slowed right down – a nail had punctured a rear Michelin! He had to crawl gently back to the pits, allowing Michele Alboreto's Tyrrell 011 through to a lucky victory. Nelson recovered to take a frustrated fourth while Patrese retired with brake trouble.

A week later the Canadian Grand Prix at Montreal saw Nelson retire from third place with a broken throttle cable, but with Arnoux winning for Ferrari and Cheever taking second for Renault, the Brazilian was still in contention for the Championship as the circus headed back to Europe. Prost had 30pts at the head of the table, but Nelson and Patrick Tambay were joint second a mere 2pts behind him.

The British Grand Prix at Silverstone on July 16 saw the Brabhams turned out in a neat reversal of the distinctive blue and white Parmalat livery, blue now being the cars' predominant colour. The mid-season break had enabled Gordon Murray to finalize a 'B' specification for the car, featuring myriad detail changes to the monocoque including the addition of lightweight bulkheads. There was also a subtly changed underbody, revised bodywork and a slightly shorter nose section, the last-mentioned developed after a Hockenheim test.

Arnoux and Tambay dominated the grid with their brand new carbon fibre composite Ferrari 126C3s, but when the race got underway it was Prost's Michelin-shod Renault which again exerted its superiority over the Goodyear-shod Italian cars. Piquet emerged from his routine pit stop in a potentially challenging position, but the alleged absence of pit signals telling him where he stood in relation to Prost lulled him into thinking the Renault was out of range. He wound down the boost pressure and cruised home second, annoyed to find that he was only 19s adrift at the flag even after he had eased his pace!

Patrese's miserable season continued with a turbocharger failure at Silverstone, but the Italian was to receive a fleeting consolation prize and a place on the winner's rostrum at Hockenheim when he came home third in the German Grand Prix on August 17. This was another Ferrari C3/Goodyear demonstration run and, although Tambay was an early retirement with engine failure, Arnoux set the

Hectic battle. Nelson Piquet's BT52B fending off Alain Prost's Renault RE40 during the 1983 Dutch Grand Prix at Zandvoort. Earlier Piquet had pulled out a commanding lead, but worn rear shock absorbers aggravated the Brabham's tyre wear and allowed Prost to close in. Anxious to get ahead of the Brazilian prior to the routine pit stops for fuel and tyres, Prost attempted a bold overtaking move at Tarzan on the lap after this photograph was taken, pushing Piquet into a tyre barrier and out of the race.

front-running pace and only allowed Piquet through briefly into the lead when he made his pit stop on lap 23. Nelson pulled in for fuel and tyres seven laps later and when the Brazilian resumed the chase, he was some 14s behind the Ferrari and there didn't look much chance that he could haul it back. But the determined little Brazilian got his head down and narrowed the gap to just over 5s with ten laps left to run. By now it seemed that René was controlling the pace of things, but Piquet was still determined to give him a run for his money.

With three laps to go the fuel pressure warning light in the Brabham cockpit flickered on as the BT52 accelerated away from the infield stadium and out into the forests. By the time he negotiated the first chicane on the outward leg the rear end of the car was blazing merrily, a haze of fuel vapour from a ruptured filter housing now ignited by the red hot exhaust system. Nelson by this stage could feel the heat build-up behind his back, so as the flames grew larger he pulled off the road just before the *Ostkurve* chicane, leaping out and running away from his fiery steed without further ado. Marshals doused the flames, but that was the end of his afternoon's work. Prost came home fourth and the Frenchman now had a nine point cushion over Piquet in the Championship points table.

The point where the Championship began to swing Nelson's way was during the Austrian GP, a race in which Alain Prost, to the casual onlooker, produced probably his best single drive of the season. Paul Rosche had been making steady progress with his neat in-line four cylinder engine throughout the season and Nelson was right in with the pace-setting bunch from the start.

Having qualified fourth, 0.7s away from Tambay's pole position Ferrari, Nelson sat confidently behind the two Italian cars in third place from the start, staying ahead of Prost's Renault RE40 with little apparent trouble. Some appalling

baulking on the part of tardy backmarker Jean-Pierre Jarrier cost Tambay the lead, allowing René Arnoux ahead and when his Ferrari made its routine stop at the end of lap 29, Nelson surged by into first place.

On lap 31 it was Piquet's turn to stop. The Brabham lads serviced their man with all the slick efficiency which was now taken for granted and the BT52 went haring out of the pits up the hill just as Arnoux came blaring by, flat-out in fifth gear. Up at the chicane it looked as though the Ferrari would haul past, but Nelson just kept ahead to the *Glatzkurve*, by which time his tyres were nicely warmed up and he could stay ahead without any trouble. One of the most impressive aspects of Piquet's performances during 1983 was the way in which he could settle back into a race rhythm immediately following a pit stop. Other drivers admitted they took two or three laps to get back into the swing of things, but, with Nelson, it was just as though you were flicking a light switch . . .

Unfortunately all this close high speed running in traffic had taken its toll and the Brabham's BMW engine began to show signs of overheating as the race drew towards a conclusion. Prudently, Piquet wound down the boost pressure, conceded the battle for the lead and conserved the machinery. At the end of the afternoon he stroked across the line in third place, easing his pace as much as he dared whilst *just* fending off the fast-approaching Cheever who was fourth. Prost won from Arnoux, but Alain went straight back to Renault's Viry-Chatillon base and warned the team that if it didn't pull its finger out on the engine development front, the Championship would be lost to Piquet.

Ironically, after this shrewd warning, Alain Prost threw away his Championship chances through a major driving error during the Dutch Grand Prix at Zandvoort. The BMW engines were now equipped with a boost control valve (provided by Paul Rosche's great friend and rival, English engine specialist Brian Hart!) which helped improve engine response at low speed and Piquet's "qualifying spare" BT52 featured a water spray cooling the air as it entered the turbocharger intercooler. Thus equipped, Nelson took pole from Tambay by half a second and the real battle for the World Championship was on!

Nelson went off like a rocket when the starting light blinked green for this 72 lap, 190.228 mile thrash and the Brabham-BMW was a good 5s ahead of Prost with ten laps completed. Gradually Prost began to haul the Renault closer towards the leading Brabham and the stage seemed set for a tense battle up to and immediately following the routine pit stops. Nelson had, perhaps, run a little too hard, too soon on that first set of Michelins and Prost was crowding him by lap 37, anxious to slip ahead so that he could be first into the pit lane for fuel and tyres – and, hopefully, first out. Later it would be found that the Brabham's rear-dampers had packed up.

Going into the braking area for *Tarzan* at the start of lap 40, Prost pulled inside Nelson in what looked like a properly legitimate overtaking manoeuvre. Yet just as it seemed that Alain had done it, the Renault began fishtailing violently, side-swiping the Brabham off the circuit and into an unyielding tyre barrier. Prost just managed to gather everything up and continue, but Nelson was out, the BT52 sustaining a bent front wishbone and a puncture in this little drama. The Brabham team leader climbed quietly out and walked away without any fuss or histrionics whatsoever, an indication of just how much mature and philosophical he had become over the past 12 months.

For a few fleeting moments this looked like the bonus of bonuses for Prost. His arch-rival was out of the contest, leaving the way clear for an easy Renault victory. Not so. Mid-way round that very same lap, Alain went plunging off the road into a guard rail, his RE40's handling impaired by a wayward front aerofoil which had been damaged in the collision. Rough justice, perhaps, but justice none the less. Patrese, who had retired with a cracked block in Austria, drove splendidly at Zandvoort and was challenging for second place six laps from the end when his engine suddenly lost power and he slipped back to a lapped eighth at the chequered flag.

There were now only three races left on the Championship calendar and Piquet was 14pts behind Prost in the chase for the title. But the tide was now running in

Under development. One of the M12/13 engines on the test bed at the BMW Motorsport base in Munich.

Nelson's favour, even though the mathematics seemed stacked against him. For the Italian Grand Prix at Monza on September 11, Patrese qualified on pole position with a 1m 29.1122s, the crowd not knowing whether to laugh or cry at the sight of an Italian in one of the loathed "Bernie Brabhams" beating Tambay, a Frenchman in one of their beloved Ferraris, to number one slot on the grid!

Riccardo bounded into the lead at the start, but on lap four his BMW's turbo expired in a cloud of blue smoke, allowing team-mate Piquet through into the lead. From then on he was never challenged, holding on at the head of the field through a stupendous 10.1s pit stop for fuel and tyres. Prost retired with turbo problems, so Nelson was left with a routine run through to the end of the 52 lap, 187.403 mile race, winning by just over 10s from René Arnoux's Ferrari C3. Prost now had 51pts, Arnoux 49 and Piquet 46 – but the real battle was between Alain and Nelson.

Tests at Snetterton revealed that it would be worthwhile running 'Ferrari-style' rear wing side extensions at Brands Hatch where the Grand Prix of Europe was scheduled to take place on September 25. The Brabhams were obviously still the cars to beat, even though Pirelli's rubber performed sufficiently well for the new Gerard Ducarouge-designed Lotus 94Ts to show promising form. Patrese took pole again, with the Lotus twins next up and Piquet fourth. Riccardo sprinted into the lead at the start, but Elio's impetuosity resulted in both cars spinning at Surtees on lap 11 when the Lotus driver attempted to barge inside the Brabham – and failed to do so!

Piquet was thus handed the race on a plate, taking over the lead at that point with the added luxury that his team mate was now holding second ahead of Prost. From then on it was a re-run of Monza, Nelson leading all the way through his pit stop to stroke home just under 7s ahead of Prost, Patrese having faded to seventh. Prost was now a mere 2pts ahead of Piquet, with Arnoux effectively out of the equation after a poor showing at Brands.

All that remained now was the final race, the South African Grand Prix at Kyalami on October 15. What's more, a shrewd variation of the Brabham-instigated pit stop formula, suggested by no less a luminary than Bernie

Ecclestone, put the Championship title into Nelson's pocket almost before the 77 lap, 196.35 mile race had even started.

Tambay had taken pole from Piquet by 0.2s, but Michelin's race tyres were much better propositions, so this practice swansong to Patrick's Ferrari career was of little consequence. Ecclestone's idea was brilliantly simple. In order to push the opposition to breaking point, why not fill the car with a minimal amount of fuel and schedule Nelson's stop for *early* in the race? This way, he could stun his rivals into submission with a blistering spurt from the start and, with luck, emerge from his pit visit in an even stronger position than usual. Hitherto, the Brabham-BMWs had stopped late in the race, using residual fuel as ballast in the event of a post-race weight check and also benefitting from an empty pit lane.

At the start Piquet simply hurtled away from his rivals in a manner that startled even Gordon Murray. Nelson was *two seconds* ahead at the end of the opening lap, cracked fastest lap as early as lap six and sustained the lead through his pit stop with such brilliant effect that the driver himself was reluctant to believe the pit signals that indicated he was still in the lead. At the end of lap 35, Prost's challenge came to an end when the Frenchman crept quietly into the pits to retire his Renault with turbo failure, and when Nelson received the specially prepared sign to inform him of Alain's departure from the race, he eased off and allowed team-mate Patrese to catch him.

Determined to ensure that he finished with the Championship, Nelson not only allowed Patrese through to take a gratefully received victory, but also dropped behind Andrea de Cesaris in the Alfa 183T. It was good enough for him to take the Championship by 2pts from the crestfallen Prost, soon destined to leave Renault after a vicious end of season post-mortem full of recriminations. For Brabham, BMW and Michelin, however, it was a great day. Nelson Piquet was the first man to win a Championship at the wheel of a turbocharged Grand Prix car and, although the Constructors' Championship had fallen to Ferrari (through consistency as much as anything) BMW was set to capitalize on Piquet's success in its world-wide advertising campaign.

Patrese, notwithstanding his Kyalami victory, was set to leave the Brabham team because he was far too expensive a proposition, in Ecclestone's view, as a number two driver. Bernie had his enthusiasm well under control for this particular win, rounding tersely on the author during the flight back to London when it was suggested that Riccardo scored a good win. "Really?", he replied acidly, "we give him a good-bye present like that, hand him the race on a plate, and you think it's a good win?" Ouch!

BMW was on the receiving end of a most unpalatable postscript to the 1984 season when it was suggested that the fuel employed in the BT52s had contravened the rules, exceeding the 102RON maximum octane rating permitted in the Formula 1 technical regulations. This little snippet of information was published, admittedly without comment, by a rival fuel company after independent tests on samples of the BMW fuel had indicated a problem after Kyalami. But no action was ever taken and, quite predictably, Dieter Stappert reacted angrily and firmly when the suggestion was put in front of him.

"There must have been a laboratory mistake. I don't understand how people can believe such a thing," Stappert replied, "We go Formula 1 racing to win and when you win, *everything* is checked on the car, including the fuel. So what's the point in using illegal fuel to win when you know you are going to be thrown out? I mean, it is so blatantly ridiculous that I really cannot believe that people can think it. Such an infraction of the rules would do far more damage than any benefit obtained by winning the race. Anyway, I am convinced that before Paul Rosche would condone *anything* that was less than 100 per cent legal, the River Isar would have to start flowing uphill. That's how strongly I feel about these allegations!"

Certainly, the inspection procedures for checking the BMW Formula 1 fuel seem exhaustive, to say the least. The purpose-made fuel is produced by the Osnabruck-based Winterschall company, a subsidiary of the giant BASF chemicals group (the German equivalent of ICI). Winterschall mixes the fuel in

RENAULT
RENAULT
BARCLAY
WÜRTH
BARCLAY
NORDICA
parmalat
parmalat
Santal
parmalat
parmalat

Resilience. A matter of minutes after Nelson Piquet (above) clambered from this badly damaged BT53 at the start of the 1984 Detroit Grand Prix, he was strapped into the spare car in which he led the restarted race from start to finish. In the accident picture Marc Surer's Arrows has just collided with the rumpled Brabham which was pushed into the wall by an over-enthusiastic Nigel Mansell's Lotus 95T. Below, Nelson takes the spare BT53 past the pits at the end of the opening lap of the second race with Prost's McLaren leading the pursuit. It was one of the most impressive performances of Piquet's distinguished career.

batches of several thousand litres at a time and is responsible for shipping to the various races, but not before three samples are taken from each batch. Two of those samples are sent to the BASF laboratories at Ludwigshafen where one is checked by BASF technicians and one is sent for analysis at an independent research establishment. The other sample is sent to BMW Motorsport in Munich where the company chemists check part of the sample and it is also subject to an independent check. When everybody agrees that the fuel conforms to the octane rating required, only then is it released for use by the Brabham-BMWs. Says Stappert, "As far as I'm concerned, they can check any aspect of our engines any and every day. The more checking is done, the less these rumours will be made." FISA also released a detailed dossier which supported the BMW point of view, adding that "the FISA has given sufficient proof of strictness and impartiality in the application of the regulations for these unfounded accusations against it to be stopped." Not all BMW's rivals seemed satisfied, though.

For the 1984 season, Gordon Murray continued with the basic BT52 concept, although it had to be revised with a bigger fuel cell as fuel stops were banned as from the start of the 1984 season and a 220-litre fuel capacity maximum was implemented.

On paper, it was difficult to imagine the Brabham-BMWs tailing away as far as performance was concerned, but the car of 1984 was destined to be the TAG/Porsche-engined McLaren MP4/2. When the season opened at Rio de Janeiro on March 25 Alain Prost's kicked off with a victory for his new team and he and Niki Lauda seldom stopped winning right through the year.

Piquet qualified his BT53 a somewhat disappointing seventh, 1.8s away from Elio de Angelis's pole position Lotus 95T, and then celebrated the start of the new season by stalling his engine as the starting lights blinked green. His new team mate Teo Fabi, scheduled to share the second BT53 with his younger brother Corrado in order that he could dovetail an F1/CART programme, at least managed to get away from his 15th slot on the grid, but turbo failure eventually claimed him just as his senior team-mate rolled to a halt with a broken engine. It was to be the start of a heart-breaking run of misfortune for the team which had won the '83 Brazilian race so convincingly with the BT52 . . .

At Kyalami on April 7, Nelson qualified on pole for the South African Grand Prix and although he almost fluffed his start again, from lap three to lap nine, he and Teo Fabi held first and second places in impressive style. Unfortunately Nelson's early speed had taken its toll on his tyres and he was obliged to stop for a change, relinquishing the lead to Niki Lauda's McLaren which went on to win. Eventually both BT53s stopped with turbo compressor failure and Piquet's disappointing trend continued at Zolder where he suffered such a massive engine breakage during the closing stages of the Belgian Grand Prix that the BT53's side pods were bowed outwards and the cylinder block virtually sliced in half!

None the less, Nelson was a quick qualifier with that BMW engine and he grabbed pole for the San Marino Grand Prix at Imola, although he had to play second fiddle to Prost's McLaren once the race got underway. He held on in second place until 12 laps from the end of the 60 lap contest when a turbo failure again sent him scuttling for the pit lane. Hardly had the Brazilian pulled to a stop in front of the Brabham garage than Teo Fabi followed him in with an identical problem.

By the time the French Grand Prix at Dijon-Prenois was over, the pit lane was circulating an in-joke, speculating whether Bernie Ecclestone could continue being President of the Formula 1 Constructors' Association if his cars could no longer qualify his team for membership! At the rate they were going, the Brabham-BMWs would never be in a position to score sufficient points to keep the team in play as a front-running contender – and thus perhaps end up losing its important travel benefits which accrue to the 10 top points scoring teams, taken on a half-yearly basis.

The prospect of this happening was seemed to be increased when Piquet, having qualified third behind Tambay's Renault RE50 and de Angelis's Lotus 95T, came smoking into the pits after only 11 laps with another mammoth turbo failure. The

Player's
POSITIONS
1 01
2 07
3 11
16 4
26 5
27 6
TOURS
St-Hubert
HONDA
Player's
HONDA
LONGINES
parmalat
parmalat

Nelson Piquet in command of the 1984 Canadian Grand Prix, his BT53 having just taken the lead from Alain Prost's McLaren MP4/2. The Ferrari C4s of Michele Alboreto and René Arnoux are third and fourth ahead of Elio de Angelis's Lotus 95T. (Inset) Corrado Fabi waves team leader Piquet through as the World Champion comes up to lap him.

overheated turbocharger had also set fire to the Brabham's side pod, so Nelson had to hop smartly from the cockpit as his mechanics doused the car in foam. The only consolation to emerge from this weekend was Teo Fabi's ninth place finish, proving that a Brabham BT53 could, after all, complete a race. It was not terribly competitive, but it finished . . .

Teo's absence at the Milwaukee CART race gave younger brother Corrado the chance to make his Brabham debut at Monaco, his experience allied to electrical problems during practice and torrential rain during the race hardly aiding his cause. Nelson found his car plagued with turbocharger boost control problems and could only qualify ninth at Monaco, falling to the tail of the field at the start and struggling in to retire with waterlogged electrics after 24 embarrassing laps, by which time Fabi *minimus* had himself spun off at Portier and had been similarly unable to restart his sodden engine . . .

What worried Gordon Murray more than anything else was the fact that most of the engine failures did not seem to be related: "Normally, if you start a season with one particular problem, you have to write off a couple of races while you sort it out. But, this year, once we sorted out one problem, another totally unrelated failure occurred, with the result that we've just been chasing breakages backwards and forwards throughout the engine . . ."

"The main changes on the BT53 over the BT52 were a mixture of aerodynamic alterations and improvements for turbocharger cooling, but much of our trouble was down to qualify control problems with the KKK turbochargers and the Behr intercoolers which are supplied by BMW." Without the 1983 luxury of as much fuel as one cared to use, within limits, the prohibition of fuel stops meant that additional attention had to be concentrated on an efficient intercooling and producing a turbocharger capable of withstanding increased loads and temperatures. Of course, Brabham's pool of 25 BMW engines was continuously shouldering the brunt of the Munich firm's test and development work, but there was a limit to how much consequent unreliability could be allowed to compromise the Brabham racing programme.

During practice at Zolder an incorrectly mixed batch of fuel accounted for no fewer than ten engine failures, highlighting just how crucial the correctly prepared "brew" had become in this high technology era of turbocharged Formula 1 engines. But, underlying this frustrating sequence of failures was an inherent strand of speed and competitiveness emphasized by a string of pole positions. If the Brabham-BMW would only last, then most people expected it to win.

Despite feeling distinctly unwell with an upset stomach, Nelson Piquet started the 70 lap, 191.82 mile Canadian Grand Prix at Circuit Gilles Villeneuve from pole position. Prost briefly led for the first half lap, but Nelson powered into the lead as they came out of the first hairpin and that was the end of the race. The BMW engine stood the pace on this occasion and Piquet won convincingly to celebrate the second anniversary of the Brabham-BMW partnership's first such success. His only complaint at the end of the race was a badly burnt foot, toasted by the new nose-mounted oil radiator which had been prepared for the sweltering heat anticipated in Dallas some three weeks hence.

A week later, Piquet dished out another defeat to his rivals when he won the Detroit Grand Prix over 63 laps, 157.50 miles of the "Motor City" street circuit. This time his achievement was even more praiseworthy for Piquet achieved this success at the wheel of the team's spare BT53 which he had been obliged to take following a startline shunt which saw the race stopped at the end of the first lap. Nigel Mansell had attempted to thread his Lotus 95T through a gap between Piquet and Prost on the front row, but the Englishman's challenge just was not on. The result was a multiple pile-up which involved several cars, the most badly damaged of which was Piquet's BT53 which riccochetted backwards into the concrete retaining wall and was severely damaged as a result. Nelson, nursing a stiff neck, climbed into the spare car and led from start to finish. Teo Fabi backing him up with a cautious run to fourth.

Dallas proved to be a total fiasco for the Brabham-BMWs, Piquet never getting with it all weekend and actually qualifying behind Corrado Fabi who wound up a distant seventh at the end of two hours' slog in the unyielding Texas sun. Piquet grappled manfully with a sticking throttle during the race, but it eventually caught him out and he slid into an escape road, retiring ignominiously right in front of a television camera which beamed his indiscretion round the world . . .

For the British Grand Prix at Brands Hatch Gordon Murray came up with what he termed "a fairly new motor car, the BT53B. This involved a *lot* of work in the middle of the season – new rear wing, body top, aerodynamics, radiators, intercoolers, engine inlet . . . It looked good in the wind tunnel, but we abandoned it as an entity after practice at Brands where, although it handled well, we were unable to generate sufficient tyre temperature. We did keep the rear body underwings and the rear suspension layout, though, on the regular BT53 . . ."

Over the balance of the year, Piquet continued to demonstrate generally brilliant form. He was in with the two McLarens during the Brands race, only to fade to seventh place with loss of turbo boost pressure. At Hockenheim he had the legs of both Prost and Lauda again until the six-speed gearbox suffered pinion bearing failure and he made one of his rare errors by failing to pressure Niki Lauda's ailing McLaren in the closing stages of the Austrian Grand Prix. "I thought he was stroking it home to win," said Nelson ruefully, "my tyres were blistered, so I thought I would settle for second place. I didn't know he was in trouble. It was my mistake . . ." Still, with Fabi finishing fourth again, it was not a bad result for the team as a whole. The diminutive Italian had now chosen to concentrate on Formula 1 for the second half of the season and, having made that decision, his driving form improved significantly over the last few races.

A loose oil union leaked away most of the oil from Piquet's BT53 at Zandvoort, robbing him of a chance of a runaway Dutch Grand Prix victory while he was the class of the field in the Italian Grand Prix at Monza (where he started from pole yet again) until his BMW engine expired yet again. A lurid slide over the high kerbing at Lesmo on the second lap may or may not have damaged a water radiator, causing the coolant to leak away as a prelude to engine failure. However, what that slide over that kerb *did* do was to produce an impact which snapped off the clutch master cylinder, leaving Piquet to change gear without it for the balance of his tenure in the lead. Fabi, despite an early spin, also hung onto the leading bunch at Monza, earning vociferous praise from his compatriots when he abandoned his blown-up BT53 right in front of the main start/finish grandstand after 43 impressive laps. Another broken oil union was diagnosed as the cause of this mechanical failure.

The first Grand Prix of Europe at Nurburgring saw Piquet on pole, as did the final round of the Championship at Estoril in Portugal. However, in Germany a stiff gearchange frustrated Nelson's efforts on BMW's home soil and he struggled home third, running out of fuel on the last lap and pipped to the line by Michele Alboreto's similarly fuel-starved Ferrari. Then, at Estoril, another rare error saw Nelson spin on the opening lap: he recovered to haul back to sixth place, but all chances of another victory had vanished. Manfred Winkelhock was drafted in to drive the second BT53 after Teo Fabi hurried home to Italy on the death of his father: the German driver performed unspectacularly to finish 10th.

With fourth place in the Constructors' Cup and Piquet only managing fifth in the Drivers' Championship, the 1984 season had turned out to be a spectacular anti-climax following Piquet's title-winning success of the previous year. But the Brabham team could at least console itself with the knowledge that its number one driver had been right on the pace throughout the year. The BMW side of the equation, rarely the Brabham ingredients, had been predominantly responsible for this disheartening lack of achievement.

BMW MPower
2

Teo Fabi's BT53 spins to a halt on the outside of Tarzan during the 1984 Dutch Grand Prix at Zandvoort. The Italian driver kept the engine running and resumed to finish fifth.

Appendix

KEY TO ABBREVIATIONS

Ret	Retired
DNF	Did not finish
NC	Not classified
DNQ	Did not qualify
DNS	Did not start
DNA	Did not arrive

(Capital letters denote World Championship qualifying rounds)

1962

Aug 15, GERMAN GRAND PRIX, Nurburgring
J. Brabham BT3/F1-1-62 Climax Ret: throttle linkage
Sept 1, Gold Cup Oulton Park
J. Brabham BT3/F1-1-62 Climax 3rd
Oct 7, UNITED STATES GRAND PRIX, Watkins Glen
J. Brabham BT3/F1-1-62 Climax 4th
Nov 4, Mexican Grand Prix, Mexico City
J. Brabham BT3/F1-1-62 Climax 2nd
Dec 29, SOUTH AFRICAN GRAND PRIX, East London
J. Brabham BT3/F1-1-62 Climax 4th

1963

April 15, Glover Trophy, Goodwood
J. Brabham BT3/F1-1-62 Climax 6th
April 15, Pau Grand Prix, Pau
J. Schlesser BT2/FJ-5-62 Ford Ret: ignition
April 21, Grand Prix of Imola, Castellaccis
J. Schlesser BT2/FJ-5-62 Ford 4th
April 27, Aintree 200, Aintree, Liverpool
J. Brabham BT3/F1-1-62 Climax DNS: engine
May 11, International Trophy, Silverstone
J. Brabham BT3/F1-1-62 Climax 7th
D. Gurney DNS: car not ready
May 26, MONACO GRAND PRIX, Monte Carlo
J. Brabham BT3/F1-1-62 Climax DNS: engine (took spare Team Lotus 25)
D. Gurney BT7/F1-1-63 Climax Ret: transmission
June 9, BELGIAN GRAND PRIX, Spa-Francorchamps
J. Brabham BT3/F1-1-62 Climax Ret: injection pump
D. Gurney BT7/F1-1-63 Climax 3rd
June 23, DUTCH GRAND PRIX, Zandvoort
J. Brabham BT7/F1-2-63 Climax Ret: accident
D. Gurney BT7/F1-1-63 Climax 2nd
June 30, FRENCH GRAND PRIX, Reims-Gueux
J. Brabham BT7/F1-2-63 Climax 4th
D. Gurney BT7/F1-1-63 Climax 5th
July 20, BRITISH GRAND PRIX, Silverstone
J. Brabham BT7/F1-2-63 Climax Ret: engine
D. Gurney BT7/F1-1-63 Climax Ret: engine
July 28, Solitude Grand Prix, W. Germany
J. Brabham BT3/F1-1-62 Climax 1st
Aug 4, GERMAN GRAND PRIX, Nurburgring
J. Brabham BT7/F1-2-63 Climax 7th
D. Gurney BT7/F1-1-63 Climax Ret: gearbox
Aug 11, Kanonloppet, Karlskoga, Sweden
J. Brabham BT7/F1-1-63 Climax 3rd
D. Hulme BT3/F1-1-62 Climax 4th
D. Prophet BT6/FJ-5-63 Ford 11th
Aug 18, Mediterranean Grand Prix, Enna-Pergusa
J. Brabham BT7/F1-2-63 Climax 12th
Sept 1, Austrian Grand Prix, Zeltweg
J. Brabham BT3/F1-1-62 Climax 1st
Sept 8, ITALIAN GRAND PRIX, Monza
J. Brabham BT3/F1-1-62 Climax 5th
D. Gurney BT7/F1-1-63 Climax Ret: fuel feed
Sept 21, Gold Cup, Oulton Park
J. Brabham BT7/F1-2-63 Climax 4th
D. Gurney BT7/F1-2-63 Climax Ret: oil leak
Oct 6, UNITED STATES GRAND PRIX, Watkins Glen
J. Brabham BT7/F1-2-63 Climax 4th
D. Gurney BT7/F1-1-63 Climax Ret: cracked chassis
October 27, MEXICAN GRAND PRIX, Mexico City
J. Brabham BT7/F1-2-63 Climax 2nd
D. Gurney BT7/F1-1-63 Climax 6th
Dec 14, Rand Grand Prix, Kyalami
D. Prophet BT6/FJ-5-63 Ford 6th
Dec 28, SOUTH AFRICAN GRAND PRIX, East London
J. Brabham BT7/F1-2-63 Climax 13th
D. Gurney BT7/F1-1-63 Climax 2nd
D. Prophet BT6/FJ-5-63 Ford Ret: oil pressure

1964

March 14, Daily Mirror Trophy, Snetterton
J. Brabham BT7/F1-1-63 Climax Ret: scavenge pump
I. Raby BT3/F1-1-62 BRM Ret: accident
March 30, News of the World Trophy, Goodwood
J. Brabham BT7/F1-2-63 Climax Ret: broken wheel rim
I. Raby BT3/F1-1-62 BRM
April 12, Syracuse Grand Prix, Syracuse, Sicily
I. Raby BT3/F1-1-62 BRM 8th
April 18, Aintree 200, Aintree, Liverpool
J. Brabham BT7/F1-2-63 Climax 1st
D. Gurney BT7/F1-1-63 Climax Ret: transmission
I. Raby BT3/F1-1-62 BRM 15th
D. Hulme BT10/F2-1-64 Ford 10th
A. Rees BT10/F2-2-64 Ford Ret: out of fuel
May 2, International Trophy, Silverstone
J. Brabham BT7/F1-2-63 Climax 1st
D. Gurney BT7/F1-1-63 Climax Ret: brakes
R. Anderson BT11/F1-5-64 Climax Ret: clutch
I. Raby BT3/F1-1-62 BRM Ret: piston
J. Bonnier BT11/F1-4-64 BRM DNS: practice fire
May 10, MONACO GRAND PRIX, Monte Carlo
J. Brabham BT7/F1-2-63 Climax Ret: fuel injection
D. Gurney BT7/F1-1-63 Climax Ret: gearbox
R. Anderson BT11/F1-5-64 Climax Ret: gearbox mounting
May 24, DUTCH GRAND PRIX, Zandvoort
J. Brabham BT7/F1-2-63 Climax Ret: ignition
D. Gurney BT7/F1-1-63 Climax Ret: broken steering wheel
J. Bonnier BT11/F1-4-64 BRM 9th
R. Anderson BT11/F1-5-64 Climax 6th
J. Siffert BT11/F1-6-64 BRM 13th
June 14, BELGIAN GRAND PRIX, Spa-Francorchamps
J. Brabham BT7/F1-2-63 Climax 3rd
D. Gurney BT7/F1-1-63 Climax Ret: out of fuel
J. Bonnier BT11/F1-4-64 BRM Ret: driver unwell
J. Siffert BT11/F1-6-64 BRM Ret: engine
R. Anderson BT11/F1-5-64 Climax DNS: practice problems
June 28, FRENCH GRAND PRIX, Rouen-les-Essarts
J. Brabham BT7/F1-2-63 Climax 3rd
D. Gurney BT7/F1-1-63 Climax 1st
J. Siffert BT11/F1-6-64 BRM Ret: clutch
R. Anderson BT11/F1-5-64 Climax 12th
July 11, BRITISH GRAND PRIX, Brands Hatch
J. Brabham BT7/F1-2-63 Climax 4th
D. Gurney BT7/F1-1-63 Climax 13th
J. Bonnier BT11/F1-4-64 BRM Ret: brake pipe
J. Siffert BT11/F1-6-64 BRM 11th
R. Anderson BT11/F1-5-64 Climax 7th
I. Raby BT3/F1-1-62 BRM Ret: accident
F. Gardner BT10/F2-4-64 Ford Ret: accident on grid
July 19, Solitude Grand Prix, Solitude, W. Germany
J. Brabham BT7/F1-2-63 Climax Ret: accident
J. Siffert BT11/F1-6-64 BRM 7th
J. Bonnier BT11/F1-4-64 BRM 5th
R. Anderson BT11/F1-5-64 Climax 3rd
Aug 2, GERMAN GRAND PRIX, Nurburgring
J. Brabham BT7/F1-2-63 Climax Ret: transmission
D. Gurney BT7/F1-1-63 Climax 10th
J. Bonnier BT11/F1-4-64 BRM Ret: electrical
J. Siffert BT11/F1-6-64 BRM 4th
R. Anderson BT11/F1-5-64 Climax Ret: suspension
Aug 16, Mediterranean Grand Prix, Enna-Pergusa
J. Siffert BT11/F1-6-64 BRM 1st
F. Gardner BT10/F2-4-64 Ford Ret: engine

Aug 23, AUSTRIAN GRAND PRIX, Zeltweg

J. Brabham	BT11/F1-1-64 Climax	9th
D. Gurney	BT7/F1-1-63 Climax	Ret: suspension
J. Bonnier	BT7/F1-2-63 Climax	6th
J. Rindt	BT11/F1-4-64 BRM	Ret: steering
J. Siffert	BT11/F1-6-64 BRM	Ret: accident
R. Anderson	BT11/F1-5-64 Climax	3rd

Sept 6, ITALIAN GRAND PRIX, Monza

J. Brabham	BT11/F1-1-64 Climax	Ret: engine
D. Gurney	BT7/F1-1-63 Climax	10th
J. Bonnier	BT7/F1-2-63 Climax	12th
G. Russo	BT11/F1-4-64 BRM	DNQ
J. Siffert	BT11/F1-6-64 BRM	7th
R. Anderson	BT11/F1-5-64 Climax	11th
I. Raby	BT3/F1-1-62 BRM	DNS

Oct 4, UNITED STATES GRAND PRIX, Watkins Glen

J. Brabham	BT11/F1-1-64 Climax	Ret: engine
D. Gurney	BT7/F1-1-63 Climax	Ret: engine
J. Bonnier	BT7/F1-2-63 Climax	Ret: stub axle
J. Siffert	BT11/F1-1-64 BRM	3rd
H. Sharp	BT11/F1-4-64 BRM	NC

Oct 25, MEXICAN GRAND PRIX, Mexico City

J. Brabham	BT11/F1-1-64 Climax	Ret: electrical
D. Gurney	BT7/F1-1-63 Climax	1st
J. Bonnier	BT7/F1-2-63 Climax	Ret: broken wishbone
H. Sharp	BT11/F1-4-64 BRM	13th
J. Siffert	BT11/F1-6-64 BRM	Ret: fuel pump

Dec 11, Rand Grand Prix, Kyalami

G. Hill	BT11/F1-4-64 BRM	1st
R. Anderson	BT11/F1-5-64 Climax	3rd
P. Hawkins	BT10/F2-2-64 Ford	2nd
D. Prophet	BT10/F2-10-64 Ford	18th

1965

Jan 1, SOUTH AFRICAN GRAND PRIX, East London

J. Brabham	BT11/F1-1-64 Climax	8th
D. Gurney	BT11/F1-2-64 Climax	Ret: ignition
J. Bonnier	BT7/F1-2-63 Climax	Ret: clutch
J. Siffert	BT11/F1-6-64 BRM	7th
R. Anderson	BT11/F1-5-64 Climax	16th
F. Gardner	BT11/F1-4-64 BRM	12th
P. Hawkins	BT10/F2-2-64 Ford	9th
D. Prophet	BT10/F2-10-64 Ford	14th

March 13, Race of Champions, Brands Hatch

J. Brabham	BT11/F1-1-64 Climax	Ret: oil leak
D. Gurney	BT11/F1-2-64 Climax	Ret: engine
J. Bonnier	BT7/F1-2-63 Climax	3rd
J. Siffert	BT11/F1-6-64 BRM	6th
R. Anderson	BT11/F1-5-64 Climax	Ret: throttle linkage
F. Gardner	BT11/F1-4-64 BRM	4th
I. Raby	BT3/F1-1-62 BRM	9th
R. Bloor	BT14/FL-6-65 Ford	Ret: steering

April 4, Syracuse Grand Prix, Syracuse, Sicily

J. Siffert	BT11/F1-6-64 BRM	Ret: engine
J. Bonnier	BT7/F1-2-63 Climax	4th
R. Anderson	BT11/F1-5-64 Climax	6th
I. Raby	BT3/F1-1-62 BRM	8th

April 19, Sunday Mirror Trophy, Goodwood

J. Brabham	BT11/F1-1-64 Climax	3rd
D. Gurney	BT11/F1-2-64 Climax	9th
J. Bonnier	BT7/F1-2-63 Climax	5th
J. Siffert	BT11/F1-6-64 BRM	Ret: accident
R. Anderson	BT11/F1-5-64 Climax	Ret: disqualified
F. Gardner	BT11/F1-4-64 BRM	DNS: practice problems
R. Bloor	BT14/FL-6-65 Ford	12th
J. Cardwell	BT14/FL-8-65 Ford	11th

May 15, International Trophy, Silverstone

J. Brabham	BT11/F1-1-64 Climax	Ret: gearbox
D. Hulme	BT11/F1-2-64 Climax	Ret: oil leak
J. Bonnier	BT7/F1-2-63 Climax	5th
R. Anderson	BT11/F1-5-64 Climax	14th
F. Gardner	BT11/F1-4-64 BRM	Ret: clutch
I. Raby	BT3/F1-1-62 BRM	12th

May 30, MONACO GRAND PRIX, Monte Carlo

J. Brabham	BT11/F1-1-64 Climax	Ret: engine
D. Hulme	BT7/F1-1-63 Climax	8th
J. Bonnier	BT7/F1-2-63 Climax	7th
J. Siffert	BT11/F1-6-64 BRM	6th
R. Anderson	BT11/F1-5-64 Climax	9th
F. Gardner	BT11/F1-4-64 BRM	Ret: engine mounting

June 13, BELGIAN GRAND PRIX, Spa-Francorchamps

J. Brabham	BT11/F1-1-64 Climax	4th
D. Gurney	BT11/F1-2-64 Climax	10th
J. Bonnier	BT7/F1-2-63 Climax	Ret: ignition
J. Siffert	BT11/F1-6-64 BRM	8th
R. Anderson	BT11/F1-5-64 Climax	DNS
F. Gardner	BT11/F1-4-64 BRM	Ret: ignition

June 27, FRENCH GRAND PRIX, Clermont Ferrand

D. Gurney	BT11/F1-2-64 Climax	Ret: engine
D. Hulme	BT11/F1-1-64 Climax	4th
J. Bonnier	BT7/F1-2-63 Climax	Ret: electrical
J. Siffert	BT11/F1-6-64 BRM	6th
R. Anderson	BT11/F1-5-64 Climax	9th

July 10, BRITISH GRAND PRIX, Silverstone

J. Brabham	BT11/F1-1-64 Climax	DNS: gave car to Gurney
D. Gurney	BT11/F1-1-64 Climax	6th
D. Hulme	BT7/F1-1-63 Climax	Ret: electrical
J. Bonnier	BT7/F1-2-63 Climax	7th
J. Siffert	BT11/F1-6-64 BRM	9th
R. Anderson	BT11/F1-65 Climax	Ret: gearbox
F. Gardner	BT11/F1-4-64 BRM	8th
I. Raby	BT3/F1-1-62 BRM	11th

July 18, DUTCH GRAND PRIX, Zandvoort

D. Gurney	BT11/F1-2-64 Climax	3rd
D. Hulme	BT11/F1-1-64 Climax	5th
J. Bonnier	BT7/F1-2-63 Climax	Ret: engine
J. Siffert	BT11/F1-6-64 BRM	13th
R. Anderson	BT11/F1-5-64 Climax	Ret: engine
F. Gardner	BT11/F1-4-64 BRM	11th

Aug 1, GERMAN GRAND PRIX, Nurburgring

J. Brabham	BT11/F1-1-64 Climax	5th
D. Gurney	BT11/F1-2-64 Climax	3rd
D. Hulme	BT7/F1-1-63 Climax	Ret: fuel leak
J. Bonnier	BT7/F1-2-63 Climax	7th
J. Siffert	BT11/F1-6-64 BRM	Ret: engine
R. Anderson	BT11/F1-5-64 Climax	DNS: practice accident
F. Gardner	BT11/F1-4-64 BRM	Ret: gearbox
I. Raby	BT3/F1-1-62 BRM	DNQ

Aug 15, Mediterranean Grand Prix, Enna-Pergusa, Sicily

J. Brabham	BT11/F1-1-64 Climax	6th
D. Hulme	BT7/F1-1-63 Climax	4th
J. Bonnier	BT7/F1-2-63 Climax	Ret: engine
J. Siffert	BT11/F1-6-64 BRM	1st
F. Gardner	BT11/F1-4-64 BRM	3rd
A. Rees	BT16/F2-10-65 Ford	Ret: engine

Sept 12, ITALIAN GRAND PRIX, Monza

D. Gurney	BT11/F1-2-64 Climax	3rd
D. Hulme	BT11/F1-1-64 Climax	Ret: suspension
G. Baghetti	BT7/F1-1-63 Climax	Ret: engine
J. Bonnier	BT7/F1-2-63 Climax	7th
J. Siffert	BT11/F1-6-64 BRM	Ret: gearbox
F. Gardner	BT11/F1-4-64 BRM	Ret: engine

Oct 3, UNITED STATES GRAND PRIX, Watkins Glen

J. Brabham	BT11/F1-1-64 Climax	3rd
D. Gurney	BT11/F1-2-64 Climax	2nd
J. Bonnier	BT7/F1-2-63 Climax	8th
J. Siffert	BT11/F1-6-64 BRM	11th

Oct 24, MEXICAN GRAND PRIX, Mexico City

J. Brabham	BT11/F1-1-64 Climax	Ret: oil leak
D. Gurney	BT11/F1-2-64 Climax	2nd
J. Bonnier	BT11/F1-2-63 Climax	Ret: suspension
J. Siffert	BT11/F1-6-64 BRM	4th

1966

Jan 1, South African Grand Prix, East London

J. Brabham	BT19/F1-1-66 Repco	Ret: injection pump
D. Hulme	BT22/F1-1-64 Climax 4	Ret: transmission
R. Anderson	BT11/F1-5-64 Climax 4	Ret:
D. Charlton	BT11/F1-2-64 Climax 4	4th
J. Siffert	BT11/F1-6-64 BRM V8	2nd

May 1, Syracuse Grand Prix, Syracuse, Sicily

J. Brabham	BT19/F1-1-66 Repco	Ret: metering unit
D. Hulme	BT22/F1-1-64 Climax 4	Ret: piston
R. Anderson	BT11/.F1-5-64 Climax 4	DNS: practice problems
J. Bonnier	BT11/ F1-6-64 BRM V8	5th

May 14, International Trophy, Silverstone

J. Brabham	BT19/F1-1-66 Repco	1st
D. Hulme	BT22/F1-1-64 Climax 4	4th
J. Taylor	BT11/F1-4-64 BRM	6th
R. Anderson	BT11/F1-5-64 Climax 4	7th

May 22, MONACO GRAND PRIX, Monte Carlo

J. Brabham	BT19/F1-1-66 Repco	Ret: transmission
D. Hulme	BT22/F1-1-64 Climax 4	Ret: transmission
R. Anderson	BT11/F1-5-64 Climax 4	Ret: transmission
J. Siffert	BT11/F1-6-64 BRM V8	Ret: clutch

June 13, BELGIAN GRAND PRIX, Spa-Francorchamps

J. Brabham	BT19/F1-1-66 Repco	4th
D. Hulme	BT22/F1-1-64 Climax 4	Ret: accident damage

July 3, FRENCH GRAND PRIX, Reims

J. Brabham	BT19/F1-1-66 Repco	1st
D. Hulme	BT20/F1-2-66 Repco	3rd
J. Bonnier	BT22/F1-1-64 Climax 4	NC
J. Taylor	BT11/F1-4-64 BRM V8	6th
R. Anderson	BT33/F1-5-64 Climax 4	7th

July 16, BRITISH GRAND PRIX, Brands Hatch

J. Brabham	BT19/F1-1-66 Repco	1st
D. Hulme	BT20/F1-2-66 Repco	2nd
C. Irwin	BT22/F1-1-64 Climax 4	7th
J. Bonnier	BT7/F1-2-63 Climax V8	Ret:
J. Taylor	BT11/F1-4-64 BRM V8	8th
R. Anderson	BT11/F1-5-64 Climax 4	13th

July 24, DUTCH GRAND PRIX, Zandvoort

J. Brabham	BT19/F1-1-66 Repco	1st
D. Hulme	BT20/F1-2-66 Repco	Ret: ignition
J. Taylor	BT/11/F1-4-64 BRM V8	8th
R. Anderson	BT11/F1-5-64 Climax 4	Ret: suspension

Aug 7, GERMAN GRAND PRIX, Nurburgring

J. Brabham	BT19/F1-1-66 Repco	1st
D. Hulme	BT20/F1-2-66 Repco	Ret: ignition
J. Taylor	BT11/F1-4-64 BRM V8	Ret: accident
R. Anderson	BT11/F1-5-64 Climax 4	Ret: transmission

Sept 4, ITALIAN GRAND PRIX, Monza
J. Brabham *BT19/F1-1-65 Repco Ret: oil leak
D. Hulme BT20/F1-2-66 Repco 3rd
R. Anderson BT11/F1-5-64 Climax 4 6th
C. Amon BT11/F1-6-64 BRM V8 DNQ
Sept 17, Gold Cup, Oulton Park
J. Brabham *BT19/F1-1-65 Repco 1st
D. Hulme BT20/F1-2-66 Repco 2nd
R. Anderson BT11/F1-5-64 Climax 4 Ret: engine
Oct 2, UNITED STATES GRAND PRIX, Watkins Glen
J. Brabham BT20/F1-1-66 Repco Ret: engine
D. Hulme BT20/F1-2-66 Repco Ret: engine
Oct 23, MEXICAN GRAND PRIX, Mexico City
J. Brabham BT20/F1-1-66 Repco 2nd
D. Hulme BT20/F1-2-66 Repco 3rd
FOOTNOTE: *BT19 renumbered thus after introduction of "second" BT20 chassis

1967
Jan 2, SOUTH AFRICAN GRAND PRIX, Kyalami
J. Brabham BT20/F1-1-66 Repco 6th
D. Hulme BT20/F1-2-66 Repco 4th
R. Anderson BT11/F1-5-64 Climax 4 5th
D. Charlton BT11/F1-2-64 Climax 4 NC
L. Botha BT11/IC-5-64 Climax 4 NC
March 12, Race of Champions, Brands Hatch
J. Brabham BT20/F1-1-66 Repco 9th
D. Hulme BT20/F1-2-66 Repco Ret: electrical
R. Anderson BT11/F1-5-64 Climax 4 Ret: ignition
April 15, Spring Cup, Oulton Park
J. Brabham BT20/F1-1-66 Repco 1st
D. Hulme BT20/F1-2-66 Repco 2nd
R. Anderson BT11/F1-5-64 Climax 4 7th
April 29, International Trophy, Silverstone
J. Brabham BT20/F1-1-66 Repco 2nd
D. Hulme BT20/F1-2-66 Repco Ret: off circuit
R. Anderson BT11/F1-5-64 Climax 4 8th
May 7, MONACO GRAND PRIX, Monte Carlo
J. Brabham BT19/F1-1-65 Repco Ret: engine
D. Hulme BT20/F1-2-66 Repco 1st
R. Anderson BT11/F1-1-64 Climax 4 DNQ
June 4, DUTCH GRAND PRIX, Zandvoort
J. Brabham BT19/F1-1-65 Repco 2nd
D. Hulme BT20/F1-2-66 Repco 3rd
R. Anderson BT11/F1-5-64 Climax 4 9th
June 18, BELGIAN GRAND PRIX, Spa-Francorchamps
J. Brabham BT24/1 Repco Ret: engine
D. Hulme BT19/F1-1-65 Repco Ret: engine
R. Anderson BT11/F1-5-64 Climax 4 8th
July 2, FRENCH GRAND PRIX, Bugatti Circuit, Le Mans
J. Brabham BT24/1 Repco 1st
D. Hulme BT24/2 Repco 2nd
R. Anderson BT11/F1-5-64 Climax 4 Ret: ignition
July 15, BRITISH GRAND PRIX, Silverstone
J. Brabham BT24/1 Repco 4th
D. Hulme BT24/2 Repco 2nd
G. Ligier BT20/F1-2-66 Repco 10th
R. Anderson BT11/ F1-5-64 Climax 4 Ret: engine
Aug 6, GERMAN GRAND PRIX, Nurburgring
J. Brabham BT24/1 Repco 2nd
D. Hulme BT24/2 Repco 1st
G. Ligier BT20/F1-2-66 Repco 6th
A. Rees F2 BT23/ Cos. FVA 2nd class
G. Mitter F2 BT/23/ Cos. FVA Ret: engine
Aug 27, CANADIAN GRAND PRIX, Mosport Park
J. Brabham BT24/1 Repco 1st
D. Hulme BT24/2 Repco 2nd
Sept 10, ITALIAN GRAND PRIX, Monza
J. Brabham BT24/1 Repco 2nd
D. Hulme BT24/2 Repco Ret: engine
G. Ligier BT20/F1-2-66 Repco Ret: engine
Sept 17, Gold Cup, Oulton Park
J. Brabham BT24/1 Repco 1st
F. Gardner BT19/F1-1-65 Repco Ret: ignition
G. Pitt BT23B-3 Climax 4
Oct 1, UNITED STATES GRAND PRIX, Watkins Glen
J. Brabham BT24/1 Repco 5th
D. Hulme BT24/2 Repco 3rd
G. Ligier BT20/F1-2-66 Repco Ret: engine
Oct 22, MEXICAN GRAND PRIX, Mexico City
J. Brabham BT24/1 Repco 2nd
D. Hulme BT24/2 Repco 3rd
G. Ligier BT20/F1-2-66 Repco 11th
Nov 12, Spanish Grand Prix, Jarama
J. Brabham BT19/F1-1-65 Repco 3rd

1968
Jan 1, SOUTH AFRICAN GRAND PRIX, Kyalami
J. Brabham BT24/1 Repco Ret: engine
J. Rindt BT24/2 Repco 3rd
J. Love BT20/F1-1-66 Repco 9th
D. Charlton BT11/F1-2-64 Repco Ret: transmission
Race of Champions, Brands Hatch
S. Moser BT20/F1-2-64 Repco Ret: engine
May 12, SPANISH GRAND PRIX, Jarama
J. Brabham BT26/1 Repco DNS: mechanical
J. Rindt BT24/3 Repco Ret: engine
May 26, MONACO GRAND PRIX, Monte Carlo
J. Brabham BT26/1 Repco Ret: suspension
J. Rindt BT24/3 Repco Ret: accident
S. Moser BT20/F1-2-66 Repco DNQ
P. Gethin BT21 BMW 4 10th
A. Lanfranchi BT23B-3 Climax 4 7th
June 9, BELGIAN GRAND PRIX, Spa-Francorchamps
J. Brabham BT26/1 Repco Ret: fuel pump
J. Rindt BT26/2 Repco Ret: engine
June 23, DUTCH GRAND PRIX, Zandvoort
J. Brabham BT26/1 Repco Ret: accident
J. Rindt BT26/2 Repco Ret: driver withdrew
D. Gurney BT24/3 Repco Ret: driver withdrew
D. Moser BT20/F1-2-66 Repco 5th
July 7, FRENCH GRAND PRIX, Rouen-les-Essarts
J. Brabham BT26/1 Repco Ret: fuel system
J. Rindt BT26/2 Repco Ret: split fuel tank
July 20, BRITISH GRAND PRIX, Brands Hatch
J. Brabham BT26/1 Repco Ret: engine
J. Rindt BT26/2 Repco Ret: electrical fire
S. Moser BT20/F1-2-66 Repco NC
Aug 4, GERMAN GRAND PRIX, Nurburgring
J. Brabham BT26/1 Repco 5th
J. Rindt BT26/2 Repco 3rd
K. Ahrens BT24/2 Repco 12th
S. Moser BT20/F1-2-66 Repco DNQ
Aug 17, Gold Cup, Oulton Park
J. Brabham BT26/1 Repco Ret: engine
J. Rindt BT26/2 Repco Ret: engine
Sept 8, ITALIAN GRAND PRIX, Monza
J. Brabham BT26/1 Repco Ret: engine
J. Rindt BT26/1 Repco Ret: engine
S. Moser BT20/F1-2-66 Repco DNQ
Sept 22, CANADIAN GRAND PRIX, Ste. Jovite
J. Brabham BT26/1 Repco Ret: exhaust
J. Rindt BT26/3 Repco Ret: engine
Oct 6, UNITED STATES GRAND PRIX, Watkins Glen
J. Brabham BT26/1 Repco Ret: engine
J. Rindt BT26/3 Repco Ret: engine
Nov 3, MEXICAN GRAND PRIX, Mexico City
J. Brabham BT26/1 Repco Ret: engine
J. Rindt BT26/3 Repco Ret: ignition

1969
March 1, SOUTH AFRICAN GRAND PRIX, Kyalami
J. Brabham BT26/2 Cos DFV Ret: handling
J. Ickx BT26/3 Cos. DFV Ret: engine
S. Tingle BT24/2 Repco 8th
P. de Klerk BT20/F1-1-66 Repco NC
March 16, Race of Champions, Brands Hatch
J. Brabham BT26/2 Cos. DFV Ret: leaking fuel pipe
J. Ickx BT26/3 Cos. DFV Ret: sticking throttles
P. Courage BT26/1 Cos. DFV Ret: split fuel tank
R. Pike BT23B-3 Climax 4 DNS
March 30, International Trophy, Silverstone
J. Brabham BT26/2 Cos. DFV 1st
J. Ickx BT26/3 Cos. DFV 4th
P. Courage BT26/1 Cos. DFV 5th
May 4, SPANISH GRAND PRIX, Montjuich Park, Barcelona
J. Brabham BT26/2 Cos. DFV Ret: engine
J. Ickx BT26/3 Cos. DFV Ret: suspension
P. Courage BT26/1 Cos. DFV Ret: engine
May 18, MONACO GRAND PRIX, Monte Carlo
J. Brabham BT26/2 Cos. DFV Ret: accident
J. Ickx BT26/3 Cos. DFV Ret: broken hub carrier
P. Courage BT26/1 Cos. DFV 2nd
S. Moser BT24/3 Cos. DFV Ret: transmission
June 21, DUTCH GRAND PRIX, Zandvoort
J. Brabham BT26/2 Cos. DFV 6th
J. Ickx BT26/3 Cos. DFV 5th
P. Courage BT26/1 Cos. DFV Ret: clutch
S. Moser BT24/3 Cos. DFV Ret: steering/ignition
July 6, FRENCH GRAND PRIX, Clermont-Ferrand
J. Brabham BT26 Cos. DFV DNS: injured in testing accident at Silverstone
J. Ickx BT26/3 Cos. DFV 3rd
P. Courage BT26/1 Cos. DFV Ret: loose bodywork
July 19, BRITISH GRAND PRIX, Silverstone
J. Ickx BT26/4 Cos. DFV 2nd
P. Courage BT26/1 Cos. DFV 5th
August 3, GERMAN GRAND PRIX, Nurburgring
J. Ickx BT26/4 Cos. DFV 1st
P. Courage BT26/1 Cos. DFV Ret: accident
P. Westbury F2 BT30 Cos. FVA 5th in F2 class
R. Attwood F2 BT30 Cos. FVA 2nd in F2 class
X. Perrot F2 BT23C Cos. FVA 6th in F2 class
Aug 16, Gold Cup, Oulton Park
J. Ickx BT26/3 Cos. DFV 1st
Sept 7, ITALIAN GRAND PRIX, Monza
J. Brabham BT26/4 Cos. DFV Ret: oil leak
J. Ickx BT26/3 Cos. DFV 10th
P. Courage BT26/1 Cos. DFV 5th
S. Moser BT24/3 Cos. DFV Ret: fuel system
Sept 20, CANADIAN GRAND PRIX, Mosport Park
J. Brabham BT26/4 Cos. DFV 2nd
J. Ickx BT26/3 Cos. DFV 1st
P. Courage BT26/1 Cos. DFV Ret: fuel leak
S. Moser BT24/3 Cos. DFV Ret: accident

J. Cordts	BT23B-3 Climax 4	Ret: oil leak
Oct 5, UNITED STATES GRAND PRIX, Watkins Glen		
J. Brabham	BT26/4 Cos. DFV	4th
J. Ickx	BT26/3 Cos. DFV	Ret: engine
P. Courage	BT26/1 Cos. DFV	2nd
S. Moser	BT24/3 Cos. DFV	6th
Oct 19, MEXICAN GRAND PRIX, Mexico City		
J. Brabham	BT26/4 Cos. DFV	3rd
J. Ickx	BT26/3 Cos. DFV	2nd
P. Courage	BT26/1 Cos. DFV	10th
S. Moser	BT24/3 Cos. DFV	11th

1970

March 7, SOUTH AFRICAN GRAND PRIX, Kyalami		
J. Brabham	BT33/2 Cos. DFV	1st
R. Stommelen	BT33/1 Cos. DFV	Ret: engine
P. de Klerk	BT26/1 Cos. DFV	11th
March 22, Race of Champions, Brands Hatch		
J. Brabham	BT33/2 Cos. DFV	4th
April 19, SPANISH GRAND PRIX, Jarama		
J. Brabham	BT33/2 Cos. DFV	Ret: engine
R. Stommelen	BT33/1 Cos. DFV	Ret: engine
April 26, International Trophy, Silverstone		
J. Brabham	BT33/2 Cos. DFV	Ret: engine
May 10, MONACO GRAND PRIX, Monte Carlo		
J. Brabham	BT33/2 Cos. DFV	2nd
R. Stommelen	BT33/1 Cos. DFV	DNQ
June 7, BELGIAN GRAND PRIX, Spa-Francorchamps		
J. Brabham	BT33/2 Cos. DFV	Ret: clutch
R. Stommelen	BT33/1 Cos. DFV	5th
D. Bell	BT26/4 Cos. DFV	Ret: gear linkage
June 21, DUTCH GRAND PRIX, Zandvoort		
J. Brabham	BT33/2 Cos. DFV	11th
R. Stommelen	BT33/1 Cos. DFV	DNQ
July 5, FRENCH GRAND PRIX, Clermont-Ferrand		
J. Brabham	BT33/2 Cos. DFV	3rd
R. Stommelen	BT33/1 Cos. DFV	7th
July 18, BRITISH GRAND PRIX, Brands Hatch		
J. Brabham	BT33/2 Cos. DFV	2nd
R. Stommelen	BT33/1 Cos. DFV	DNS: car damaged in practice
Aug 2, GERMAN GRAND PRIX, Hockenheim		
J. Brabham	BT33/2 Cos. DFV	Ret: oil leak
R. Stommelen	BT33/3 Cos. DFV	5th
Aug 16, AUSTRIAN GRAND PRIX, Osterreichring		
J. Brabham	BT33/2 Cos. DFV	13th
R. Stommelen	BT33/3 Cos. DFV	3rd
Sept 6, ITALIAN GRAND PRIX, Monza		
J. Brabham	BT33/2 Cos. DFV	Ret: accident
R. Stommelen	BT33/3 Cos. DFV	5th
Sept 19, CANADIAN GRAND PRIX, Ste. Jovite		
J. Brabham	BT33/2 Cos. DFV	Ret: oil leak
R. Stommelen	BT33/3 Cos. DFV	Ret: steering
Oct 4, UNITED STATES GRAND PRIX, Watkins Glen		
J. Brabham	BT33/2 Cos. DFV	10th
R. Stommelen	BT33/3 Cos. DFV	12th
Oct 25, MEXICAN GRAND PRIX, Mexico City		
J. Brabham	BT33/2 Cos. DFV	Ret: engine
R. Stommelen	BT33/3 Cos. DFV	Ret: engine

1971

March 8, SOUTH AFRICAN GRAND PRIX, Kyalami		
G. Hill	BT33/4 Cos. DFV	9th
D. Charlton	BT33/3 Cos. DFV	Ret: engine
March 21, Race of Champions, Brands Hatch		
G. Hill	BT34/1 Cos. DFV	Ret: engine
T. Schenken	BT33/1 Cos. DFV	4th
March 28, Questor Grand Prix, Ontario Motor Speedway, California		
G. Hill	BT34/1 Cos. DFV	Ret: oil leak
T. Schenken	BT33/1 Cos. DFV	5th
April 18, SPANISH GRAND PRIX, Montjuich Park, Barcelona		
G. Hill	BT34/1 Cos DFV	Ret: damaged steering
T. Schenken	BT33/1 Cos. DFV	9th
May 8th, International Trophy, Silverstone		
G. Hill	BT34/1 Cos. DFV	1st
T. Schenken	BT33/1 Cos. DFV	3rd
May 23, MONACO GRAND PRIX, Monte Carlo		
G. Hill	BT34/1 Cos. DFV	Ret: accident
T. Schenken	BT33/1 Cos. DFV	10th
June 20, DUTCH GRAND PRIX, Zandvoort		
G. Hill	BT34/1 Cos. DFV	10th
T. Schenken	BT33/3 Cos. DFV	Ret: driver withdrew
July 4, FRENCH GRAND PRIX, Paul Ricard		
G. Hill	BT34/1 Cos. DFV	Ret: spun off
T. Schenken	BT33/3 Cos. DFV	12th
July 17, BRITISH GRAND PRIX, Silverstone		
G. Hill	BT34/1 Cos. DFV	Ret: collision
T. Schenken	BT33/3 Cos. DFV	Ret: transmission
Aug 1, GERMAN GRAND PRIX, Nurburgring		
G. Hill	BT34/1 Cos. DFV	9th
T. Schenken	BT33/3 Cos. DFV	6th
Aug 15, AUSTRIAN GRAND PRIX, Osterreichring		
G. Hill	BT34/1 Cos. DFV	5th
T. Schenken	BT33/3 Cos. DFV	3rd
Aug 21, Gold Cup, Oulton Park		
C. Craft	BT33/2 Cos. DFV	5th
Sept 5, ITALIAN GRAND PRIX, Monza		
G. Hill	BT34/1 Cos. DFV	11th
T. Schenken	BT33/3 Cos. DFV	Ret: suspension
Sept 19, CANADIAN GRAND PRIX, Mosport Park		
G. Hill	BT34/1 Cos. DFV	Ret: accident
T. Schenken	BT33/3 Cos. DFV	Ret: ignition
C. Craft	BT33/2 Cos. DFV	DNS: engine trouble
Oct 3, UNITED STATES GRAND PRIX, Watkins Glen		
G. Hill	BT34/1 Cos. DFV	7th
T. Schenken	BT33/3 Cos. DFV	Ret: engine
C. Craft	BT33/2 Cos. DFV	Ret: chassis breakage
Oct 24, Rothmans World Champion Victory Race, Brands Hatch		
G. Hill	BT34/1 Cos. DFV	8th
T. Schenken	BT33/3 Cos. DFV	5th
C. Reutemann	BT33/1 Cos. DFV	9th

1972

Jan 23, ARGENTINE GRAND PRIX, Buenos Aires		
G. Hill	BT33/3 Cos. DFV	Ret: engine
C. Reutemann	BT34/1 Cos. DFV	7th
March 4, SOUTH AFRICAN GRAND PRIX, Kyalami		
G. Hill	BT33/3 Cos. DFV	6th
C. Reutemann	BT34/1 Cos. DFV	Ret: engine
March 30, Brazilian Grand Prix, Interlagos, Sao Paulo		
C. Reutemann	BT34/1 Cos. DFV	1st
W. Fittipaldi	BT33/3 Cos. DFV	3rd
April 23, International Trophy, Silverstone		
G. Hill	BT37/1 Cos. DFV	7th
May 1, SPANISH GRAND PRIX, Jarama		
G. Hill	BT37/1 Cos. DFV	10th
W. Fittipaldi	BT33/3 Cos. DFV	7th
May 14, MONACO GRAND PRIX, Monte Carlo		
G. Hill	BT37/1 Cos. DFV	12th
W. Fittipaldi	BT33/3 Cos. DFV	8th
June 4, BELGIAN GRAND PRIX, Nivelles-Baulers, near Brussels		
G. Hill	BT37/1 Cos. DFV	Ret: suspension damage
C. Reutemann	BT37/2 Cos. DFV	13th
W. Fittipaldi	BT34/1 Cos. DFV	Ret: gearbox
July 2, FRENCH GRAND PRIX, Clermont-Ferrand		
G. Hill	BT37/1 Cos. DFV	10th
C. Reutemann	BT37/2 Cos. DFV	12th
W. Fittipaldi	BT34/1 Cos. DFV	8th
July 15, BRITISH GRAND PRIX, Brands Hatch		
G. Hill	BT37/1 Cos. DFV	Ret: accident
C. Reutemann	BT37/2 Cos. DFV	8th
W. Fittipaldi	BT34/1 Cos. DFV	Ret: suspension
July 30, GERMAN GRAND PRIX, Nurburgring		
G. Hill	BT37/1 Cos. DFV	6th
C. Reutemann	BT37/2 Cos. DFV	Ret: transmission
W. Fittipaldi	BT34/1 Cos. DFV	7th
Aug 13, AUSTRIAN GRAND PRIX, Osterreichring		
G. Hill	BT37/1 Cos. DFV	Ret: fuel injection
C. Reutemann	BT37/2 Cos. DFV	Ret: fuel injection
W. Fittipaldi	BT34/1 Cos. DFV	Ret: brakes
Sept 10, ITALIAN GRAND PRIX, Monza		
G. Hill	BT37/1 Cos. DFV	5th
C. Reutemann	BT37/2 Cos. DFV	Ret: suspension
W. Fittipaldi	BT34/1 Cos. DFV	Ret: suspension
Sept 24, CANADIAN GRAND PRIX, Mosport Park		
G. Hill	BT37/1 Cos. DFV	8th
C. Reutemann	BT37/2 Cos. DFV	4th
W. Fittipaldi	BT34/1 Cos. DFV	Ret: gearbox
Oct 8, UNITED STATES GRAND PRIX, Watkins Glen		
G. Hill	BT37/1 Cos. DFV	11th
C. Reutemann	BT37/2 Cos. DFV	Ret: engine
W. Fittipaldi	BT34/1 Cos. DFV	Ret: engine

1973

Jan 28, ARGENTINE GRAND PRIX, Buenos Aires		
C. Reutemann	BT37/2 Cos. DFV	Ret: gearbox
W. Fittipaldi	BT37/1 Cos. DFV	6th
Feb 11, BRAZILIAN GRAND PRIX, Interlagos, Sao Paulo		
C. Reutemann	BT37/2 Cos. DFV	11th
W. Fittipaldi	BT37/1 Cos. DFV	Ret: overheating
March 3, SOUTH AFRICAN GRAND PRIX, Kyalami		
C. Reutemann	BT37/2 Cos. DFV	7th
W. Fittipaldi	BT37/1 Cos. DFV	Ret: engine/gearbox
Mar 18, Race of Champions, Brands Hatch		
G. Hill	BT37/ Cos. DFV	Ret: accident
J. Watson	BT42/1 Cos. DFV	Ret: accident
April 29, SPANISH GRAND PRIX, Montjuich Park, Barcelona		
C. Reutemann	BT42/3 Cos. DFV	Ret: transmission
W. Fittipaldi	BT42/2 Cos. DFV	10th
A. de Adamich	BT37/1 Cos. DFV	Ret: accident
May 20, BELGIAN GRAND PRIX, Zolder		
C. Reutemann	BT42/3 Cos. DFV	Ret: engine
W. Fittipaldi	BT42/2 Cos. DFV	Ret: engine
A. de Adamich	BT37/2 Cos. DFV	4th
June 3, MONACO GRAND PRIX, Monte Carlo		
C. Reutemann	BT42/3 Cos. DFV	Ret: gearbox
W. Fittipaldi	BT42/2 Cos. DFV	Ret: fuel system
A. de Adamich	BT37/2 Cos. DFV	7th
June 17, SWEDISH GRAND PRIX, Anderstorp		
C. Reutemann	BT42/3 Cos. DFV	4th
W. Fittipaldi	BT42/2 Cos. DFV	Ret: off circuit
July 1, FRENCH GRAND PRIX, Paul Ricard		
C. Reutemann	BT42/3 Cos. DFV	3rd
W. Fittipaldi	BT42/4 Cos. DFV	Ret: throttle seized
A. de Adamich	BT37/2 Cos. DFV	Ret: transmission

July 14, BRITISH GRAND PRIX, Silverstone
C. Reutemann BT42/3 Cos. DFV 6th
W. Fittipaldi BT42/2 Cos. DFV Ret: oil leak
A. de Adamich BT42/4 Cos. DFV Ret: accident
J. Watson BT37/2 Cos. DFV Ret: throttle control
July 29, DUTCH GRAND PRIX, Zandvoort
C. Reutemann BT42/3 Cos. DFV Ret: tyre burnt
W. Fittipaldi BT42/2 Cos. DFV Ret: accident
Aug 5, GERMAN GRAND PRIX, Nurburgring
C. Reutemann BT42/3 Cos. DFV Ret: engine
W. Fittipaldi BT42/2 Cos. DFV 5th
Aug 19, AUSTRIAN GRAND PRIX, Osterreichring
C. Reutemann BT42/3 Cos. DFV 4th
W. Fittipaldi BT42/2 Cos. DFV Ret: fuel injection
R. Stommelen BT42/6 Cos. DFV Ret: wheel bearing
Sept 9, ITALIAN GRAND PRIX, Monza
C. Reutemann BT42/3 Cos. DFV 6th
W. Fittipaldi BT42/5 Cos. DFV Ret: oil leak
R. Stommelen BT42/6 Cos. DFV 12th
Sept 23, CANADIAN GRAND PRIX, Mosport Park
C. Reutemann BT42/3 Cos. DFV 8th
W. Fittipaldi BT42/5 Cos DFV 11th
R. Stommelen BT42/6 Cos. DFV 12th
Oct 7, UNITED STATES GRAND PRIX, Watkins Glen
C. Reutemann BT42/3 Cos. DFV 3rd
W. Fittipaldi BT42/5 Cos. DFV 17th
J. Watson BT42/6 Cos. DFV Ret: engine

1974
Jan 13, ARGENTINE GRAND PRIX, Buenos Aires
C. Reutemann BT44/1 Cos. DFV 7th NR
R. Robarts BT44/2 Cos. DFV Ret: gearbox
J. Watson BT42/2 Cos. DFV 12th
Jan 27, BRAZILIAN GRAND PRIX, Interlagos, Sao Paulo
C. Reutemann BT44/1 Cos. DFV 7th
R. Robarts BT44/2 Cos. DFV 15th
J. Watson BT42/2 Cos. DFV 18th
Feb 3, Grand Premio Presidente Medici, Brasilia
C. Reutemann BT44/1 Cos. DFV Ret: engine
W. Fittipaldi BT44/2 Cos. DFV 5th
March 17, Race of Champions, Brands Hatch
C. Reutemann BT44/3 Cos. DFV Ret: accident
R. Robarts BT42/3 Cos. DFV 12th
March 30, SOUTH AFRICAN GRAND PRIX, Kyalami
C. Reutemann BT44/1 Cos. DFV 1st
R. Robarts BT44/2 Cos. DFV 17th
J. Watson BT42/2 Cos. DFV Ret: fuel pipe
April 7, International Trophy, Silverstone
R. Robarts BT42/3 Cos. DFV 14th
April 28, SPANISH GRAND PRIX, Jarama
C. Reutemann BT44/1 Cos. DFV Ret: driver withdrew
R. von Opel BT44/2 Cos. DFV Ret: oil leak
J. Watson BT42/2 Cos. DFV 11th
May 12, BELGIAN GRAND PRIX, Nivelles-Baulers
C. Reutemann BT44/3 Cos. DFV Ret: engine
R. von Opel BT44/2 Cos. DFV Ret: engine
J. Watson BT42/2 Cos. DFV 11th
G. Larrousse BT42/6 Cos. DFV Ret: electrical
T. Pilette BT42/3 Cos. DFV 17th
May 26, MONACO GRAND PRIX, Monte Carlo
C. Reutemann BT44/3 Cos. DFV Ret: accident
R. von Opel BT44/2 Cos. DFV DNQ
J. Watson BT42/2 Cos. DFV 6th
June 9, SWEDISH GRAND PRIX, Anderstorp
C. Reutemann BT44/1 Cos. DFV Ret: fuel pressure/oil leak
R. von Opel BT44/2 Cos. DFV 9th
J. Watson BT42/2 Cos. DFV 11th
June 23, DUTCH GRAND PRIX, Zandvoort
C. Reutemann BT44/3 Cos. DFV 12th
R. von Opel BT44/2 Cos. DFV 9th
J. Watson BT42/2 Cos. DFV 7th
July 7, FRENCH GRAND PRIX, Dijon-Prenois
C. Reutemann BT44/1 Cos. DFV Ret: damaged suspension
R. von Opel BT44/2 Cos. DFV DNQ
C. Pace BT42/3 Cos. DFV DNQ
J. Watson BT42/2 Cos. DFV 16th
G. Larrousse BT42/6 Cos. DFV DNQ
July 20, BRITISH GRAND PRIX, Brands Hatch
C. Reutemann BT44/1 Cos. DFV 5th
C. Pace BT44/2 Cos. DFV 8th
L. Lombardi BT42/3 Cos. DFV DNQ
Aug 4, GERMAN GRAND PRIX, Nurburgring
C. Reutemann BT44/1 Cos. DFV 3rd
C. Pace BT44/3 Cos. DFV 12th
J. Watson BT44/4 Cos. DFV Ret: suspension
Aug 18, AUSTRIAN GRAND PRIX, Osterreichring
C. Reutemann BT44/1 Cos. DFV 1st
C. Pace BT44/2 Cos. DFV Ret: fuel leak
J. Watson BT44/4 Cos. DFV 4th
Sept 8, ITALIAN GRAND PRIX, Monza
C. Reutemann BT44/1 Cos. DFV Ret: gearbox
C. Pace BT44/2 Cos. DFV 5th
J. Watson BT44/3 Cos. DFV 7th
Sept 22, CANADIAN GRAND PRIX, Mosport Park
C. Reutemann BT44/1 Cos. DFV 9th
C. Pace BT44/2 Cos. DFV 8th
J. Watson BT44/4 Cos. DFV Ret: suspension
E. Wietzes BT42/3 Cos. DFV Ret: engine
I. Ashley BT42/2 Cos. DFV DNQ
Oct 6, UNITED STATES GRAND PRIX, Watkins Glen
C. Reutemann BT44/1 Cos. DFV 1st
C. Pace BT44/2 Cos. DFV 2nd
J. Watson BT44/4 Cos. DFV 5th
I. Ashley BT42/2 Cos. DFV DNQ

1975
Jan 12, ARGENTINE GRAND PRIX, Buenos Aires
C. Reutemann BT44B/1 Cos. DFV 3rd
C. Pace BT44B/2 Cos. DFV Ret: engine
Jan 26, BRAZILIAN GRAND PRIX, Interlagos, Sao Paulo
C. Reutemann BT44B/1 Cos. DFV 8th
C. Pace BT44B/2 Cos. DFV 1st
March 1, SOUTH AFRICAN GRAND PRIX, Kyalami
C. Reutemann BT44B/1 Cos. DFV 2nd
C. Pace BT44B/2 Cos. DFV 4th
April 13, International Trophy, Silverstone
C. Reutemann BT44B/3 Cos. DFV 8th
April 27, SPANISH GRAND PRIX, Montjuich Park, Barcelona
C. Reutemann BT44B/1 Cos. DFV 3rd
C. Pace BT44B/2 Cos. DFV Ret: accident
May 11, MONACO GRAND PRIX, Monte Carlo
C. Reutemann BT44B/1 Cos. DFV 9th
C. Pace BT44B/2 Cos. DFV 3rd
May 25, BELGIAN GRAND PRIX, Zolder
C. Reutemann BT44B/1 Cos. DFV 3rd
C. Pace BT44B/2 Cos. DFV 8th
June 8, SWEDISH GRAND PRIX, Anderstorp
C. Reutemann BT44B/1 Cos. DFV 2nd
C. Pace BT44B/2 Cos. DFV Ret: spun off
June 22, DUTCH GRAND PRIX, Zandvoort
C. Reutemann BT44B/1 Cos. DFV 4th
C. Pace BT44B/2 Cos. DFV 5th
July 6, FRENCH GRAND PRIX, Paul Ricard
C. Reutemann BT44B/1 Cos. DFV 14th
C. Pace BT44B/2 Cos. DFV Ret: transmission
July 19, BRITISH GRAND PRIX, Silverstone
C. Reutemann BT44B/1 Cos. DFV Ret: engine
C. Pace BT44B/2 Cos. DFV 2nd
Aug 3, GERMAN GRAND PRIX, Nurburgring
C. Reutemann BT44B/1 Cos. DFV 1st
C. Pace BT44B/4 Cos. DFV Ret: suspension
Aug 17, AUSTRIAN GRAND PRIX, Osterreichring
C. Reutemann BT44B/1 Cos. DFV 14th
C. Pace BT44B/4 Cos. DFV Ret: engine
Aug 24, Swiss Grand Prix, Dijon-Prenois
C. Pace BT44B/3 Cos. DFV 6th
Sept 7, ITALIAN GRAND PRIX, Monza
C. Reutemann BT44B/1 Cos. DFV 4th
C. Pace BT44B/4 Cos. DFV Ret: throttle linkage
Oct 5, UNITED STATES GRAND PRIX, Watkins Glen
C. Reutemann BT44B/1 Cos. DFV Ret: engine
C. Pace BT44B/3 Cos. DFV Ret: accident

1976
Jan 25, BRAZILIAN GRAND PRIX, Interlagos
C. Reutemann BT45/2 Alfa f-12 12th
C. Pace BT45/1 Alfa f-12 10th
March 6, SOUTH AFRICAN GRAND PRIX, Kyalami
C. Reutemann BT45/2 Alfa f-12 Ret: engine
C. Pace BT45/1 Alfa f-12 Ret: engine
March 16, Race of Champions, Brands Hatch
C. Pace BT45/1 Alfa f-12 Ret: engine
P. Neve BT44B/1 Cos. DFV 7th
L. Kessel BT42/2 Cos. DFV Ret: engine
March 27, UNITED STATES GRAND PRIX WEST, Long Beach
C. Reutemann BT45/2 Alfa f-12 Ret: accident
C. Pace BT45/1 Alfa f-12 9th
April 11, International Trophy, Silverstone
C. Pace BT45/1 Alfa f-12 9th
P. Neve BT44B/2 Cos. DFV 11th
L. Kessel BT44B/1 Cos. DFV 12th
May 2, SPANISH GRAND PRIX, Jarama
C. Reutemann BT45/1 Alfa f-12 4th
C. Pace BT45/3 Alfa f-12 6th
L. Kessel BT44B/1 Cos. DFV DNQ
E. de Villota BT44B/2 Cos. DFV DNQ
May 16, BELGIAN GRAND PRIX, Zolder
C. Reutemann BT45/2 Alfa f-12 Ret: engine
C. Pace BT45/1 Alfa f-12 Ret: electrical
P. Neve BT44B/2 Cos. DFV Ret: transmission
L. Kessel BT44B/1 Cos. DFV 12th
May 30, MONACO GRAND PRIX, Monte Carlo
C. Reutemann BT45/2 Alfa f-12 Ret: accident
C. Pace BT45/1 Alfa f-12 9th
June 13, SWEDISH GRAND PRIX, Anderstorp
C. Reutemann BT45/1 Alfa f-12 Ret: driver unfit
C. Pace BT45/3 Alfa f-12 8th
L. Kessel BT44B/1 Cos. DFV Ret: accident
J. Nelleman BT44B/2 Cos. DFV DNQ
July 4, FRENCH GRAND PRIX, Paul Ricard
C. Reutemann BT45/2 Alfa f-12 11th
C. Pace BT45/3 Alfa f-12 3rd
D. Magee BT44B/2 Cos. DFV DNQ
L. Kessel BT44B/1 Cos. DFV DNQ

July 18, BRITISH GRAND PRIX, Brands Hatch

C. Reutemann	BT45B/3 Alfa f-12	Ret: oil leak
C. Pace	BT45B/1 Alfa f-12	9th
R. Evans	BT44B/1 Cos. DFV	Ret: gearbox
L. Lombardi	BT44B/2 Cos. DFV	DNQ

Aug 1, GERMAN GRAND PRIX, Nurburgring

C. Reutemann	BT45/3 Alfa f-12	Ret: injection pump belt
C. Pace	BT45/4 Alfa f-12	4th
R. Stommelen	BT45/1 Alfa f-12	6th

Aug 15, AUSTRIAN GRAND PRIX, Osterreichring

C. Reutemann	BT45/3 Alfa f-12	Ret: clutch
C. Pace	BT45/4 Alfa f-12	Ret: brakes/accident
L. Kessel	BT44B/1 Cos. DFV	13th
L. Lombardi	BT44B/2 Cos. DFV	12th

Aug 29, DUTCH GRAND PRIX, Zandvoort

C. Reutemann	BT45/3 Alfa f-12	Ret: clutch
C. Pace	BT45/1 Alfa f-12	Ret: engine

Sept 12, ITALIAN GRAND PRIX, Monza

C. Pace	BT45/3 Alfa f-12	Ret: engine
R. Stommelen	BT45/1 Alfa f-12	Ret: fuel system

Oct 3, CANADIAN GRAND PRIX, Mosport Park

C. Pace	BT45/3 Alfa f-12	7th
L. Perkins	BT45/3 Alfa f-12	17th

Oct 10, UNITED STATES GRAND PRIX, Watkins Glen

C. Pace	BT45/5 Alfa f-12	Ret: accident
L. Perkins	BT45/3 Alfa f-12	Ret: broken suspension

Oct 24, JAPANESE GRAND PRIX, Fuji

C. Pace	BT45/3 Alfa f-12	Ret: driver withdrew
L. Perkins	BT45/1 Alfa f-12	Ret: driver withdrew

1977

Jan 9, ARGENTINE GRAND PRIX, Buenos Aires

C. Pace	BT45/5 Alfa f-12	2nd
J. Watson	BT45/3 Alfa f-12	Ret: broken gearbox mounting

Jan 23, BRAZILIAN GRAND PRIX, Interlagos, Sao Paulo

C. Pace	BT45/5 Alfa f-12	Ret: accident
J. Watson	BT45/3 Alfa f-12	Ret: accident

March 5, SOUTH AFRICAN GRAND PRIX, Kyalami

C. Pace	BT45/B Alfa f-12	13th
J. Watson	BT45/3 Alfa f-12	6th

March 20, Race of Champions, Brands Hatch

J. Watson	BT45/1B Alfa f-12	3rd

April 3, UNITED STATES GRAND PRIX WEST, Long Beach

J. Watson	BT45/3B Alfa f-12	DIS
H. Stuck	BT45/1B Alfa f-12	Ret: brakes

May 8, SPANISH GRAND PRIX, Jarama

J. Watson	BT45/5B Alfa f-12	Ret: fuel pump
H. Stuck	BT45/1B Alfa f-12	6th

May 22, MONACO GRAND PRIX, Monte Carlo

J. Watson	BT45/5B Alfa f-12	Ret: gearbox
H. Stuck	BT45/1B Alfa f-12	Ret: electrics

June 5, BELGIAN GRAND PRIX, Zolder

J. Watson	BT45/5B Alfa f-12	Ret: accident
H. Stuck	BT45/1B Alfa f-12	6th

June 19, SWEDISH GRAND PRIX, Anderstorp

J. Watson	BT45/6B Alfa f-12	5th
H. Stuck	BT45/3B Alfa f-12	10th

July 3, FRENCH GRAND PRIX, Dijon-Prenois

J. Watson	BT45/6B Alfa f-12	2nd
H. Stuck	BT45/3B Alfa f-12	Ret: spun off

July 16, BRITISH GRAND PRIX, Silverstone

J. Watson	BT45/1B Alfa f-12	Ret: fuel pressure
H. Stuck	BT45/3B Alfa f-12	5th

July 31, GERMAN GRAND PRIX, Hockenheim

J. Watson	BT45/1B Alfa f-12	Ret: engine
H. Stuck	BT45/3B Alfa f-12	3rd

Aug 14, AUSTRIAN GRAND PRIX, Osterreichring

J. Watson	BT45/5B Alfa f-12	8th
H. Stuck	BT45/3B Alfa f-12	3rd

Aug 28, DUTCH GRAND PRIX, Zandvoort

J. Watson	BT45/5B Alfa f-12	Ret: oil leak
H. Stuck	BT45/3B Alfa f-12	7th

Sept 11, ITALIAN GRAND PRIX, Monza

J. Watson	BT45/5B Alfa f-12	Ret: accident
H. Stuck	BT45/3B Alfa f-12	Ret: engine

Oct 2, UNITED STATES GRAND PRIX, Watkins Glen

J. Watson	BT45/6B Alfa f-12	12th
H. Stuck	BT45/3B Alfa f-12	Ret: accident

Oct 9, CANADIAN GRAND PRIX, Mosport Park

J. Watson	BT45/6B Alfa f-12	Ret: accident
H. Stuck	BT45/1B Alfa f-12	Ret: engine

Oct 23, JAPANESE GRAND PRIX, Fuji

J. Watson	BT45/6B Alfa f-12	Ret: gearbox
H. Stuck	BT45/1B Alfa f-12	7th

1978

Jan 15, ARGENTINE GRAND PRIX, Buenos Aires

N. Lauda	BT45/7C Alfa f-12	2nd
J. Watson	BT45/8C Alfa f-12	Ret: engine

Jan 29, BRAZILIAN GRAND PRIX, Rio

N. Lauda	BT45/7C Alfa f-12	3rd
J. Watson	BT45/8C Alfa f-12	8th

March 4, SOUTH AFRICAN GRAND PRIX, Kyalami

N. Lauda	BT46/4 Alfa f-12	Ret: engine
J. Watson	BT46/3 Alfa f-12	3rd

March 19, International Trophy, Silverstone

N. Lauda	BT45/7C Alfa f-12	DNS

April 2, UNITED STATES GRAND PRIX WEST, Long Beach

N. Lauda	BT46/4 Alfa f-12	Ret: ignition
J. Watson	BT46/3 Alfa f-12	Ret: explosion in oil tank

May 7, MONACO GRAND PRIX, Monte Carlo

N. Lauda	BT46/4 Alfa f-12	2nd
J. Watson	BT46/3 Alfa f-12	4th

May 21, BELGIAN GRAND PRIX, Zolder

N. Lauda	BT46/4 Alfa f-12	Ret: accident at start
J. Watson	BT46/3 Alfa f-12	Ret: accident

June 4, SPANISH GRAND PRIX, Jarama

N. Lauda	BT46/6 Alfa f-12	Ret: engine
J. Watson	BT46/4 Alfa f-12	5th

June 17, SWEDISH GRAND PRIX, Anderstorp

N. Lauda	BT46/6B Alfa f-12	1st
J. Watson	BT46/4B Alfa f-12	Ret: stuck throttle

July 2, FRENCH GRAND PRIX, Paul Ricard

N. Lauda	BT46/6 Alfa f-12	Ret: engine
J. Watson	BT46/4 Alfa f-12	4th

July 16, BRITISH GRAND PRIX, Brands Hatch

N. Lauda	BT46/6 Alfa f-12	2nd
J. Watson	BT46/5 Alfa f-12	3rd

July 30, GERMAN GRAND PRIX, Hockenheim

N. Lauda	BT46/6 Alfa f-12	Ret: engine
J. Watson	BT46/5 Alfa f-12	7th

Aug 13, AUSTRIAN GRAND PRIX, Osterreichring

N. Lauda	BT46/6 Alfa f-12	Ret: accident
J. Watson	BT46/5 Alfa f-12	7th

Aug 27, DUTCH GRAND PRIX, Zandvoort

N. Lauda	BT46/7 Alfa f-12	3rd
J. Watson	BT46/5 Alfa f-12	4th

Sept 10, ITALIAN GRAND PRIX, Monza

N. Lauda	BT46/7 Alfa f-12	1st
J. Watson	BT46/5 Alfa f-12	2nd

Oct 1, UNITED STATES GRAND PRIX, Watkins Glen

N. Lauda	BT46/7 Alfa f-12	Ret: engine
J. Watson	BT46/6 Alfa f-12	Ret: engine

Oct 8, CANADIAN GRAND PRIX, Ile Notre Dame, Montreal

N. Lauda	BT46/7 Alfa f-12	Ret: brakes
J. Watson	BT46/8 Alfa f-12	Ret: collision damage
N. Piquet	BT46/5 Alfa f-12	11th

1979

Jan 21, ARGENTINE GRAND PRIX, Buenos Aires

N. Lauda	BT48/2 Alfa V12	Ret: fuel pressure
N. Piquet	BT46/7 Alfa f-12	Ret: accident

Feb 4, BRAZILIAN GRAND PRIX, Interlagos, Sao Paulo

N. Lauda	BT48/2 Alfa V12	Ret: gear linkage
N. Piquet	BT48/1 Alfa V12	Ret: driver unwell

March 3, SOUTH AFRICAN GRAND PRIX, Kyalami

N. Lauda	BT48/2 Alfa V12	6th
N. Piquet	BT48/3 Alfa V12	7th

April 8, UNITED STATES GRAND PRIX WEST, Long Beach

N. Lauda	BT48/2 Alfa V12	Ret: accident
N. Piquet	BT48/3 Alfa V12	8th

April 15, Race of Champions, Brands Hatch

N. Lauda	BT48/2 Alfa V12	5th
N. Piquet	BT48/1 Alfa V12	2nd

April 29, SPANISH GRAND PRIX, Jarama

N. Lauda	BT48/2 Alfa V12	Ret: water leak
N. Piquet	BT48/3 Alfa V12	Ret: injection malfunction

May 13, BELGIAN GRAND PRIX, Zolder

N. Lauda	BT48/4 Alfa V12	Ret: engine
N. Piquet	BT48/3 Alfa V12	Ret: engine

May 27, MONACO GRAND PRIX, Monte Carlo

N. Lauda	BT48/4 Alfa V12	Ret: accident
N. Piquet	BT48/3 Alfa V12	7th

July 1, FRENCH GRAND PRIX, Dijon-Prenois

N. Lauda	BT48/2 Alfa V12	Ret: spun and stalled
N. Piquet	BT48/3 Alfa V12	Ret: accident

July 14, BRITISH GRAND PRIX, Silverstone

N. Lauda	BT48/4 Alfa V12	Ret: brakes
N. Piquet	BT48/3 Alfa V12	Ret: accident

July 29, GERMAN GRAND PRIX, Hockenheim

N. Lauda	BT48/4 Alfa V12	Ret: engine
N. Piquet	BT48/3 Alfa V12	Ret: engine

Aug 12, AUSTRIAN GRAND PRIX, Osterreichring

N. Lauda	BT48/4 Alfa V12	Ret: engine
N. Piquet	BT48/3 Alfa V12	Ret: engine

Aug 26, DUTCH GRAND PRIX, Zandvoort

N. Lauda	BT48/4 Alfa V12	Ret: driver withdrew
N. Piquet	BT48/2 Alfa V12	4th

Sept 9, ITALIAN GRAND PRIX, Monza

N. Lauda	BT48/4 Alfa V12	4th
N. Piquet	BT48/3 Alfa V12	Ret: accident

Sept 16, Gran Premio Dino Ferrari, Imola

N. Lauda	BT48/4 Alfa V12	1st

Sept 30, CANADIAN GRAND PRIX, Ile Notre Dame, Montreal

N. Piquet	BT49/2 Cos. DFV	Ret: gearbox
R. Zunino	BT49/3 Cos. DFV	7th

Oct 7, UNITED STATES GRAND PRIX, Watkins Glen

N. Piquet	BT49/2 Cos. DFV	Ret: transmission
R. Zunino	BT49/1 Cos. DFV	Ret: spun off

1980

Jan 13, ARGENTINE GRAND PRIX, Buenos Aires

N. Piquet	BT49/4 Cos. DFV	2nd
R. Zunino	BT49/5 Cos. DFV	7th

Jan 27, BRAZILIAN GRAND PRIX, Rio
N. Piquet BT49/4 Cos. DFV Ret: accident
R. Zunino BT49/5 Cos. DFV 8th
March 1, SOUTH AFRICAN GRAND PRIX, Kyalami
N. Piquet BT49/4 Cos. DFV 4th
R. Zunino BT49/5 Cos. DFV 10th
March 30, UNITED STATES GRAND PRIX WEST, Long Beach
N. Piquet BT49/6 Cos. DFV 1st
R. Zunino BT49/5 Cos. DFV Ret: accident
May 4, BELGIAN GRAND PRIX, Zolder
N. Piquet BT49/6 Cos. DFV Ret: accident
R. Zunino BT49/2 Cos. DFV Ret: transmission
May 18, MONACO GRAND PRIX, Monte Carlo
N. Piquet BT49/7 Cos. DFV 7th
R. Zunino BT49/3 Cos. DFV DNQ
June 1, Spanish Grand Prix, Jarama
N. Piquet BT49/7 Cos. DFV Ret: gearbox
R. Zunino BT49/4 Cos. DFV Ret: gear linkage
June 29, FRENCH GRAND PRIX, Paul Ricard
N. Piquet BT49/8 Cos. DFV 4th
R. Zunino BT49/6 Cos. DFV Ret: clutch
July 13, BRITISH GRAND PRIX, Brands Hatch
N. Piquet BT49/8 Cos. DFV 2nd
H. Rebaque BT49/6 Cos. DFV 7th
Aug 10, GERMAN GRAND PRIX, Hockenheim
N. Piquet BT49/8 Cos. DFV 4th
H. Rebaque BT49/6 Cos. DFV Ret: gearbox
Aug 17, AUSTRIAN PRIX, Osterreichring
N. Piquet BT49/7 Cos. DFV 5th
H. Rebaque BT49/6 Cos. DFV 10th
Aug 31, DUTCH GRAND PRIX, Zandvoort
N. Piquet BT49/7 Cos. DFV 1st
H. Rebaque BT49/6 Cos. DFV Ret: gearbox
Sept 14, ITALIAN GRAND PRIX, Imola
N. Piquet BT49/9 Cos. DFV 1st
H. Rebaque BT49/6 Cos. DFV Ret: suspension
Sept 28, CANADIAN GRAND PRIX, Ile Notre Dame, Montreal
N. Piquet BT49/9 Cos. DFV Ret: engine
H. Rebaque BT49/6 Cos. DFV 6th
Oct 5, UNITED STATES GRAND PRIX, Watkins Glen
N. Piquet BT49/9 Cos. DFV Ret: spun off/pushstart
H. Rebaque BT49/6 Cos. DFV Ret: engine

1981
February 7, South African Grand Prix, Kyalami
N. Piquet BT49/10 Cos. DFV 2nd
R. Zunino BT49/7 Cos. DFV 8th
March 15, UNITED STATES GRAND PRIX WEST, Long Beach
N. Piquet BT49C/11 Cos. DFV 3rd
H. Rebaque BT49C/12 Cos. DFV Ret: accident
March 29, BRAZILIAN GRAND PRIX, Rio
N. Piquet BT49C/11 Cos. DFV 12th
H. Rebaque BT49C/12 Cos. DFV Ret: suspension
April 12, ARGENTINE GRAND PRIX, Buenos Aires
N. Piquet BT49C/11 Cos. DFV 1st
H. Rebaque BT49C/12 Cos. DFV Ret: electrical
May 3, SAN MARINO GRAND PRIX, Imola
N. Piquet BT49C/11 Cos. DFV 1st
H. Rebaque BT49C/12 Cos. DFV 4th
May 17, BELGIAN GRAND PRIX, Zolder
N. Piquet BT49C/11 Cos. DFV Ret: accident
H. Rebaque BT49C/12 Cos. DFV Ret: accident
May 31, MONACO GRAND PRIX, Monte Carlo
N. Piquet BT49C/11 Cos. DFV Ret: accident
H. Rebaque BT49C/12 Cos. DFV DNQ
June 21, SPANISH GRAND PRIX, Jarama
N. Piquet BT49C/11 Cos. DFV Ret: accident
H. Rebaque BT49C/12 Cos. DFV Ret: gearbox
July 5, FRENCH GRAND PRIX, Dijon-Prenois
N. Piquet BT49C/11 Cos. DFV 3rd
H. Rebaque BT49C/12 Cos. DFV 9th
July 18, BRITISH GRAND PRIX, Silverstone
N. Piquet BT49C/11 Cos. DFV Ret: accident
H. Rebaque BT49C/12 Cos. DFV 5th
Aug 2, GERMAN GRAND PRIX, Hockenheim
N. Piquet BT49C/14 Cos. DFV 1st
H. Rebaque BT49C/12 Cos. DFV 4th
Aug 16, AUSTRIAN GRAND PRIX, Osterreichring
N. Piquet BT49C/14 Cos. DFV 3rd
H. Rebaque BT49C/12 Cos. DFV Ret: transmission
Aug 30, DUTCH GRAND PRIX, Zandvoort
N. Piquet BT49C/14 Cos. DFV 2nd
H. Rebaque BT49C/12 Cos. DFV 4th
Sept 13, ITALIAN GRAND PRIX, Monza
N. Piquet BT49C/14 Cos. DFV 6th
H. Rebaque BT49C/12 Cos. DFV Ret: electrical
Sept 27, CANADIAN GRAND PRIX, Ile Notre Dame, Montreal
N. Piquet BT49C/15 Cos. DFV 5th
H. Rebaque BT49C/12 Cos. DFV Ret: spun off
Oct 17, CAESARS PALACE GRAND PRIX, Las Vegas
N. Piquet BT49C/15 Cos. DFV 5th
H. Rebaque BT49C/12 Cos. DFV Ret: spun off

1982
Jan 23, SOUTH AFRICAN GRAND PRIX, Kyalami
N. Piquet BT50/3 BMW t/c Ret: accident
R. Patrese BT50/2 BMW t/c Ret: turbo
March 21, BRAZILIAN GRAND PRIX, Rio
N. Piquet BT49D/16 Cos. DFV DIS
R. Patrese BT49D/17 Cos. DFV Ret: driver fatigue
April 4, UNITED STATES GRAND PRIX WEST, Long Beach
N. Piquet BT49D/11 Cos. DFV Ret: accident
R. Patrese BT49C/15 Cos. DFV 3rd
May 9, BELGIAN GRAND PRIX, Zolder
N. Piquet BT50/3 BMW t/c 5th
R. Patrese BT50/1 BMW t/c Ret: accident
May 23, MONACO GRAND PRIX, Monte Carlo
N. Piquet BT50/3 BMW t/c Ret: gearbox
R. Patrese BT49D/17 Cos. DFV 1st
June 6, UNITED STATES GRAND PRIX, Detroit
N. Piquet BT50/3 BMW t/c DNQ
R. Patrese BT49D/17 Cos. DFV Ret: accident
June 13, CANADIAN GRAND PRIX, Montreal
N. Piquet BT50/3 BMW t/c 1st
R. Patrese BT49D/16 Cos. DFV 2nd
July 3, DUTCH GRAND PRIX, Zandvoort
N. Piquet BT50/3 BMW t/c 2nd
R. Patrese BT50/4 BMW t/c 15th
July 18, BRITISH GRAND PRIX, Brands Hatch
N. Piquet BT50/3 BMW t/c Ret: injection
R. Patrese BT50/4 BMW t/c Ret: accident
July 25, FRENCH GRAND PRIX, Paul Ricard
N. Piquet BT50/3 BMW t/c Ret: engine
R. Patrese BT50/4 BMW t/c Ret: engine
Aug 8, GERMAN GRAND PRIX, Hockenheim
N. Piquet BT50/3 BMW t/c Ret: accident
R. Patrese BT50/4 BMW t/c Ret: engine
Aug 15, AUSTRIAN GRAND PRIX, Osterreichring
N. Piquet BT50/3 BMW t/c Ret: engine
R. Patrese BT50/4 BMW t/c Ret: engine
Aug 29, SWISS GRAND PRIX, Dijon-Prenois
N. Piquet BT50/5 BMW t/c 4th
R. Patrese BT50/4 BMW t/c 5th
Sept 12, ITALIAN GRAND PRIX, Monza
N. Piquet BT50/2 BMW t/c Ret: clutch
R. Patrese BT50/4 BMW t/c Ret: clutch
Sept 25, CAESARS PALACE GRAND PRIX, Las Vegas
N. Piquet BT50/5 BMW t/c Ret: broken spark plug
R. Patrese BT50/4 BMW t/c Ret: clutch

1983
March 13, BRAZILIAN GRAND PRIX, Rio
N. Piquet BT52/3 BMW t/c 1st
R. Patrese BT52/2 BMW t/c Ret: turbo
March 27, UNITED STATES GRAND PRIX WEST, Long Beach
N. Piquet BT52/3 BMW t/c Ret: throttle malfunction
R. Patrese BT52/2 BMW t/c 10th
April 10, Race of Champions, Brands Hatch
H. Rebaque BT52/1 BMW t/c Ret: damage sustained during pit stop
April 17, FRENCH GRAND PRIX, Paul Ricard
N. Piquet BT52/3 BMW t/c 2nd
R. Patrese BT52/1 BMW t/c Ret: engine
May 1, SAN MARINO GRAND PRIX, Imola
N. Piquet BT52/3 BMW t/c Ret: engine
R. Patrese BT52/4 BMW t/c Ret: accident
May 15, MONACO GRAND PRIX, Monte Carlo
N. Piquet BT52/3 BMW t/c 2nd
R. Patrese BT52/4 BMW t/c Ret: electric
May 22, BELGIAN GRAND PRIX, Spa-Francorchamps
N. Piquet BT52/3 BMW t/c 4th
R. Patrese BT52/4 BMW t/c Ret: engine
June 5, UNITED STATES GRAND PRIX, Detroit
N. Piquet BT52/3 BMW t/c 4th
R. Patrese BT52/1 BMW t/c Ret: brakes
June 12, CANADIAN GRAND PRIX, Circuit Gilles Villeneuve, Montreal
N. Piquet BT52/3 BMW t/c Ret: throttle cable
R. Patrese BT52/1 BMW t/c Ret: gearbox
July 16, BRITISH GRAND PRIX, Silverstone
N. Piquet BT52B/5 BMW t/c 2nd
R. Patrese BT52B/6 BMW t/c Ret: turbo
Aug 7, GERMAN GRAND PRIX, Hockenheim
N. Piquet BT52B/3 BMW t/c Ret: fuel leak/fire
R. Patrese BT52B/6 BMW t/c 3rd
Aug 14, AUSTRIAN GRAND PRIX, Osterreichring
N. Piquet BT52B/5 BMW t/c 3rd
R. Patrese BT52B/6 BMW t/c Ret: engine
Aug 28, DUTCH GRAND PRIX, Zandvoort
N. Piquet BT52B/5 BMW t/c Ret: accident
R. Patrese BT52B/6 BMW t/c 9th
Sept 11, ITALIAN GRAND PRIX, Monza
N. Piquet BT52B/5 BMW t/c 1st
R. Patrese BT52B/6 BMW t/c Ret: engine
Sept 25, GRAND PRIX OF EUROPE, Brands Hatch
N. Piquet BT52B/5 BMW t/c 1st
R. Patrese BT52B/1 BMW t/c 7th
Oct 15, SOUTH AFRICAN GRAND PRIX, Kyalami
N. Piquet BT52B/5 BMW t/c 3rd
R. Patrese BT52B/6 BMW t/c 1st

1984
March 25, BRAZILIAN GRAND PRIX, Rio
N. Piquet BT53/5 BMW t/c Ret: engine
T. Fabi BT53/2 BMW t/c Ret: turbo

April 7, SOUTH AFRICAN GRAND PRIX, Kyalami

N. Piquet	BT53/5 BMW t/c	Ret: turbo
T. Fabi	BT53/2 BMW t/c	Ret: turbo

April 29, BELGIAN GRAND PRIX, Zolder

N. Piquet	BT53/5 BMW t/c	Ret: engine
T. Fabi	BT53/2 BMW t/c	Ret: spun off

May 6, SAN MARINO GRAND PRIX, Imola

N. Piquet	BT53/5 BMW t/c	Ret: turbo
T. Fabi	BT53/2 BMW t/c	Ret: turbo

May 20, FRENCH GRAND PRIX, Dijon-Prenois

N. Piquet	BT53/5 BMW t/c	Ret: turbo
T. Fabi	BT53/2 BMW t/c	9th

June 3, MONACO GRAND PRIX, Monte Carlo

N. Piquet	BT53/5 BMW t/c	Ret: waterlogged electrics
C. Fabi	BT53/2 BMW t/c	Ret: waterlogged electrics

June 17, CANADIAN GRAND PRIX, Circuit Gilles Villeneuve

N. Piquet	BT53/5 BMW t/c	1st
C. Fabi	BT53/2 BMW t/c	Ret: turbo

June 24, UNITED STATES GRAND PRIX, Detroit

N. Piquet	BT53/3 BMW t/c	1st
T. Fabi	BT53/2 BMW t/c	4th

July 8, DALLAS GRAND PRIX, Texas

N. Piquet	BT53/4 BMW t/c	Ret: jammed throttle/hit wall
C. Fabi	BT53/2 BMW t/c	7th

July 22, BRITISH GRAND PRIX, Brands Hatch

N. Piquet	BT53/4 BMW t/c	7th
T. Fabi	BT53/2 BMW t/c	Ret: electrical

Aug 5, GERMAN GRAND PRIX, Hockenheim

N. Piquet	BT53/4 BMW t/c	Ret: gearbox
T. Fabi	BT53/2 BMW t/c	Ret: turbo

Aug 19, AUSTRIAN GRAND PRIX, Osterreichring

N. Piquet	BT53/4 BMW t/c	2nd
T. Fabi	BT53/5 BMW t/c	4th

Aug 26, DUTCH GRAND PRIX, Zandvoort

N. Piquet	BT53/4 BMW t/c	Ret: oil leak
T. Fabi	BT53/5 BMW t/c	5th

Sept 9, ITALIAN GRAND PRIX, Monza

N. Piquet	BT53/4 BMW t/c	Ret: engine
T. Fabi	BT53/5 BMW t/c	Ret: engine

Oct 7, GRAND PRIX OF EUROPE, New Nurburgring

N. Piquet	BT53/6 BMW t/c	3rd
T. Fabi	BT53/4 BMW t/c	Ret: gearbox

Oct 21, PORTUGUESE GRAND PRIX, Estoril

N. Piquet	BT53/6 BMW t/c	6th
M. Winkelhock	BT53/5 BMW t/c	10th

Winner! Piquet takes the flag to win the 1984 Canadian Grand Prix at Montreal with Niki Lauda's second place McLaren just coming into view in the distance.

Owing to a printer's error, this photograph was omitted from page 226, where an incorrect photograph appears. The publishers and author regret this mistake which was totally beyond their control, and hope it will not detract from the reader's enjoyment of the book.